A History of
Modern Greek Literature

A History of

Modern Greek Literature

By C. Th. Dimaras

Translated by Mary P. Gianos

State University of New York Press

Albany, New York 1972

A History of Modern Greek Literature

First Edition

Published by State University of New York Press,
99 Washington Avenue, Albany, New York 12210

Originally published in 1948 as
'Ιστορία Ιῆς Νεοελληνικῆς Λογοτεχνίας
Translation made from 4th edition.

Printed in the United States of America
Book designed by Richard Hendel

Library of Congress Cataloging in Publication Data

Dimaras, C   Th   1904–
    A history of modern Greek literature.

    Translation of Historia tēs Neoellēnikes
logotechnias.
    Bibliography: p.
    1. Greek literature, Modern—History and criticism.
I. Title
PA5210.D513   880'.9   73-112610
ISBN 0-87395-071-2
ISBN 0-87395-230-8 (pbk)
ISBN 0-87395-171-9 (microfiche)

Contents

880.9
D58

50706

Preface

The title of this book is *A History of Modern Greek Literature*. If we analyze each term in the title, we have a precise idea of its content. The term *logotechnia* (literature) contains the notion of art of expression. However, this book considers literature in its broader aspect as the totality of written works, excluding those concerned with a specific discipline. Even so, such a definition lacks essential breadth. Indeed, we should not forget that what distinguishes Greek letters is the contribution of oral transmission originating principally from the folksong. It also happens that some works of a scientific character, particularly those concerning the so-called theoretical sciences, are written in such a painstaking form that they should be included among literary works despite their scientific basis. Further, we should also keep in mind that certain branches of knowledge express an orientation of the mind that corresponds to the predominant artistic records of each period. Philosophic, historic, and geographic interests of a period, as well as those which treat of natural sciences, also leave their imprint on literary production. Hence, such works also have their place in this study, not from their scientific viewpoint but as an aid to a more precise understanding of the spirit dominating literature during a given period. From the moment these works are integrated with the intellectual life in their more specialized character, they cease to interest the historian of letters. What is important is the moment of change not the later evolution of the various branches of science. Hence, history of letters and history of culture are recurrent terms in the history of literature as presented here.

The term *modern Greek* delimits our subject. Only modern Greek texts will be examined. However, since we are concerned with monuments of expression, the definition should be understood in linguistic, not political, terms. This book will be concerned exclusively with works written in modern Greek. Those written in ancient Greek, irrespective of date of composition, will be excluded.

Yet, even in this area, we will have numerous occasions to mention writers whose language was archaic, if they constitute or present evidence that informs about the spirit of the period to which they belonged or about the authors. Also excluded from this book—considering the reservations formulated above—are texts written in languages other than modern Greek. On the other hand, all works written in modern Greek, irrespective of their author's nationality, are examined.

Lastly, this book is a history, an attempt, that is, to capture the flow of time and to enclose it in a narration, in something inevitably static and structured to some degree. The extent to which this objective can be accomplished will lead us to something far different from what a series of specialized monographs arranged in chronological order would have done. One would like to arrange the material into a continuous narration; to grasp the infinite variety of life in an infinite synthetic view. However, the nature of our subject sometimes makes it necessary to distribute an author's work through various points in the narration, while at other times the unity of the subject compels us to go beyond the chronological demarcations adopted.

These ideal objectives are limited by the nature of this study's subject and by the limitations of the mind. First of all, for example, the modern Greek language does not consist of a separate body and should not be isolated from earlier forms of the Greek language. G. Hadjidakis, in speaking about the periods in the history of language, writes: "These periods are not separated from one another by the wall of China; on the contrary, the older periods exercise their influence on the later ones." Generally, the Greek language after classical times tends to become more and more analytical and to have more standardized and unified forms. Atticism posed an artificial barrier to this natural tendency; transmission of the Greek language among people whose maternal language was not Greek contributed, along with other historic causes, to impeding the normal linguistic evolution. Foreigners are inclined to the archaic. Nonetheless, the language that was disregarded by the cultured was accepted and adopted by Christianity. When we go to the Greek language of the Middle Ages, we find a simplified syntax, impoverished form, and analytical structure. From this point on, we should include in our study all the nonarchaic literary texts that we encounter. An analogous modification in the area of metrics, the passage from ancient prosody to the new, facilitate in the purification of language. It is pointless to emphasize that the *katharevousa,* a purely neo-Hellenic phenomenon that is a combination of recent historic factors, is examined along with other literary documents.

Although the course of both political and intellectual history is not disjunctive, we can still observe signs of change, moments when the slow evolution reaches new forms. Hence, we must admit the existence of a succession of periods whose limits are imprecise. Seeds of the new forms were contained in the old, and in the new forms we find survivals of the old. We must also take into account those conditions particular to Greece. The Byzantine Empire became increasingly more homogeneous as the more distant provinces were lost and the empire tended to concentrate on Greek soil. The Greek element which early had given its own imprint to the different races constituting the Byzantine Empire now asserted itself entirely. After 1261 we can say that Byzantium and Greece were one. Furthermore, the decline of the empire promoted the power of eastern piety; an intense religious life characterized the end of the Byzantine Empire. Language, customs, and faith tended toward a conscious Hellenic unity. Around the fall of Constantinople, Byzantine intellectuals appeared purely Greek. "We are of the Hellenic race, as evidenced by our language and our ancestral culture," wrote Gemistos. Two days before the fall, Constantine Paleologus called Constantinople "the hope and joy of all the Greeks." The passage from Byzantium to Greece was accomplished. And as we see the birth of neo-Hellenism emerging out of Byzantium, so in neo-Hellenism we see a Byzantium which continues to live.

We should not attribute greater importance to the divisions introduced by later periods of Greek literature. We must not forget that literature is a social phenomenon and that all its manifestations are closely associated with other expressions of a period. The cause and effect that exists between two series of phenomena, the literary and nonliterary, is of no concern to us here; points of contact between the two are easily discernible. In studying the history of literature, we are forced by the unity of the different manifestations of a civilization not to ignore the events and developments of the political or cultural history. Related references pertain to matters that are, or that should be, known to the reader. In any case, the same reason permits us, and even obliges us at times, to utilize the dates of political history for the divisions in literary history. Political dates acquire importance and constitute a natural demarcation between two periods, particularly where a lack of abundant literary activity deprives literature of its relative autonomy. Of course, even here the coincidence is not absolute, but it is perceptible. In any case, and

whatever reservations temper our judgment, the date 1453 constitutes an important point in the history of culture as well. In 1669,
when the expansion of the Ottoman Empire on Greek soil was
completed, we also have a series of phenomena in the intellectual
history associated with the political history of Greece. A century
later, the treaty of Kuchuk Kainarji, with the privileges this treaty
accorded Hellenism, is reflected in the history of Greek culture. We
can say the same for 1821.

The dates cited raise an observation. The first modern Greek
texts used in this study refer back to the ninth century. Between the
ninth century and 1453 approximately six hundred years elapsed;
from the fall of Constantinople to 1669 approximately two hundred
years elapsed; one hundred years elapsed from 1669 to 1774; and
not quite fifty years from 1774 to the War of Independence in 1821.
The isolated segments, in other words, become increasingly short.
This formation is not only a question of historical perspective, which
makes us see subsequent events in greater detail, but it also has a
more essential explanation. New Hellenism was rising toward its
height; the intellectual life was becoming more compact and should
be examined in greater detail. After the War of Independence, conditions changed and we are forced to use demarcations imposed by
the abundance of material available. Finally, the autonomous life of
literary genres could not be rendered in a narration without some
basic classification by genres. As emphasized below, method is subordinated to the object of research.

Genre consists each time of the point of encounter between two
opposing forces, that is, between the force which tends toward its
repetition and that which tends toward its renewal. The moment itself is determined by time and space. We discussed the matter of
time above. Before turning to the matter of space, we should say a
few words about the respective forces that tended to maintain or
even restore the genre. By its very nature genre tends to repeat itself
unaltered. Ever since their first appearance, tragedy, sonnet, and
novel would have needed no modification had external conditions
foreign to the genre not imposed change. These foreign conditions
were history—to which I have referred above—and the individual,
who in each case transmits the tendencies of a particular time.

The geographic center of this *History* consists of Greece proper
—continental and insular—with extensions spreading fan-like over
greater or lesser areas at the various moments of this history. It con-

sists of the small area of Epirus divided by mountains into much smaller ones; it consists of numerous islands. It is a sterile land where communication is difficult and the coastline is largely fragmented. Hence, this small piece of land presents an extended coastal area. Were the coasts to be placed end to end, they would form a straight line longer than the distance between Greece and America. The difficulties of land communication, the poverty of soil, and the multitude of coastlines and islands caused the inhabitants of Greece to travel and to emigrate, which contributed to the great differentiation between the sedentary and the mobile populations. All the external facts contributed to the differentiation.

The climate of Greece, temperate on the whole, is nonetheless vastly different from one region to another. In limiting our observations to the actual mainland, we will note that the most southerly point of Crete is as far from Thrace as England is from Spain. The differences this distance creates in the climate and in men, added to the causes already mentioned, produce tendencies toward regionalism and variety in character, temperament, and inspiration.

The result is individualism. Each time that a Hellenic harmony succeeds in establishing itself, it always becomes a polyphonic harmony. The tendency toward synthesis, emerging from a common awareness, a common language, and a common faith is unquestionably one of the characteristic traits of modern Greek intellectual history. The development of communications, and later, the constitution of a Greek state accomplished this synthesis, even though we often still sense the presence of the regional within the general.

The characteristics of interest to us that have constantly contributed to this formation of Greece are the following: the Greeks are an intelligent race, enduring, curious, fond of novelty, assimilative. Their tendency toward displacement, which is also a permanent trait, will be encountered in this *History* each time that it appears as an influence on letters. And the geographic position of Greece accentuates these characteristics. The country lies between two large blocks of civilization that remain distinct from one another even though the course of history creates some alterations of boundary and some blending, which is not of interest to us here. East and West are united on Greek soil and at the same time in constant collision. As a bridge to the opposing civilization, Greek territory was often subject to conquest. But what constituted a tragedy for the Greek race simultaneously constituted one of its cultural splendors. In this way, Hellenism received a wealth and variety of influences which brought about its originality. Greece managed to utilize these influences both to affirm her originalities and to exercise her assimilative powers. The geographic position of Hellenism brought about another distinctive characteristic of this race. Aristotle observed that the people of Europe appeared to be energetic but lacked intellectual acuity, while the reverse was true of the Asiatics. He concluded that the Greeks, living in a climate that partook both of Europe and of Asia, assimilated the best of each group.

Greek civilization is thus regularly renewed by contact with foreign civilizations and the constant brilliance of its own genius. Here we are concerned with the influences the Greeks received. In general terms, Greek ability to assimilate has demonstrated the autonomy of their intellectual history from very ancient times to our own day. But the Greeks had a second, unique, response to assimilation. Nations, like any organization, assimilate so long as they are alert, and the more alert they are, the better and greater the assimilation. The decrease in assimilation expresses a biological decline of the organization; only dead organizations cease to assimilate. Intellectual self-sufficiency is a myth. Wherever an attempt has been made to impose this self-sufficiency, we note tragic consequences for the nations involved. What we are considering is the ability for a true assimilation, that is to say, for the creation of a new and original element in the appropriation of the foreign contribution. Such is the meaning that we must give to the words of Plato, which, in my estimation, are valid even today: what the Greeks accepted from the barbarians, they improved. Other, more specialized reflections with regard to the influences exercised on Hellenism have their place in this *History*.

The last constant characteristic of modern Greek intellectual life which we will discuss presents very delicate nuances. It should not, however, be omitted. Even though various reasons contribute to this phenomenon, it is a fact that most of the greatest moments in the history of Greek letters come at some point of contact between Greek and foreign civilizations. This is true when we speak about the akritic character of Greek literature, the flowering of Crete, and the Ionian Islands school. It appears that contact with foreign elements fortified the Hellenic character of the literary production in the long run. These observations should not be applied to the physical territory of Greece, but to its intellectual territory; that which would permit us to attribute an akritic character even to the folksong of the Ottoman domination and to the rise of the generation of 1880.

We have already said that each genre is realized in the individual work. Objective definitions always exist, but each *creation* is individual. Hence, the ideal history would be that in which we could follow simultaneously the conditions that make a genre possible and the individual coefficient that gives it life. In fact, the more important the work and the less it fits common definitions, the greater the importance of the subjective factor.

In the following pages, inclusion of biographical material was dictated by the fact that this is not a history of writers but a history of literature. This explains the presence of minor writers and some analysis of their works. Often where individual literary genius is lacking, the characteristics of the period appear more clearly than they would have with more important writers.

But the relationship between the individual and society has other aspects which should be mentioned. Social currents are expressed through the individual; a work can interest us even if it has remained unpublished, because it acquaints us with the period to which the work belonged and consequently with other contemporary works. A work also generally exercises a certain influence when it is published, and so a work that was not published when it was written but was published perhaps centuries later would become an influence on society at the moment it appeared. *Digenis Akritas,* the first manuscripts of which were revealed to the public around 1870, is one such example. Each work, therefore, should be examined for its significance at the time it was written and its effect when published. An attempt has been made to discuss fully works that pose such problems.

We have already touched on the question of method. It is clear that we are concerned with developing a structure out of the facts and not with straining reality by superimposing a preconceived structure. Generally, my observation is that, depending on the material examined and the influence it has exercised to the present, and depending on the literary importance of the texts under examination, the development of a subject is oriented either toward combining elements or toward individual analyses of these. The aesthetic or historic importance of a writer or a work, in my estimation, emerges basically from a detailed examination of him or his work. But even this we must qualify, for we are concerned with history, not criticism. This, however, only increases the historian's obligation. Besides his own opinion, which of necessity is more or less that of his period, there is also the opinion of the period to which the work pertains. Further, there are the successive opinions expressed by intervening generations. We should not neglect any contribution of opinion. The history of criticism is inseparable from the history of literature in the dimensions given here. We are interested, for example, in the opinion earlier writers had of *Erotokritos,* while we seek at the same time to examine the position that work actually occupies today in the world of letters. This explains some phenomenal disproportions in reputation and space alloted here to individual authors. For a century Dapontes was famous as a great poet. We cannot ignore him, even though today we have a different opinion of him. To ignore him would prevent us from seeing clearly both earlier and later events. Finally, we have the writer whose opinions gave him great influence at one time, though they are now considered erroneous. To mention this influence will maintain a balance between his former position and the place he occupies in literature today.

This subject poses a problem that cannot possibly find practical, rational resolution. From the first appearance of their works, the Soutsos brothers exercised a very long and profound influence on Greek intellectual history. Consequently, their place in the history of letters is unique. Solomos, on the other hand, and Kalvos, and until recently Cavafy exercised a belated influence. Their work, an expression of their period, has its place, but it a historical one, if we are considering the influence these works exercised. Slight displacements, sometimes a simple mention and at other times a distribution of our analysis throughout various chapters, correct this inevitable irregularity to a certain extent. Naturally, under such conditions, when attempting to describe intellectual life in its infinite variety, all grouping of authors by the dates of their birth or death, their literary height or their generation has only an auxiliary and fortuitous character.

Finally, I wish to make some observations which perhaps can assist the reader. This book is divided into parts, each of which corresponds to an historical unity; the chapters which compose the parts do not necessarily follow a chronological order. In order to render a fluid and protean reality without offending the rational demands of understanding, in each part I examine the material from different angles within a chronological unity. Naturally, I make an exception for the first part, which constitutes an introduction to the entire history of modern Greek literature. The other exceptions result from concessions to reality. My observation is that a greater number of subdivisions could have been introduced in our text, but certain disjunctions would have been very conventional and lacked detail. This would have distorted the true image of the facts.

I have attempted to cite characteristic passages of the various authors, because I believe that without these a precise knowledge of the aesthetic facts would have been incomplete. I hope there are enough of these passages. Poetic texts are more numerous; we should not forget that up to our period the modern Greek soul has been expressed principally in verse. This fundamental statement releases us from enumerating all the other reasons why verse texts are preferable in a history of letters to prose ones.

Numerous histories of modern Greek literature have already appeared, both in our own time and in the past. There is no reason for me to express a critical opinion about them. The mere fact that I am producing another history shows that I do not consider it an unnecessary task. It is nonetheless an obligation to express gratitude to those who undertook this arduous task before me and to emphasize my indebtedness. If their works had not existed, my own efforts would have been more unsatisfactory than they are. Science is not the work of one man or even of one generation. Those who come later profit from the experience and knowledge of the past. In the same way, I hope that my history will assist those who undertake the composition of a similar work in the future.

I would also like to add that I attempted to use, insofar as possible, existing monographs on the subject of modern Greek literature. My purpose, indeed, has not been to offer new material to the reader, and I regret that such monographs as would have prepared the way for that kind of history are so limited. Unfortunately, there are entire chapters in the history of modern Greek literature where the historians must do the work of a researcher. I feel that if we wish to improve our knowledge of modern Greek culture, our principal concern should be the examination of subjects that have been neglected until now. I would like to believe that the potential work to which these pages serve as an introduction will not remain unwritten.

C. TH. DIMARAS

Part One
The Roots
Modern Greek Literature
before the Turkish Domination

*As we approach modern Greek literature, we distinguish
three broad categories. First, the folksong, which does not
contain the scholarly elements of the Attic language,
perpetuates the tradition of ancient song. Second, and
operating concurrently with the first, an erudite inspiration
emerges with the creation and refinement of a mixed form,
such as appears in the akritic or frontier songs, in the epic*
Digenis Akritas, *in the Byzantine romances, and elsewhere.
Finally, there is a scholarly production which is addressed to
the people and which makes use of the popular language.
Thus, there are three coexisting currents at the beginning;
their synthesis will occur by degrees and will be completed
at the height of modern Greek literature in the nineteenth
century with such writers as Koraes, Kalvos, and Solomos.*

Chapter I

The Ancients Live Forever

The Folksong

Introduction

The configuration of the Greek land, as we have seen in the Preface, consists of a formation of small islands, isolated from the large routes of land and sea communication. It is these islands which interest us at the beginning of this literary *History* because the degree of purity in elements which constitute their civilization, from all evidence, was much greater here than anywhere else. An economic system, more or less closed, was necessarily established on each of these islands, whose consequences, in proportion to our interests, must be set forth from the materialistic point of view, as well as from the psychological one. Small colonies, with few inhabitants, with limited wealth, lived on each of these small islands. Their technical skills are not renewed from the outside; thus an obvious tendency toward repetition of form is manifested in them. It is well known that in certain regions of Greece, household utensils, tools of farm life, and products of art crafts present a surprising uniformity throughout the centuries. This uniformity of social institutions involved, at the same time, their continuation without essential modification. Indeed, only unchanging social life can satisfy the unaltered forms of a materialistic civilization. Thus, we can deduce, with fair assurance, that national life was renewed at a slow pace on these isolated islands until that moment when the general political conditions transformed the economy of the country into an open economy. The population of these regions also gives evidence throughout the centuries of the same fundamental reactions to the important ceremonies of their daily lives (baptism, marriage, burial) as to the artistic manifestations relating to their professional occupations (work songs), or to their social life (festival songs and poems commemorating local events).

The psychology of isolated populations must also appear static. The more the traveller, the itinerant merchant, the sailor, became curious and developed a taste for novelty as a result of contacts with foreign populations, the more a population dedicated to immobility gave evidence of a psychological conservatism and a tendency to repeat indefinitely the same rites according to tradition.

It is well known even today in Greece that development of means of communication has relieved, to a certain extent, the isolation of the countryside, but we see how slowly the rural populations assimilate technical progress. The stable populations resisted all attempts at change of the conditions of life, even when that change consisted of an obvious improvement for them. These general remarks reinforce the hypothesis of the inflexibility of social institutions in a great portion of the Greek territory. Applied to remote times, during the periods when the technical evolution did not present the accelerated rhythm of today, these facts become all the more significant.

Finally, I would like to mention the stability of form which the crafts present. Certain decorative motifs, certain ornaments, certain symbols of domestic life persist in their traditional form from prehistoric times to our own day. This last observation, an abstraction on the particular character which the area of Greece presents, allows us to say that the stability of forms in folk life could well have its equivalent in the literary manifestations of the people. Also, when we will encounter in the folksong the motifs and morphological elements surviving from earliest antiquity, it will be expedient to establish a certain correlation between this phenomenon and the survival of ancient forms of civilization.

A number of foreigners penetrated Greece. More often, they advanced by means of the large communication routes, but they also reached the most remote regions. These military bands did not carry a constituted civilization with them. Women, habitual carriers of folk culture, seldom participated in these incursions. Most of the invaders rarely established themselves in the regions they crossed. Hence, the traces of culture left by their passage were superficial and negligible and did not cause notable changes in the traditional usage and customs of an essentially conservative society. The assimilating force which characterizes the Greek race allowed it to absorb foreign elements to such a degree that, even today, despite all available research, there is no way of isolating the foreign elements and of distinguishing the original civilization. The force and violence of these invasions were so great that they sometimes completely obliterated the Greek element in the smaller regions. On the other hand, we are in no way justified in saying that the deep incursions were profound enough to disrupt the historical cohesion of the Greek race in a definitive manner and to create a culture whose roots were not Greek. The foreign incursions certainly had their effect on the sedentary populations of Greece, but the various traces, going back to antiquity, which research has succeeded in isolating, prove that the heterogeneous action failed to cause the Greek civilization to deviate from its ancestral orientation.

Similarly, the foreign cultural elements which did not form a body with the indigenous elements, or better, were not assimilated in time, formed clusters clearly contrasting with the traditional Greek civilization; thus, not only are these groups easy to isolate, but they also constitute evidence throughout of the permanent character of the Hellenic tradition. The cohesion of Hellenic culture is such that it is less the language which distinguishes the oral Greek landmarks than the manner in which the subjects were treated. This choice of episodes, description of morals and characters, and even techniques which governs the entire development differentiates the positive manner of the song and the Greek tale from those we have encountered elsewhere. Without doubt, we can make the same observation about the folk production of other countries. But in Greece, where folklore studies have sometimes been carried out with great chauvinistic energy intent on proving that the Greek nation descended directly from the ancient Greeks, countless examples of the survival of ancient Greek customs have been collected. Generally, they concern modern Greek folklore, and particularly, they prove the survival of morphological elements of ancient folksong in the modern. Though these comparisons sometimes lead to conclusions which today appear exaggerated, in their totality, the relationship uniting the collective life of contemporary Greece with that of antiquity is nonetheless evident. As for the oral landmarks, the origin from antiquity of a quantity of traditions, stories, and songs springs from the same theme, the manner in which this theme was treated, or the psychic universe which they expressed. The perfected form which these Greek songs attained necessitates their individual examination.

Folksong

In this land, on that dry, barren earth, generations of men lived, rejoiced, loved, and died without interruption. As the daughter shed tears over the loss of her mother, so, in time, her own daughters would shed tears over her. The songs that the young man sang at dances and festivals were the same songs that he, as an old man, would teach his grandchildren, thereby linking the past to the present, and to the future, without interruption. The rhythm with which the mill turned and accompanied the song of the miller, the rhythm with which the young man pulled on the oars, easing his burden with song, the cadences of these songs, remained the same throughout the centuries. Rhythm perpetuated the song. But we also find a conservative element here. It has been said that once something had been invented, experimented, and approved by the people, it was not easily discarded.

When we speak about folk poetry, we should not forget that this also includes chanting. The vogue which attracted Greek and foreign scholars to the Greek folksong created an artificial dissociation between word and music. The words were studied separately and their charm brought about imitation, or, on another level, it allowed for recitations of the folksong. However, these imitations were artificial elaborations which should not confuse our research concerning the genesis and morphology of the folksong. "We should not separate what is inseparable, poetry and song," wrote George Tertsetis, a judicious scholar of modern Greek culture. Thus, the study of the folksong had led modern musicologists to conclusions which are useful, though they are beyond the scope of our subject, because they reveal the uninterrupted bond between classical music and contemporary folksong, for music has conveyed the words of the folksong throughout the centuries. This fact, which admits the relationship of the music to the word, no longer permits us to deny a parallel relationship of word with music.

We must also bear in mind that the dance had a close relationship with the folksong. Σέρνω τό χορό (pull the dance) is the technical term still used today by the Greek people. Συρτός (syrtos) is also the term for one of the most popular Greek folk dances. This dance has its own melodies and its own songs, appropriate, as the people say, to these dances. An ancient inscription reveals at a glance that the "syrtos" was not only of classical, but in fact of most ancient, origin. We are at the time of Caligula. Subjugated Greece has conquered her conqueror. The vision of ancient glory is lodged not only in the spirit of the Romans, but also in the spirit of the Greeks: the nostalgic return to antiquity, which will be accomplished a century later with the Antonini, has already begun. Somewhere around Roumeli in northern Boetia, a wealthy landowner desires to revive the ancient customs of his region, to return to tradition. An inscription informs us that, "He executed religiously the dance of the 'syrtos' inherited from his ancestors." It is not only evident from this inscription that the Greek people, even at that time, performed a dance called the "syrtos," but even more, it informs us that the "syrtos" was considered a very ancient dance belonging to local traditions and customs. This written testimonial forces us to recognize that a manifestation of the ancient civilization continues even to our times; nor can we exclude from this, naturally, the music and chanting which accompany the dance.

As with music and dance, so with words, we find living indications relating the modern Greek song to the ancient. Among the worksongs of antiquity, there is one, for millers, which begins with these words: "ἄλει μύλε, ἄλει (grind, mill, grind)." Today, the song begins with the same words, though pronunciation differs. So it is with certain festival songs. The historian Theognis mentions that, on the island of Rhodes, a very ancient custom associated with the tradition of Cleobulus had the children going from house to house on certain holidays, singing songs and collecting gifts. The song began with these words: " Ἦλθε, ἦλθε χελιδών (It has come, it has come, the swallow)." We find this same custom and the same song, known as the *swallow song,* in Byzantine times, and it has been observed that in various Greek regions this same custom has survived to our era with the same words. On the first of May, it is customary for children to make the rounds from house to house singing this same song and collecting gifts. It should not appear strange that among the places where this ancient custom has been preserved is Rhodes. For centuries, the Franks and Turks controlled the island, but the evidence is of a characteristic historical unity of its civilization which has survived the devastation and disasters. Even had we no evidence, we could still say that mothers in aniquity sang lullabies to their children and that rhythmic lamentations accompanied the funeral processions of the dead. The popular cultural element has only become a subject for study in European civilization in recent times. For this reason, we have little written evidence of these elements and they are in no systematic form. Yet, even this evidence suffices to inform us that the ancients also had their lullabies, which they called "vaukalismata" or "katavaukaliseis" and that they also had professional mourners, the ancient "Carinnes," who were paid to lament over the dead. We saw above that we possess some written evidence from antiquity for the festival and work songs; in fact, explicit evidence. We have every right, from what we know about these songs, to extend that knowledge by analogy to other cases on which we have insufficient evidence. Customs, songs, and language have moved together throughout the centuries, not only in the classical period but even during the preclassical.

We have little evidence of the persistent survival of the ancient songs in the mouths of the people, because very few songs were recorded formerly, so that a comparison with the oral tradition cannot be established. But in times where such evidence can be ascertained, the force of tradition is revealed with astonishing persistence. Thus, Samuel Baud Bovy has established that the celebrated song of Armouris, which has been preserved in manuscript, dating perhaps to the fifteenth century (but attributed to the tenth century), contains verses which have been preserved intact in the oral tradition of the nineteenth century.

προτοῦ τὸ πιάσει ἐπιάνετον, προτοῦ τὸ σείσει ἐσιέτον
(γραπτὴ παράδοση)

πρὶ νὰ τὰ πιάσει, πιάνουοτο, πρὶ νὰ τὰ σείσ᾿ ἐσειόττο
(προφοριχὴ παράδοση Καρπάθου)

Before it was grasped, it had been grasped already.
(written tradition)

Before it could be shaken, it was shaken already.
(oral tradition of Karpathos)

We also find impressive coincidences with oral tradition in songs published recently from later manuscripts. A manuscript probably dating to the sixteenth century contains the following verses:

Μόνε νά σου κι ᾿Αντρόνικος στὴν πόρτα καβαλλάρης

But here before the door is Andronikos the horseman.

And in oral tradition we have:

Καὶ νά τος κι ὁ ᾿Ανδρόνικος στοὺς κάμπους καβαλλάρης.

And here on the plains is Andronikos the horseman.

(These evidences are convincing because they concern texts which were never printed; the printed texts always ran the risk of alteration by oral tradition.) Among the few folksongs found stored as treasures in old printed copies, we note one in a book dating to around 1584.

I love my dearest one, I want my darling.
Work magic spells on me, cause me to forget her.
Clothe me in irons and put me in a deep hole,
So the iron can press on me and the earth can cover me.
And put a serpent on my breast, a three-headed serpent,
So the serpent's sting will cause me to forget her.

Despite the fact that this song exists in bad condition, which renders the reading difficult, its presence among our sources is valuable because it constitutes an incontestable link between the ancient folksong and that of modern times.

The question of morphology of the folksongs will be examined in a later chapter which treats of the highest achievement of the folksong during the eighteenth century. However, we should observe here that even the themes of the folksong probably were inherited from the ancient folksongs. Thus, the theme of "vain questions," as I. Th. Kakrides recently termed them,

μήνα σὲ γάμο ρίχνονται, μήνα σὲ χαροκόπι;

Is it at a wedding, is it at a feast,
(Where those gunshots are being fired?)

appears to have passed into modern Greek folksongs from pre-Homeric folksongs. The same can be said about the theme of the *adynaton* (impossible), which is often found in the folksongs, and is probably of ancient origin.

ἂν τρέμουν τ' ἄγρια βουνά, νὰ τρέμει τὸ γιοφύρι,
κι ἂν πέφτουν τ' ἄγρια πουλιά, νὰ πέφτουν οἱ διαβάτες,

When the rude mountains tremble, then the bridge trembles
And when the wild birds fall, then the travellers fall. . . .

The term Τραγούδι (song), with the double interpretation of poem and song, naturally aroused the curiosity of researchers because of its evident relationship to the ancient term τραγῳδία (tragedy). Already in 1859, Spiros Zambelios, known for his penetrating and original observations on neo-Hellenic matters, published an essay called *"From Whence the Modern Term Sing."* The contents of the work, unfortunately, do not correspond to the title; hence, the reader has before him a text which lacks the charming and fascinating theses that distinguish the work of Zambelios. In our time, Stilpon Kyriakides elaborated on an original system for interpreting the term τραγουδῶ. Song actually proceeds from ancient tragedy and has been handed down to us through the mediation of the orchestral dramas of the Romans. This affiliation is such that a contemporary folklorist associated it with the evolution of the term παραλογή (ballad), which we encounter later and which unquestionably is linked to the Byzantine forms καταλόγιν, καταλογίτσην, and καταλογίμαν (to reckon among).

This interesting theory, which has not been contradicted or even supplanted to our times, nonetheless fails to cover all the attending problems. Indeed, such an origin to the modern folksong could have been supported if we had found it surviving in urban centers, because it could have been maintained there from the Byzantine period. But the phenomenon is essentially extraurban. At any rate, the correlation between τραγωδία and τραγούδι undeniably exists, and the multiple observations and comparisons made by Kyriakides link neo-Hellenic folklore firmly with ancient Greek literature. The number of strong arguments in favor of an ancient origin of the folksong, independent of its morphology, forces us to place it at the beginning of this *History*. The folksong forms an organic bond between classical and modern literature.

Division of the Folksong

If we examine the folk poetry collected to date, we will ascertain that it can be classified, without difficulty, into three groups. The first and most important is composed of a great variety of songs, all of which refer to different stages and different aspects of human life. In this division, broadly speaking, we should group the songs of love, weddings, lullabies, songs for children, carols, Palm Sunday songs, carnival songs, and other festival songs, as well as songs of exile, dirges, gnomics, professional and work songs, and lastly, satires.

In the second group should be assembled the songs whose character or historical origin is evident. The songs are separate from those which treat of real events in life, as, for example, the satiric songs. Here we include, on the one hand, the songs originally inspired by a historical figure or a manner of life pertaining to a concrete historical period, as do the akritic or klephtic songs. The nature of these songs places their interest in a broader regional and chronological context. On the other hand, we also include all kinds of songs which are generated by some historical moment, even though this moment is unknown to us, but which maintain their special regional color and the moment which produced them. If we were to broaden the scope which pertains to history, we would lose the divisional basis. This second large group, as we have delimited it, requires further subdivision. Most of the klephtic songs refer to *klephtes* by name or describe their lives. A common heroic character links these songs. But there are also other songs, which, though they maintain the same characteristics, names, heroic life, and the rest commemorate persons who do not belong to the world of the klephtes, or which celebrate enemies other than the Turks (for instance, the Saracens), and which certainly take us outside the period of the klephtes. These songs, which have a fundamental unity, form the akritic group of folksongs; they will be examined in the following chapter.

Finally, the third group consists of the ballads to which we have referred. They are short narratives which have the rapid epic rhythm and, generally, a complete resolution. They resemble a popular story given in verse form.

The more we advance into these subdivisions, the greater the difficulties we encounter in the divisions proper, because, in reality, the Greek people included some songs under ballads which research shows belong to other groups particularly the akritic one. Furthermore, we should not forget two fundamental difficulties which often forestall any attempt at differentiation. Time presents the first difficulty; that is, the antiquity of the songs has permitted successive generations of a song to change a name, to omit a characteristic passage, or to suppress those elements unfair to a particular period or region. The second difficulty comes with corruptions; that is, the well-known phenomenon where the singer, either consciously, in order to create something new, or unconsciously, through faulty memory, or even through a complete lapse of memory, assembles passages from songs of different origins. The literary works devoted to the folksong have proved that it is sometimes possible to restore, with relative certainty, the original form of a poem altered by corruption. Studies of this genre, however, are few at present, if one excludes the significant contribution of John Apostolakis. Moreover, the difficulties in such a study are often organic, because corruption of text is the most common process for creating new songs.

Beware of Collections of Songs

The reader of published collections of folksongs should bear in mind that many editors of folksongs, particularly older ones, started out with different premises from ours, and thus were not concerned with a faithful transcription of the songs. On the contrary, they believed that they had an editorial obligation to alter the songs and to improve them according to their own conception, linguistically as well as aesthetically. Besides, they did not hesitate to interpolate entire songs composed by other scholars on the model of the folksong. Not only foreign collections, as those of Fauriel, Haxthausen, and Passow, but also certain Greek collections have been interwoven with folksongs written by scholars. Without going into details, which are beyond the scope of this *History*, we should emphasize that extreme caution must be exercised by anyone intending to use a text which at first sight appears to contain folksongs. The collection of folklore published in 1914 by Nicholas Politis is the best such collection we possess today. Even though the texts have been altered somewhat by the editor, this alteration is limited to combining authentic verses borrowed from different variants.

We will now examine the songs of life, the historical songs, and the ballads separately. In the following chapter, the reader will find the akritic songs, then, in their historical order, the songs of the klephtes. We will there examine the more recent historical songs as well, and the morphology of the folksong, which, as we know today, is also of a later period.

General Characteristics

The folksong, a sincere, authentic, and unaltered expression of the folk spirit, reveals the Hellenic people to be as temperate in disposition as they are frugal in life, a people who are classical in the expression of their sensibility. A girl would express to her mother the sentiments she nourished for someone she loved in these words: "Mother, when you see him, you will envy his beauty."

These people show a great capacity for perceiving the physical world, and more generally, the external world, as well as possessing a remarkable sensibility. Their familiarity with the physical world and the love they hold for it sometimes permits them to project and thus objectify these sentiments.

Blossom, trees, if you want, if you want, wither.
I will not sit under your shade, I don't want your freshness,

or even

The trees weep, weep, the branches weep,
The lairs where I once hid also weep.

The Greek people sometimes personified the physical world completely:

Olympos and Kissavos, the two great mountains quarrel,
Over which will make the rain fall, which will drop the snow.

From here passage is made wtihout difficulty to the folksong and even to allegory, but always preserving the same direct sensibility:

A proud eagle, an eagle with striking carriage,
By reason of his pride and of his striking carriage,
Refuses to spend the winter pleasantly in lower regions.

Religious sentiment is rarely expressed directly in the folksong. More often it is indirect and appears through discrete and restrained mysticism, born of contact between the human spirit and the physical world; invisible forces govern both man and nature, and these forces express interest in man through nature. Nobility and elevated emotions, ardent attachment to family life, contempt for psychic abnormality—such are the tendencies of the folksong. On this point, we recall the song that Nicholas Politis has entitled "The Loving Brothers and the Wicked Woman." Social formality, the notion of hospitality, should also be associated with the conservative, patriarchal character of the Greek folksongs. Respect for the stranger presupposes and demands a differentiation from him and requires that he be aware of the limits of hospitality. Sociability is above all an indication which reveals the flexibility of the Greek consciousness. The Greek is bound to the external world through all his senses; his neighbor is a primeval and integral part of his world.

Finally, we find a remarkable psychological capacity in the folksong, as well as a great acuity in expressing with precision characteristics of various social categories constituting the human group. Aside from these, the intense aspiration for all forms of liberty, which we will explore later, and the overflowing imagination, of which the folksong gives an example from beginning to end, should in no way be considered a contradiction to all that has been said above.

His shoulders are like two mountains, his head is like a fortress.

Love

The general observations made above apply equally to the songs of love. The lover-singer—and it is not rare that the words be given to a woman in love—is modest and reserved in expressing love. Often a faint smile, which never becames ironical, illuminates the song and reveals a certain flexibility of sentiment.

But I am a thief of kisses and a cheat in love.
Why have you given your lips that I have kissed so tenderly?

This quality, however, considered along with the absence of all amorous mysticism, often confers an intensely carnal character on the songs of love. The presence of this element involves no distortion, but, on the contrary, is associated with the extreme simplicity of the folksong in all its themes and should be interpreted as an expression of the simple and natural life of the people who created it. When it is not restricted by social prejudices and conventions, natural and self-controlled carnal desire finds expression in a normal life and reveals the fundamental importance it really has for man. Perhaps we should atttribute this same meaning to the immodest songs, whose production has always been great.

Even in the songs of love, one distinguishes an awareness which should be qualified as regional or patriarchal, according to how one views the subject. In actuality, the stranger is not considered a desirable love object, either by the lover, or by the family; in general, the young man or the young girl desires a love intrigue with someone from his own region. When this does not occur, the family intervenes to oppose a union that appears incompatible, simply because the beloved is of foreign origin. And "stranger" or "foreigner" in their eyes is not only one of another race or faith; it is even a Greek who comes from another region. For the young girl of the mountains, a man of the plains is a stranger.

> Mother, why did you plan a bad marriage for me
> When you sent me to the plains?

Further, one can distinguish a conservative element that aims at marriages between individuals of the same social group. This voluntary obstruction of the amatory horizon, or rather of the family perspective, should be considered along with the general observations made at the beginning of this chapter concerning the conservative character of the Greek social group. This conservative spirit is expressed in numerous songs whose subject is the "abandoned one." Nicholas Politis has classified one of the earliest folksongs known in this group, a folksong which has been preserved in manuscript form dating from the fifteenth century.

> He journeys, the friend of the beautiful girl with fair complexion and blond hair. He has departed for distant shores, long is his journey. And the maiden in her sorrow curses the months. "Burn, February, as you burn me! And you, March, who have caused me to wither. And you, April, with your procession of flowers. And you, scorching May, what does it matter to me that you have strewn the earth with roses! You have filled my heart with pain and tears!"

The same psychological content displayed in the songs of love will also be encountered in the wedding songs (only method separates the songs that describe marriage customs from the others) and in the lullabies, where naturally the mother expresses her aspirations and hopes for her child. The prayer for social elevation of the child is often formulated in the Greek lullabies. This prayer is expressed simply, in the consciousness of the poor mother who seeks the improvement of an economic position. Imagination here is unbridled and leaps outward to distant lands, represented, in extant manuscripts, specifically by Constantinople and Venice, and sometimes even by the world of dreams.

> Sleep. I have ordered jewels from Constantinople,
> And from Venice your trousseau and your diamonds.

A characteristic trait of these songs, as of those in the other categories, is the extent and importance that prayer assumes in them.

The feeling that man is surrounded by portents and the desire to interpret these in order to prevent future evil constitute a principal element in the spiritual life as it is expressed in the Greek songs and confirms their ancient origin. This ancient origin is also confirmed by the numerous curses that one encounters in folksongs, which proceed from the same psychological motivation. The songs of children, naturally, and the festival songs are full of imagination and abound in wishes of all kinds.

Songs of Expatriation

The songs of expatriation are particularly significant and are distinguished by their content. They should be associated with the larger group of songs exhibiting literary inspiration. Poor land, which drives the Greek far from his homeland, is a subject which often recurs in Greek poetry and helps us understand how intimate the bonds were between the Greek and his country. The permanent motif of the songs of expatriation is the nostalgia for return. The foreign land is unfriendly to the expatriate, and he, in turn, feels no love for the new land. The woman he encounters exhibits no sympathy or pity for him. In his soul, he misses the motherland and his family, which render separation all the more painful. All the songs are a hymn to his childhood land and to the paternal home.

> Expatriation, loss of parents, bitterness, and love:
> All four were placed on the scales:
> It was expatriation that weighed the heaviest.

Death

The idea of death for the Greeks and the image that the folksong gives of death are subjects which have been of special interest to researchers of modern Greek folk poetry. We receive a particular concept of death for the Greek people from the mourners who chant before the dead, improvising from memory, and from songs where death is evoked. For the Greek people, death is primarily separation, the departure without a return. The dead are deprived of earthly possessions; death is worse than illness and old age, both of which are hateful because they deprive one of the possible enjoyment of life. When the dead one is brought back to life in the song and he speaks, he expresses a regret at having been torn from the joys of the physical world. It is neither a question of chastisement nor of recompense. It is neither paradise nor hell. Christian faith has not penetrated the eschatology of the folksong. The regions to which the dead are returned belong to the "world below," the world where one feels an emptiness for all that relate to the senses. Hence, the insensibility of death has been projected to the places where the dead reside, in the same way that we saw human emotions projected to the physical world. Lights, odors, and sounds, all of which add charm to life, are absent from the world below. The dead move without joy, possessed by the disconsolate memory of the living world.

> Tell me, have you found anything enviable in the infernal world? There, to the dance of violin, to the dance of musical instrument? There, one never sees two men seated together, nor three, in a mood for conversation.

Moreover, this memory—a unique bond between the dead and the living—softens the fate of the dead and offers consolation to the living. The dead would like, in some manner, to be able to participate again in life and the bereaved hope that the dead have not tasted of the water of Lethe and thus rendered separation a permanent one. The center of the drama is the physical world, the world above the earth. This concept is certainly associated with the ancient pagan faith. In the folksong, life is never a nonexistence between two realities, and death never marks the passage to a world of justice and rewards or punishments. This pre-Christian sentiment is reinforced by the fact that death is often personified in these songs. "For the Greek people, the death agony is a struggle of the dying against death." Death appears in numerous songs, either as inviting a young girl to follow him, or as challenging a young man to do battle with him. Death is evil, inflexible, and quarrelsome. His inevitable appearance spurs man to enjoy life on earth without delay. The gloomy note of the folksongs, their tendency toward sadness, often have been stressed. Some have pointed to this as evidence only of the sad experiences to which Ottoman rule subjected the Greek people, but actually the evidence has much deeper historical roots and shows a propensity toward enjoyment of life now:

> Eat, friends, be gay; let us rejoice in this good year!
> Who knows if next year we will be alive,
> Or dead and gone to another world!

So in gnomic poetry, where the philosophy of the Greek people is formulated in verse, the idea of death is a spur to the enjoyment of life. However, despite this aspect, it is still a pessimistic concept of life which predominates in these poems.

> I have not encountered a more reliable friend and a more
> true brother than my sword and my purse.

Gnomic Poetry

Perseverance, patience, prudence, shrewdness, guarding against ambition are qualities that emerge from the Greek gnomic songs and make up their general psychology. Parallel with this, individualism, and its faithful acolyte mistrust, are associated also with gnomic poems from all we know about them today. Omitting the work songs, whose content places them in various other categories, this same attitude toward life appears in the ironic poems as well. Their irony often shows that great appearances are not befitting a wise man and that a sumptuous exterior often conceals poverty and internal misery. Among the ironic poems, we further note those which ridicule an unfortunate marriage. The bitter comments about a bride they have forced on a groom, or the protestations of a wife concerning the sick old man or scoundrel imposed on her in marriage are common subjects for these songs. I believe this element should be pointed out because it illustrates the essential family character of the folksong.

Byzantine Songs

Along with satire, it is appropriate to mention the oldest known historical poems attributed to the Byzantine period. Since grievances could not be expressed openly in the asphyxiating, autocratic Byzantine state, the malcontents or the displaced were reduced to violence or raillery as weapons to obtain satisfaction. The people often broke into songs which more or less overtly expressed their irritation. A few songs, often only verses, that have been preserved by the Byzantine chroniclers, who were contemptuous of folk life, can be considered the oldest neo-Hellenic folksongs.

Ballads

We have already seen that we can postulate, without fear of mistake, the ancient origin of all the songs of life, to whichever category they belong. The last group of songs left to examine here takes us back to the early roots of Greek civilization. In fact, in the ballads, we find the basic themes that belong to ancient Greek literature and to the remote mythological tradition. The relationship of these songs with analogous myths or analogous songs of other Indo-European peoples constitutes additional proof of their very ancient origin. We should mention this here because of their wide diffusion in the Balkans and because of the many controversies that have arisen over the *Song of the Dead Brother*. Thematically, the myth of the dead brother who returns from Hades to fulfill a promise he had made gave researchers the occasion to associate this myth with that of Adonis, even though this situation is not the only one that gives rise to the song, nor is it the most obvious one. The murderess mother who feeds the flesh, more specifically the entrails, of the child to her husband, also takes us to the pre-Hellenic cosmology, where the theme of the father eating his children is common. Nicholas Politis observed that this song presents two categories. In the first, the murder of the child is justified by the desire of the mother to assure that her transgressions will not be revealed. However, there is no motivation in the second, where the liver of the child is served to the father. The only explanation we can give is a comparison with the most ancient myths where the father is compelled to eat the entrails of his child without knowing it. I note further that the return of the absent one, with the basic theme of recognition by one of his relatives, the theme of the swimmer, the theme of the godmother who becomes the bride, or the theme of the bridge of Arta constitute on the whole, with their wide diffusion, convincing evidence of survivals from remote antiquity. The savage and primitive tendencies expressed in the oldest ballads should be considered indications of an ancient origin. Thus, in concluding this chapter, we can state that the ancients continue to live in the souls of the modern Greek people and survive in their songs.

But on closer examination, and considering the folksong as a whole, I would have this to add. The folksong, free from the elaborate technique of a literary author, presented only as an unaltered expression of the natural soul, helps us to approach, outside considerations of time and space, the very essence of poetry. This perspective reveals the great importance of separation as the inspirational theme at the base of the folksong. The aspiration to return, the nostalgia for something lost, aversion for that which is strange, which belongs to others, or for existence far from birthplace create a psychological disposition where the various themes typify an ardent and a universal desire for return. The persistent presence of this desire in the folksongs, clothed in a variety of themes, reinforces the hypothesis that the lyrical expansion of the Greek people as a whole is only a manifestation of man's ancestral desire to return to something better.

Chapter 2

Fascination with Narration

The Byzantine Romance

As we have seen, corruption and change of names in the Greek songs sometimes impede our tracing with accuracy the precise line of demarkation between the different categories of folksongs. Besides, we can admit readily, without requiring evidence, that most ancient poetic themes, whose diffusion was extensive, were the same as those singers exploited in more recent periods. Here it is no longer a question of corruption or change in names, but of utilization in a new poem of a fragment borrowed from ancient songs. Moreover, it must always be borne in mind that divisions and classifications tend, in the history of literature, to inspire systemic and methodological urgencies and that, in fact, they rarely correspond to the essence of things. Thus, the songs classified as akritic are differentiated from those songs based only on the names of their heroes. The collecting and study of folksongs, to the extent that it has been done, reveal that often akritic names fell into disuse and were replaced by others; or the inverse happened, the prestige of certain akritic names, as much for the audience as for the singers, introduced those names into later songs devoid of all akritic character.

Digenis

Akritic names which properly serve to differentiate the akritic group are all Byzantine; for example, Andronikos, Alexios, Doukas, Nicephoros, and many others. The name of Digenis, the original Digenis, dominates all the others. Then there are all the place names, as Ankara, Amorium, Arabia, Armenia, Babylon, Candace, Cappadocia, to mention a few. Elements of another nature also help us compose this aggregate that places them with certitude in the Byzantine period and within the confines of the Asiatic Orient of the Byzantine Empire. These akritic songs and the so-called epic of

Digenis Akritas, which constitute the subject of this chapter, have become, from a historical and topical point of view, an object of thorough research which has yielded significant discoveries. In a series of studies extending over a long period of time, Henri Gregoire arrived at concrete conclusions. Though all these conclusions have not been confirmed, they nonetheless present a perfectly coordinated interpretative thesis. The historical correlation begins with the name of Digenis. Indeed, this name of Digenis figures in Byzantine history; that is to say, as a superior officer, "a very capable man," as the chronicle writers called him, who was killed in 788 in a battle between the Byzantines and the Arabs somewhere in Taurus. The song of Armouris seems to be a committing to memory of an expedition of Michael III around 860. Andronikos recalls the general Andronikos Doukas who lived at the beginning of the tenth century. An old Russian variant of this period permits us to deduce that the elements forming part of the akritic songs served at some moment to glorify the battles of the Paulicians (Karoës, who died in 863, Chrysocheris, who died around 872). But the researcher even found the name of the Amazon Maximo on an inscription dating to the beginning of the third century A.D. Thus, the historical source of the entire group, independent of details, can be considered certain. It only remains to examine closely the different records of the akritic songs.

These are divided into two large groups; on the one hand, we have all the akritic songs, and on the other hand, the different variants of the metrical romances which are titled after the principal hero, Digenis Akritas. The relationship between the two groups is clear and undeniable. We find the same names, the same places, the related episodes. One question has greatly concerned the specialists: the relative antiquity of the two groups; that is, did the songs precede the romance, or was it the inverse? The opinion of such qualified scholars as Politis, Kyriakides, and Gregoire are based on the widespread opinion that *Digenis Akritas* is an epic; and on the generally admitted theories with regard to the birth of the epic genre, it is proper to say that originally a vast cycle of heroic songs existed which glorified the exploits of Byzantine heroes, and at some moment these various songs combined with one another to form the epic. As this opinion is based on a generally admitted theory concerning the genesis of the epic, one must question first, is this theory sufficiently defended; second, is *Digenis Akritas* truly an epic; and third, does the internal evidence compel us to revise this concept insofar as the work in question is concerned.

The first objection would take us beyond the scope of Greek literature, therefore it will not concern us here. As for the second, indeed, one would have to observe that *Digenis Akritas* clearly presents the characteristics of a metrical romance which associate it with romances of love rather than with epics. The numerous elements of scholarly origin have been traced: the Muslim elements are taken from the epic of Saïd-Batal and from other sources; the classical elements are taken from the ancient erotic poets and from sophist expressions; and finally, the religious elements are taken from the Credo of Faith and similar elements of the Christian religion. Let us add that the presence of elements pertaining to folk life do not disprove these observations; they only add another dimension to the already diverse origin of the epic. Finally, in recent times another researcher particularly interested in this aspect of the question detected in the akritic songs indications which tended to prove that they proceeded from the epic. More specifically, he found literary elements from the ancient erotic poets that appear in entirety in the epic, but which were altered in the songs. The extreme position adopted by this researcher in the enthusiasm of his discovery, which consists of maintaining that the entire body of songs was later than the complete work, remains to be proved. Nonetheless, the present state of literary knowledge permits us the possibility that the folksongs could have originated from a scholarly work. Hence, the most conservative opinion that can be formulated on this subject is that a portion of the akritic songs are a secondary creation and originated from the fragmentation of the original work.

However, the main body of these songs must have originated from the direct experience of the folk singer. We know that heroism in battle inspires the spontaneous praises of a singer. During World War II when the processes which give birth to the folksong were more inhibited, songs of glory appeared. Such songs were composed either with morphological elements of the folksong or elements of a more learned form, but from a most authentic source.

Καὶ εἰς τὴν ῎Ηπειρο ἐκεῖ
θὰ κάμουν θαύματα οἱ Γραικοί,
θὰ δουλέψει τὸ τουφέκι
σὰ βροντὴ κι ἀστροπελέκι.

And down there in Epirus
The Greeks will work marvels,
The guns will go into action,
Like thunder and like lightning.

An illiterate soldier composed this song in 1940. One hundred years earlier, another illiterate singer named Tsopanakos had described the battle of Lala in similar versification:

> Ἀπ' τὸ τουφέκι τὸ πολὺ
> στὸν Ἅδη πῆγεν ἡ βοή,
> καὶ τ' ἀκούσαν οἱ ἀντρωμένοι
> καὶ χαρῆκαν οἱ καημένοι.

There were so many guns fired
That the sound went down to Hades
And the courageous men there heard it
And, poor souls, were much enheartened.

Between these two improvisors, we can place the blind singers that we of our generation have seen, or those on whom we have evidence from older times; those who, going from house to house or circulating in the streets, sang the exploits of soldiers in the War of 1912 or of those who participated in the Macedonian battles or in the Revolution of 1821. It was thus that they earned their living. This custom was almost a requirement for the older chieftains: "most of the chieftains of the klephtes and the captains of the Insurrection of 1812 had, for the most part, their own rhapsodists." The proposition of Karaïskakis to Panayotis Soutos is still mentioned as the poet himself has handed it down to us: "I will act, you will write." We need alter nothing in this familiar statement in order to imagine, going back a thousand years, the Byzantine scholar, Arethas. He tells us that the Paphlagonians composed some songs relating the ordeals of illustrious heroes and went from house to house singing for money. If we turn to the past, we see the ancients had their rhapsodists; later we find the folksongs, both historical and klephtic. During the time of Arethas, the period that concerns us here, it is the Paphlagonians who sing the akritic songs.

Akritic Songs

The Byzantines called the frontiers *akres;* the *akritas* is a border guardian. Akritic songs were inspired, naturally, by military exploits and heroic enterprises that took place on the Asiatic borders with all the savagery of that time and place. The Asiatic element of exaggeration, which we find in the ballads, appears here as well in all its grandeur. The heroes of these songs are not tailored to human measure, but appear as supermen with titanic powers. Their weapons are those a human hand cannot raise; even their horses are supernatural.

> The horse of Kostas eats iron, that of Alexis rocks,
> And that of the young Vlach uproots the trees.

A hero of the akritic songs never fights against a single enemy, but always against many:

> There were neither five, nor eighteen,
> Seven thousand enemy and I was all alone.

Savage loves and hard battles are the materials of these songs. The exaltation of bravery and prowess is their exclusive purpose. However, in addition, the akritic songs touch on all the general themes found in the folksongs. In fact, their epic character combined with the descriptions of battles and conflicts or the swift racing of horses confers on the akritic songs a more condensed and more epigrammatic rhythm.

The Story of *Digenis Akritas*

It appears that some scholarly compiler thought to recast these songs and create a long romance in verse, in which he would exalt the grandeur of the akritic heroes while simultaneously making an entertaining and edifying narrative. The central hero of this compilation is Digenis Akritas, born of a Mohammedan father and a Greek mother, whose name with its old, forgotten historical origin perhaps expresses his double background. The plot varies in the different extant forms of the work. In general outlines, however, we can summarize it as follows. The story begins with a long narration about the birth of the mother of Digenis, the beauty of the castle in which she lived, and her own beauty:

> Her face was sparkling as the snow,
> She blushed a little, taking a crimson hue.

The maiden learns about love from the statue of Eros in the garden of her palace. One day, while she is out walking with her servant girls, she encounters an emir, who abducts her. But the maiden has five brothers who seek him out and find him so enamored by her beauty that he consents to become a Christian in order to marry her. Digenis Akritas is born of this marriage. Even as a young child, he exhibits superhuman strength and an exceptional bravery. As he grows older, he follows in his father's footsteps, and he also abducts a young maiden and marries her. Many other exploits of Akritas follow, exploits of war and love, as well as descriptions of the castle that Digenis builds on the banks of the Euphrates River. Then we have the death of his father, of his mother, the illness and death of Digenis, and finally the death of his wife.

This composition of thousands of verses is characterized by the total lack of proportion; an insignificant detail will lead the compiler to long digressions totally unrelated to the principal subject. The manner in which this work has come down to us and the relatively recent variants in the different manuscripts do not permit us to form concrete ideas about the original, which in all probability can be attributed to the tenth century. However, there is every reason to believe that this particular disorder should be attributed to the initial redactor, and that, if he frequently digresses from his subject, it is with the intention of charming, through his long descriptions, the naive public to whom he addressed himself. On closer examination of various sections composing this romance, we distinguish a qualitative unevenness between them. This is obviously the result of multiple origins of the work. Certain verses and certain passages are worthy of the best folk poems and are perceptibly inspired by them. Digenis mourns the death of his mother in these words:

Who then has torn the roots of my life?
Who has turned off my light so I no longer see?

But, on the other hand, the long descriptions of the gardens reveal a scholarly origin. For this reason, the work has been compared to Byzantine chronicles or hagiographies, where the principal line of the narration is episodic. These same characteristics and the same content, which associate love with heroism, is found, moreover, in all the metrical romances of love during the Byzantine period. From this point of view, therefore, it would be incorrect to call this work an epic, and especially a national epic of the modern Greeks, as Nicholas Politis, the folklorist, characterized it.

It is a fact that Akritas was born during a great epic moment, not only in Byzantine history, but also in that of European and Oriental literature, where similar creations were produced. The romance of Akritas is the fruit of an advanced civilization with a long literary tradition, and a comparison with those nearly contemporary works of the West and East is possible only after this differentiation has been made. Moreover, we do not have the original in our hands; the manuscripts we have are not older than the fourteenth century. The Grottaferrata manuscript is of the fourteenth century; those of Athens, Trebizond, and Eskorial are of the sixteenth century; the prose version of Andros and that of Ignatios Petritzis from Chios are both of the seventeenth century. The most popular version of language is the Eskorial manuscript. This manuscript was first examined during the most combative period of demoticism and was considered to represent a much older version of the work. Today, this thesis is no longer commonly accepted, which reinforces the arguments about the scholarly character of the composition. Nonetheless, interest in this work is not diminished by these findings. Aside from the linguistic and historical interest, we come to what is worth emphasizing, the psychological point of view: the chivalric spirit of the heroes, the exalted position of women, and the strong feeling of sin. These elements, all basically Christian, soften the primitive and savage instincts of the heroes. The delicate and barely perceptible irony that suffuses the work transfers our interest to the aesthetic value of the work; that, certainly, is uneven and varies from one section to another and from one variant to another. At its best moments, the work recreates the plasticity and sensation of the physical world which characterizes the folksongs. Moreover, in pure morphology, the fifteen-syllable verse, whose second hemistich amplifies the meaning of the first, brings us quite close to the morphology of the folksong.

Akritas had already been praised and cherished during Byzantine times. In the twelfth century, a poet who sought to honor the emperor, addressed him in these terms: "The gallant warrior, the new Akritas."

The Chronicle of Moreas

The epic of *Digenis Akritas* brings us to another long poem, this one of the fourteenth century, known as *The Chronicle of Moreas* which relates the conquest of the Peloponessus by the Franks in chronicle form. Battles are described with an abundance of details, which recreate the life of French chivalry on Greek soil. The importance of this work is considerable from a historical, as well as a linguistic, point of view, because the versifier, uninfluenced by the literary tradition of Byzantine scholars, gives us a faithful picture of the language in use during his time. *The Chronicle of Moreas* bears witness to the fruitful coexistence of Greek and Western civilizations on Greek soil. But the poet's aesthetic insufficiency, which usually places him outside the history of literature proper, forces us to examine the importance of this Greek-West union and the rich aesthetic literary results it produced when we consider the primitive poetry of Cyprus and the Dodecanese. *The Chronicle of Moreas* is nothing more than a versified chronicle and does not admit of any literary pretentions.

In vain will a reader search through the nine thousand verses of the most complete version for the slightest lyrical note, for some outburst of inspiration. The descriptions drag on endlessly; the narration intends to omit no single detail. Dramatic interest, which rarely appears, proceeds not from the narrator but from the events themselves. *The Chronicle of Moreas,* though written in blank verse, precedes both chronologically and in magnitude that particular group of metrical works we will see below, those we will classify as *verse chronicles.* We mean those chronicles written in blank verse known in Greek under the name of *rimes.* Their subject matter constitutes a spiritual monument to the cultural exchanges between the Greeks and the West that resulted from the Crusades and extended with greater intensity the earlier relations of the same order. The importance of these exchanges for Greek culture is manifested throughout the entire literary history which follows.

Achilleid

The unknown poet of the *Achilleid* appears to be following the *Digenis Akritas* quite closely. This time we have a chivalric romance whose heroes, despite their ancient names, show traces of a clearly modern Greek character in their psychic texture and in their social awareness. In its initial form, this work appears to belong to the beginning of the fifteenth century. The poet is inspired by *Digenis* in the general plan, but in the details he uses the knowledge he has acquired from the ancient romances, from ecclesiastical literature, and from the folksongs, which he drew on for psychology, sometimes even borrowing their language:

> I found a bird in a cage, which knew nothing of love,
> Which was ignorant of the servitude of Eros, of love.
> I took the partridge, and I left the cage.

In a popular song such as this one, or more precisely, in a work intended for the popular classes, it is worth noting and stressing an element that is encountered in all periods of neo-Hellenic literary production and that thus assumes particular importance in our eyes. Ancient Agamemnon is a symbol of Hellenism; he is the pride of the Greeks. He has vanquished the Frank in single combat as later, in *Erotokritos,* the young Cretan will vanquish Karamanites.

The conscious memory of antiquity, though deformed and disfigured, continues to live and even to flourish during these years. Thus, contemporary with the *Achilleid,* the bishop of Epirus, John Comnenus, commissioned Constantine Hermoniakos to paraphrase the *Iliad.* Since the transposition was executed from a secondary source, it has only a vague resemblance to the original, and it would not bear mentioning except that it does help us imagine the particular climate of the fifteenth-century Hellenism.

> King Agamemnon took Cassandra, sister of Hector,
> Daughter of Priam, the prophetess, the diviner,
> Beautiful and wise.

The poem continues in this tone for nearly nine thousand verses. The *War of Troy,* dated at about the same time, also presents only a cultural interest. It is a translation of more than eleven thousand political verses * of the romance of Benoît de Sainte More. The *History of the Long-Suffering Apollonius of Tyre* also returned to Greece from the West. This probably can be traced to the fourteenth century, when a direct Greek source of the history of Alexander the Great existed (inspired by the *History of Alexander the Great* by Pseudo-Callisthenes), a work which in all probability dates back to the same century. The original forms of these two works are in free political verse, but they are devoid of any literary inter-

---

*Unrhymed accentual lines of fifteen syllables. The term "political" comes from Polis (Constantinople) where this form originated.

est. However, we will refer to them again when we treat of a later historical period, because they were printed and circulated widely during the years of Turkish enslavement.

Metrical Romances

The romantic side of *Digenis Akritas* and the influences exercised by the Western world on the Byzantine period bring us to another group of works, to the Byzantine metrical romances of love, which perpetuate the ancient tradition of "erotica" in prose and in the "epyllia."

They are directly related with the works of the same genre which we will encounter in the ancient Byzantine literature of this same period or slightly earlier than the works under discussion. The principal verse romances which concern us here are titled after the names of their heroes: *Imperios and Margarona, Florios and Platziaflora, Kallimachos and Chrysorrhoe, Belthandros and Chrysantza, Libistros and Rodamne*. Let us observe further that the final example of this kind of work was a translation of Boccaccio's *Teseida*, executed, as it seems, at the end of the fifteenth century. John Schmitt, who was concerned with a systematic study of this subject, observed that we have here the connecting link between the older Byzantine endeavors and the later Cretan achievements. Enrica Follieri, on the other hand, insists in a series of recent works that folklore elements were grafted by the Greek adapter on an Italian original. We should add that, even morphologically, the work occupies an intermediary position, because its political verses, unrhymed in other respects, rhyme only at the end of each octet, in order to give somehow the impression of the octet strophe of the original.

If we look on the group of romances as a whole, we can easily trace their common characteristics. All were written at approximately the same period, that is, around the fourteenth or fifteenth centuries. Their Western influence is obvious; for some romances, we even have the French originals. They have only one subject: two young people in love are cruelly afflicted by Fate until the day of their happy union. This monotonous outline is ornamented with abundant incidents which often have a supernatural character. The heroes are pale shadows, conventional puppets, serving as a pretext for adventures and sensational episodes. All these romances are written in iambic verse of fifteen syllables. Their language is char-

acterized by a tendency to use the diminutive, by the facility in composing words, and by the laborious passage from synthetic to analytical syntax.

But a closer examination of nearly all these romances reveals in
each distinctive elements which force their individual study and
separate classification. In a work such as *Imperios,* the assimilation
of foreign texts is more advanced than the assimilation of foreign
culture. Its verse, purely Greek in form, presents clearly Western
chivalric morals. The recasting of the work has been executed by
someone skilled in manipulating language and verse and who reveals the existence of a former culture. But the Western original
appears under a strong Greek form. The reader formulates the same
impression in *Florios* and in *Callimachos.* However, when we come
to such works as *Libistros* or *Belthandros,* we ascertain that the
Greek assimilating power transmuted the European civilization expressed in these works and greatly accentuated their Greek character.

The elevation of a new aesthetic is also appreciable, for we are
concerned with entirely assimilated elements. Moreover, it is obvious
that the versifiers interpolated entire sections of folksongs, either because they were familiar with them, or because the folk audiences
desired them. Hence, in *Libistros,* we have:

> The mountains sigh, the plains partake of my sorrow, the cliffs
> lament, the prairies thunder. The trees under which I pass and
> the rocky mountain passes still carry my pain and sigh in my
> stead. They say: A soldier afflicted with sorrow has passed by;
> he was seized by desire for a lovely maiden. He poured out
> torrents of tears, his sobs rumbled like thunder, and his un-
> happy breathing covered the mountains with smoke. He had
> the sun as witness, that which covered the clouds on the spot
> where he passed, which sympathized with his sadness.

We find the same motifs here that charmed us in the folksongs;
further, we find human relations which are familiar to us from contact with Greek life. There is no break in continuity between the
folksongs and these romances:

> You have consumed and set my heart on fire;
> So may your own heart be consumed by flames of love,

we read in *Belthandros.* Or even,

> So great is my sorrow that even the rocks split open.

One ascertains further in these last works a superior psychology of character. The heroes are painted in relief, light and shade are distributed better. The folk accent of these late romances is explained less perhaps by their chronological differences, that they are of slightly later creation, than by the more advanced assimilation of European cultural elements which permitted their most direct folk elaboration.

We should also note some differences in composition; for example, in the loose structure of *Callimachos*, where the various sections rely on one another, it is evident that the compiler had reassembled many myths, while in *Libistros* he interwove two parallel accounts. The problem of sources, on the other hand, is more complicated, because the Western models, direct or even remote ancestors of these works have also been perceptibly influenced by classical antiquity or its tradition. This caused Krumbacher to characterize one of these works, the *Florios*, as "the termination of a literary circuit," which returned an originally Greek subject to Greece from the West. We should also observe that the titles of these works conform morphologically to a Greek tradition that takes us back to classical antiquity. The Oriental element observed in these romances, the fairy-tale element, the use of magic and miracle, and even the more precise comparisons that have been made between their episodes and corresponding episodes in the *Thousand and One Nights* or *Barlaam and Josephat*, gives evidence once more that these metrical romances do not come from a unique source, but that their unknown Greek versifiers composed them by assimilating not only Western and Greek but also Oriental material. Chronology can help resolve some of the problems we have enumerated, but even here we find difficulties. These texts have not come down to us in their original versions; we do not even know if they were originally in written form. It has been maintained, with some likelihood, that these works were created by rhapsodists, and only later written down, after they had been altered greatly, either intentionally, or very simply to fit them to the written language in use at the time. The alterations in a text within the space of two centuries or more should make us cautious with regard to linguistic as well as cultural indications and we should not draw chronological conclusions.

Only in rare instances can we attribute one of these works to a specific author or to a restricted chronological period. *Kallimachos* we can consider the work of someone called Andronicus Comnenus and it was probably written between 1310 and 1340, as Michel Pichard has established. But it is usually even difficult to determine in which country these works were recast. Internal evidence, such as place names, reveal a contact with the Turks, which would bring us to those regions of Byzantine Asia where the empire came into conflict with the advancing Turks. On the other hand, certain linguistic indications bring us to the islands along the coast of Asia Minor, Rhodes, Cyprus, or even Crete.

We can hope that more recent literary research will clarify somewhat their topical and chronological origin and at the same time refine their aesthetic form by removing later alterations. In their present condition, it is difficult to place them in the history of the genre insofar as time and place are concerned. These poems prepare the way for the flowering of Cretan literature; they herald the moment when, following a long literary apprenticeship and a progressive familiarity with Western culture, a Greek land attained one of the heights of national creation. Oriental, Western, and classical elements, assimilated by literary men in whom the folk tradition continued to live, gave this genre at its height a maturity of which we have seen only the beginnings.

Having reviewed a purely folk production and then a mixed production, that is, one in which folk and scholarly elements coexist in the same work, we will now turn to the cultivated production, or more precisely, the urban production, which is removed from folk tradition. During the period with which we are concerned here, we can take the *ptochoprodromika* poems as a typical example of the latter genre. Along with these, however, we will examine some other products written in the same or a similar spirit.

Chapter 3

"Accursed be Letters"

Ptochoprodromos

Ptochoprodromos

Digenis participated in love and war in the valleys and mountains of Asia. The heroes of the romances circulated around unreal feudal castles. But poor Prodromos wandered under the windows of the palace of the emperor of Constantinople seeking charity. It appears here that the folk tradition has been interrupted. We are in a large city in a cosmopolitan center where language, customs, and spirit have been profoundly altered by all kinds of movement and by a mixture of populations. Ptochoprodromos was begging. His only dream was to eat somewhat better and to find rest from the torments engendered by poverty. As all the other characters we have come to know—Digenis, Belthandros, and Callimachos—Ptochoprodromos was also a hero in his own way; that is to say, he was representative of a certain class of men. His faulty morality, his lack of pride, his lack of higher aspirations should not be attributed to him personally, but to the class to which he belonged, and was expressed through his supplications and his fundamental mediocrity. Moreover, even though we have a group of poems that have come down to us under the name of Ptochoprodromos, we are not certain whether the name designates one or more than one literary personality. In the twelfth century, Byzantium knew a man of the court, a poet and writer, who was called Theodore Prodromos. His life is unknown to us. His works, written in an archaic manner, have been determined. But his name is associated with a group of poems composed in the folk language of the period and present the poet himself as the hero who recounts his torments and who seeks protection from the emperor. At first, the archaic poet and the folk poet appear to be one and the same man. They lived at approximately the same period, that of the Comneni. If the one was a courtier, it is clear that the other also had some connection with the court. However, certain biographical details lead us to believe that the two persons should be distinguished from one another. The controversy around the single or double personality of Prodromos has gone so far as to support the theory that there were three authors by the same name. But if we examine the poems of Ptochoprodromos more closely, we find another solution that today appears more probable. The poems of Ptochoprodromos were not the works of a single author, nor do they belong chronologically to a period that corresponded to a single life span.

The poems that survive under that name are six in number. In the first, Ptochoprodromos traces his conjugal life; in the second he laments over his poverty; in the third and fourth, he is a monk and reproaches the abbots of the convent; in the fifth and sixth, he describes the poverty of the intellectuals in somber colors and compares their careers to less honorable but more lucrative professions. Even if we were to stop at this point in our investigation, this would suffice to show us that the only distinctive characteristics of the hero-author, common in all the poems, were poverty and misfortune. As for the rest, he sometimes appears as a married man, father of many children; sometimes he appears as a monk; and at other times, he appears first endowed with a solid culture and then as an individual with an elementary education. These incompatibilities between the different portraits and the real linguistic and chronological difficulties prevent us from attributing all these works to a single poet. We should add further than in the two pairs of poems mentioned earlier, the third and fourth and the fifth and sixth, the manner in which the subject is treated corresponds to the manner described in the preceding chapter where different traditional versions of the same romances were treated. Consequently, we can postulate here as well that the primary source, written or oral, was altered by later redactors. This reinforces the hypothesis that we have a hero of the urban folk poems—an indigent and undignified type—who was presented each time by a different author and placed by him in social situations with different professions.

In any case, these poems, which have no clear formal value, excite a very vivid interest as much for their profound folk sagacity as for their rich portrayal of manners. The first is addressed to the Emperor Mavroyannis, John Comnenus. The poet appears to have an air of pleasantry, but in reality he is suffering cruelly:

But I am suffering greatly, and I am experiencing profound grief,

> I suffer from a cruel malady, and I endure torments, O what
> torments!

The emperor need not imagine some severe illness; he is harrassed

> By a shrewish woman with a very witty tongue.

And here, Ptochoprodromos begins to describe his torments:

> I certainly fear her tongue, I fear her anger.

Her principal weapon, certainly, is her language:

> Sir, you are not neat. Sir, what have you to say?
> Sir, what have you brought home? Sir, what have you brought?
> What dress have you designed? What cloth for me have you
> woven?
> What petticoat have you given me? I've never seen the Easter
> festivals.
> Only twelve years of misery and privations have I endured with
> you.
> Nor have I put a buckle on my feet that came from your work.

She continues her grievances in a dozen verses. She is wellborn, while he is of humble origin: "You are you, Ptochoprodromos, and I am a Mantzoukini." She does nothing but complain. She tyrannizes her husband in a thousand other ways. She gives him no food to eat. They fight. The author continues in this tone for two hundred seventy verses and ends by appealing for charity so that the emperor will not lose Prodromos, "his best courtier."

In the second poem, addressed to an unknown august person, we find a description of misery and hunger that Ptochoprodromos suffers which ends also with a supplication for charity. The third is dedicated to Manuel Comnenus. Prodromos is now a monk and he writes "against the abbots." There are two superiors in the monastery who sieze every opportunity to plague the unfortunate monk. Punishment follows every offense, interdictions multiply, nor do they cease to remind him of the inferiority of his condition before the other monks.

> He is a student, he is a scholar author.
> You, you cannot even recite the alphabet.

The heaviest and most painful tasks are reserved for the poor monk. Fasting is not the same for everyone. The meals of the superiors are described in glowing colors and in titilating details. The other monks eat only bread. As for money, the situation is the same.

> For themselves they collect money in abundance,
> For us they preach sermons on avarice.

The fifth poem is addressed to Manuel Comnenus himself. Ptochoprodromos remembers the time when his father pressured him to get an education.

> My son, learn letters, if you want to be successful. See that one?
> He used to walk on foot, but now he is covered with gold,
> He has a horse at a triple portal and he jogs around on a grey mule.

With magnificent examples his father convinces Ptochoprodromos:

> And I learned letters, but at the price of what efforts!
> And later when I became a clerk, I lacked for bread and even crumbs.
> I cursed the letters, and I said with tears,
> "O Christ, accursed be letters and accursed whoever cultivates them."

Then he goes into comparisons with the most scorned professions. There is the embroiderer in gold, his neighbor the leatherer, the tailor, the baker, the sour-milk man, the dyer, the textile merchant, his neighbor, the screen maker, who all, throughout the interminable descriptions of starvation, eat well.

We cannot deny that these texts have a certain aesthetic value, owing to the imagination and descriptive abilities of the narrator. However, his language lacks the cultivation of the language of the folksong; that is, his urban origin is visible. Behind the laments of Ptochoprodromos, there is no single cultural tradition to elevate them to the level of art. But though this essential element is lacking, other elements of the folksong abound. There is the rich imagination of the narrator that permits the hungry man to describe in lavish details the banquets to which he is not invited, the joys of a luxurious life that does not belong to him; there is the descriptive ability that permits him to revive before our eyes the thousand aspects of a city with its characteristic noises and cries of ambulatory merchants, the swarming streets; he restores for us the Byzantine home, alternating humble sufferings with obscure pleasures.

Moreover, this aspect of the poems of Ptochoprodromos contributes considerably, with its extreme precision and evocative force, to our knowledge of the daily life of the Byzantines. But it is the ironic element, the self-satire or mockery, which actually associates these poems most closely with the tradition of the folksong. Ptochoprodromos knew how to see, how to make us see, how to distinguish the ridiculous, and how to make us laugh. We have found and stressed this element of irony in the folksong. The comparison between the two, the songs inspired by the open country and the urban creations, permits us to evaluate these latter and to define them. One could say that the spirit of the folksong, the results of a traditional popular culture was entirely lost in the composite milieu of the city. On the contrary, the spirit of the folksong, with the intelligent vision of a man of the people, lost none of its acuity in being transported to the city. Prodromos is the displaced man of the city, he is mischievous, a man alive and versatile, disciplined, whose business sharpens the spirit to a point of making him search for all kinds of profitable occasions. The humor in the Ptochoprodromos poems is of the same quality as the gibes of actual idlers. This comparison helps us find a better solution to the problems posed by the personality of Prodromos. Indeed, it is the people who speak through his mouth.

Glykas

Irony, then, appears to be the common characteristic found on the one hand in the folksongs and on the other in the urban manifestations of the Byzantine people or in the folk poet of this period. We find irony again in a work somewhat analogous with the poems of Prodromos that has been preserved under the title *Poems of Michael Glykas, Written in Prison Where He Was Sent at the Accusation of a Malevolent Person*. Glykas explains to Michael Comnenus that he has been imprisoned unjustly, he describes his torments in prison, and he entreats his freedom. This more literary versifier has a tendency to alternate scholarly elements and folk elements. The folk accent is characterized by a wise banter which predominates in his work, as we see in the following: "The donkey kicks his feet; they beat the saddle to revive him and to prevent him from lashing out."

The same irony is found in a series of other works which also have their roots in Byzantine folk life and which respond to its spiritual demands. It is natural that we begin with those relating to religious life. This life was a rich source of inspiration for the monks or the secular moralists. However, as these works often touched on religious matters, a characteristic of strongly religious historical periods similar to the one under consideration here, they create a familiarity in the awareness of the faithful that appears entirely incompatible with the reverence attached to objects of worship. During all periods when faith flourished, in all countries, East and West, where religiosity expanded, one perceives a particular form of humor that we can call "a monkish humor" which did not venerate the object of worship but often took it as a subject in order to express a general religious way of life.

Religious Satire and Parody

We can classify among the products of such a religious inspiration a certain number of folk creations, such as the *Philosophy of the Drunkard,* which is attributed to the twelfth century and is not, in reality, a religious parody, though it refers constantly to religious matters. It is characteristic that this poem has been attributed to Theodore Prodromos, that is, to Ptochoprodromos.

The Book of the Life of the Honest Donkey has no religius content, but its title is significant and the entire story it relates rests on the confessions of an innocent man to a cunning one:

> I begin by making a sincere confession,
> After that, I will confess my sins,
> And last, it will be the donkey's turn.
> We will hear one another out.

This is also satire, similar to that found in *Against the Abbots* by Prodromos. The work is dated in the fifteenth century. Satire against the clergy, those who "swallow the camel and filter the mosquito," is full of wit. The donkey is accused of a crime he had not committed with the sole purpose of condemning him to be eaten by the wolf and the fox. His confession does not contain any basic accusation; once in a while he eats a lettuce leaf belonging to his master. But the judges find in this admission a mortal sin: "Is there a more execrable sin in the world?" All this is expressed with a great intemperance of language.

The Mass of the Beardless Man is slightly older in form as it has come down to us. This obscene parody of religious texts reminds us of the ceremonies of the Middle Ages and primitive Christianity which parodied the Mass. Here one has difficulty isolating a passage that does not contain obscenities.

Though this work can neither charm nor move us, still it provokes unreserved admiration for the flexible linguistic and imaginative talent of the unknown composer. The recent editor of this work, Emile Legrand, mentions (eventually to disregard the fact) that this might have been a personal satire. But if we were in the presence of a personal satire, or more generally, of a religious parody against the beardless monks, it becomes clear that we have here a genre extending from Byzantine times to our own period, a genre cultivated by such later religious scholars as Dapontas and Papadiamantis. The extension of the ecclesiastical forms to subjects entirely alien to religion exhibits how profound were religious roots in the Hellenic consciousness.

Books of the Lives of Saints and Exhortatory Literature

But the religious experience was not exhausted in satire and in parody. The simplest forms of spiritual life were ministered to in folk life by books of saints' lives written in the folk language and the different edifying poems. This group of works constituted the spiritual nourishment of the Greek people during the entire Byzantine period and even in later years. Much as this group of texts has been praised and their importance stressed in our days, they have not become an object of the scientific study they merit. Influences, morals, and history are some of the areas from which these works could be investigated. Yet, their clearly narrow religious character classifies them as religious literature with which we are not concerned here. However, the more general exhortatory literature should not go unmentioned.

Spaneas goes back to the twelfth century, or even a little earlier.

In it we see a father teaching his son the social virtues. The direct influence of *Discourse of Demonikos* by Isocrates has been detected in this work. Without doubt, a methodical investigation of later Greek texts reveals the presence of abundant traces of the Attic teacher down to the days of Koraes and perhaps later.

From this same period, around the twelfth century, we find sixteen beautiful political verses under the title "Prayer of a Sinner." The dramatic struggle between passion and aspiration for virtue is manifested with vehemence and with great force of expression:

> I should mourn from day to day,
> I should eat the dust of earth, the leaves of trees,
> I should drink my tears spilled for my sinful deeds.

Expatriation

The different poems inspired by expatriation and by nostalgia for birthplace form a separate group in this scholarly production. The relation existing between the inspiration of the scholar-poet and that of the folk singer is clearly visible. Even if we did not possess a great number of other indications, the songs of expatriation would suffice of themselves to convince us that the boundaries between these two forms of creation are hardly distinct. Naturally, here as well there is a relationship between the inspiration of the scholarly poet and the folksinger. The bird that transmits a message is an element of the folksong and it has passed to the scholarly poetry:

> And the birds bent down and picked up the piece of paper,
> From afar I saw it; what will they do with it?
> I watched them as they gathered around each other,
> They held a council and often whispered to each other. . . .

The nostalgia evoked by life in a strange land accords with the tragic destinies of the Greek people. We possess three pieces in verse devoted to this subject. Their initial form dates to the Byzantine period. All three are written in free verses of fifteen syllables.

> What misfortunes those pitiful foreigners endure!
> See how voyages in foreign lands have withered me.
> I have suffered, I have been tossed about;

> I have seen, I know henceforth what expatriates endure,
> I know the many evils that crush life in foreign lands.

There is reason to believe that these poems were circulated widely in manuscript form among the Greek people before and after the fall of Constantinople. One of the three is in the form of an alphabet. These acrostics, known as *The Alphabet*, should be mentioned for their ancient origin, their great diffusion, and their tenacious survival to our times. The genre encompasses various subjects; we know of one other alphabet, aside from the one on expatriation, that is called *Alphabet, Pious and Edifying, On the Vanity of the World*.

This alphabet presents material of no great interest. The acrostics come after every fifth verse and form a total of one hundred twenty verses with numerous repetitions. The period to which this work is attributed is determined not only by the language, but also by an opening rhyme. It is written in free verse with a fifteen-syllable line which every so often rhyme.

> See how concupiscence has conquered and made you lose your
>   soul!
> Be penitent, refrain from concupiscence.
> Fast, impose sacrifices on yourself, stay away from women.
> For good or evil, abstain from all desire,
> In the end to gain celestial glory and the respect of men.

In these verses, which begin with the letter π in Greek, we again find the theme of female malignity, which was converted to a monkish malignity and profoundly stamped the neo-Hellenic intellectual production.

As for the edification poems, we should not pass over *Comforting Discourse on Unhappiness and Happiness*, which should be attributed to the late Byzantine period. Unhappiness, happiness, and time are personified and romanticized in this allegorical narrative in political verses and relate the vicissitudes of an unfortunate youth in quest of happiness. But the gnomic and moralistic elements of this prosaic work are overwhelmed by the narration and description.

History and Chronicle

The religious texts did not suffice to satisfy the intellectual needs of the Byzantine people. Some texts satisfy other curiosities and different interests. First of all, there are those concerned with history.

Parallel with the great historical writings of Byzantium, the official ones with their archaic language and Thucydidean allure, we are offered some modest documents. Under regimes like the Byzantine Empire, history assumes a political purpose. It did not suffice that history address itself only to the cultured public. Works were needed, simply written yet comprehensible to auditors and to readers with a limited culture. At that time, history was not meant to expose fact primarily; it required narration that at the same time would entertain those whom it would instruct, not only children, but also the mass of adults, and in general all those who were accustomed to marvelous tales. Hence, even in a centralized civilization that was not concerned with the diffusion of instruction, one saw a history written more simply, a history in a popular form and language called the chronicle.

The chronicle was also a heritage from classical times. But in Byzantium, it acquired a particular importance; it became popular with the common people and continued in vogue throughout the Turkish domination. Here we touch on the marvelous narratives. The chronicle became a tale; the accent was placed on that which attracted by its strangeness, on that which varied from the rule and aroused the imagination of the simple man. The chronicle writers usually began with the creation of the world and arrived at their own times, regularly following only one source for every historical period treated, sometimes with such fidelity that it is difficult to resolve questions asked by critics. At other times, they copied one another or used foreign texts, altering them arbitrarily. Fate, and the manner in which these texts were used, places them rightfully where they belong, among the anonymous, impersonal folk productions. The same fate was reserved for the various popular pamphlets that were published, particularly in Venice during the Turkish occupation of Greece. These pamphlets contained irresponsible changes and revisions, and arbitrary adaptations from older sources.

The first chronicle writer to make use of the folk language, that is, of the *koine* in use during his time, appears to have been John Malalas, who lived in the sixteenth century. The long and almost uninterrupted chain of Byzantine and post-Byzantine chronicles begins with him. In the ninth century, the Patriarch Nicephoros distinguished himself with a simplicity of language and with a clearly apologetic tone. A little later, the monk Georgios, while he had no linguistic importance, gave us samples of a warm, living folk speech, as, in the eleventh century, did John Skylitzes, who was distinguished for the simplicity of his style, Zonaras, in the twelfth century, who was more conservative in language, and Michael Glykas, an exceptionally spirited Byzantine figure of whom we spoke earlier in this chapter. Certainly, the manner in which the chronicle writers worked in general did not permit them to show great achievement in style and language. Remaining close to their sources, they differed in language each time they changed sources. Here the declaration of Zonaras at the beginning of his work is characteristic:

> If the style is lacking in unity and is not in all respects similar to itself, no one should be astonished. . . . Drawing on different sources, I have made use of situations and phrases employed by the authors who inspired me. Consequently, in places where I have imitated them and have written somewhat in their manner, I have varied my style so that my text will present no incoherence.

During the last years of Byzantium, the renascent spirit that marked the period of the Paleologi and the oppositions inherent in all humanism brought certain writers closer to the spoken language of their contemporaries, while other writers, on the contrary, adopted an extreme archaic language. Hence, we find living linguistic elements in John Kanonos, Doukas, and George Phrantzis, all three of whom belonged to the fifteenth century. The works of these three writers present, in different proportions, forms and aspects of language as we come to know them in writings during the Turkish domination and later. Doukas and Phrantzis had no hesitation in using Italian and Turkish words in their texts; the archaic ideal competed successfully with the contemporary intellectual requirements of the times. The tendency toward translating older historians into the spoken language should be attributed to similar requirements of reality and was encountered even during the Turkish domination where historical awareness is presented without interruption.

Allegorical Satire

We should also mention, though practical recitations and popular prescriptions of medicine are not a part of our subject, the popular works of natural science, which in various ways were intended to satisfy human curiosities about the world or which simply served to recall things that should be remembered.

The satiric element reappears. Such a method is found in the *Book of Fruit,* whose early form perhaps belongs to the twelfth century. From all evidence, this is an adaptation from memory of folk wisdom. Here we have a trial of various fruit articulated in the pompous diction of Byzantine court etiquette:

> Under the reign of the celebrated Quince,
> And supervised by the very illustrious Quince,
> Assisted by the Pomegranate. . . .

The *Book of Fruit* was enjoyed even in later years and was read widely when this short text was published in the popular pamphlets from Venice. Even recently there was mention of it by an old man from the island of Naxos. Parallel with the *Book of Fruit,* we have the *Book of Fish,* whose theme is the same but with names of fish: "And at once the fish exclaimed and said in a single voice, 'Long may you live, our Prince.' "

Three other metrical works seem to have had greater variety and served other purposes. These works were *Narrative of the Quadrupeds, The Book of Fowl,* and the older and more significant *Bestiary.* The *Quadruped* (in unrhymed political verses) should perhaps be dated to the second half of the fourteenth century. The lion, king of the animals, summons all the quadrupeds to assess their virtues and vices. One by one, all the animals appear; they present their own virtues and denounce the vices of their colleagues. In the end, a quarrel breaks out among the animals, and the herbivorous animals vanquish the carnivorous:

> Thus the prophesy of the singer is fulfilled:
> "The king, for all his might, cannot be saved,
> Neither can a giant be saved
> For all his strength."

According to the introductory verses, the work had a dual purpose: "For this story was written to combine utility with pleasure." The burden, however, falls on the side of didacticism. The habits of the animals and their distinctive characteristics are the main theme of this long metrical work. The experience of things in nature is combined with imaginary stories about the peculiarities of different animals. The unknown author is spirited in his descriptions and his remarks are judicious. The horse is presented as proud and assured:

He reared, he descended, he stopped,
He craned his neck, he shook his mane.

Not lacking from the work is a certain quality of folk humor. When the war is renewed between the animals, the poet remembers the heroic accents of the folksongs:

The panther cried below:
"Where are you comrades, brothers, carnivorous animals?
You stand there looking and come not to my aid."

A sarcastic tone, moreover, which characterizes the recriminations among the animals, becomes witty, and there is great freedom of language. Also, the different parts of the work are more artistically unified. We see a narrative that is linked in a perfectly coherent manner.

These latter qualities are lacking from the *Book of Fowl*. The king of birds, the eagle, summons the birds to the wedding of his son. Each of the guests finds an opportunity to criticize his neighbor. This work appears older than the *Narrative of the Quadrupeds*, perhaps because it contains more folk elements. It is in unrhymed political verses; the story is imperfectly formed and the connection between the different episodes is purely external. Otherwise, the resemblance to the *Narrative* is great, especially the common curiosity about things in nature. The origin of both works can be traced to the *Bestiary*.

The origin of the *Bestiary* takes us back to antiquity. But the form which interests us here is in a manuscript probably dating to the fifteenth century. It is also in unrhymed political verses, except where prose is inserted in a few places. In forty-eight short chapters, we have the description and habits of different animals, real as a rule but sometimes imaginary. The description of each animal is followed by what each symbolizes. Ancient scientific knowledge alternates with folk inspirations, with erroneous observations, or with religious beliefs. The work in its various forms circulated during the Middle Ages, both in the East and the West. It was a precious source of knowledge and served as a comparison between classroom teaching and the physical world.

Part Two
Survival and Renewal
Hellenism from 1453
to 1669

The folksong continues its journey. The mixed forms, enriched by Western elements, reach their peak in Crete. The dispersion adopts in theory and practice a doctrine advocating the formation of a language based on the spoken language elaborated by scholars. The period, placed conventionally between 1453 and 1669, is clearly an extension of the past, particularly in what concerns the mixed form. The cultural tone is given by the progressive and courageous spirit of the church: by religious humanism. The rise of the ruling class among the Hellenes is assured in 1669. The Phanariots will assume leadership.

Chapter 4

Out of the Ruins

Greece Under Turkish Domination

1453. The Byzantine Empire was now only a name, a symbol that had almost no reality. Ever since the Byzantines recaptured Constantinople from the Franks, the empire had been confined to its capital city. Incapable of procuring food from the outside, it was a monster that gradually consumed its own flesh. In the East there was the Empire of Trebizond; in the West the Despotate of Epirus and Moreas. The islands were small principalities, more or less autonomous, without organic dependence on the center. Poverty reigned everywhere. In the countryside, the lack of security reduced the supply of working hands, while the cities and monasteries overflowed. The more mobile and enterprising people became expatriates, either to lands occupied by the West or to the West itself. Yet in the metropolis, Constantinople, attempts were made for the continuance of outdated forms, condemned from the beginning because they had no correspondence to reality. Poverty ruled the metropolis. The schools, the Institutes, were unable to support their professors. Gennadios has left us a vivid description of this impoverishment and its consequences:

> Once the material wealth, which formerly had been the pride of Constantinople, was gone, not even the glory of letters remained to her misfortune. Truth to tell, she still maintained vestiges of former wealth, but her literary glory was only a false appearance. Shortly, she lost even that, for time revealed the ignorance that had taken possession of her.

Beyond the seas, however, in the hateful schismatic West, new cities were being organized; new families, full of ardor, dynamism, and wealth took the political administration and the intellectual renaissance into their hands. The West, which had never completely disavowed her interest in the classical tradition, regained her old curiosity and turned avidly to every source of knowledge now that she was renewing her wealth, now that her ships were bringing precious cargo and messages from different worlds. Through the study of Latin, the vision of ancient Greek wisdom was revived in their eyes. Knowledge of the Greek language became the ideal of every cultivated Italian or Frenchman. But treasures of Greek beauty and Greek wisdom were not to be found in the West. The Greek manuscripts were preserved in monasteries and in libraries of the Greek Orient. This obliged the wealthy Franks, avid for knowledge, to go to the East to acquire the wisdom of the Greeks. Expeditions were organized, missions were created, whose purpose it was to assemble and to transport the Greek manuscripts from Greek soil to the West. Along with the manuscripts would come those who could decipher their secrets; the Greek scholars, fleeing from poverty and stagnation in the Greek state, departed for the West. And the greater the danger became, the greater the uncertainty and indigence in the East, the greater was the current of those fleeing to the West. The few scholars that Greece had continued to nurture departed one by one to secure their bread in the cities of Italy and France. There the Greek language continued to survive. As one writer put it, "Now in Italy the Greeks live better than those who live here." In Greece, only those who united their fate with religious struggles remained; those who believed that "it is far better to see the turban of the reigning Turks in Constantinople than the Latin mitre."

East and West

Indeed, on the intellectual level, the religious struggles at this time once more posed the eternal problem of Hellenism between East and West. In more ancient times, the strong Byzantine Empire had created a reality that was simultaneously a synthesis and an outgrowth of opposing forces, but now this reality no longer existed. Hellenism, which had absolute awareness of itself, must either lean toward the West or associate itself organically with it, or it must await its inevitable end. Hellenic religious awareness, on the one hand, and a lack of historical awareness, on the other, prevented the last representatives of the Byzantine faith from perceiving that the Western church had not sought to neutralize the racial idiosyncrasies nor had it ever been able to do so. Greek Orthodoxy, obstinately closing its eyes to reality, continued to rest on the same arguments she had used during the years when her faith was imposed and reinforced by a powerful empire. A group of bright intellectuals and politicians attempted to change this situation. Despite a myriad difficulties and pusillanimous controversies, the last Byzantine emperors were forced to realize the ecclesiastical union that they believed could save Byzantium. A few theologians supported their efforts. These political attempts did not take into account the spiritual problems, nor even the fundamental political reality of the moment. Constantinople was weak before the irresistable force of the Ottoman drive. All the attempts she made to survive were condemned to failure. Money was lacking, men were lacking, spirit was lacking, "And she waited for the Turk to capture her."

In this situation, one could observe three reactions taking shape among the scholars. The vast regions populated by the Greeks lived either in relative autonomy or under strong dynasties. It was in these regions that those who no longer believed in the empire sought refuge; and there, under relatively more favorable conditions, they attempted to survive and to transmit their knowledge. George Gemistos was installed at Mistra and he established a school which overshadowed with its brilliance the fading lights of Constantinople, the Queen of Cities. In Crete, where the Venetian domination was older, increasingly more stable conditions of life were created and a meritorious literary life began to develop. In other Greek islands as well, which early had passed into the hands of the Frankish dynastic rulers, a civilization was created which was a curious mixture of Greek and Western customs. This will be discussed in the following chapter. A certain number of Byzantines solved the problem by going to Italy or France. Among these were Chrysoloras, Laskaris, and Bessarion. There were others who did not leave Byzantium and who attempted to perpetuate in a vacuum what had once been the spirit of the empire and thus transmit it to future generations. But Constantinople, long before its fall, was already void of intellectual life. The Greek forces were scattered or had gone underground. When, in the last days of May 1453, the conqueror Mohammed entered Constantinople with his armies, this event only confirmed a state of events that had existed for a long time.

The number of scholars, those who chose to remain on Greek soil or those who emigrated to the West, were classified among the survivors of ancient literature by reason of the language they used. Nevertheless, they have a place in modern Greek literature to the extent that they displayed the spirit of their times. Furthermore, certain of these scholars used the spoken language of the times in some of their secondary works, a fact which also gives them a place in modern Greek literature. The earliest among the refugees to the West were Manuel Chrysoloras and Bessarion, contemporaries of the fall of Constantinople, and Janus Laskaris, who lived somewhat later. Their activities in the West should be mentioned. They made great efforts first to prevent the city from falling into Turkish hands and later toward a crusade which would regain the city. Here we should also mention Anthony Eparchos, who composed a long poem called *Lamentations on the Enslavement of Greece,* in which he deplored the fate of Greece and expressed a hope for her liberation. The few texts these men wrote in the spoken language show that the use of the ancient language had been responsible, to a large extent, for the lack of reality that characterized the literature of this period. Whenever the living language was used in a letter or any secondary text, we see that it corresponded plainly to the truth and reality of the moment. Thus, when Bessarion wrote as tutor to the children of Thomas Paleologus, he said:

> It is essential above all to attend to their education and to the formation of their moral character so that these children can become well educated, if you want them to be respected here. Otherwise, they will be scorned here, and you as well, and no one will turn to look at you. Their deceased father and I agreed on this. He also wished that they should dress and live entirely as Franks.

The fate of those who remained behind in Constantinople was worse. Reality forced the sultan to assure the survival of the Greek populations in the lands he had conquered, and his desire to prevent contact between Hellenism and the West brought him, in fact, to measures that would protect the Orthodox church. Within the Turkish state the patriarchate became an administrative mechanism with considerable authority over the Orthodox population.

First of all, such a measure naturally reinforced the barrier that had been raised between East and West. Further, the Turks granted special privileges to the *rayahs* in exchange for these Greeks keeping some order and preventing rebellions among their own people. This had complex results for the Greek population; it made possible the physical survival of the Greeks, but it did not contribute to the advancement of the nation. The loss of Constantinople and the subjugation of Greece were bitter experiences; however, sheer survival demanded the Greeks take advantage of the conditions the Turks imposed in order to reconstruct and reshape their lives. But peaceful coexistence was superficial; the flame sparked by the heroic actions of Constantine Paleologus not only illuminated the death of one world but also shone as the distant dawn of a new one.

Gennadios Scholarios, the first ecumenical patriarch enthroned after the fall of Constantinople, abandoned the sterile discussions with the Franks and began more profitable work which would benefit the Orthodox church and Hellenism. He attended to the establishment of a school near the Patriarchate from which the future dignitaries of the church would emerge. The necessity to maintain contact with the people who were ignorant of the archaic language led him to approximate the language of the people from time to time. Some of the texts in which he used the simpler idiom have been preserved: "Because you asked to learn what God sought in becoming man, listen to the reason: God had no need to be embodied in flesh, but mankind was praying for salvation. . . ."

The Folk Language Serves the Church

It must be observed, furthermore, that this phenomenon was not unique; it constituted one weapon which the Orthodox church, abandoning theological research, employed each time it sought to approach the folk consciousness directly or even in matters of refutation. The spiritual battles with the Turks, with the Hebrews, and with those in the West, and later the differences and the polemics with the disciples of the Enlightenment consecrated to a large extent the use of the folk language as a quasi-formal organ of the church. This pattern of operation did not proceed from a spirit of doctrine, nor did it presuppose it. The various propaganda attacks were not concerned with preserving the patrimony of the past or the conservative spirit of tradition; hence, they always utilized the *koine* language in order to attain their purpose better. The only means offered to the church to counteract the enterprises of the enemies was to imitate them. Hence, from this period until Napoleonic times and even later, we will observe campaigns of proselytism and the propaganda of Turks, Russians, British, French, Catholics, and

Protestants using the folk idiom spontaneously and without any attempt at theoretical justification. Parallel with this, we also observe the Eastern church operating in the same manner. Further, we will see the Greek people, also without any attempt at a theoretical justification, using the folk idiom each time they addressed the people and spoke about the people. It was so in the case of Rigas; it was so somewhat later, in the years before the War of Independence.

Insofar as church matters which arose in the period under discussion, the phenomenon of the *koine* was more evident in rhetoric. This was for the good reason that writing works in the popular language could hardly serve a people, the majority of whom were illiterate. No matter in which language a book was written, it would have been incomprehensible to them. The sermon of the church was another matter. Here, very early, we find texts rendered methodically in a language intended to be understood by the common people. And this was being done consciously and with great effort. In the sixteenth century, the church orators affirmed that they had great difficulty composing sermons in the folk language and that they preferred to compose in the archaic rather than in the new idiom. Models were lacking, examples were lacking, linguistic preparation was lacking. Paraphrases of religious texts in a simple language were also lacking. Every so often, from Byzantine times on, such religious paraphrases appeared, sometimes in verse form and at other times in prose. And even though they received no praise from the scholars, who remained indifferent to such manifestations, and even though they were exposed by the unskilled language to which they resorted, some of these translators and paraphrasers did attain the ends they sought. The diffusion of their redactions and the repeated editions for years testify that their efforts were not in vain. Though George Houmnos, who in the fifteenth century paraphrased the Old Testament in fifteen-syllable couplets, failed to receive a wide response, there were others who bequeathed a productive work for later generations. The libraries in the monasteries of the Greek Orient were full of religious paraphrases, patristic and ascetic treatises, written in a relatively simple language or even in the folk language. Many of these paraphrases were not published, but even this did not prevent their wide diffusion, which often extended beyond the monastery. By all indications, the apostolic spirit inspired the transcription of these edifying works, which includes efforts at translating the Bible into a simpler language.

Laments

While subjugated Hellenism sought to reconstitute itself in a manner to be indicated later, we see a series of texts appearing, some purely folk works, others scholarly, but all inspired by the popular tradition which revealed how profound the emotions aroused by the fall of Constantinople were. In this category, we can without hesitation include the *Song of Saint Sophia,* recently restored by our contemporary John Apostolakis.

> God calls, the earth calls, Heaven calls, Saint Sophia, the great monastery of the forty-five sounding boards and the sixty-two bells, calls. For each bell there is a priest and for each priest a deacon. When the Holy Relics and the King of the World arrive, a voice from Heaven will say: "Cease your psalmetry, lower the Relics, and send a message to the Franks to tell them to come for the Relics, for the Cross of gold and the Holy Bible and the Holy Table of Sacrifice, so that they will not be profaned." When the Virgin heard these words, Her icons wept. "Do not weep, Lady Virgin, do not let Your tears fall. One day, in years to come, all will be ours again."

Many texts exist which express amazement or emotion but also the hopes of the Greek people. We should not forget that the empire did not fall apart at one stroke, as though under a sudden great blow, or that the fall of Constantinople was the final stage in the advancing conquest of the Turks. This conquest, realized in successive stages of powerful aggression and feeble resistance, could have given the Greek people the notion that they were not observing the last act of a drama, but that it was simply one more episode in a long history. It would be a great mistake if, projecting our own historical awareness to those troubled times, we thought we had a clear perception of the importance of these crucial events. Constantinople fell, as Adrianopolis had fallen earlier, as Trebizond was to fall later.

The prestige of the Queen of Cities was immense, and for this reason her fall produced profound emotions. But for this reason as well, hopes were greater. One of the significant laments, inspired by the fall of Constantinople, expresses this psychology clearly:

Whoever is a Christian, let him weep for Constantinople, This
Queen of Cities was a home to all, to Greeks and Latins.

The empire could never be reestablished through its own powers.
But those from the West were also interested in stopping the advance of the Turks, in stopping their onrush:

The time has come for Christians, for Latins and for Romans,
For Russians and for Vlachs, Hungarians, Serbs and Germans,
All to unite in harmony, to become as only one,
And all the Christians to cry out with single voice,
And raise on high the Cross, the sign of Christ.

The unknown poet, who concealed his name because he was living
under Turkish domination, proceeded, as did all his colleagues who
had fled to the West, to detail the forces of the Turks and the possibility of liberating the city by means of a crusade. And he continued with details of military strategy for such an enterprise.

Other laments, also nearly contemporary with the fall of Constantinople, were less analytical and closer to folk improvisation:

"Ship, from whence come you, and where do you go?"
"I come from that accursed place, and from profound
darkness,"

writes one of these laments. Its rapid rhythm and the dialogue between the two ships met at sea gives the lament a number of elements similar to those of the folksong. Another lament, with fewer
folk elements and perhaps more artificial, describes the immensity of
the disaster:

You mountains weep, and rocks split open
Rivers diminish and fountains dry
.   .   .   .   .
And you celestial Moon, give no light to earth,
And you, flowing waters, stop running and stand still,
And you, O sea, proclaim the disaster, the Fall of Constantinople.

Even more scholarly in language and style is another lament in
which the destruction is described briefly and an appeal is made to
Christ to destroy the Turk. Lastly, we shall mention a lament in
dialogue, perhaps of later origin. The four patriarchates are con-

versing about the disaster and lamenting over the misfortune. In these verses also, one finds traces of a prayer that is full of hope:

> Only the Lord God can bring me comfort,
> And to me unhappy creature, only He can grant mercy.

Predictions

The phenomenon is characteristic. The fall of Constantinople, this material symbol of the empire, did not seem an end in the consciousness of contemporaries. On the contrary, the abundant prophetic production that accompanied all the historical accounts of the imperial court testify to a significant change after the fall of the city. All prophecies before the fall were pessimistic and predicted destruction and extinction because the fundamental scheme inherited from Hebrew prophetism desired that grandeur carry within it the seed of decay, the height, the first signs of future ruin. But once the fall of Constantinople had been accomplished and the city reduced to ruins, the same scheme was imposed to project the promise of salvation.

> The great misfortune of the Nation is situated exactly at the intersection of fears and hopes, of discouragement and encouragement. And thus, because prior to these terrible ordeals, the prophesies were sinister and announced disaster and ruin; after the Fall of Constantinople the diametrically opposed predictions gave evidence of a change which was produced in the state of the spirit of the nation.

At this moment, as is always the case in times of disaster and despair, the particular psychological conditions are created which urge man to accept the security that life has refused him, to accept the security emanating from unknown, mysterious powers. Even during the early Turkish domination, an organized group of prophesies began to appear which predicted "the end of the kingdom of Ishmael." They are included here from fifteenth and sixteenth century manuscripts:

> The time of grape gathering has come
> As though to cause the entire race
> Of Ishmael to disappear . . . .
> The river Rompheas will fill

> And wash away the weapons
> Of the Agarenes up to the Saracens,
> Up to the white fountain.

Of course, those who are prudent react to prophecies which have a dangerously optimistic hold on the souls of men:

> We place our hopes on oracles, on false prophecies,
> We waste our time on vain words,

writes Matthew, the Metropolitan of Myrees, at the beginning of the seventeenth century. We encounter this prophetic utterance later in a more energetic and profitable form, as a precious political instrument utilized for its own ends by foreign propaganda. In the meantime, it served only as evidence of the ceaseless agitation and hope which never stopped living under the cruel mantle of Ottoman domination.

However, thick as this mantle was, we have seen that it was to the Turk's interests not to stiffle all activity among the Greeks. The Greek population of the Turkish Empire, surrounded by potential invaders, were those which assured the wealth and taxes. They should live, at least so long as it was possible for them to furnish revenues for the conqueror. They should remain faithful to the dogmas of their religion, so long as that was essential to guarantee the collection of taxes. Thus, we see even during the worst hours of Turkish conquest, but in a much more systematic manner around the end of the sixteenth century when this aggressive drive fades, the Greek people begin to organize; they are offered administrative freedom, a judicial autonomy with its resultant advantages, and the possibility of acquiring wealth and education. The patriarchates, with the privileges they received, were perceptively improved, and Contantinople, which became a significant arena for diplomatic struggles with the West, exalted the patriarch and ethnarch. But the liquid assets of Turkish dominated Greece were not large enough to furnish a significant hierarchy at the patriarchate of Constantinople and important men of letters for enslaved Hellenism. Nonetheless, some scholars do emerge out of the Turkish-dominated regions.

Aitolos and Others

Such is the case, around 1580, with George Aitolos. Aitolos wrote some praiseworthy poems in folk language about important personalities of his time. He also versified fables in the folk language and meter. The continuation of ancient letters is significant to mention during this period. The phenomenon should not be explained only by Western Renaissance, for judging from correspondence carried on in the ancient language and from other similar manifestations, we are obliged to admit that the classical tradition is perpetuated even during the early Turkish domination. Almost all the 144 fables of George Aitolos demonstrate this for they belong to the tradition of the fables of Aesop and Babrius. Recollections of ancient works are not lacking.

> Tale of a Rhodian,
> A man said, in bragging about himself,
> that he had taken a leap, to his just glory,
> And someone replied: "Here is Rhodes,
> Hear it, and perform your leap, if you can."

We perceive here the presence of a scholar cultivated in ancient Greek letters, who considers that it is not unwarranted or futile to give the ancient myths in popular verse, that is, in a language which is not taught in the schools, but which serves the intellectual needs of the people directly. Our evaluation of Arsenios, or of all who wrote verse chronicles, is the same. On the other hand, we should stress the survival of classical literary tradition among Turkish-dominated Greeks.

At the end of the sixteenth century when the Turkish wave began to stabilize, and when those from the West turned their attention to political exploitation, the patriarchate of Constantinople, strong now and organized, aspired to play a primary role in the diplomatic activity centering around Constantinople. Jeremiah II, the Magnificent, was one of the great figures of Orthodox hierarchy during this period. He served repeatedly as patriarch of Constantinople between the years 1572 and 1595. The church underwent ordeals both internally and externally, but her position was sufficiently great to create certain demands in the mind of its chief leader. Jeremiah was a strong monastic personality with vast knowledge, moral rectitude, and will power. His adversaries tell us that "he never listened to the counsel of anyone, but neither did he take advantage of any of his subordinates." He loved letters and the luxuries of the church, and even more he delighted in perfect administrative operation. In his time ordination could not be bought. Also, during his years as patriarch, it was decided that the metropolitans in certain regions should undertake to create and support schools. He travelled widely to Roumeli and to the Peloponnesus. He came in contact with the

Protestant church and he specifically participated in important decisions concerning the Russian church. Finally, in 1588, he went to Moscow and was ordained as Job, the first patriarch of the Russian church. This formal recognition had grave consequences for the evolution of Orthodox Hellenism during the years of Turkish domination. Arsenios, bishop of Elasson, was part of the escort which accompanied Jeremiah to Russia and he has given us an interesting account of this long voyage. Though he writes in political verses, Arsenios is not a literary man, but he is a careful observer and transmits conscientiously all that he sees with a simplicity which is not lacking in charm.

> When the king saw us from the throne on which he sat,
> He arose and descended with sceptre in his hand.

Arsenios has also left us his memoirs in prose, where he gives proof of a linguistic culture which is more refined than in his verses. Something similar can be said about Matthew, bishop of Myrees, a contemporary and friend of Arsenios. Matthew is especially known for his Chronicle of Hungro-Vlachia, written in political couplets. This work, which leaves us cold, was widely read in its time and found many imitators. The author is inspired by a similar work by Stavrinos, entitled *Exploits of the Venerable and Most Courageous Michael Voevada*. As for Stavrinos, he also had originality. He interests us mostly because of the various folksong sources he used. The Cretan Gregory Palamides exhibits a superior lyrical quality during the same years in the metrical history of Michael the Brave, which he composed in 1607 while in Poland. We should stress further the emotion aroused in the subjugated Greek people by the battles of Michael against the Turks. Literary works and folksongs alike glorify him. A hope for freedom illuminates his efforts. Palamides was also inspired by Stavrinos, but he used language and verse better than Palamides. He also used forms from the *Iliad* to explore the events of his time. Even more remarkable and original for their internal arrangement are the metrical translations of the Psalms of David, which have remained unpublished.

The work of Stavrinos continued to serve as a model throughout the following century. Diakrousis imitated him, as did Matthew. Ignatios Petritsis, who wrote a variant to *Digenis Akritas* in 1670, also imitated him, and even a century later, in the verses of John Spontis, we find concrete passages reminiscent of Stavrinos. Cross currents like those presented in the work of Stavrinos or Spontis indicate how tenacious is the tendency of Greek poetry toward a unified poetic tradition. But this unification demanded the pre-existence of certain objective and subjective conditions which were only realized much later, in the years of Solomos during the nineteenth century.

Still greater difficulties are presented by linguistic unification which, even today, has not been realized. But it is worth mentioning that writers like Arsenios, Palamides, and Matthew were not the only writers of their period in subjugated Greece who made conscious use of the folk language and morphology.

Chronicle Writers

Enslaved Greece, poor in schools and more generally in culture, still lacking in a modern Greek literary tradition, found it difficult certainly to achieve intellectual or literary forms. Perhaps the most noteworthy attempt in this direction was made by Manuel Malaxos, who, continuing the Byzantine tradition, wrote a *Chronicle* in 1750 in the language of the people. This, as well as other Western and Greek sources, was used by the redactor of another chronicle known today under the title *Chronicle of the Turkish Sultans*. This composition, which apparently remained unpublished to our times, follows its sources very closely; yet, it is praised for the literary charm of the anonymous redactor, whose warm folk spirit brings us close to the later *Chronicle of Galaxidi*. The *Chronicle of the Turkish Sultans* seems to have taken the form we know today during the sixteenth century. It also utilizes, among other works, the *Book of History,* attributed to Dorotheos, Bishop of Monemvasia. This latter work is in part based on the *Chronicle* by Malaxos, and was first published late in 1631. It circulated widely in manuscript form, in several variants, and later was published repeatedly. In the same spirit, but more expanded, we have also the *New Collection of Various Histories,* a work by the Cypriot Matthew Kigalas, published in 1650. Finally, the abridged *History on Profane and Sacred Subjects* also belongs to this series; it is a work written in 1659–60 by the Cretan Nektarios, patriarch of Jerusalem, and published many times between 1677 and 1805. Its spirit remains that of the chronicle, but one is aware of scientific thought breaking through, a criticism of sources, an awakening interest in epigraphic monuments. The language is simple, "so that it can be understood by every Greek," writes Nektarios. But we still have no awareness of history; precise reporting on historical events encumbers form; perspective is lacking.

Loukaris

Many of the writers mentioned in this chapter came from the regions which had not submitted to the Turks. What the subjugated Greek people could not offer, other areas not exposed to Turkish violence could. Hence, Crete supplied Constantinople with some great prelates, such as Maximos Margounios, Meletios Pigas, and above all, Cyril Loukaris. The first two are examined later where their activities are considered in connection with the diaspora. Loukaris, however, deserves special attention here.

Loukaris became an expatriate after a brilliant career. As many Cretan youths, he had studied in Italy, in Padua, that is, in a school which had escaped Catholic influences. From a good family, endowed with natural beauty and pride, he had need to overcome within himself many irresistible forces before he could enter the path of virtue and sainthood. Before he became patriarch of Constantinople, he served as patriarch of Alexandria, successor to Pigas; he assumed various missions in regions where Catholic propaganda operated, and these missions, from his early years, caused Catholics to accuse him of being a Protestant. In 1612, he accepted the post of guardian of the patriarchal throne, replacing Neophytos, who had been accused of favoring the Latins. Loukaris approached the Protestants of Constantinople, applied himself to reestablishing order in his patriarchate, and, at the same time, wrote many literary works, some of which were in the spoken language. In 1620 he was elevated to patriarch. His first patriarchate is marked by the systemization of Western proselytism; the Catholics accused him of fomenting a rebellion on the islands with the connivance of the Russians. In the course of his second patriarchate, Loukaris organized education; he sought to bring to Constantinople the best that Hellenism had to offer in the area of letters. He introduced printing, thereby realizing, for the first time, the dream of his enlightened predecessors. The printing press, however, survived only a few short months because sympathizers of the Roman church denounced it to the Turkish government as pursuing subversive ends. His last patriarchate, which lasted about a year, ended in 1638. Once more he was denounced for having an agreement with the Russians to foment a revolution. He was arrested and remained in prison for seven days; then he was taken and strangled to death. This was the first time the Turks executed a Greek patriarch. A year later, a similar fate awaited his adversary and successor. In these struggles, which had a political as well as a spiritual character, with the patriarchal throne as prize, the Turks found it expedient to strike first the one faction and then the other, thus weakening both.

Loukaris was a progressive. He sought to enlighten the nation and it seemed that he approved of the efforts at translating the Scriptures into the spoken language. He was accused of seeking to subjugate the Orthodox church to the Reformed English church. Documents prove that he made serious concessions in this direction. Cyril Loukaris had crystallized and systematized the latent tendencies of Hellenism which were beginning to organize toward contact with Western civilization. When one considers the strong distrust of the Greek people for the activities of Rome, one comprehends better its spirit of conciliation with the rest of the Western Christian world.

It is characteristic that every movement toward a revival which the historian encounters has its beginning in some way with Loukaris or one of his enterprises. His action, insofar as it could be exercised without offending Orthodoxy, had a political character. Loukaris acted as the head of a nation. He attempted to exploit the political antagonisms of Western diplomacy in Constantinople in order to ameliorate the situation for the subjugated Greeks. Since the Greek forces available during this period were insufficient for his efforts, his attempts were destined to fail. But from the point of view of Orthodoxy, which we must not forget constituted at that time the principal factor assuring the cohesion of the Greek nation, one can consider that his activities attained their end. One sees, indeed, from this moment on, that the activities of the Roman church became less intense and, renouncing proselytism on a vast scale, it clung only to an individual proselytism. All the activities of Loukaris were exclusively Greek in sentiment and aspirations. At a time when Galileo was being prosecuted in the West, condemned and imprisoned by the church, the patriarch of Constantinople was establishing schools, printing houses, favoring translations of the Scriptures, resorting to the folk language, all in order to enlighten the faithful. We are already at the beginning of religious humanism. The Orthodox clergy has grown in value and become prestigious. It holds culture in its hand and gives it impetus.

It is noteworthy that during these years, the attitude of Loukaris is not the only position taken. About this same time, another cleric, Gerasimos Spartaliotes, considered that it was preferable to have "ignorance with piety . . . than science with impiety."

Evidence of the Greek attitudes of Loukaris is also the fact that he did not wish to send the young Greeks to the West to study; he sent only one, Mitrophanes Kritopoulos. Constantinople once again became a great intellectual center, despite the earlier, and even later, violent religious controversies and personal animosities manifested here. We should mention among the contemporaries of Loukaris, Meletios Syrigos, a professor and preacher from Crete, and George Koressios, a physician, professor, and theologian from Chios. The latter lived principally in the West and in Chios, but he was also employed by the patriarchate for dogmatic polemics.

Theophile Korydaleas

The most significant figure among the scholars who circulated around Loukaris was Theophile Korydaleas. When the great patriarch sought to reorganize the Patriarchate School, he called upon Korydaleas, the famous "philosopher" of the times, despite the doubts created by his strict orthodoxy and his attachment to ecclesiastical rites of the church. George Koressios attacked him for his religious concepts. More violent were the attacks against Korydaleas by Meletios Syrigos because of personal and professional rivalries. At such moments, the scholars of the patriarchate, regardless of how they used the archaic language, did not hesitate to use the simple language in order to achieve their objectives with greater certainty.

Syrigos and Koressios did the same, even though both as a rule used the archaic language in their works. From a literary standpoint, Korydaleas does not belong to the subject under discussion, but rather to classical literature. His production consists almost exclusively of commentaries on Aristotle, dissertations on logic and

philosophy, and a small number of writings discussing moral questions or dogmatics. It is by exception that he writes in the folk language, as it is by exception that he writes works relating to dogmatics. It has been observed that "without doubt, in his writings, he
does not theologize, but he philosophizes." His philosophy is not
concerned with enlightenment of the popular masses, but is directed
to the initiate, to "clerks." His orthodoxy became controversial even
while he was living. It was said that in matters of religion, he limped
first on one foot, then on the other. He was accused both of being a
Calvinist and being an atheist. However, the thirst for culture which
possessed Hellenism at that time had become so imperious that all
these grave accusations became secondary to the impressive bulk of
his methodical work, so for about two centuries, his teaching, called
korydalism, became the basis of the philosophic formation of the
new Hellenism. His works were considered at the time great progress
over the scholarly Byzantine manuals which had been in use. The
praises of which he was the object are significant: "a great philosopher, surpassing by far the Italian philosophers, equally as well as
the Greek philosophers." Even Voulgaris said that Korydaleas "was
a brilliant philosophical star in the sky of Greece." His manuscripts
flooded the Greek libraries. Eminent scholars made synopses of
them, criticized them, and even translated them. Nonetheless, as
J. Moisiodakas rightly observed, they belong to the more austere
scholastic tradition and ultimately greatly retarded the development
of enlightenment in Greece, since we find them used in teaching
even as late as 1827.

Another of his short works, printed in the form of letters during
the years of the Turkish domination, had an equally significant influence. This is his famous *Epistolary,* which circulated even in
manuscript copies and was reprinted many times. "Author and
father" of the epistle form his contemporaries called him. And indeed, we see the archaic correspondence of subjugated Hellenism
conforming to his models until the time of Adamantios Koraes
(early nineteenth century), and even later. If his work and its influence helps us to understand better one time in Greek culture, his
personality helps us even more in learning about the early Greek
Renaissance. In him is concentrated the first stormy wave to stir
neo-Hellenism. In his figure, we are reminded of the restless and dissatisfied personalities of the Renaissance in the West. Capable of
good or bad, versatile, quick-tempered, quarrelsome, he gives evidence of continually renewed interests and an inflexible egotism

which can be suddenly shattered by unexpected goodness, the spontaneous appearance of which was strange to his nature.

Korydaleas was born in Athens around 1560. He was educated in Italy and repeatedly attempted to be appointed a professor in Venice. But Athens always beckoned him, and after long peregrinations and adventures, after having put on the vestments only to discard them, after having been seated on the episcopal throne only to resign, he returned to his country where, greatly honored, with a large number of students around him, he died in a state of acute neurasthenia. "Beloved country," he had written earlier, "for whom I have renounced the universities of Europe, and for whom I have preferred the yoke of tyranny to the sweetness of liberty."

Athens

We are now in the years when thirst for knowledge, which is crystallized by Loukaris and spread through his efforts, has not yet reached its peak. Nevertheless, the favorable disposition of the clergy, the protection and support of the world of merchants, whose condition was better under subjugated Hellenism, favored the formation of intellectual cores in some commercial centers, as in Jannina, or in cultural centers of antiquity, as in Athens. The Athenians were aware of their classical origin and proud of it. When the Capuchins bought, in 1669, the house which enclosed the monument of Lysikrates, the old owner placed characteristic restrictions in the terms of sale: the new tenants were to permit access to the ancient monument to anyone who came to Athens to visit the vestiges of the past. In 1675 a Macedonian scholar, George Kontaris, published a history of ancient Athens in a simple language. This work is dedicated to two wealthy Athenians, and the dedication exalts the bond between ancient and modern history. "We are descendants of men so great and so wise," while the Turks are called "impious and barbarous people." At the end of the work, the author expresses the hope that God will destroy the Turks and that freedom will return to the nation.

A few years later, in 1681, Antonios Bouboulis, a Cretan established in Venice, published a poem in fifteen-syllable couplets, a complaint to Athens for the murder of Michael Limbonas, an Athenian. Limbonas had been assassinated by the Turks of Athens because he had defended the freedom of his country. In order to honor him, the poet recalls the ancient glories of Athens, of antiquity: Odysseus, Tyrtaius, Aeschylus, Euripides, Herodotus, Thucydides, and others. In the epilogue, he cites an incident that occurred in Venice between an Athenian and a foreigner who maintained that the Greeks had fallen into decadence. The Athenian replied: "His arguments twist like a whirlwind."

A traveller from France describes his visit to a school in Athens after the death of Korydaleas. The monk Damaskinos, one of the professors in Athens who speaks ancient Greek, Turkish, Latin, Italian, and a little French, is speaking:

> The Frank who comes to Athens, who sees how different our present condition is from the ancient one, deplores this condition; he mourns that such a glorious city should live usurped by the barbarians, and with a reverent zeal reproaches the ambitions of the European leaders, who fight among themselves instead of allying themselves to our best interest, and to their own, against the infidels. . . . Your wise men mock our ignorance. But are they not justified in mocking us? We were not content in antiquity to communicate to you the lights of our most beautiful sciences, but when you forgot all that you had been taught by Plato, Aristotle, Epicurus, and the other ancients, we sent you for a second time, during the middle of the fifteenth century, the wise Argyropoulos, Theodore of Gaza, George Trebizond, and George Gemistos. Now my words astonish you. But what did you take the Athenians of today to be?

Then, speaking of the servitude into which the Greeks had fallen and their aspirations for freedom, he continues: "As for us, we only wish for an opportunity to shake off this yoke. The ancient courage of our Nation has not degenerated." But this same kind of extreme rivalry is witnessed among the students of the various schools. When, following the death of Korydaleas, his last students continued to assemble to study from his manuscripts, a student from a school in Jannina came to Athens and attempted to embarrass them by projecting the teachings of his own professor. Such a zeal testifies to the flourishing awareness of culture in Jannina, as well as in Athens.

The Phanariots

Several names among the older students and followers of Korydaleas should be mentioned: Panayotis Nikousios, who will be discussed later, Eugene Aitolos, and John Karyophyllis. The latter, who was accused of being a Lutheran Calvinist because of his lyrical work, interests us here for his *Ephimerides;* that is, the journals he left us. Journals were written in the spoken language of Constantinople at the time, with a certain tendency toward mixing purism and archaism, which does not exclude the presence of a number of popular elements. *Ephimerides* continued to circulate widely in the following century; they were something between chronicle writing and memoirs, which, along with the correspondences, aid us in grasping the living thought and psychology of the scholars of the times.

An entirely different kind of influence from that of his teacher is produced in the Greek world by Eugene Yannoulis, an Aetolian. A comparison between student and teacher is of interest. Both were harsh, as befits men of a rising generation. But whereas years of restlessness brought Korydaleas to extrovertism and instability, they incited Eugene to introspection and brought him to asceticism. Familiar and fervent admirer of Loukaris, he composed a mass for the prelate following his death. His aspirations were divided between knowledge and sainthood. But cities could not contain him. With Loukaris dead, he abandoned Constantinople and returned to the mountains of his birthplace. He went to Arta, to the Aitolikon, to Missolonghi, and even to Karpenissi and Vraniana. He taught, he catechized, he corresponded with patriarchs and bishops, with dignitaries from every corner of the Greek East who sought his counsel and instruction. His work consisted of teaching and correspondence. Some of his letters were in the style of Korydaleas; others were written in the folk language. In the latter, we admire the simplicity, the gentle tone, which, however, are combined with a natural grandeur and an inflexible ascetic harshness. His student and biographer, Anastasios Gordios, who undertook to collect his letters, says about those written in the folk language: "They were admired by all the world, scholarly or not, more for their elegance than for the quality of their style." We are especially charmed by his tone, both the patriarchal and the prophetic. Whenever he addressed official personages, patriarchs and bishops, he preferred to use the archaic language. And in these cases, his severe moral tone often pierced through the scholarly tradition of his style.

Manolakis was a wealthy fur merchant from Kastoria, hence his surname Kastorianos. The commercial prosperity which already had lifted the exiled Greek people and had given them power and an impulse toward culture, began to extend even to the subjugated Greeks. Manolakis Kastorianos was one of the first merchants to work systematically in subjugated Greece to introduce schools and develop letters. This tradition of merchants who turned their attention to the culture of their compatriots will be continued and reinforced to the nineteenth century; so long, that is, as the mercantile class continued to develop and to assume leadership. Eugene served as counsellor to Manolakis Kastorianos, and he exhorted him especially to give money to establish schools in continental Greece, a region where intellectual culture had been totally neglected. "It is a rare thing there," writes Eugene, "that a priest knows how to read and write. For this reason, many children die without having taken the bath of repentance and without having received the sacraments. Even if we suppose that a priest is educated somewhat, he appears as a tragic monster or a comic scarecrow."

But already, the more lively and mobile children of these barren lands had discovered the road to Constantinople and to the other large cities of Hellenism, where they went to trade or to work and become wealthy. During the time of Eugene, we find on the mainland a flowering of religious art based on the wealth amassed by immigrants originally from these regions. Eugene himself, as he attended to the schools, did not neglect the churches, nor anything that could contribute to the welfare of the nation.

Characteristic of Eugene's interest in art is the long inscription he placed behind the icon, which he dedicated to the monastery of Myrtia in Aetolia: "In these times, nearly all the inhabited world is troubled by upheavals and an unbearable burden. It is above all in Crete that the war is being waged." What profound prayers must have been concealed in this dedication of the icon and the cold, impersonal inscription? In Crete at this moment the last of the cruel and heroic battles between Turks and Venetians were taking place, which ended in the submission of Crete and the most extensive expansion of Turkish domination on Greek soil.

Another Greek, perhaps a Cypriot, named Panayotis Nikousios, the first Christian dragoman of the Sublime Porte, assisted Kapoudan Pasha at the conclusion of the treaty of 1669. Nikousios was a physician and scholar, a friend of Eugene. But his career was chiefly diplomatic. From dragoman to foreign embassies, he went on to the service of the Sublime Porte. His culture and native ability gave a distinctive prestige to his office of dragoman. After him, the Phanariots, that is, the inhabitants of Phanar in the neighborhood of the Patriarchate in Constantinople, began to distinguish themselves in other offices of the Ottoman administration. They had already distinguished themselves in the lay offices of the patriarchate. The knowledge, experience, dexterity which their positions at the patriarchate demanded, were turned to profit by the Turkish nation. The first Phanariot to achieve the great distinction of Grand Dragoman, as we have seen, sanctioned the clauses of a treaty which subjugated the Greek population to the Turks. For an entire century, known as the century of the Phanariots, the Greek men in the service of the Turks acquired an influence destined to profit their own interests as well as those of Hellenism. Eugene wrote: "As for me, I admire these natures capable of serving tyrants, and I continue to admire them as long as their activities are for good and not for evil purposes." But before we attempt to evaluate the proportion of good or evil which the Phanariots introduced to Greek culture, we must turn to other Greek regions which had known slavery, and observe the degree of their evolution around this same period, that is, to about 1669.

Chapter 5

Signs of Conviviality

Cyprus, the Dodecanese, Crete

The Turkish conquest, as we saw, was not accomplished in a single blow, nor even in a few decades. From the twelfth century, when the Turks began to push into Asia Minor, one saw populations, or more accurately, the mobile elements of the Greek population, moving from East to West thereby displacing the adjacent populations. We saw the conquest reaching the Mediterranean shores of Asia and then passing to the neighboring islands, to Cyprus, to the Dodecanese, and elsewhere. There, an exceptionally fertile encounter occurred between the cultural tradition of Hellenic Asia and the particular civilization of the islands. The sea exercises a well-known influence on shore populations; spiritual calm, gentle manners, inspired a desire for renewal and inclined the people toward a consideration of foreign examples and influences coming from the outside. But if these characteristics are common to all island cultures, they were stronger in the Aegean, or generally, in all the Greek seas, whose numerous islands, so close to one another, produced an element of unity and not of separation between the islands and the distant mainland. Furthermore, the Greek islands situated along the Asiatic shores came in contact very early with Western civilization, and this contact lasted for many centuries. Rhodes lived under Western rulers from 1097 to 1522, Chios from 1124 to 1566, and Cyprus from 1189 to 1570. The civilization brought by the West was new without being primitive; that is, it was a dynamic and evolved civilization. The chivalric spirit animating it linked the first appearance of humanism with Christian tradition. It was a civilization where the feminine element was exalted, where love tended to occupy an essential place, and where the sentiment of honor dominated. The violent customs of the Middle Ages survived only schematically in an organized and delicate world, which was more charmed by love tournaments than by passion, by the display of chivalric dexterity than by battles of war. Lovers, flowers, songs, single combats whose prize was the smile of a woman, contests where poets were crowned

—such were the ideals of the world which came into contact with that of the Greek islands. The encounter of such a spirit and sensibility could not easily assume a hostile character. The gentle and friendly islander was charmed by such a civilization, and he took over its forms to a great extent. Thus, in these Greek islands, we see the happy encounter of a primitive Asiatic heritage with Western chivalry; that is, of two civilizations which were not fundamentally dissimilar, because the akritic civilization was also chivalric in origin, as the Western civilization was also heroic in origin. The interpenetration occurred in an environment that was prepared for its acceptance—the island environment. All the new elements created by this meeting of civilizations appeared in the content and form of the literary production of these regions.

Rhyme

In terms of form, the most important point that one can make concerns rhyme. Henceforth, rhyme no longer appeared as in older Greek times in a haphazard form with end rhyme, that is to say, as the evidence of speech in poetry. It now appeared in a regular manner, as a musical element of language consciously sought by the writer. The origin of rhyme in modern Greek versification has become a matter of great research and long discussions, from which one positive conclusion may be drawn; independent of rhymes encountered sporadically in the prose and verse of much older Greek texts, it was only after direct contact of Greek civilization with the Western world that we see rhyme in the new Greek literature. And this contact was systematically established and maintained first on the Greek islands along the Asiatic coastline. Perhaps it is of deeper significance to cite a very old document dating back to 1436 which attests to the use of rhyme in modern Greek literature; moreover, it is a poem in tercets, written by the Italian poet Kyriakos of Ancona.

Cyprus and the Dodecanese Islands

In Cyprus, besides the numerous vestiges of the akritic cycle found —softened and weakened by the minor poets in their verse chronicles—we have a very early development of a purely literary poetry with obvious Italian roots. Love was the exclusive theme of the

Cypriot songs, not love as primitive passion, but as a sentiment exhibiting courtesy and refinement. These love songs were not only rhymed, but very often they consisted of subtle metrical assemblages, such as the octet or the sonnet. Their impeccable versification appeared predominantly as a brilliantly executed eleven-syllable verse, which like rhyme was of Western origin. The Italian influence in these works was not only indirect, but also direct. The translations of Petrarch's sonnets were found mixed with original works in this group. The language of these poems is so strongly idiomatic that to penetrate their meaning without particular preparation is difficult. But even as they have been handed down to us, their grace, their lightness, and their elegance are clearly evident.

> Wait, my lady, wait, I wish to gaze on you; it is not well that thus you should be concealed, for how can one celebrate your beauties if you keep them hidden? My lady, there is no need for me to remind you of the wise precept: if something is beautiful, one takes only that which one sees.

Naturally, such a quality of language presupposes a long culture. Literary research dates these poems to around 1560. Indeed, we know that the popular language had been cultivated in Cyprus in earlier times, since we encounter it in such prose works of the fourteenth century as *Assises of Cyprus,* that is, in the Greek variant of the legislation of the kingdom of Cyprus. The *Chronicle* by Mahairas, also in the spoken language, and the *Chronicle* by Voutronios, which followed the first, belong to the next century.

A similar linguistic elaboration of speech, with more apparent popular survivals, appears in a group of songs which seems to be of Dodecanesean origin which are comparable to the Cypriot love songs. The technique of these poems is less refined than the Cypriot one, but what they lose in technique is compensated by their naturalness. These are clearly a popular form of the Greek distich, but worked by a scholar; these verses probably date to the fifteenth century. One often encounters rhyme in the poems, but the verse is iambic, octasyllabic or even fifteen-syllable, or more often octasyllabic trochaic; in all cases, the language is the popular one. The subject again is love, but in an urban form, yet with abundant pastoral elements.

> I want to kiss you when the trees are blooming,
> And when the birds on the branches are singing.

Somewhat later in the same period, we also find in the Dodecanese islands a type of versification which we already know, the *Alphabet.* Here is a poem of love, remarkable for its elegance of verse:

> I am dizzy, my lady, and my mind is troubled.
> I have no one to tell it to, except you, my beloved.

Some other *Alphabets,* slightly older, found in a manuscript of the fifteenth century, have also been published. They certainly originate from the islands, though we cannot affirm that they were originally from the Dodecanese.

> I am in a hurry to see you, to breathe for a moment.
> I see you for an instant, and I leave more dead than living.

Crete

Because the occupation of Crete by the Venetians was prolonged and continuous, and because it created conditions auspicious to an evolving cultural development, it is in Crete that the island civilization finally attained its full flowering, and it is to Crete that we are indebted for the highest literary achievements of this civilization.

The Venetians conquered Crete in 1211 and maintained the occupation without interruption until 1669. A cultural contact for four and a half centuries could only bring about fruitful exchanges of a profound nature. The flowering of Cretan literature is the result of this occupation. But we must not imagine that these exchanges were accomplished peaceably and smoothly, or that the flowering appeared without an intense intellectual preparation. Freedom-loving Crete did not accept readily the foreign ruler, and for centuries we have a series of insurrections, more or less important, whose purpose was either to ameliorate the situation for the native population or to seek deliverance from the foreign yoke. The last great uprising was in 1572. It was followed by a hundred years of peace with a corresponding cultural production. But the exchanges had started much earlier. The occupation had economic reasons which outweighed even the strategic value of the island. The Venetians neither desired nor sought a religious or a national assimilation of the population. From a religious point of view, it suffices to remember how loose the bonds were with the Catholic church. Venice was essentially a commercial state; its motivation and reactions were thoroughly commercial. And from a nationalistic point of view, the measures they were obliged to take every so often were not for expansion, but simply to safeguard their interests. They opposed religion by not tolerating the presence of Orthodox bishops in Crete. They hindered the development of Greek culture by obstructing all teaching programs.

But on the other hand, the Venetians did allow the people to live in peace so long as they remained quiet. As compensation for the occupation and its distressing consequences, they were responsible for an economic flowering for the island. But even while they lived under the Venetians, the Greek people clung to their Byzantine identity, knowing that they belonged organically to the Byzantine Empire. The inscriptions dating to the Venetian occupation, preserved in churches of Crete, are characteristic examples: "under the reign of Andronikos Paleologos and the pious Augusta Irene. . . ." (1303–04); "under the reign of John and Helen Paleologos" (1360).

Moreover, irrefutable evidence convinces us that, though superior schools did not exist in Crete, nonetheless, a higher culture had developed. The great personalities of letters and of the church, Cretan in origin, suffice to prove that, from the fifteenth century, the intellectual life was not stagnant, though perhaps it was limited. Joseph Bryenios, Mark Mousouros, Meletios Vlastos, Meletios Pigas, Cyril Loukaris, and many other Cretans, who were distinguished in Byzantium, in subjugated Greece, or among the expatriate Greeks, could not have emerged from a devastated and uncultured land. During the time of the Venetians, we see the workshops of hagiographers and copyists prospering in Crete, which testifies to an organized cultural tradition. We know there existed in Heracleion the monastery of the monks of Mount Sinai and the adjoining school of Saint Catherine.

Cretan culture was stimulated and enriched by the human exchange to which the Venetian occupation gave rise; though it is difficult to believe that the Venetian colonies brought elements of culture to the island, they nonetheless brought Western culture with them. On the other hand, the absence of advanced schools in Crete drove those who thirsted for greater knowledge to Italy.

The pamphlets published in Venice, particularly early in the occupation, first circulated in areas governed by the Venetians, and this helped to raise the level of culture and create favorable conditions for a literary production. In such fashion a work in verse, written by Koronis and published in Venice (1524, 1543), called *Mourning of Death, Vanity of Life, and a Return to God* influenced the poets of *Erophile* and of *Erotokritos*. The translation by Zakynthinos M. Soumakis (1658) of Guarini's *Pastor Fido* certainly has a connection with *Erophile* (1637); however, the problem is so complex that we cannot indicate the two dates with any accuracy.

Theodore Montzelezes from Zakynthos appears to have worked in the same intellectual milieu and with the same material during this period. He was the versifier of *Eugena*. This is a religious theatrical presentation resembling the older mystery plays of Western origin, and simultaneously exhibiting the strong moralistic tendency of the period. It adds nothing to the Greek aesthetic tradition, but does allow us to analyze better the style of the period. The Zakynthian poet accepts the Cretan technique at the same time enriching it with linguistic elements of his own regional speech. In the internal texture of the work, as with Soumakis, or later Katsaïtis, the provincial element becomes clear; the center is elsewhere, memories of older periods of literature still survive. At any rate, what concerns us in all these intellectual exchanges is that, without doubt, they do not express personal circumstances but a collective education, some of whose characteristics are discernible.

We also note that the principal cities of Crete had become commercial centers, with all that this implies. The cities acquired the characteristics of large seaports; they exhibited a quasi-cosmopolitanism, which produced a freedom of morals sometimes bordering on licentiousness. Parallel with this, however, was a rise in the level of civilization. We know a theater existed in Heracleion in the seventeenth century.

The Seduction of the Maiden

The rise of the new culture naturally affected the literary production of the island, which inevitably appears as the result of the cultural exchanges with the West. But many circumstances altered before the flowering of Cretan literature. We spoke earlier about the

objective conditions of civilization. Let us remember how they affected the refinement of the language and that of verse. The passage
from the folk element to the scholarly followed the cultural development which we have already observed. Thus, *The Seduction of the
Maiden,* which appears to belong to the fifteenth century or the
beginning of the sixteenth century, was written in a popular form,
but it carries signs of a scholarly elaboration. The verse is rhymed
political, and its numerous linguistic awkwardnesses and imperfections do not deprive it of a spontaneous charm and a sufficiently
advanced cultural evolution. The subject of this poem is a young
man's conquest of a young girl:

> The youth asks for a kiss, the maiden for a ring,
> But the youth refuses to give this maid his ring.

And in the end, he succeeds in obtaining his desires without grant-
ing an exchange. To the laments of the young girl for her misfortune, the young man replies with a sarcasm that provokes her
curses. A more cultivated love element is combined with the folk
curse of the abandoned woman. We also should mention the theme
of the *adynaton* (impossible) which appears in the beginning of the
poem.

> When the crow turns white as the dove,
> When you see the sparrow hawk chase the bear,
> When the sea is planted with wheat and oats,
> When you see fish walking on the mountains. . . .

Dellaportas

Already in this period, and without interruption through the entire
Venetian occupation of Crete, we have an abundant poetic production from known poets. A recent discovery has identified a number
of fourteenth-century poets. Among them is Leonardo Dellaportas,
whose production is of a remarkable quality. He left us a number
of poems, the most important being a dialogue between the poet and
truth. Besides their lyrical quality, these texts have a particular interest for our *History* because they constitute a bond between Byzantine folk production and the later accomplishments of Cretan
literature.

Other Cretan Writers

Clearly of later date, toward the end of the fifteenth or the early
sixteenth century was Stephen Sachlikis. He became discrete and
bitter after a restless life full of ordeals and counselled young men
against following his disappointing example. Sachlikis was an attorney by profession and his literary ambitions were modest, but he
was lively, full of description, and often acrimonious in his satire,
which presents an extremely clear picture of Cretan urban life during this period.

He was a sinner himself and he speaks to us about sinners. It is
evident that harlots were abundant in Heracleion and that many
young men flocked around them. Revelry, strolling by night, songs,
and quarrels are the environment in which we encounter the de-
pravity of Sachlikis's harlots. Study is a distasteful burden for the
young men:

> And I began to abandon my master and to stroll through the
> alleys of our fortress.
> I wanted to stroll with the musicians, with the good sportive
> youths, the promenaders.

Hence, fortunes were lost and debts accumulated, which led to
situations and to prison. Sachlikis, from within prison and even after
his release, never stopped preaching. His verses abound in sententious elements:

> What one does in the night is mocked by day: they are the
> games of fools, the pranks of youth. The singers promenade,
> the musicians strum on their instruments. They are accosted,
> they are amused, they laugh, they sing. They believe them-
> selves to be important, and the more important they believe
> themselves, the more they are degraded.

The theme of the *adynaton* is found also in Sachlikis:

> I wish to count the waves of the sea.
> I'm in a hurry to count the innumerable stars.

Chronologically it is not far from Stephen Sachlikis to the poet
Bergadis, from whom we have a poem called *Apokopos* (The Man
Cut Off from Life), published for the first time in 1519. The subject

of *Apokopos* is a dream, a descent to Hades. The title of this work, which appears to have been printed and circulated widely in Turkish-dominated Greece, comes from the first verse:

> One day, fatigued from work, I sought to sleep.

The rhymed political verses in time reveal the poet's moralistic purpose. The work contains a number of archaisms and some awkwardness, which do not diminish, however, its good points, where the author attacks sin with violence, imagination, and a certain sense of rhetoric. He decries the facility with which the living forget the dead; he denounces the cupidity of the clergy, and, in general, the insensibility of men. The infidelity of women also concerns the poet:

> Whoever takes their tears seriously,
> And believes what they say,
> Hunts for wild game in the lake,
> And fishes for fish on the hills.

Independent of the Eastern or Western models that may have influenced Bergadis's choice of subject and organization in his work, he expressed the Greek folk concept of death artistically and warmly. The dead long for light, for the senses they have lost:

> If there are gardens and mountains, if the birds sing,
> If the mountains smell fresh, and if the trees blossom. . . .

The poet himself was attracted by the charm of the material world:

> By the grace of the tree, the enchantment of the place,
> And by the melody of birds. . . .

Some sections in Bergadis are also distinguished for their lyrical quality and the descriptive force. On the whole, *Apokopos* is one of the significant achievements in Cretan literature, superior to similar contemporary works, to which it perhaps served as a model.

The dream-vision appears to have been in vogue in Crete, probably due to the influence of Bergadis, for we find it again in other works of this period. Thus, the poet John Pikatoros from Rethymnos left us the *Complaints in Rhyme on the Bitter and Insatiable Hades*. Pikatoros also had a deep and embittering experience with life, but the composition of his work was more complex. The story centers around the dream of the poet. He sees himself descending to Hades where he encounters Charon, who serves as his guide.

Charon informs the poet on matters of the underworld, uses the occasion to instruct him on virtue, and begins to describe Paradise. Here the poem was interrupted abruptly and remained unfinished. The small literary value of this ambitious project is compensated by the important folkloristic material which it contains and by the comparison it invites between the ancient world and the new.

A dream-vision is also the theme of at least one of the poems of someone known as "the very noble Seigneur Marie Phalieros," who lived in the sixteenth century. This poet treats of love or admonitions, and he is content to employ older models. Moreover, as we point out elsewhere, we cannot be certain how the cultivated Cretan scholars of that period borrowed their themes, ideas, or verses, and so cannot judge them by present standards of morality.

Two poets who also emerged from other Venetian-occupied regions and who were exposed to strong Venetian influences in the same environment as Pikatoros and Phalieros were Tzane Ventrano from Nauplion and Mark Dephanaras from Zakynthos.

Parallel with didactic works and some works of pure imagination, the Cretans also cultivated their verse and language in historical narrative poems. We mention here the poem of Manuel Sklavos entitled *The Disaster of the Great Earthquake in Crete,* which refers to an actual earthquake in 1503. Written in rhymed political verses, this work combines the moralistic element with the historical. Much longer, but more skillful, is the poem of Anthony Achelis, *The Siege of Malta,* which describes the actual seige of Malta by the Turks in 1565. The poet translates an Italian text in prose, modifying it somewhat. This fact permits us once more to see the manner in which the Greek spirit assimilated foreign models; that is, while all prose elements of the original are present in the poem, we see the poet introducing elements borrowed from his classical tradition or from neo-Hellenic folklore and from literary tradition, which gives a strong Greek color to the work.

The works of Anthimos Diakrousis and of Marinos Tzane Bounialis belong to this category. Their chronicles, inspired by the Cretan War, which ended in the subjugation of the island in 1669, were written in political couplets. Diakrousis had neither spirit nor originality, and Bounialis, despite this emotional intensity, which at certain times is transferred to the reader, was unable to go beyond the metrical chronicle. But as a historical document, his long work has an exceptional value. He gives evidence that the cohesion of the Greek nation was intact.

> That they fell into the hands of the Turks.
> That they fell into the hands of the Franks.
> Or in any other hands, such is the fate of the Greeks.

With the submission of their island, a number of Cretans sought refuge in foreign lands.

> When they meet, they do not know each other, they are content to ask: "From where do you come, stranger?" They can say nothing more. "From Crete," they say, and one grasps the hand of the other while bursting into tears.

These verses show us how strong the poetic tradition in Crete was at this time that it could offer such impeccable creations even in a simple rhymed chronicle. The poet himself had left Crete and gone to another Venetian-occupied region, the Heptanese. The connection between Crete and the Ionian Islands, which is suggested by Dephanaras, Soumakis, and Diakrousis who are Heptanesians, must be emphasized from now on. The natural route that mature Cretan literature followed after the fall of Crete was toward the Ionian Islands; that is, toward lands that offered the strongest geographical and cultural analogies with Crete. First, however, we must stop to examine this period of maturity in Cretan literature.

The production of Cretan poetry, which flourished during the sixteenth century, appears simultaneously in narrative and in theatrical works. For narratives, we have *The Shepherdess* and *Erotokritos*. A number of dramas have been preserved, among which are *King Rodolinos, Zeno, Erophile, The Sacrifice of Abraham,* an idyllic comedy called *Panoria,* and three other comedies, *Stathis, Katsourbos,* and *Fortunatos.* We can assume that *Panoria, Katsourbos,* and *Erophile* were written by a single poet, George Hortatsis from Rethymnon, and that *The Sacrifice of Abraham* and *Erotokritos* were written by Vincentio Kornaros. The evident Italian origin of all this literary production has been emphasized by all. We even have the Italian originals of most of these works. On the other hand, we should also mention how profound was the Hellenic variance that the Cretan writers gave to their foreign sources; this allowed them to create works whose essence was perfectly original. It is unnecessary, moreover, to stress that subject matter in literature is nothing more than primary material, which becomes a simple learned narration or a masterpiece, according to the creative abilities of the author.

Even if the nature of these matters did not lead us to such a conclusion, the example of the Golden Age of Crete would suffice to convince us.

The Shepherdess

The Shepherdess is obviously associated with the great pastoral idyllic production which began with the Renaissance in Europe and continued to the seventeenth century. *The Shepherdess* is a pastoral poem, that is to say, a scholarly work inspired by nostalgia of the urban man for a life close to nature. All the exaggerations which characterize the pastorals of the Renaissance are found here as well. But the contribution of the poet is in the sensibility, in the harmony of language, in the elegance of expression, and in the charm of images. On the other hand, the poet lives in the external world, he handles the element of naïveté artistically, and he reveals himself as a true creator in the subtle psychological nuances of his characters. Even the verse form is of foreign origin; it is the iambic eleven-syllable one, about which we spoke earlier, but it is also completely assimilated. With consummate skill the poet produces a rhymed couplet and a language resonant in simplicity of style.

> Blond was her hair, her body was a splendor,
> Her dress was white and sparkled as the starlit sky.
> I turned to her, I gazed into her eyes.
> My heart then cracked into three parts.

The subject is simple. It describes the meeting of a shepherd and a shepherdess, and love is born of this encounter. The two lovers live side by side for a time, but the moment comes when the shepherd must depart. He promises to return soon.

> Goodby, my dove, and do whatever you choose. If I should live, I shall return within a month to find your angelic beauty.

But accident obliges the shepherd to prolong his absence, and when he returns, he finds his beloved dead. The poem ends with the lamentations of the shepherd. The morals described in this poem are free, as undoubtedly were the urban morals of that time in Crete. We have no reason, however, to attribute these morals to the actual life of the countryside. The writer here composes a poem with the elements at his disposal and conforms to the tradition of this genre. Earlier admirers of this pastoral work were mistaken when they believed they had found evidence of a true-life episode, and that they had before them a true-life story, a chronicle in rhyme. The work is scholarly; its poet successfully utilizes his classical training, which he combines with the poetic tradition of his island.

Panoria

The Shepherdess in all probability belongs to the beginning of the great period of Cretan literature, that is, to the end of the sixteenth century. The other bucolic work, *Panoria* by Hortatsis, earlier entitled *Gyparis,* appears to have been written later, perhaps around 1585. The main body of this poem is inspired by the pastoral comedy *Calisto* by L. Groto. The theme centers around the love of two shepherds for two shepherdesses who reject them. The youths invoke the aid of Aphrodite, who grants them their wish and sends Eros to pierce the two shepherdesses with his arrows. The two couples are united. The work in five acts, written in political couplets, contains long monologues and other amplifications, for which the high quality of the verse sometimes compensates. The absence of stage action and the lack of real characters are no less obvious. The intervention of *deus ex machina* and the use of elements from Greek classicism should not go unobserved.

Erophile

The subject of *Erophile* is equally archaic. It is a savage, bloody tragedy. The father of Erophile has mounted the throne of Egypt after killing his brother. Erophile loves a prince who lives in the same court; they are married secretly. But the father discovers the marriage and kills the bridegroom. Erophile commits suicide and the slave girls, in turn, kill the king. Between the acts of this work, inspired by a foreign model, *Orbecche* by G. Giraldi, interludes are inserted that are translations of a dramatic variant taken from Tasso's *Jerusalem Delivered*. *Erophile* was first published in 1637, after the death of its author, George Hortatsis of Rethymnos. The technique is highly developed and, despite the lengthy dialogues, shows all the signs of absolute theatrical maturity. The slave girls of Erophile form a chorus which expresses itself in impeccable tercets of eleven-syllable verse. The dialogue is in political couplets. The sententious spirit and reminders of classical antiquity are also found here. Though the subject of the work recalls the *Antigone* in very broad terms, it is actually the chorus which recalls the play more directly and more agreeably:

> Love, you often dwell in the hearts of the most noble and the most generous, for you hate the others, the lowly; you are strong and powerful and your arms are so forceful that you always become the victor.

Or

> Gracious ray of heaven,
> With your great flame,
> You give light to all the universe.

The poet stands firmly at the height to which his inspiration has elevated him:

> Insatiable greed for riches, desire for glory, accursed thirst for gold, how many have perished for your sake! How many unjust wars have you incited! How many quarrels are caused by you, daily, in the entire world.

When the dialogue does not unravel in interminable monologues, it sometimes exhibits a gripping dramatic character. When Erophile learns of the brutal death of her beloved, a rapid dialogue follows between her and her father in a scene of remarkable artistry. The couplets succeed one another in the mouths of the two protagonists until the departure of the king, whereupon the girl breaks into a magnificent lament:

> O gracious mouth with sweet-smelling breath, fountain of all virtues, mouth full of sweetness! Why don't your sweet lips call, alas, your Erophile? Why this silence before my sorrow, my tears? Why do you not say some word to comfort me?

Katsourbos

Hortatsis also attempted comedy with equal success, if, as is probable, *Katsourbos* is his work. It is not known if this comedy was published; we know it only in manuscript form. Recent research places the work before 1601, but later than *Erophile*. Its plot is absolutely schematic: two young people are in love, a rich old man desires the young girl, he is finally revealed to be her father, and the young people marry. The principal characters are standard figures from Italian comedy, the brave man and his servant, the cunning valet, the pedant, the pander, and others. The dialogue is excellent, and character revelation is executed with brilliance. The stage action is lively and rapid and shows dexterity when it is not drowned out by the abundant obscenity. At no moment, not even during the less lyrical scenes, can we forget that we are in the presence of a true poet.

Stathis and Fortunatos

The two other comedies known to us are *Stathis,* perhaps later than *Panoria,* and *Fortunatos,* which should be dated at the end of the Venetian occupation, perhaps even during its last year. The plot and technique are similar to those of *Katsourbos.* In *Stathis,* the subject is complicated by introducing two pairs of lovers. The plot is treated in a less perfect manner, the poetic language is less polished; consequently, the effort at comedy is more evident. The poet of *Stathis* is unknown; *Fortunatos,* on the other hand, is attributed to Mark Anthony Foscolo. The Italian name of the poet should not surprise us, for we know that the Cretans often took the names of their noble Venetian patrons. Despite his intemperance of language, which creates a problem with the publication of this work, Foscolo is charming. He is full of verve and communicates his liveliness directly without resorting to technical overelaborations. Despite all the ancient names and the reminders of antiquity which abound in *Fortunatos,* as, moreover, in all the other comedies, it is entirely evident that this work was not written to please a cultivated audience, but to be performed in the noisy halls of the popular theater. The verse of this work is the epitome of the Golden Age of Crete. In meter and rhyme, it expresses all that is perfect.

> Love, which school have you frequented, or where have you learned about horrible and sinful intrigues? Who was your heartless master that taught you to dole out bitterness and torments, to provoke quarrels, pain, and passions?

Rodolinos and Zeno

Before passing on to the great writer Kornaros, we should mention two other tragedies, *King Rodolinos* by John Andreas Troïlos, published in 1647, and *Zeno* by an unknown poet writing later than 1648. Both are variants of foreign works; the first is of *Il re Torrismondo* by Tasso, and the second of a Latin tragedy of the same name by the English Jesuit, Joseph Simonis. The subject of *Rodolinos* is classical, and that of Zeno, Byzantine. Neither the one nor the other merit examination of stage-craft, since they both follow their originals very closely. But whereas *Zeno* presents flat metrics and rare flights, *Rodolinos* contains a certain maturity and a remarkable elaboration of technique. This tragedy closes with a sonnet recited by the chorus. It is the first time, following the Cypriot sonnet, that we again encounter this verse form in Greek literature. Along with the tercets in *Erophile,* it reveals how far Crete had advanced in artistic elaboration of language.

> For this thing which is called life and which is considered the supreme good and which is honored by crowns and scepters, all men should cry with sorrow. For false hope which brings pleasure dies when it is illuminated. One can consider it a dream, or an uprooted tree about to fall. Treasures, youth, are nothing; power of the great sovereign is nothing; death commands. The example of fallen rulers shows men that they must not hope in this transient and deceitful world.

The Sacrifice of Abraham

The religious drama, *The Sacrifice of Abraham,* dating to 1635, is also a variant of a foreign model, the *Isaac* by L. Groto. The variant, however, is by a poet of genius. In all probability, it is the work of Vincentio Kornaros, the poet of *Erotokritos*. Taking great liberty with the original, he follows the Biblical tradition only to satisfy the exigencies of the stage. His deletions accentuate the dramatic character of the work and accelerate the rhythm of the drama. The additions make the tragedy of the father more poignant and increase the humanity, the tenderness, and sympathy. Furthermore, viewed as a whole, we note that the tone always remains elevated, in perfect accord with the elevated subject. In order to succeed in his plan, the author goes to the roots of Cretan tradition and utilizes a great number of folk elements. The aphorisms, the blessings, the parables bring us the best that folk tradition had to offer.

> On which road can my loving son be travelling?
> What sent the light of my eyes into exile?

or even:

> How can my eyes look on this spectacle?
> How can my hand make this gesture?
> What assistance is given to my body,
> Which trembles as a broken reed?

Here is no mechanical imitation of folklore elements, but an artistic exploitation in the hands of a master. The scene of Abraham's sacrifice is followed by increasing dramatic intensity up to its happy conclusion. The tender age of Isaac renders the tragedy of the father more poignant. Isaac tells his father:

> That you remember what I tell you, I will give you a sweet kiss,
> Today, I entrust my mother to you; talk with her, comfort her,
> Always be united. Tell her that I go joyfully to Hades.

The lamentations of Sarah are not equalled in neo-Hellenic letters except by her outburst of joy when she sees Isaac returning:

> What news, what voice, what anguish of heart! What fire burns me, what terror do I feel in all my body! What daggers, what swords, piercing my body, have given me a hundred wounds! How can I live, how can I restore my soul, when I have lost my son so suddenly, dedicated to such a death?

Her joy gushes from the same impetuous source:

> I can no longer wait. I leave before my son so as not to become foolish! My living son! Oh, my soul abandons me, my heart cannot contain such joy!

By an error committed when the Italian original of this work was still unknown and when it was thought to be of very ancient origin, *The Sacrifice of Abraham* was considered a mystery play of the Middle Ages. Today, it is clear that it has no connection with the medieval mystery plays, and that it is as far removed from them as is the unaffected medieval hagiography from the paintings of the Greek Renaissance masters. The scholarly element, the teachings from classical and post-classical tradition, predominate here. Though the internal evidence could be disputed, the prologue of the Italian *Isaac* places it indisputably within the spirit of the Renaissance. Indeed, the poet feels the need to apologize to an audience accustomed to classical works because this time they will not be seeing bucolics in mythical Arcady or a repertoire of classical tragedies, but a work drawn from the Bible. Moreover, as we have observed already, the work does not center on religious emotions, but on a delicate elaboration of character psychology. In this, the success of *The Sacrifice of Abraham* is unsurpassed. The tendency toward amplification, characteristic of dramatic works of the Cretan period, is entirely lost in the action and in the emotions which it arouses. This success is multiplied by the remarkable techniques of metrical elaboration which charms the audience from beginning to end. Perhaps this is the place to praise the assimilating power of the Greeks who could Hellenize every kind of material. But we will reserve examination of this subject for *Erotokritos*.

Erotokritos

Erotokritos must belong to the end of the great period of Cretan literature, that is, to the years of the Cretan War. More specifically, we can say that *Erotokritos* was probably begun in 1646 and completed before 1669. Its poet, Vincentio Kornaros, recounts the love of Erotokritos and Aretousa in ten thousand political couplets. The Princess Aretousa loves a noble youth at her father's court called Erotokritos. The inequality in their social stations, however, is an obstacle to their marriage, and Erotokritos is forced into exile. Later, through courageous action, he saves his country from enemy attack without revealing his identity. He is recognized and the marriage of the two lovers follows. The plot, both in general outline

and in numerous episodes, is borrowed from a Western work called
Paris et Vienne. Kornaros, in any case, knew the French original
from one of its many Italian adaptations by Orvietano. Here, however, we have a perfect example of how the Greek poet used his
foreign model.

In broad lines, in the schematic development of the work, the
variant remains close to the original. One cannot fail to note an essential difference, however. In the Western work, Vienne leaves with
her beloved without her father's consent, but Kornaros is extremely
careful with Aretousa's morality. She remains at her paternal home
and hopes. Another difference worth mentioning is that the Christian
element is stressed in the Western original, whereas Kornaros places
his story

> In ancient times when the Greek people were masters,
> Or their faith had neither roots nor foundation.

The religious element has disappeared entirely in Kornaros and been
replaced by a magical element wherever essential to plot intrigue.
Finally, the resolution of this work shows an important difference.
In the original, the cunning of Paris saves the king from captivity.
Erotokritos rescues the king and his kingdom in combat. A heroic
inspiration infuses the work and furnishes the poet occasions to develop epic episodes.

The story is not set in a precise historical and geographic framework. The king is Hercules, King of Athens, and surrounding him
are the rulers of Macedonia, Koroni, Sklavonia, Patras, the kings
of Nauplion, Cyprus, and Byzantium. The Karamanites, Vlachs,
Saracens, and Franks are present as well in this work. But in essence, it is the civilization of Crete during the last period of Venetian occupation which is portrayed: love, songs, chivalric tournaments, and the particular character formed by the combination of
Eastern and Western civilization on the Greek islands. Basically, the
men described by the poet are Greek men, with Greek customs,
Greek traditions, and a Greek temperament. In the Western romance, for the French maiden to fall in love with Paris, it is essential
that he distinguish himself in her eyes through heroic deeds. Erotokritos is no less courageous than Paris, but it is his song that causes
Aretousa to fall in love with him. In the Greek adaptation, one
senses the living soul of the Greek nation. Karamanitis, who will be
vanquished in the tournament by a Cretan, is a despicable man; he
is a Turk. We have spoken already about the Hellenization of the

story, as well as the general epic character of the episode which resolves the conflict.

In exploitation of subject, Kornaros surpasses his prosaic model; he introduces a warm lyrical fervor in the details, he decorates them with poetic images and poetic comparisons. The French text says: "When the knights completed their narration, Vienne, who had been listening to their words, was greatly displeased." And in another place, "Monsieur Jacques, on hearing the insane request of his son, was so amazed that he did not know what to do." The Greek text is animated by a lyric moment: "Aretousa listened to the words: it was as though a tree had been planted in her heart, then blossomed. The branches entwined around her heart and increased her concern and torment." The transformation of the second passage is also significant: "When the old man heard what he had not suspected, his eyesight blurred as though a cloud had covered it. His body trembled, the little blood remaning in him drained away. He became, on the spot, blind and mute."

In expression, we have a poet whose language and melody are mature. His versification is an impeccable fifteen-syllable verse which follows the pattern of Greek folk verse and Greek thought. If we exclude certain questionable instances, his rhyme is not of lesser quality. An imagination, simultaneously elevated and balanced, presides in this poetry. It is a creative imagination in the morphology and external characteristics of the poem and in the way content is refashioned. Only a simple form of the original work remains.

Out of one romance, the Greek poet has designed a masterpiece. The assimilating force of Hellenism is manifested here with exceptional power. Nicholas Politis, analyzing this work before the Western model had been discovered, proposed that this was an original Greek work and that it was perfectly futile to search for a Western model. One final comparison with *Digenis Akritas,* the other metrical romance of neo-Hellenic literature, will complete our inspection of *Erotokritos.* Both works are marked by foreign influences, both show a cultural interchange, and in both we see a strong Greek imprint. The differences between the two express the different moments of Greek civilization which had assimilated foreign models. Though on the one hand chivalry, plastic consciousness, the sense of measure proper to the Greeks remain unaltered in the two poems, on the other hand, we see the Oriental influences being supplanted by Western influences and the savagery of mountain morals by the sweet softness of an island civilization. Heroism gives way to passions of love; that is to say, not only has the Greek spirit continued to assimilate the foreign contributions, but it assimilated whatever influences responded to the cultural needs and expressions of the moment.

This Hellenization, fundamental to Greek works and emphasized by Greek scholars, was felt profoundly by the Greek people. Successive editions kept *Erotokritos* alive among the people, and certain verses are still recited from memory in our own time. Entire sections of the poem, large or small, have been transmitted orally, and in earlier times recitations of verses from *Erotokritos* were associated with folk festivals. The charm exercised by this work was such and its circulation so great that during the period of Greek neoclassicism a scholar named Denis Photinos considered it opportune to give a version in the cold language of his own time.

The work continues to delight us today. The modest and ardent Aretousa, once we have come to know her, retains our love. When Erotokritos sings under her window,

> Without seeing him, but only through his songs, she was caught in the web of love and desire overwhelmed her. She awakened her nurse and spoke to her. With cunning and stealth, she revealed how love had struck her.

When their passion is revealed, she turns her eyes toward the external world and seeks to justify this passion:

> Who has come into the world and never known love? Who has not been tried by love, who has not pursued it? Not only men who have reason and words run to this tree of love to eat of its fruit; the stones, the trees, the metals, and the animals of the universe know well that desire grants them life.

When Aretousa thinks her beloved dead, her passion rises to a lament:

> Your life is the source of mine, it is through your eyes I see.
> Thinking of you, I endure my tribulations as best I can.
> I renounce myself, I am with you.
> My life and death are in whatever you desire.
> Awake I think of you, asleep I see you in my dreams.
> And this evocation is for me a constant cure.

But Erotokritos also loves. His bravery is combined with passion and with prudence.

> He was eighteen, but he possessed the wisdom of old men.
> One could be nourished by his words and by his counsels.

Passion inflames his heart:

> The first blows were insignificant, imperceptible.
> But nothing is ever completed without becoming sizeable.
> I think I see her, and she holds me there.
> I live with her image, and I seek for nothing more.
> But little by little desire overwhelms me.
> And becomes roots and branches, birds and flowers.

When he fights in combat, he is a veritable beast who cannot be restrained by anything; he becomes a lion and a wolf:

> As the hungry wolf falls on the lambs and slaughters them,
> Wherever he can find them, wherever they take refuge,
> So is Erotokritos in combat.
> The Vlachs tremble as the sheep; and he is a wolf.

When, however, he meets Aretousa for the first time, we sense all the tremor of his distressed soul:

> She trembled on the one hand, he trembled on the other. The one waited for the other to speak. They stood thus for an hour, without saying a word. The thousand things they had to say remained unsaid. They did not venture to say all they wished to say, they did not know where to begin, relating their tribulations.

The gnomic theme and the theme of the *adynaton,* so familiar in Greek works, abound in this poem as well. And while the descriptions gush forth in a succession of impetuous verses, gnomic distichs and the proverbial verses are chiselled in an epigrammatic style:

> What speaks with wisdom and in an appropriate manner,
> Causes the eyes of men to cry and to laugh,

or

> In time, the difficult and painful become easier to bear.
> Many times, Art vanquishes Nature.

If the entire work shows a certain platitudinous quality, a tendency that follows from the folk tale, in details, on the contrary, which are extensive or compressed into litotes, the total impression is not one of superfluity. In these thousands of verses, beauty evolves endlessly and often with a perfection of form.

The dawn had appeared and poured out the dew. It revealed the signs of the holiday: the grass had sprung forth, the trees had blossomed, a soft wind was blowing from the embrace of the sky; the shores glistened, the sea was sleeping, the trees and waters sang tenderly.

Equal accomplishments are rare in modern Greek poetry; superior ones, however, there are none.

Kornaros is a cultivated artist. Fundamentally, he possesses the classical tradition and is concerned with invigorating it; he enjoys ornamenting his work with classical allusions. Similarly, he exploits the folk tradition, as his compatriots had fashioned it. The height he attained was full of future promise, which was cut off brutally when Crete fell into Turkish hands in 1669. But if it took 150 years before Solomos, pouring over the venerable text, discovered its secret and fulfilled its promises, the people did not wait. They recognized themselves in *Erotokritos* and claimed it, and they have placed this praiseworthy poem, even in our time, first among the treasures of their national heritage. Thus, under the cold artistic expressions of the Phanariots, we know that the spirit of Hellenism was still alive, sustained by the spirit of *Erotokritos*. Crete, as it fell in 1669, transmitted a flaming torch first to the Ionian Islands and later to all enslaved Greece.

Chapter 6

The Diaspora

Expatriate Hellenism

We have seen how bonds were made between Venetian-occupied
Crete and the other islands in the hands of the Venetians. Of course,
there were bonds with the city of Venice as well. Thus, after the
Turkish conquest, when many Cretans left Crete, they found a
familiar atmosphere in Venice and in the Ionian Islands. As we will
see, the Cretan tradition was still alive in the Ionian Islands, where
conditions of life were propitious to it.

In Venice and other cities of Italy the immigrants found flourishing Greek colonies. The present chapter discusses the history of Hellenism of the diaspora and of the Ionian Islands around 1669. This
Hellenism maintained a life fairly independent of the head of
Orthodoxy during the early period of Turkish domination. An organized Greek colony already existed in Venice around the middle
of the fifteenth century. Common religious expression united these
Greeks, even though there was some pressure from Bessarion and
other members of the Eastern clergy who had accepted the dogma
of the Western Church. The change, however, of religious affiliation
—and this is characteristic of the period—did not lessen interest in
the destiny of the Greek nation. A certain number of scholars, certainly, and particularly Hellenists, were lost to Hellenism, because
they ended by writing their works in Latin, the scholarly language
of the period. But the Orthodox who were converted to Catholicism
generally developed a continuous energetic activity in favor of
Greece. They changed their faith, not to deny their race, but on the
contrary, in the hope that they would serve its cause better. There
were also practical considerations: the dignities and positions that
the Western church dispersed generously to all who joined it, attracted them. At the same time, as it is not our purpose here to examine what was lost in the Greek diaspora, but to trace the intellectual history under Ottoman domination, we take our tone from
the men who worked with passion, with extravagance, with fanaticism to proselytize their compatriots to Catholicism. Their action
created inside the Ottoman Empire a class of Graeco-Franks.

Karyofyllis

Matthew Karyofyllis should be mentioned among the most aggressive partisans of the Catholic church. A near contemporary of Loukaris, he produced a series of neo-Hellenic apologetics besides works in Latin. He fought violently against Meletios Pigas and Loukaris, censuring their erroneous opinions. Nor was he content with denouncing their base morals and railing at their imperfect knowledge of the Greek language. His principal accusation was that with the destruction of faith they were also destroying the nation:

> Traitor to the Faith,
> Traitor to the Greeks,
> Traitor to the ancients,
> Traitor to the moderns.

Allatios

Karyofyllis was originally from Venetian-dominated Crete; Leon Allatios (1586–1669), who also embraced the Church of Rome, came from the island of Chios, where he was born twenty years after the island had passed from the Genoese to the Turks. Western influence, naturally great during the Genoese period, persisted under Ottoman domination, thanks to the Jesuits on the island. Allatios received his early education from the Jesuits. Later, however, when he established himself in Italy, though he pursued a career dedicated to the Western church, he never for a moment lost his strong Hellenic conscience. True to the older tradition, he wrote in an archaic language a short poem called "Hellas," expressing his hopes and prayers for the liberation of his country. A prolific writer, the major part of his work belonged to Western Latin literature. However, when he addressed his compatriots in order to convert them, he used their language with ease.

The exquisite realism of the Italian Renaissance influenced those Greeks who lived in Italy. Imitation of Italian examples, the sense of reality, and the material and intellectual departure from Eastern ecclesiastical tradition created favorable conditions for an intellectual flowering. It came where these elements could root in Greek soil. Hence, the miracle of Crete was accomplished.

Trivolis

On the Ionian Islands, during the early period, the local conditions (schools, instruction, and other), were not conducive to the cultivation of language. Nonetheless, a movement parallel to the cultural growth in Crete was manifested early. We should mention Jacob Trivolis (c. 1557 or 1558), a "gay and gracious poet," according to his compatriot Nicholas Sofianos. Trivolis wrote and published two poetic works: *The History of Tagliapiera* (c. 1528) and *The History of the King of Scotland and the Queen of England* (1540). In the latter work, he borrowed his plot from Boccaccio and composed in political couplets. The former work described and praised, in trochaic octasyllabic couplets, the exploits of a certain Venetian sailor who fought successfully against the Turks. The honor bestowed upon the sailor was related to the Greek consciousness of the poet. The small literary value of both these compositions would have consigned them, if not required their passage, to oblivion, but it is essential to mention them, for later their successive editions and wide distribution made them favorite folk readings in subjugated and dispersed Hellenism. Moreover, the exodus of Cretans after the capitulation of their island to the Turks, in large measure aided the intellectual movement of the Ionian Islands.

Sophianos

Though the climate in Italy was favorable, the terrain was not fertile. It was only in Venice, where the Greek colony was deeply rooted that we eventually see a certain flowering of Greek letters. Isolated efforts were not lacking in other places. Nicholas Sophianos occupied a place of primary rank. Originating from Kerkyra in the Ionian Islands, he also lived in Italy during the first half of the sixteenth century and there he ended his days. What interests us in his work and in his personality is the meeting of the ancient culture on the one hand with the tendency toward a systematic use of the neo-Hellenic language in the different genres on the other. The ancient culture was undoubtedly the result of the Greek heritage, but in any case it was reinforced by the orientation to the Western Renaissance. The use of contemporary language probably should be attributed to Venetian influences of the time such as the dialogues of Sperone Speroni and other Italian models. The comparison between progress realized in the West and the intellectual decadence in the East was obvious. Sophianos admired the ancients: "Our Race has fallen into decadence, and it has no memory of the degree of perfection to which our ancestors had climbed." He envied those in the West for their achievements in letters and sciences. Their language was not superior to the Greek language, "which possesses such order, harmony, and beauty, which, to my thinking, has never been approximated." He believed, as did many others with whom he discussed the problem, that the Greeks would be able to take their place once more among civilized nations, "if they would read and study the books left by those virtuous men of antiquity." It was in this spirit, which appears to be the spirit of a circle of Greek scholars who were influenced by Italy, that Sophianos composed a grammar in the demotic language, unpublished until our times, and he published in 1544 a translation of *On the Education of Children* by Pseudo-Plutarch. Also, moved by the humanistic spirit, he pursued many branches of knowledge, particularly geography. He annotated the geography of Ptolemy, published a comparative study of astrolabes, and drew a map of Greece. In this work, Sophianos established a connection between the ancient and new toponyms, attempting to prove the continuity of new Greece with the ancient one.

Among the scholars mentioned by Sophianos as approving the translation of classical texts into modern Greek were Jacob Trivolis, Anthony Eparchos, and Hermodoros of Zakynthos, a scholar known under the name of Listarchos, who became famous for his teaching activity in Chios. But we should mention that Trivolis was the only one among these three eminent scholars who wrote systematically in the spoken language. One sees for the first time, a number of writers, whose language was the archaic, now editing in a contemporary language works of a practical nature, those which testify to a civilizing effort on the part of Hellenes in Italy. For instance Emmanuel Glyzinos from Chios established himself in Venice, wrote verses and letters in an archaic language, and published, in 1568, a practical arithmetic in spoken Greek. This book was published repeatedly throughout the 250 years following its first edition.

Kartanos

The tendency to use the popular language is, of course, equally manifested in religious matters. We mention here the attempt made by Jonathan Kartanos from Kerkyra to make the teachings of the church accessible to the uninstructed. Toward this end, he published, in 1536, in simple language, a work which contained "the flower and essence" of the Old and New Testaments, along with some sermons, also in the folk language. Kartanos believed it was necessary to educate the masses with words written in their own language. "And this I have done not for the masters, but for those without instruction, like me, so that all the artisans and all the uninstructed might understand the Divine Scripture. . . ." This work appears not to have been heterodox, but its language could only dissatisfy those who continued to live in the archaic climate of Byzantium and imagined that language, along with other traditions bequeathed by the past, could remain unaltered in the new times.

This opposition is obvious between Kartanos and his violent persecutor, Pachomios Rousanos, who referred to himself as the monk "clothed in rags." Rousanos was originally from Zakynthos, but his life and activity were confined to Turkish-oppressed Greece. This religious writer died while still young, in 1553, leaving behind a quantity of works, treatises, and letters. His diatribes against Kartanos extended even to the question of language. "It is impossible to write otherwise than in the ancient tradition. It is futile that the Ancients composed and bequeathed this admirable work to their descendants, I wish to say the Grammar. But why, one asks, did they not bequeath the usual words, but other unknown terms?" Rousanos's material and the language of his writings is not within the scope of our present study. He is mentioned only to illustrate the profound difference which at that time existed between Greek regions influenced by Constantinople and those which gravitated toward Venice. On the one hand, there was a need for revival; on the other a desire to safeguard the ancestral heritage. The latter tendency should not be confused with ignoring reality. The national-religious group which was constituted in the East and formed of all the traditional elements was regarded by its guardians as an entity whose least rupture could become fatal.

Along with Kartanos and still within the older Venetian circles, we should also mention Damaskinos Stoudites and Alex Rartouros, who joined several others in a movement favoring a popular religious teaching. The former published, in 1528, a collection of predictions under the title *Thesauros*, which was much admired, reprinted many times, and became a popular reading during the years of Turkish domination, and even much later. The didactic spirit took different forms in Damaskinos. One work, concerned with natural sciences and written in the spoken language, made a tentative conciliation between the old Byzantine traditions and the new tendencies of Western origin. This conciliation found its fullest expression in the work of Sophianos. The predictions of Rartouros (1560) followed the same course. They were not of exceptional quality, but one senses in them a constant interest in approaching the common people.

Pigas

Perhaps the most eminent representative of this period which produced Loukaris and other writers of his century was Meletios Pigas (1549–1601); moreover, he was the main defender of Loukaris. Pigas also used the spoken language in his sermons; he attributed special significance to those he preached around 1587 in Constantinople from the patriarchal pulpit. His rhetoric was judicious enough to combine naïveté with simplicity; but there was also a force of persuasiveness mixed with humor and irony, which contributed effectively to the didactic purpose of the discourse.

> One holds beans and tosses the beans and predicts extraordinary events. O vanity! Come, beans, you ignominious prophets of shame, and tell us how you reveal prophesy. . . .

Maximos Margounios and Maximos the Peloponnesian

The two Maximi, Margounios and the Peloponnesian, also used intentionally the popular idiom for their predictions. Margounios, who divided his life between Crete and Venice, belonged to the end of the sixteenth century. He translated religious texts in the spoken language and addressed his sermons in this same language; he also used the archaic language with skill, which was not rare during those years. The same can be said about the slightly later Maximos the Peloponnesian, who for a time also lived in the Ionian Islands. Neither man was a theoretical supporter of the spoken language, nor incapable of using the ancient language. The intention of both was clear; they used the language of the people in order to encourage the uninstructed flock toward Orthodoxy.

There were many from one end of the Greek world to the other who applied themselves to this end during this period and later. We should mention one more example, the Athenian Nathaniel Hykas. He also alternated between the two languages. He wrote masterfully in the archaic, but his religious polemics and in his sermons he did not scorn the spoken idiom. A contemporary of Cyril Loukaris, he exercised his literary activity both in Constantinople and in Venice. But the opposition between the two regions continued no less fiercely even when the destiny of the patriarchate in Constantinople was entrusted to Loukaris. When the latter founded the printing office in Constantinople under the direction of Nikodemos Metaxas, he received a work from Venice by Gabriel Seviros for publication. The editor deemed it his duty to apologize for the language of the work in these terms: "The work is written in the spoken and vulgar language because the people expressly have demanded it." This phrase permits us to measure the breach between the Greeks of the West and those who continued to live under the influence of the patriarchate. And though Metaxas was originally from the Ionian Islands, he had received his education in the West and he was animated by the desire to elevate the intellectual level of the Greek people. After the failure of the premature enterprise of Loukaris, Metaxas departed for the West and attempted to established a printing office in Cephalonia. This desire to multiply texts by printing them, an interest that carried over into the schools, characterizes the sixteenth century.

The Athenian Leonard Philaras divided his life between Italy and France. As a young man in 1633, he wrote a work in the spoken language dedicated to Cardinal Richelieu. Later, he had a brilliant career. The honors bestowed on him in the West did not alienate him, however, from his mother tongue. In 1652, his picture appeared in print along with a quatrain in modern Greek which he addressed to his "honorable Mother":

Madame, there is still no possibility for my return
To our country to see you and to kiss your hand.
Rejoice when looking at my picture and know my heart is with
    you,
And that it is only my body which is in foreign lands.

Vlachos, Varouchas, and Palladas

The Cretans Gerasimos Vlachos (1607–1685), Athanasios Varouchas (1631–1708), and Gerasimos Palladas (c. 1714) distinguished
themselves during these years with their contributions to Greek
culture. Vlachos and Varouchas lived under Venetian influence,
the former both in Venice and in the Ionian Islands, the latter in
the Ionian Islands. Neither man had a literary disposition. Both dedicated their intellectual faculties to different aspects of the cultural
advancement of their compatriots. While the scholarly elements
predominated in the former, the latter preferred the folk elements.
The migration from Crete to the Ionian Islands and Italy, where the
culture was similar, does not surprise us; what holds our attention
is a certain change in the orientation of Cretan culture. Besides the
fall of Crete, the end of the seventeenth century was characterized
by a change, a development away from creative production to more
theoretical and more critical forms of expression. This phenomenon
has generally been considered in the history of letters as marking
the end of the classical period and the beginning of neoclassicism;
but there was also a tendency to refer the spoken language to its
source, to the ancient speech. Indeed, during the last years of the
Venetian occupation Crete perhaps had lost a little of its old radiance and was more receptive to the influences coming from the
progressively organized ecumenical patriarchate, powerful and
aware of its mission and its doctrine.

Vlachos composed a number of philosophical and theological
works destined for education and written in the ancient as well as
in the spoken language. Most of these, and his ecclesiastical sermons
written in the spoken language, remained unpublished. He is mentioned here particularly for his dictionary in four languages, which
represents the first serious attempt at modern Greek lexicography
and which served as a model for later publications on the same

order. Varouchas specialized in religious publications and paraphrased various sacred texts in the spoken language. The oratory of his discourses gives evidence of a primitive awkwardness that was not lacking in charm. Moreover, his fervor and the living language in which he wrote, the extensive circulation which his homilies enjoyed throughout the entire eighteenth century, assured him an eminent place in the culture of this period.

Gennadios Palladas, who ascended the patriarchal throne of Alexandria, is mentioned specifically because he was in communication with the circle of friends of Gerasimos Vlachos. It is with Palladas that the passage in Cretan civilization from literature to meditation, from poetry to prose, becomes clear. Palladas appears to have written his juvenilia in verses in which techniques of the time coexisted with traditional religious music. This is the way he laments the fall of Crete:

> She who was a flower, who sparkled as the sun,
> Who was the ornament of all the cities,
> Of all the earth, and the entire Universe.

Nonetheless, his main contribution consists of purely philosophical or religious works, among which one should note the sermons in a simple spoken language. Poetry gives way to prose.

The work of Petros Katsaïtis furnishes contrasting evidence to the natural decline of the Cretan period in Greek letters, for he produced even when the Turks occupied Crete. Born in Cephalonia, he lived in the Venetian-occupied Peloponnesus and then in Crete after its conquest by the Turks. Thus, in the Ionian Islands, in the Peloponnesus, or in Crete, we find Katsaïtis wherever the fusion of two civilizations has been accomplished. He was the author of several tragedies and a verse chronicle called *The Complaint of Peloponnesus,* wherein he described the conquest of Peloponnesus by the Turks. And though the Cretan influence was especially strong in him, particularly in his tragedies, *Iphigenia* (1720), *Thyestes* (1721), creative inspirations is lacking from his work. It is clear that we are concerned with simple survival. This sense of termination becomes much stronger when one recalls that Katsaïtis sought his prototypes in the works of the Italian poet Lodovico Dolce of two centuries earlier. *The Complaint of Peloponnesus,* a long chronicle written in eleven-syllable couplets, offers nothing more than a considerable historical interest.

Skoufos

Francis Skoufos is the most significant man of Greek letters treated
in this chapter. He was born in Crete in 1644, but lived in Italy
from the time he was a year old. Skoufos belonged to the last stage
of the period under examination here. His work is one more manifestation of the gradual rise in the intellectual level of the Greeks
living in the West and the strengthening of their national awareness.
Other manifestations consist of the contributors mentioned above,
who also are placed in this period, that is, around 1669. Furthermore we observe that, while in earlier periods, around the fall of
Contantinople, the scholars who went to the West were assimilated
to a great extent by their new milieu and were lost to Greek letters,
now such cases become rare, although they do not disappear entirely. The Greeks found a way, even while living in the West, to
earn a living by working at whatever required knowledge of modern
Greek. These men were clerics, professors, writers, editors, or printers. Also, during this same period, the number of Greek schools in
the areas governed by the Venetians had increased. This phenomenon will be repeated in subjugated Greece in the following period.
Perhaps these factors can be attributed to the increasing Greek
wealth in the regions which interest us, to a decline in centralization,
which permitted the development of a certain peripheral autonomy,
to an enfeebled local aristocracy indifferent to modern Greek culture, and to a parallel advance in social classes which were more
closely allied to Greek traditions. Finally, we are on the eve of the
establishment in Venice of two Greek printing offices, that of Glyki-
don in 1670 and Sarros in 1686.

Francis Skoufos wrote little. Absorbed in the effort to spread the
Catholic rites, he left only two important books. The one is his
Rhetoric; the other is an epistolary manual which remained unpublished. Religious rhetoric, in contrast to other kinds of rhetoric,
always flourished in the East, as we have seen already. But the
proselytizing endeavors of the Catholic church contributed to perfecting this genre. Moreover, in the West, the exigencies of the
court offered occasion to cultivate eloquence. Skoufos composed his
Rhetoric in the spoken language and promised, if his work was successful, to write another such book in the ancient language. His
work discussed the art of religious rhetoric and he declared that his

examples would be taken from religious texts. In addition to educating, his book would thus be useful for the edification of the reader. This dual purpose would have sufficed to explain the composition of such a work in the spoken language: "In order that my work may become useful to all the world, I have expressed myself in the spoken language; my desire is that it will be accepted with open arms, not only by the scholars and the best of men, but also by the simplest of people." But even without this admission, we know that the art of religious rhetoric was exercised in the folk language even in the regions of the East. A *Rhetoric* in the ancient language, or one containing examples from ancient texts, would have been less useful. Imitating both Western and ancient models of rhetoric texts, Skoufos inserted examples in his work. A well-known example, later imitated by Maniates, expressed his passionate love for his country. His sentiments in this respect were declared in the prologue: "I have wished to be of service to my people, rich formerly in every virtue and in science, reduced at present by the rigor of destiny to nakedness and indigence." In order to give an example of the Supplication, he prayed

> to Christ, the liberator of the world, to liberate the Greek nation from the Turks one day. How long must a glorious and noble people prostrate themselves before the impious turban installed on the throne? All these countries on which this visible Sun rises, and in which, under human form You appeared, invisible Sun, how long must they submit to the domination of the half-moon?

Thus, Catholic propaganda and the cult of liberty travelled side by side. But it was combined with something more: the awareness of the connection between pre-Christian Hellenism and neo-Hellenism. This connection was affirmed often, but it became particularly evident in the numerous references to the classics and to ancient mythology, which Skoufos inserted, despite his original intention. A profound knowledge of antiquity and the ancient texts in conjunction with the popular language—characteristic traits of Skoufos—are manifested again without restriction in his epistolary guide. The *Epistolario* in vogue was that of Korydaleas, which employed archaic formulas. Skoufos proved the need to offer to the public, parallel with his *Rhetoric,* a collection of epistolary formulas renewed and alive. He collected 150 letters, many of which were personal in nature. His epistolary guide also contained a large number of epigrams, because Skoufos wished to give additional proof that the cultivation of ancient Greek was normally allied to love of the new language. In eloquence and in the attachment to a continuity of the Greek tradition, Skoufos had a worthy successor in Elias Miniates. Miniates became the most celebrated orator during the Turkish occupation.

Part Three

A Century of Endeavors

Hellenism from 1669
to 1774

This is the century of the Phanariots. The homogeneity created on Greek soil by the foreign conquest is disturbed by movements of new classes with new intellectual needs: the Phanariots and later the merchants. Their needs were those of knowledge and of an ethic. The Phanariots give the tone and the tendency toward development of instruction and the examination of moral problems. Furthermore, we see the appearance of a certain literary sense, but it is incoherent. At the end of this period and at the beginning of the next one characteristic signs appearing in Hellenism are: the greatest period of the folksong and the first dissensions between the ecclesiastical and folk cultures. The end of this period comes around 1774, when the rising bourgeoisie acquire a more coherent character and when it begins to express its own particular intellectual needs.

Chapter 7

Three Generations

Intellectual Matters

Miniates, whose name closed the preceding chapter, will not be examined here as an isolated manifestation of Greek culture. And this is because the century of the Phanariots, which we are entering, actually qualifies somewhat as the first partial Greek synthesis. By this we mean that the line we have been obliged to draw between East and West now begins to disappear. In the East, the sovereign church at its height expressed a religious humanism of a conciliatory character, while the Catholic church, absorbed in its own difficulties with the Enlightenment, gave secondary importance to its efforts at proselytism. The persistent hostility of the patriarchate toward the Papal church diminished. The Phanariots who held jurisdiction over the Danubian principalities turned to the West and contributed in spreading Western influences to Constantinople. Greek commerce, which had developed in the bowels of the Ottoman Empire, now extended to the West, and the multiple bonds created by these exchanges went beyond the economic area. The movement back and forth between subjugated Hellenism and the diaspora became incessant. Intellectual manifestations tended more and more to coincide.

The Mavrokordatos Family

Alexander Mavrokordatos, who presided over Hellenic life for a century, is the representative figure of this Phanariot spirit. Panayotis Nikousios, originally from Chios, took as his secretary in 1671 a young man of thirty named Alexander Mavrokordatos. Mavrokordatos had studied abroad, begun a brilliant career and married into wealth, and, as a doctor and a philosopher, occupied a chair at the Patriarchal Academy where he became famous. He later detached himself from letters and was able, with his gifted intelligence and versatility, to succeed Nikousios when he died suddenly two years later. From this moment a period of splendor and glory began for Mavrokordatos. He was showered with dignities by the church, rich presents from foreigners, titles and favors from the Turks. Mavrokordatos participated in important delegations and diplomatic missions, which offered him the opportunity to become acquainted with the ingratitude of Ottoman administration. However, before he died in 1709, he proudly saw one of his sons installed as Prince of Moldavia and another son as Grand Dragoman of the Sublime Porte. He himself held the title of Exaporite (Secret Counsellor), under which he is known in history. Throughout his long life, he remained dynamic and always efficient. His success came through his kindness; but when diplomacy was insufficient, he became extremely violent.

This is not the place to examine his political activities, for which he was greatly honored, especially by his contemporaries. But if we consider the various official and family obligations that absorbed his time and thought, we can say that his writing activity is quantitatively remarkable. His early works, written during the period of his life devoted to education remained unpublished for the most part. These, the *Rhetoric, Grammar, Commentaries on Aristotle,* permit us to observe the rapid pace of his production. He also wrote a sacred history called *History of the Hebrews;* all these works were in the archaic language. The exceptional praises awarded him by his contemporaries and even by later generations testify more to his personal prestige and the power of his lineal descendants than to objective and impartial judgment. The more personal writings of his maturity, composed when his aristocratic consciousness was already formulated, interest us, not as works of art, but as an official expression of the principles of a newly forming world. This second group of works is composed of his *Thoughts,* which were published for the first time in 1805, and his letters. Mavrokordatos wrote in the archaic language, except in letters to his intimate friends; the spoken language, even in its most cultivated form, was for him only a servant destined for humble use. His directives and his recommendations are summarized in the following: study the ancient language and cultivate rhetoric. *Thoughts,* a collection of reflections inspired by the experience of life, constitutes a document of unique value; it is the fruit of political maturity freed from all dangerous idealism: "We do not forge an incorporial and immaterial rule of conduct; we hold body and matter accountable."

It is certain that he had read Machiavelli and La Rochefoucauld. His philosophy is simple; it is regulated by prudence, in which one sees, furthermore, an excellent foundation for ethics: "I have seen that the fortunate truths are those which are content to be and know how to restrain their desires. I have found those who do not love what they possess to be most unfortunate." Elsewhere he recommends, "With downcast eyes we will act according to the times; we will learn nothing more than we should or say more than will be to our benefit." Those who become involved in public administration, "become inwardly blind and outwardly deaf." As for his fellow men, "prudence will cause us not to benefit them without some assurance. We will pretend to them to be righteous even when we are not," because, he explains, fundamentally a righteous appearance is not assumed "with the intention of deceiving someone" but constitutes an homage to virtue. These last counsels are found in the chapter entitled "On the Simulation of Virtue." A similar teaching is found in his letters. In addressing his children, he never ceases to counsel them in wisdom, in circumspection, and in the necessity of subduing heart to reason. He also emphasizes the value of good conduct, of a solid culture, and of wealth: "indigence is the greatest of evils." A pretense at virtue is not reprehensible in his eyes because this avoids scandal. "Do nothing simply because you wish, or nothing simply because you can, but only because it serves your best interests."

These counsels and requirements do not appear to have been given in vain. Political sagacity and assiduous cultivation of letters distinguished the successive generations of the Mavrokordatos family. Their line went from success to success until the nineteenth century. At that time, the War of Independence revealed the diplomatic ingenuity of another great Mavrokordatos. We return, however, to the immediate successor as Secret Counsellor, to the son Nicholas, who also wrote at a time when politics was not his main concern. Nicholas was not endowed with the exceptional dynamic character of his father nor with his remarkable activity. He was a member of the third generation, which not only had need to create, but also to preserve what it had inherited. Being more refined, it was only natural that he should incline toward intellectual matters. We find him disturbed by violent passions of the soul—an inheritance from his father—and sometimes he breaks out into verbal attacks. In cupidity and in plunder, he rivalled his father, if not surpassed him; he learned prodigality as a means of retaining power. But we note in him a certain detachment from the ancient tradition to which his father had adhered with such fidelity.

His official works also were rendered in archaic language. He wrote a philosophical treatise entitled *Concerning Death* and another work entitled *Minor Works of Philotheos*, an attempt at creating a novel, but it remained unpublished until the end of the nineteenth century. He also wrote dialogues modelled on Lucian. His philosophy, composed of the four cardinal virtues of the classical tradition, reminds us, from one point of view, of the teachings of his father: "Thoughtless generosity causes many errors and is wasteful," or even, "He who tolerates evil in one man commits an injustice to the entire race." Prudence for him is also "the mother of all virtues." Certain of this thoughts, nonetheless, reveal that times had changed. He judged superstition harshly and hypocrisy even more severely: "There is nothing worse than injustice which simulates justice while it is injustice."

But in his translations he hazarded to use a more simple language. We have his translation from the Latin of *Political Theater* by Ambrosio Marliano. It is a kind of manual for princes; the new ruling class prepared these manuals for educational purposes. There would be no reason to cite the text of this foreign work if the Greek version did not present, here and there, some interesting verses from the point of view of metrics and language.

> When the people are hungry and when they suffer,
> They are embarrassed by no one, they fear no one.

Moreover, Nicholas made concessions to the popular language when he wrote verses, and he composed with a charm which, in his time, was not continued by the school of the Phanariots. At this stage in the evolution of Phanariot society, literature did not respond to an aesthetic need but constituted an instrument destined to conquer the world and gain material possessions. Nicholas remained unique for his period:

> She walks in the garden.
> The grass on which she walks
> Kisses her footsteps.
> See, at once it begins to bloom.

We find the same human tenderness, the same sweetness in expression, in the manuscripts of instruction that he left to his son Constantine: "Do not be prodigal, be economical. Do not be greedy, but manage well what you have. Stretch your legs only as far as they will carry you." And, "unnecessary gifts, whether to strangers or to members of the family, procure a bad name. They are intolerable to the inhabitants of the country, and all the subjects become discontented. If your father was at fault on this point, let his example serve as a lesson to you." This last advice refers to the various extremes which the course of events and his own cupidity had led Nicholas.

Such were the counsels of Nicholas to his son Constantine, who, in turn, would succeed to sovereignty over the Danubian provinces. Such high place is never attained without sacrifices and significant concessions to even the most elementary moral laws. Intrigues between relatives and even between brothers are not infrequent; the reign of even the mildest prince is marked by bloodshed. Constantine Mavrokordatos became a ruler ten times over. He was still in power at the time of his death in 1769.

For an entire century, the prestige and authority of the Phanariots had continued to develop. This is the moment to evaluate their activity. Constantine Mavrokordatos became famous for his culture. In 1741 one of his panegyrists, the Phanariot Drakos Soutzos, assured us in verse that,

> as he was liberated from occupations and from responsibilities inherent in his station, he listened to the reading of ancient texts and modern history. He applied himself to the study of historical books, works of his forebears. They were his only pleasure, his only occupation. He studied the Scriptures, philosophy, geography, and even other sciences. Always before him were piled all the books of the ancients and the moderns.

He was honored as well for all that he did for the benefit of culture and for raising the level of life of his subjects. In this his forty years' activity was remarkable. Though his father had written verses inspired by violent anti-Frankish sentiments, Constantine oriented the Danubian provinces toward the French Enlightenment. A French scholar dedicated a book to him in 1743, in which he congratulated him for honoring French authors by procuring their works, thereby expressing his love for France. He said, further, that Constantine ruled in a land which preferred the French language to all other modern languages. The French language, which had been imposed and recognized as the official diplomatic language, was studied systematically by the Phanariots; their children learned French and absorbed French culture. This period marks the most important stage in modern Greek culture. The consequences of this decisive association with an enlightened European culture—as Western culture was being called—will be discussed later. Here we need only observe that the new cultural orientation has as its point of departure religious humanism which unites the church and the Phanariots in common action.

Dositheos, Patriarch of Jerusalem

The new rising class was possessed by a passion for knowledge; schools were constructed, books published, scholarships awarded, thanks to the generosity of the Phanariots. Dositheos, patriarch of Jerusalem (1641–1707), was a figure much in view during the initial stage of this new attitude. He was not only an active man, a prolific writer, a severe defender of strict Orthodoxy, but he also worked indefatigably for the diffusion of culture. He set up a printing office in Jassy and restored another in Bucharest. His objective was to have all ecclesiastical works and religious books printed, but very shortly he also turned to works of a more general character. He printed the first historical compositions of the time—Dositheos himself had attempted writing history—and even *The History of the Hebrews* by the Exaporite and translations of ancient texts in a simple language. In 1704 we see a translation of *Parallels Between Greeks and Romans,* a treatise ascribed to Plutarch, executed by Constantine J. Bassaraba Brancovan, appearing from the printing press in Bucharest. Once more progressive tendencies were manifested in the work of the ruling classes. Dositheos was interested in establishing a printing office in Moscow and a school in Jerusalem; faith and letters were identified in his mind: "This school is destined to inspire faith in children more than piety, thanks to the study of letters." The clergy should be instructed. "The monks and priests should learn letters and music; they should learn how to copy books." Books contain a charm for Dositheos, a splendor characteristic of religious humanism. He orders for the monastery: "Send us the *Treatise of the Trinity* by St. Augustine; cover it with canvas and tell the Fathers that, should anything happen, God forbid, everything else can be destroyed but, for nothing in the world, that book."

The impetus toward letters during this period was a universal phenomenon. At the end of the eighteenth century, we see the pat-

riarch prohibiting the ordination of illiterate priests. A patriarch of
Antioch named Sylvester wrote: "There is nothing more praiseworthy in the eyes of God and men than the path to study and the
reward which accompanies it."

Miniates

Elias Miniates was born in Lixouri in 1669 of a scholar father. Having terminated his studies in Italy, he became a professor, a
preacher, and bishop in the regions of Greece still in the hands of
the Venetians. He died at the age of forty-five (1714). He distinguished himself with his precocity. At the age of twenty, he left the
university, he was named professor at the Flangunian College, and
he wrote the preface to an encomium for Denis IV of Constantinople by Gerasimos Kakavelas. The young deacon did not hesitate
to associate his name with a bold text in which Vlachia was called
"the school of debauchery," and in which there was an allusion to
"the avarice of certain ecclesiastics and dignitaries of Constantinople, men of little faith."

His writing activities were quite restricted; we have a work of his
directed against the papacy entitled *Stone of Scandal*, which was
not published until after his death. But during his life he was famous
for his teachings and his sermons. A year before he died, an illiterate
monk noted that he was "greatly miraculous." The scholarly circle
honored him no less; his *Sermons* were translated into Rumanian
during his lifetime. It is from him that Meletios, his contemporary,
and Damodos took their examples when they composed their
Rhetorics. Dapontes called him the new Chrysostom and his fame
persisted throughout the eighteenth century. Kodrikas, who spoke of
him as a man in the classical mode, wrote: "He has elevated the
popular language with the eloquence of Demosthenes." The many
editions of his works prove he was accepted by a vast public. The
Stone of Scandal was reprinted five times between 1718 and 1783,
the *Sermons* ten times between 1716 and 1800.

His language was simple: "As for me, I am inspired by the example of the great teacher of nations, the apostle Paul, who says, 'I
am indebted to the wise and to the illiterate,' and I strive to teach
as simply as possible in order to be understood by all." The central

point of his teaching was ethics; he avoided theoretical controversies, "which do not clarify but rather create confusion." It is clear that with him the spirit of Korydaleas was endangered, and that the interest of new Hellenism began to concentrate on action. The future of the country preoccupied Miniates greatly; he used the words of Skoufos to call for the liberation of Greece. But his faith remained strong and he depended on the church: "Would it not be better to spend on the Church and the monasteries all that is being spent now on the theaters and in the houses of prostitution?" His language was simple, his thought was practical; but his technique was very elaborate rather than simple. The form of discourse obeyed all the strict rules; the figures of rhetoric, the objections, the retorts to objections, the images, the parables, the visions, and the dialogue, all abound within a fixed framework. All this gives life and movement to his prose; one imagines a preacher with ample and emphatic gestures. Miniates's prose is decorated with all the ornaments and ribbons of the Italian baroque. He sought to arouse, to charm, and to captivate, not to convince. To this end, he played the entire scale from tenderness to passion. The power of imagination and courage sustained his efforts:

> At a time when Orthodoxy sparkles like the sun at noontime, I also light the lamp of the Evangelical Gospel, I come to a church full of Christians, and I search for a Christian, I search for a Christian. But how? Those I see here and elsewhere, in the cities, in the fortresses, in the provinces, in the kingdoms, in most of the world, are they not Christians? .... I search for one, in the greater part of the world, and I fail to find him. I search for a Christian. I search for a Christian. I go from city to city to find one. I search for him in the market places among the nobles: I find arrogant pride. But no Christian. I search in the bazaars, among the merchants: I find an insatiable avarice. But no Christian!

Today the reader is satiated by such an abundance of images and in their obstinate prolongation:

> She advances from the bright gate of the Orient, this luminous announcer of the sun, I should say the radiant dawn, rosy-fingered. And from where she advances, in a silvery-golden sky, the appearance of the fair Apollo, the choir of numerous stars seek to disappear. The profound darkness of

night disappears entirely. The crescent of the moon cannot suffer this brilliant light and covers her face with shame. One hears the harmonious music of melodious chants of birds in the green and gold forests. Men, slumbering soundly, begin to awaken to go to work. And finally, the gracious messenger announces to the four corners of the earth the good news: Day has come. See the light.

But it is the first time that we are concerned seriously with the question of style in a prose text distributed during the Turkish occupation. We should note the manner with which it treats of prayer in favor of Greece. The supplication is not addressed to the Lord but to the Virgin, to a woman. The element of tenderness is enriched thereby and the sentimentality is increased.

Until when, most Holy Virgin, must the unhappy Greek people remain prisoners of an insufferable slavery? Until when must the barbarous Thracian foot continue stepping on its noble neck? Until when must these lands be ruled by the Crescent, these lands where the mystic Sun of Justice assumed human form, from Your sacred bowels. O Holy Virgin!

We have the same spirit, the same elevation that we found in Skoufos. But the language here is ornamented with delicate flowers, the presence of the Virgin is enriched with sonorous adjectives, which Miniates deliberately sought. The conventional worship here takes a visionary acuity: "the foot stepping on its noble neck." It is clear that Christian faith runs side by side with a more human preoccupation; in other words, with a literary concern.

Damodos

Vincent Damodos (1700–1752) was thirty years younger than Miniates. Originally from Cephalonia, he studied in Italy, and returned to his country to enter the practice of law and later to devote himself to teaching. He retired to his native village of Havriata and there established a school. Since the number of students was restricted, he found time to write a complete course in the popular language. He was also occupied with teaching rhetoric and writing purely theological works. A small portion of his works was published after his death. In his philosophy, he also was concerned with rejecting the Aristotelian yoke that had been transmitted by Korydaleas. However, though he appeared to sympathize with Descartes in essential matters, and though he disagreed emphatically with scholastic philosophy, he remained true to Aristotelian forms. All this inspired him with a critical intention which should be emphasized. The new orientation of Greek thought on ethics and on physics is evident in the work of Damodos. The new man turns to the external world and attempts to determine his place among men and in the physical universe. Damodos's moral attitude is courageous and one can almost say progressive. It is shot through with a democratic spirit: absolute authority of man over his hearth or of the bishop over his flock does not please him:

> The authority of man over woman is not despotic. Man cannot do what he wants with woman. His authority is political: he has the right to do what he wants within the limits of Justice, as the patriarchs and bishops, whose authority in the Church is a political authority. If a bishop orders something unjust, the people should resist him.

However, living in a small isolated community and not publishing any of his work, Damodos was unable to enter the mainstream of Greek letters. In spite of his talents and originality, he appears only as a local innovator, outdated, archaic. Others, such as the Zakynthian Katiphoros and the Corfiot Milias, who lived only in urban centers, influenced modern Greek culture clearly and for a longer period of time.

The theory of the popular language, soon to be systematized in a more complex form by the neo-Hellenic Enlightenment, appears in simple outline at the end of the period we are discussing. In 1759, Timothy Kyriakopoulos from Chios published *Promotion of Instruction in the Christian Religion,* a work of papist inspiration. The preface poses the problem:

> "He who reads your book, does not read it to see if he is knowledgeable in the Greek language, but to learn from it what is essential for his salvation. When you write a book on theology, on philosophy, or any other book destined to instruct scholars, write as you please; but when you write for the salvation of the people, you must write and speak in a way that the people will pay attention to you."

A step further and the Greek Enlightenment will proclaim that all knowledge is for the people and that, consequently, all culture should use the language of the people. This step will be delayed by the passage of Voulgaris in Greek letters. Voulgaris, who appears to have been a student of Damodos and who, in any case, was a student of Katiphoros, reconciled all the oppositions of the century with his powerful personality. But before discussing Voulgaris, we should take one last look at the entire century and examine certain other manifestations that had no place in this chapter.

Chapter 8

The Charm of Expression

The Man of Letters

and his Public

The manifestations we will examine now are fundamentally those that language can offer for man's exclusively aesthetic enjoyment. The century of the Phanariots helped produce the first aesthetic of the new Greek literature: verse and prose were to be cultivated in particular forms, either by continuing and expanding the insular tradition, by following foreign evolutions, or by perfecting the folksong and folk prose. The development of printing offices multiplied the output of literary activities. In this chapter, we will examine the various forms of literary production; further, we will study the diffusion of printed matter in those regions of Greece occupied by the Turks from its first manifestations to the end of the Phanariot period.

The Flowers of Piety

One stage in this history is marked by *The Flowers of Piety*, a collection of poetry edited in 1708 by the students of the Flanguinian School in Venice. Some of the conditions necessary to the development of poetry include, first of all, the coexistence of a living linguistic tradition with a tradition of artistic expression. A social group which pursues poetry is another condition. Both conditions are not wholly present for the scholarly poetry of the period we are examining, for they imply, more or less, that poetic expression can develop only when it is a local product. Hence, the cultural centers on foreign soil were not conducive to the projection of poetry, while those of the Hellenic interior still lacked maturity. Venice was the closest to offering the requisite conditions. Certainly, its soil was strange, but it was crowded with a flourishing Greek colony of long standing. Moreover, it was to Venice that many of the last representatives of Crete's Golden Age went to settle. But even in Venice, the language was removed from its source and contained some characteristics of a dead language, a fact which did not reestablish it naturally.

Despite this, *The Flowers of Piety* is precious testimony of the extent to which Greek poetic expression succeeded wherever it profited from a favorable cultural climate. The collection contains some sonnets and a certain number of poems in strophes or other forms. The sonnets are distinguished by their perfect techniques and an excellent linguistic development. We must not forget that these poets were studying literature, philosophy and rhetoric in Italy; but not one of these poets would preserve a line of poetry that appeared to have originated there. Hence, works, refreshed by a youthful spirit, contained scholarly influences of the classroom and those of the Italian environment. The school contributed an intense recollection of the Hellenic past and the sentiment that Hellenism was the civilizing unity throughout the ages. An anonymous poet, perhaps the Cretan Francis Gerardos (1691), expressed this in a verse entitled "To Greece."

> Under the shade of a tree I lay sleeping and breathing deeply, but my heart was sad because I was thinking of the joy of Greece, and her power. Then I heard a voice in my sleep. "Awaken, arise!" it said. "What despondence, what sleep is this? What causes your grief that you lie there sorrowing?" I awakened and saw over my head Athena herself, who went on to speak very frankly, there from on high: "Time can never wither the ancient glory of Greece because wisdom is ever unwithering."

The attitude, certainly, is scholarly. Greece lives through wisdom. But the passion for everything Greek is evident. Certain ancient allusions emerge from the poems; a satirical sonnet, dedicated "To an Untalented Singer Who Believes that He Has a Beautiful Voice," the work of a young Cretan, Lawrence Venerios (1694), ends as follows:

> The old women say that someone is going to die when the raven is heard at night in the neighborhood. But when you sing, it is the raven that bursts!

This reference of ancient origin comes from an epigram in the Palatine anthology. But from the Italians (independent of the tendency towards Latinization) will come the weight of the baroque style that we encountered already in Miniatis. Sighs, sweetness, ribbons and bows bind the work tightly to its period.

Much artistry, but also genuine poetic inspiration, perfects these poems which constitute the first great achievement after the Cretan Age. These are authentic flowers, with a charming variety of colors, but they are hothouse flowers; though they connect with the past, they do not create something new. The artificiality of these poems is revealed not only through their workmanship, but also because they remain without consequence. Of the dozen young men who collaborated on the collection, only a few names survive, and these from outside literary activity. The oldest of the group was Anthony Liberios Kolettis (b. 1685 or 1738 or 1739), who also collaborated on a translation of the New Testament into the spoken language. Only one, Anthony Stratigos (1692–1758), continued to appear in Greek letters. However, even though toward the end, in 1745, he remembered his Cretan origin and translated *The Frogs* in fifteen-syllable couplets, his interests lay elsewhere: ancient Greek verses which bound him with the past, translations into the spoken language of works with a strong didactic character; these latter, his essential work, give evidence of his patriotic preoccupations and associate him with the Enlightenment that is coming into being.

Dapontes

Caesar Dapontes was considered the great poet of his century. His contemporaries imitated him and subsequent generations found no words eloquent enough to extol his praises. And, indeed, he was the poet most adapted to an essentially antipoetic society, as was the intellectual society of Turkish-dominated Greece during his period and even later. This society was composed of men whose interests centered not on art but on knowledge. Successive generations were gripped by an insatiable thirst for knowledge and sensations. They sought to be informed about everything, to inquire into everything. For men animated by such a spirit, verse ended by becoming a mnemonic technique, and indeeed, the interminable fifteen-syllable verses of Dapontes are nothing more than a kind of memorization. He longed for knowledge as others longed for wine, and where they say

> My glass, my little glass, five times my glass,

he will say

> My book, my little book, ten times my book.

And it was not only about books that he was curious. It was about everything; he examined everything. All his feelings were turned toward knowledge.

> Argus had a thousand eyes, says mythology.
> As for me, I wish I had a thousand ears
> To hear stories endlessly. . . .

he writes in the preface to his *Geography*. Most observant by nature, he travelled, he examined everything; he made judgments about everything, without any lyricism, but with an acuity and intelligence.

> I saw the island of Chios, which is nothing but rock.
> I saw the inhabitants of Chios, intelligent and industrious.
> Finally, I saw that charity did not quit Chios
> Because the island prevented it from fleeing.
> But I 'did not let them damn themselves again,
> I taught them how they, too, should grant charity.

Naturally, from all his readings, he gained an absolute awareness of the historical unity of Hellenism. His verses, as well as his prose works, abound in ancient allusions. He dreamed of the resurrection of the nation and he described his dream. However, that admiration for the ancient glory, though reflected in his language, did not prevent him from exploiting the vigor of the language of his time. Though he versified old stories, he was attracted irresistably by the contemporary ones; he wrote chronicles that are precious to us today, geographies and travel works, "marvelous histories and curiosities of the world," and using religious parodies as models he enumerated the "remarkable things known in many islands and cities, of people and of animals."

But we must mention one further kind of knowledge which Dapontes was first to introduce obviously into Greek letters. Ptochoprodromos and Sachlikis had already written of their sufferings and tribulations. Dapontes did the same, but he added something new; he took pleasure in self-examination and self-evaluation. As yet, it was not a question of subjective poetry, but one notices an awakening interest in self, an attitude of curiosity, which cannot be called affectation. Hence, we have a perceptible blending of two tendencies: of the old Christian introspection and of the new spirit of curiosity, a spirit which characterizes the century of the Phanariots. Moreover, the coexistence of these two tendencies is also a characteristic of this period. Dapontes describes himself with interest and with a certain satisfaction.

> Though I hate oral gossip,
> I love to talk with others.

He talks about his psychic condition:

> A few days ago, my left eye twitched.
> I said: there will be nets and boats in my life again. . . .

In 1766 Dapontes published in Leipzig a metrical work in two volumes under the title *Mirror of Women*. It was a collection of stories about the most celebrated religious and secular women. Voulgaris, who was in Leipzig awaiting the opportunity to publish his *Logic,* said impatiently: "If I had a wife or a daughter, I would never permit either to be reflected in such a mirror." Thomas Mandakasis edited this work and added a preface. Mandakasis was a physician from Kastoria who lived and practiced medicine in Leipzig and dedicated his time and money to the publication of Greek books. He was also a writer. In 1760 he had published a book of his own under the title *Of Invisible Things Revealed Through Visible Things.* A certain looseness in thought and expression characterizes the work, but it gives evidence of a progressive spirit. "In our day, men are outspoken on a great many things, and they do not wish to spit on the faces of hypocrites and liars." Or even, "Today, men refer falsely to the rich by the title of nobleman." Now and then, he wrote verses. The intention was superior to the expression. Seeking to justify the language of Dapontes, he praised the spoken language:

> You, do not scorn the spoken language, for it is full of beauty when you come to know it. It possesses so much charm and surpasses all other languages in the world.

Editors and Books

Mandakasis was a friend of Voulgaris; he knew and exercised a certain influence on the young Koraes. His interest in intellectual matters, however, did not allow him to work superficially as an editor on the works entrusted him. It seems that, from this point of view, he badly mishandled the poems of Dapontes and the latter complained about it. However, had Dapontes known better the customs of typography at that time, perhaps he would have been more understanding. Indeed, thoughout the entire period of Turkish domination, most other editors took liberties with recent literary texts, those written in the spoken language, the same liberties that characterize the corresponding Byzantine copyists. These texts were often issued with important variants and tended toward linguistic modernization.

We would like to know what was read at this time in the Greek world. Certain figures are indicative in this regard. When, in 1707, Meletios Mitros sought to publish his *Geography*, he wrote to the publisher that he was willing to subsidize 1500 to 2000 copies, convinced that it would sell, since no comparable work existed. In 1766, Dapontes calculated that 1000 copies were printed of one of his books. In 1814, Economos printed 750 copies of his *Catechism*. Finally, in 1823, only 500 copies of the Old Testament circulated. It appears that the average circulation of editions was around 1000 copies. And indeed, we know of an epistolary guide that was printed in 1757 in 1000 copies; the following year it was almost exhausted. One thousand copies also were printed of some works of Rigas: *The Moral Tripod*, and others. It is useful to present a few more figures. *The Greek Bibliography* of Koraes was also printed in 1000 copies. Of the *Iliad*, which Koraes classified among educational works, he proposed to print 1500 copies but later reduced the figure to 1000 copies. The pamphlets published for propaganda purposes had a wider circulation: the *Proclamation* of Rigas and the *War Trumpet* of Koraes circulated in 3000 copies. Sometimes years after the original publication we find a book listed again in catalogues of the publishers or in advertisements, which means that the 500 or 1500 copies had not sold. But we also find that editions succeed one another within a few years. Desire for a book was shortly followed by a critical evaluation of it; hence, we see the life of an edition established very early: a calculated number to be printed, anticipated sales, and antagonisms in the form of criticism.

We have seen the passionate interest already aroused by books among scholars of this period. We also know there were a significantly large number of private libraries; in fact, a characteristic phenomenon appeared at this time which merits attention. Whereas formerly one saw oriental manuscripts coming to the West, now entire libraries were purchased in the West by scholars of the Hellenic East. As for the number of books published by the Greeks, it was growing constantly; there were countless publications in all genres during the five years between 1670 and 1674. One can count more than a hundred during the eighteenth century for a corresponding period.

The fate of the small popular pamphlets or books was quite different. Since they were widely read, they were reprinted frequently. *The Book of Alexander the Great* was reprinted three times during the seventeenth century and at least six times during the eighteenth. *Aesop,* his life and his fables, was printed at least five times during the century of the Phanariots and more than twenty times from 1775 to 1821. Of the *Erotokritos,* there is mention of at least seven editions in the eighteenth century. The rhythm of publications is most significant. *The Shepherdess* was printed in 1745, 1755, and 1764, or three editions in ten years. The most significant works from the point of view of circulation during this period were: *Aesop, The Book of Alexander the Great, The Book of Apollonius, The Shepherdess, Susanne* by Dephanaras, *The History of the King of Scotland* by Trivolis, *The Exploits of Michael Boevada,* and the romance of *Imperios and Margarona* in a variant later than the original.

The Book of the Donkey

The Greek spirit of satire found its way into many of these publications and was developed as a consequence. An extension of an ancient Byzantine tradition, they were directed against the nobles, against women, against bad members of the clergy. *Bertoldos,* a translation from the Italian, an edition of which we know already in 1646, favors precisely this spirit. The same can be said about *The Book of the Donkey.* This latter work, usually titled *The Amusing History of a Donkey, a Wolf, and a Fox,* is a good variant, in political couplets, of the *Book of the Life of an Honest Donkey.* It cannot be dated later than the fifteenth century. Furthermore, the excellent quality of its versification and certain linguistic elements show that it was probably of island origin. Written with spirit, this narrative is superior to its original. The work is tighter, though longer, more artistic, more delicate in psychological nuances:

You should eat that lettuce leaf without vinegar!
How is it that we weren't drowned throughout this journey!

We understand why the Greek people showed a special preference for *The Book of the Donkey,* if we compare it to the bad
rhymed prose habitually offered to them. Even the title became a
proverb and served to designate the whole of folktale literature during the Turkish occupation.

Along with these works, we should mention those in which natural science is discussed more or less in the form of a fable; these
include the *Book of Fruit* and the practical manuals such as the
Agriculture by Agapios Landos and the *Arithmetic* by Glyzonios.
These works were reprinted many times during this period. They
filled certain fundamental human needs, but they did not satisfy all
of them. Religious requirements were satisfied easily by the printed
books and by the religious life of the time. One work, which seems
to have been printed much later but which circulated widely in
manuscript form before its publication, came to inspire, to exalt, and
to satisfy the love of liberty. It was the famous *Agathangelos,* which
played a very significant role in the cultural history of Hellenism.

Written around 1750 by a cleric, Theoklitos Polyides, the work
is presented as a translation of an older Italian work. In reality,
Polyides was inspired by the ancient prophetic literature and his
style in composing an original work was destined to convince the
Greek people that their liberty would come through Russia, the
Blond Race. It was a work of propaganda, known in Greece even
to this day through its successive popular editions. One can get an
idea of the direct hold this pamphlet had on the popular masses by
reading the appeal Voulgaris addressed to Catherine the Great in
the preface of his 1770 translation. There he writes: "The simple
people think about this prediction with relation to the blond race,
and I don't know how many other prophecies formerly expressed.
. . . Greece, and the other people of the same religion, are revived
in this hope and believe that their deliverance is very near." Every
so often disillusionment followed and for an instant hope faltered,
but the discouragement was quickly surmounted. After the disappointing expedition of Orlof, Dapontes lamented:

Weep, prophets and makers of predictions: your words are carried by the wind, deceitful astrologer. Greeks, let us weep for
our antiquity. For her, we have lost our glorious fame.

Metrical Ballads

The metrical folk works, if one excludes Cretan literature or, more generally, the island literature, lack aesthetic value. Most of the pieces which circulated during this period were metrical ballads, long versified narratives without a breath of spring and without elevation. During the entire period of the Turkish occupation, poems in this genre were composed by only moderately gifted versifiers. They took as subjects of their narrations recent events which had made a special impression and aroused the interest of the local public. The custom was an old one. Stavrinos, Matthew Myreon, and Palamides had written metrical ballads. And Bounialis also had composed a long metrical ballad.

The subjects treated in the metrical ballads bring us to another area where the three literary forms, the printed, the manuscript, and the oral, are blended. The metrical ballads and the folk pamphlets circulated in urban centers, where the little culture of the time was concentrated and where the linguistic sense was blunted by contact with the language of the school, but one sees, in this period, another form of language flourishing out in the fields, up the mountain sides, in inaccessible and isolated regions. Linguistic tradition, traditional cultivation of verse, rooted in the ancestral soil, conditions indispensible to the realization of a literature, all existed in these regions. Something else was found here as well. I have already emphasized the frontier character of modern Greek literature. In a Greece oppressed by the Turks, some islands continued to remain free. Sometimes the spirit of the narrator or singer was expressed, but at other times the works were identified with the bands of klephtes who breathed the air of freedom. The externalization of the Greek spirit in texts of folk inspiration is one of the most characteristic phenomena of the century and certainly the most outstanding. For the chronicle, we note *The Chronicle of Galaxidi;* for poetry, the popular folksong; for rhetoric, Kosmas the Aetolian.

The Chronicle of Galaxidi

We already know the memoirs, where men who often scarcely knew how to write evoked the most important events of their times in a few words. These events were marked in the margins of their printed works or on blank pages of manuscripts. Likewise, another genre, the court chronicle bequeathed by antiquity to Byzantium, remained in use under Turkish domination. These were short chronicles or brief abstracts, either of world history or that of a country or a province, which insisted particularly on dates. We should include in this category a masterly work called *The Chronicle of Galaxidi.* The intention is the same here; the work serves to preserve for later generations the notable histories of the past that should be remembered. The spirit remains the same, simple, popular, descriptive. But Euthemios, the author of this *Chronicle,* had a talent for writing and managed, despite his limited knowledge, to compose a small complete work, full of life, spirit, and dramatic intensity. He possessed the art of narrating with charm: "My narrative pleases me to relate to you an unfortunate episode, provoked by the bad faith of the Franks, who always fight against the faith of the Greeks." His style is epigrammatic, without any rhetorical embellishments: "He lived two hours. When the battle was ended finally, he said, 'Now, my Lord God, I die content,' and he gave up the spirit." Euthemios should also be remembered for his heroic sentiments and his patriotism, which were combined with a profound religious faith: "All for country and all for faith, absolved of all our sins." These words were written in 1703, but the manuscript remained unpublished until 1865. The chronicle is cited because of its literary value, and also because it constitutes significant evidence of the spirit of its time.

The Folksong

It is in such an ideal atmosphere that the folksong, and especially the klephtic song, took root and developed. It is time now to continue the observations made at the beginning of this *History* by saying that the tradition of the folksong showed no interruption between the period we left it and that we are discussing. It continued to be nourished by the great events of folk life while pursuing its traditional function. When the revolt of Denis Skylososophos was quelled, Seraphim, bishop of Phanari in Thessaly, submitted to martyrdom along with many others. The official church disavowed the movement for political reasons, but Seraphim allied himself with the new martyrs. Gordios, also originally from Agrapha, composed a divine service dedicated to the memory of Seraphim and the people chanted it. In the following century we have the song of Boukou-valas. However, the klephtic song and the folksong in general, both products of the collective consciousness, were not basically inspired by hero-worship. The free life of the klephtes, the daily incidents, the acts of bravery, the psychology of men who chose freedom, their sentiments, their passions, their thoughts, all became song. We have no reason here to analyze again the folksong or its subject matter. We shall only state that it was now at its full flowering as an expression of the Greek spirit. It was ripe for courageous endeavors, for it was now a complete aesthetic achievement in literature.

The popular development of folksong had reached the point of expressing the spirit of the people accurately; it was a spirit thirsting for equilibrium, for "isometry," as it has been designated recently. The verse of the folksong expressed this desire. The original Greek folk verse, the iambic of fifteen syllables divided into two hemistichs, was perfected without unnecessary amplification, without enjambment, both of which are incompatible with the sensation of plenitude. The first hemistich is generally completed in the second. And when it is necessary for meaning, a second verse will follow, balanced and symmetrical

Νὰ κατακάτση ὁ κορνιαχτός, νὰ σηκωθῆ ἡ ἀντάρα,
'Απὸ βραδὺ μοιριολογοῦν καὶ τὴν αὐγὴ φωνάζουν.

When the dust settles, when the fog lifts,
They chant dirges in the evening and they weep at dawn.

Or in two other verses:

Βλέπουν ἐχτροὶ καὶ χαίρονται καὶ φίλοι καὶ λυποῦνται,
τὸν βλέπει κ' ἡ μανούλα του καὶ κάθεται καὶ κλαίει.

The enemies see and they rejoice and friends are sad,
His mother also sees him and she sits down and weeps.

The other meters of the folksong appear to have derived from political verse, conforming to musical or choreographic necessities, and are subject to the same rules, as for instance in the following:

Κάτω στοῦ Βάλτου τὰ χωριά,
Ξηρόμερο καὶ στ' Ἄγραφα,
καὶ στὰ πέντε βιλαέτια,
βάλτε μπρὲ νὰ πιοῦμ' ἀδέρφια.

> Down there, in the villages of Valtos
> At Xhiromero and Agrapha
> And in the five vilayets.
> Pour something to drink, brothers.

or even:

> Νά κ' ἡ ρίζα μου, καὶ δέσε τ' ἄλογό σου,
> νά κ' οἱ κλῶνοι μου καὶ κρέμασ' τ' ἄρματά σου.
>
> Here is my root, secure my horse;
> Here are my branches, hang up my weapons.

The same principle which in antiquity determined the rhetorical expression determined the form of the new folk creation, with the exception that the heritage was not transmitted through books; the carrier was the spirit. Ideas and propositions are all balanced.

Naturally, with such a verse form, the long subordination of sentences is excluded. Each verse, each distich, springs forth independently and tends to be autonomous. It gives one meaning, one image, one emotion. The universe reflected in the folksong is organized in small versatile units, clearly delineated, with positive function and clarity. The element of allusion is used, but not from abstractions, and rarely does suggestion or allusion proceed from an accumulation of ideas; more often it is created by emphasizing only one detail, the most characteristic, which, thus isolated, suffices. The part suggests the whole, the effect suggests the cause:

> ἀντιφάνηκε τὸ ποδαστράγαλό της,
> κ' ἔλαμψ' ὁ γιαλός, λάμψαν τὰ περιγιάλια.
>
> Her ankle appeared: at once the shore
> And the surroundings become radiant.

These same requirements of form suffice to impose a sobriety on all subject matter; all this contributes to a severe restriction of language. The adjective, rarely used at all, never embellishes the noun; it completes it and serves to replace long descriptions or to render explanations unnecessary. It is from a well-known song that the above verses are cited, and a single adjective serves to create the atmosphere:

> A sweet wind from the north began to blow.

In order to portray the idyllic state, the song confines itself to one particular and unusual attribute, sweetness in the north wind. The sweet north wind suffices to explain the presence of women, to render plausible the discreet lifting of the skirt, the passing of the galley, with the oars, near the shore.

There is no room for embellishment. All the elements of language should exercise a determined function in order to obtain, with as few words as possible, the integrity and plenitude of verse. For this reason, the folksong makes constant use of the historical present, which is briefer, more direct, more rapid. The result is to increase the dramatic character and render an easy passage from narrative to dialogue or from dialogue to narrative:

> The women look on them from their windows. "Who are these women who come from the Gate of Saraï? Women, what do you think? What do you see? We are the wives of klephtes, the wives of men of Lazos." Velis Pasha is watching; he stops and asks. . . .

Perhaps we should also mention the frequent use of formulaic expressions in the folksong, such as: "three birds were sitting" or "the word was in suspense" or "it offended him"; and also the use of opposites, such as: "high-low," "soft-hard," "snow-sun." As these locutions were familiar to the audience of the folksong, they aroused in it certain given images or a certain attitude of expectation, thanks to which superfluous descriptions and verbose psychological introductions were avoided.

In the same way these diverse organic causes, all of which led to the plastic integrity of form, were elaborated by the action of time and the great diffusion of the folksong. Redundancy, clumsiness of phrase, unpleasant hiatus, all the antipoetic elements were little by little eliminated. Moreover, the higher standard of living contributed to this purification, for it brought a progressive improvement to the verbal instrument. The Greek language during these years had not reached a dangerous crystallization which could lead to dead classical formulas. It could not be exposed to such a danger so long as the language remained one of oral expression and not a written one. Versatile and malleable, the language could respond at each moment to the simplest necessities of a world in evolution. Its freshness allowed it to give value to an old charm; it had gone past the stage where it was encumbered with numerous diminutives and now combined the virtues of a synthetic language with the former analytic.

This is the peak period of the folksong: a severely arranged technique, regulated by a rich and sensuous language. It is a moment of balance. Even the description of passion, in its most exaggerated form, becomes a simple and moderate form.

Kosmas the Aetolian

This chapter would not be complete without discussing the original folk teacher of the Turkish domination, Kosmas the Aetolian. Kosmas also was a true scholar in the sense that he appears to have had some education, but he acquired it during his maturity. His distinctive trait was his faith in the people and his attempt to work directly with them. He was born in 1714 in a small village of Apokouros in Aetolo-Akarnania. Later information shows him at a school in Mount Athos after 1753 studying under the guidance of Voulgaris, who was much younger. At any rate, from 1760, with the approval of the Patriarch Seraphim II, he undertook to preach his sermons throughout a large portion of Greece, from Thrace to the Ionian Islands, to the shores of the Corinthian gulf, to the mountains of Epirus and Macedonia. He circulated without any interruption for some twenty years. Then, denounced to the Turkish authorities, he was arrested and executed in 1779. His apostolate consisted of teaching and counselling the Christians in the cities, but particularly in the villages through which he passed. He never wrote a sermon. His disciples and his auditors reproduced from memory some of the sermons, which have been handed down to us more or less altered. But even in their approximate form, they exhibit an exceptional eloquence. Kosmas spoke the language of the people, formulating simple ideas with all the force of unelaborated passion. His images were also simple: "When we put a little yeast in a kneading trough of flour, that flour is soured; likewise, enmity sours all that is good, reduces it to nothing, and causes it to disappear."

He avoided matters of dogma; he preached virtue, love, good works. He criticized the bad use of wealth; he was a friend to the poor. But above all, he sought education, Greek education: "Educate your children in ancient Greek because our Church uses ancient Greek, and our nation is Greek. Whoever does not understand Greek, my brother, does not understand the teachings of our Church. Better, my brother, to have a Greek school in your province than to have fountains and rivers."

In one of his letters, written a short time before his execution, he wrote that he had established ten secondary schools (that is, schools where Greek was taught) and one hundred primary schools. He also promoted the Greek language to the foreign populations of the areas through which he travelled. His association with Voulgaris and with the Patriarch Seraphim—to be discussed in the following chapters —as well as other indications convince us that he worked along the lines suggested by Russian propaganda. What arouses our interest is that he believed he could work directly on the folk masses, and that he succeeeded. The nation had reached its maturity. He was welcomed everywhere as an "apostle." Twenty years after his death, his biography had already been written in the *New Martyrology*. Even today, in Roumeli and Epirus, they recall his words and recount his miracles. A precursor of Rigas and Koraes, he was honored by all, contemporaries and their descendants. We should mention a comment which came from Doukas and which reveals how the disciples of archaism, despite their good faith, had lost contact with reality. In one of his letters, Doukas reproached Kosmas and Koraes for "having employed their forces in vain" and for having left as legacy to their descendants the difficult task of removing the *impurities* with which they had *stained* the nation, in order that the country could progress.

Chapter 9

Greece and Hellenism

Development of Curiosity

Geographical Interest

During the century we are studying here, we have a qualitatively important portion of the Greek population moving throughout Greek regions. We are not considering the merchants, whose work obliged them to travel; rather we are considering the teachers whom we have already seen carrying out their assignments to teach by travelling often from city to city. Higher education, as Greece could provide it during this period, involved frequent displacement. The number of schools increased. Certain schools became famous for their excellent advanced studies in a particular branch of knowledge, and a young man desirous of completing his education was led successively from one school to another. Generally, he completed all his studies by practicing some profession to provide for a living; he became a teacher, a priest, a clerk. This development in the life of the intellectuals which added to the thirst for knowledge that gripped the Greek people and made them aware of the differences between each region, aroused an interest which we can term geographic. Tourism had not yet come into existence; the kind of traveller who moved from place to place simply to satisfy his own curiosity or his need to move was an exceptional phenomenon. However, these displacements, though they were compulsory, naturally produced a desire in men to describe the various regions they visited, to note their differences and similarities, and to list what should be seen in each place. Travels abroad, becoming daily easier, were more frequent and developed the taste for relating these experiences. The scholar who left Greece without wanting to return eventually became more rare as conditions of life in Greece improved. One frequently found, on the contrary, the scholar who went to the West to study, or who simply travelled abroad, and who later returned to Greece, enriched by a multitude of impressions which he yearned to express in writing, thus arousing the curiosity and admiraiton of his compatriots.

The taste for curiosities, for mirabilia, was combined with the scientific disposition of the period. The increased public curiosity and frequent contacts with other countries created the requisite conditions for the appearance and development of geographic literature. But there was also another genre ready to receive the accounts of travellers. This was the *ephemerides,* of which we have already spoken. The people who kept a journal naturally enriched it with their travel impressions which they related with particular detailed attention. We saw Arsenios describe, in former times, the marvels of his travels in Russia. We saw the curiosity of Dapontes. But between these two men, at the beginning of the century of the Phanariots, we encounter the first systematic Greek geographer who lived in Greece. This was Meleios Mitrou, a professor at Jannina, and later bishop. We should also remember the geographic interests of Constantine Mavrokordatos during the middle of the century.

Voulgaris

Eugene Voulgaris was born in Kerkyra in 1716. He was educated in the Ionian Islands and perhaps also in Italy, from where, in 1742, he went to Jannina as a professor. The vicissitudes of his professorial career—his encounters with Balanos Vassilopoulos, provoked by the liberal ideas of the former—brought him to Kozani. In 1753 the academy at Mount Athos was organized and Voulgaris was invited to direct it. But he did not remain there for long; his quarrelsome nature, known to us from other sources, as well as other reasons, brought him into opposition with the professors and officials of the establishment. In one of his letters he complained bitterly of Panayotis Palamas, who taught Greek with him. He went to Constantinople. The Patriarch Seraphim II, devoted to the Russian dream, easily influenced Voulgaris, whose liberal political ideas coincided with his own views. In 1759, Voulgaris gave the sermon at the official commemoration of the Russian national holiday of Saint Andrew at the patriarchate and thereby provoked a scandal. In the meantime, he continued teaching at the patriarchal school. But the patriarch changed, and the usual polemics, which the character and ideas of Voulgaris aroused, forced him to retire. He went to the Danubian provinces, Prussia, and ended in Leipzig with the intention of completing his studies, particularly mathematics, and of publishing his works. We have already encountered him in Leipzig. He wrote to one of his friends from there, describing his life and the house in which he lived: "In the same house is a chapel," that is, the oratory reserved for the Orthodox church, "and I am in danger of becoming a follower." We imagine him more like the free abbots of the period than a monk of Mount Athos. He published his *Logic,* a subject he had taught for a number of years. Because manuscript copies were circulating with an increasing number of errors, and because the subject was taught widely in Greek schools, Voulgaris considered it his duty to publish the work in order to reestablish the authentic text.

In the Germanic countries, the leading figure of this time was Frederick II, friend and admirer of Voltaire. In Russia, Catherine the Great ruled; her association with Voltaire is well known. The works of Voulgaris on this French philosopher and the great fame he had acquired with his own progressive teaching in the Orient aroused the interest of the empress. She was ambitious to compose a court of intellectuals and she was also beginning to prepare for the new Russo-Turkish War. Catherine had excellent reasons for wanting to attract Voulgaris to her court. Indeed, she invited him, and Voulgaris, after much hesitation and numerous services rendered her while in Germany, finally set off for Russia.

In 1772 we find him at the court of Catherine, heaped with honors, her librarian and collaborator. He remained near her until the end of the Russo-Turkish War. After the war, by her desire, he accepted ordination as a priest and consecration as bishop, and he took over the newly established Ukrainian archdiocese of Kherson. According to Dapontes, "he was sent there because, they said, the Synod of Russia was envious of the high rank to which he had risen."

In 1779, he resigned from the archdiocese in favor of Nikiforos Theotokis and returned to St. Petersburg, where he found himself once more immersed in a Russo-Turkish war. Later, in 1801, he retired to a monastery, where he died in 1806.

Theotokis

Parallel to Voulgaris's, but less pronounced, were Nikiforos Theotokis's travels. He was also originally from the Ionian Islands, from Kerkyra. Fifteen years younger than Voulgaris—he was born in 1731—he studied under the same professors. Then he went to Italy and Bologna to study, especially mathematics and physics. He returned to his country as a teacher and participated in the religious life of the islands. His fame as a preacher dates from this time. In 1765, he went to Constantinople at the invitation of the Patriarch Samuel Chadzaris. He left there discontented, went to Leipzig, published a certain number of his works, went to Jassy as director of the prince's school where he taught physics. But he was forced to leave there "as a thief in the night" in order to escape persecutions from the conservatives. In 1779 he succeeded Voulgaris to the archdiocese of Kherson, and in 1786 he went to the archdiocese of Astrakhan, resigned in 1792, then retired to a monastery in Moscow, where he died in 1800. He wrote works on physics, mathematics, geography, theology, and published his religious sermons. He had neither the abundance nor the impetuosity of Voulgaris. He was a placid man, balanced, prudent, diligent, both in the content of his writing and the elegance of his style; he appears more positive and more conservative than Voulgaris. The fifteen years separating the two men helped accentuate their temperamental differences and orient Theotokis toward conservativism. Indeed, the more courageously progressive he became, the more the church distrusted religious humanism and adopted a conservative attitude. Later, the church took purely reactionary measures, such as censures. Theotokis was farther from religious humanism than was Voulgaris, however Voulgaris lived long enough to evolve increasingly conservative ideas.

Toward Conservatism

Voulgaris's attitude toward Voltaire is characteristic. He was almost the first—so far as we know from written documents—to introduce Voltaire into Greece. If the notes to his *Logic* refer to the oral teachings of Voltaire, then his audience could have known the French philosopher even before 1766. However, Voulgaris was among the first to anathematize Voltaire. Moreover, we must not forget the role that politics played in all this. Until around 1790, the best method of flattering the intellectual pretensions of Catherine was to show liberalism and admiration for Voltaire. The church had no reason to become greatly concerned, because serious liberalism was rare and easy to suppress. But matters changed around 1790; the French Revolution came to trouble spirits. In Greece, liberal ideas displaced the class of distinguished men in favor of the merchant class and the bourgeosie generally. Catherine, burning her old idols, quickly travelled the path of conservativism and was reconciled with the Turks. The church, uneasy at indications of a rise in liberal spirit, followed this about-face with sympathy. Intellectual liberalism became repugnant, both for Russia and for the church. In 1793 Voltaire, its titled spokesman, was condemned officially by the patriarchate. Voulgaris did not wait for this condemnation before changing his attitude. Living in St. Petersburg, he sensed the change early. Already in 1790 the translator and admirer of Voltaire classified his idol, in a letter published the following year, among the "great impious" names. The battle had started: each year, a book, a pamphlet, a satire attacked Voltaire, while the progressives praised him. From 1766 to 1821 Voltaire was mentioned some one hundred times in Greek literature, either in books directed specifically against him and in satires against the progressives or in translations of his works or other publications intended to honor him. Theotokis took an active part in this battle by publishing in 1794 a long book attacking Voltaire.

Theotokis had not started out as a conservative. Despite his interest in the natural sciences, which was characteristic of the period to 1766, it is worth mentioning that his first religious sermons were published in the same year. In these early texts, conforming to a double tradition, of simple language in religious rhetoric and corresponding Italian influences, he employed a quasi-popular language. These early texts were devoid of all rhetorical intention; there was no ostentatious style, no sensibility. He did not attempt great artistic heights, and if he sometimes tried for them, he did not succeed. His language was simple, logical; mathematical, one might say, one more indication of the dominant critical spirit. But his warmth of words conveyed, on the whole, a profoundly human accent which increased the sensibility by the rhetorical sobriety and a certain natural suavity.

The intellectual climate of Hellenism accepted neither Voulgaris nor Theotokis. Both men died far from their homeland. However, we cannot say that they were persecuted. Psalidas tells us that Voulgaris left Greece without reason, without danger "either to his life or to his reputation, as is known to all. Scorning his country and all his Race, he sought refuge among strange and barbaric peoples, placing his patriotism second to his pleasures and his belly, all this for futile reasons." This criticism is unjust, but it contains a bit of the truth. The attraction for Voulgaris of life free from the Turkish yoke was associated with the idea that he could serve Greece in this manner. And the reasons which drove him to leave were not so insignificant. Moisiodakas, who experienced the same pressures, judged them otherwise: " 'Why do you waste time?' he would say to his audiences. 'Do you want arithmetic? You have the grocers. . . . These are the master who can teach you arithmetic. . . .' The great Voulgaris and the illustrious Theotokis have denied our race, because both have been treated badly by the Greeks." Both men also had strong support in their own country. Alexander Mavrokordatos was the protector of Voulgaris; Gregory Ghikas patronized Theotokis. Voulgaris's long life, which allowed him acquaintance with Theotokis, brings us to a new phenomenon, the important divergence between the church and the Phanariots. The patriarchate, imbued with a solid tradition and orientation, resisted the new ideas at the time when the Phanariots still pressed toward the Enlightenment. These divergent views and their fatal consequences for the Phanariots, the more feeble of the two parties, are revealed in the following period from 1774 to the War of Independence. This period is the subject of the next three chapters.

Part Four
Birth of a World
1770 to 1820

The rhythm accelerates. The predominant spirit is that of the popular bourgeoisie. The church passes from conservatism to reaction. The Phanariots weaken, and we see them, in their turn, doubting the new social structure. An essentially critical period, it is given to scientific investigations and to a revival of moral values; the individual is detached from the group, expression of the subjective world is affirmed, literary preoccupations are accentuated. There is an obvious tendency toward a synthesis of various currents and the beginning of preromanticism. The period is characterized by a vigor that will be intensified; it will reach its peak and will be shattered by the War of Independence.

Chapter 10

Intellectual Effervescence

Predominance of the

Western Element

We mentioned in the last chapter how early attempts to introduce teaching of mathematics in Greece were resisted. The nature of this science, which is simultaneously abstract and applied knowledge, would seem to have favored its introduction into the Greek schools. However, contact, even indirect, with trivial reality was not acceptable to the conservative scholars and the majority of the professors. When Voulgaris taught mathematics in Constantinople, his students one day saw a grocer entering their classroom. "Spreading at least fifteen or eighteen feet the stench of his trade," the visitor unexpectedly held the *Arithmetic* by Glyzonios in his hand. He had been sent by adversaries of Voulgaris on the pretext of discussing with him their common competence. Most thinkers judged then that the lesson should be limited to religious subjects and to grammar. The opposition to currents which, as we have seen, had been in progress for some time, only intensified during the period we are now entering. Both in the preceding period and in this one, wherever we encounter mathematical interests, we can be certain we are in the presence of progressive tendencies, though they are not always conscious. Algebra and geometry were not needed, nor were any of the humanistic sciences and studies. Mathematics in general was not essential because it was considered an invention of cupidity.

But mathematics was not enough; the earth did not consist of a shape that could be recreated by syllogisms and numbers. The earth was matter, it was the physical world in which the senses delighted, and whose beauty and variety Dapontes and Voulgaris extolled. The thirst for knowledge could not be gratified without the return to natural sciences, could not be satisfied so long as one neglected his study. We have arrived at the moment when the last step toward conquest of the external world was about to begin. The Phanariots supported the movement; it corresponded to a demand of Western Enlightenment, which the Phanariot culture was well disposed to satisfy. In 1779 an anonymous text of Phanariot inspiration praised curiosity.

Man is by nature so inclined toward curiosity that he always desires to search the mysterious, always loves to meddle with what, for him, is hidden and unknown. If curiosity were lacking, he would not be able to ascertain the nature of things to such an extent that he would not understand their powers and operations, he would not be able to discover so many sciences, he would not be able to understand the countless arts, assigning to each such order and adroitness, and therefore he would still be in the deep chaos of ignorance and barbarism.

We know that natural sciences were taught in the Danubian provinces around 1780; we also know that this teaching was not only theoretical but also experimental. During this same period, we find instructions concerning the most economic installations of *experimental theaters* or *chambers of natural history*. The name given to the new sciences reveals the illimitable hope that it generated; it had the same name as that in France, experimental philosophy, a wholesome philosophy. What formerly had been learned from books, henceforth would be learned from experiment, and the emotion formerly generated by the name of Aristotle was transferred to that of Newton.

The new study endangered the traditional formation of a spiritual life by limiting its scope; the danger it posed for the church was serious; the spirit which animated the experimental doctrine might cause neophytes to lose faith. The term *philosophy,* used to that time in Greek religious literature, assumed a new significance that evoked mistrust. In troubled times the play on words had always been a chosen weapon for religious battles. Philosophy was treated as a ξυλοδοφία (science of wood) or as a φιλοζοφία (love of gloom). But the physicists or philosophers did not always put aside their weapons easily. Supporting them were the Phanariots, who were anxious to see the nation enlightened by the new ideas; they were also sustained by the increasing number of cultivated people who were more or less independent of the church. "Do not harass the philosophers because you will be embarrassed," Mourouzis cried out in the patriarchate in 1810. The attacks became more direct; philosophy would deliver them from superstitions, and this term implied much that was not acceptable to tradition. The physics books published at this time informed the reader on their title pages that they were edited "to put an end to superstition." Physics became the symbol of freedom. Rigas, who published his *Physics* in 1790, noted: "Whoever thinks freely, thinks well." *Conversations on the Plurality of Worlds* by Fontenelle, translated by Kodrikas, was published in 1794 during the period of the Phanariots. Kodrikas added many of his own notes to the work; he attacked those "who, through superstitious ignorance, twisted the demonstrated truths of the Copernican system." Three years later, Serge Makraios, professor at the patriarchate school, wrote in response to Kodrikas his *Trophy of the Greek Panoply Against the Followers of Copernicus.* This consisted of three dialogues, imitating the Platonic dialogues of the ancient Greeks. The work did not pass unobserved and the criticism to which it gave rise testifies to the change that had come about in thought on Greek soil. An instructor, a steward of the church of Tyrnavos in Thessaly, hearing that Serge Makraios had refuted the Copernican system, remarked with laughter: "O! we are still faint-hearted children." However, many sacrifices had to be made before arriving to this stage.

Moisiodakas

At the beginning of the period under discussion, Joseph Moisiodakas expressed an inclination toward the new ideas. He was born probably a little before 1730 and had been educated in the intellectual centers of Hellenism, among them at the school of Mount Athos as a student of Voulgaris. He continued his studies abroad and later taught in the Danubian provinces. His interests were in natural sciences and in pedagogy. He published *Theoretical Geography: A Treatise on Pedagogy,* a translation of an ancient text by Isocrates, *To Nikokles,* and, in 1780, an *Apologia,* where he exposed the causes and manner of his persecution.

Repeatedly he was forced to resign as director of the school for princes in Jassy and in Bucharest. The grammarians made his life insupportable, his health created a complication. Sick, exhausted by his battles and efforts, he went to Italy, then to Vienna, and ended his days in obscurity in Bucharest around 1800. "Observe the recompense that our people always reserve for educated men, those who have not an enslaved spirit, not the patience worthy of Atlas," he concluded about his own persecutions and similar victims.

If we want to define the intellectual territory which Moisiodakas covered, we should begin by introducing his interests: they were the classics, mathematics, natural sciences, and pedagogy. He rejected the subject of grammar from his universe. His entire *Apologia* proclaims an antipathy toward the dry teaching of grammar which at that time and perhaps even later was the exclusive school curriculum. He also rejected Aristotelianism: "The schools of the scholastics always have been the vessels in which one beats water, patiently and noisily; however, water continues to remain water." Finally, he asked that the spoken language be introduced in teaching and used for all purposes. However, his dislike of grammar and Aristotle, even associated with his linguistic convictions, should not be taken to show he did not honor classical antiquity; we saw that he translated Isocrates. His attitude, however, toward the ancients was original and personal. He acknowledged, as did other contemporaries, that "Europe today surpasses even ancient Greece in knowledge." But his originality lies elsewhere:

> Today, Greece suffers from two faults, incompatible with her glory: respect for and indifference to antiquity. The first has given rise to a prejudice that consists of finding good and just all that has been elaborated by antiquity. The second is caused by the scarcity, or rather the total absence, of most works of antiquity. Prejudice inspires one with an implacable hatred of all that is modern, and scarcity of texts deprives one of knowledge of the most important ancients.

It is the first time that we see manifested a creative disposition with regard to antiquity: the new conservation was to be abandoned and there was to be a return to ancient tradition. It suffices to make a comparison with Voulgaris to see in which direction the creative spirit moved.

We already know all that concerns geography, physics, and mathematics. There remains the question of pedagogy. Here also we have evidence of a notable change; here, however, Moisiodakas appears as an expression rather than an instigator. In society the educator acquired a place never known before; he felt conscious of a special mission. This aimed at a more general education, destined to form character and to develop moral sense. The numerous treatises on pedagogy published during these years show how extremely great was the interest in problems of this nature. The educator acquired a status commensurate with the importance attributed to education by a society concerned with a renewal of its moral values. Theoreti-

cal guide in this movement, directly or indirectly, was Locke, whose
works were now translated into Greek for the first time. All the living names in Western literature of the period are found in Moisiodakas's works: Newton, Locke, and others. In a triumphal lecture
in 1765 before the prince of Moldavia, Moisiodakas cited Voltaire.

But we should add some observations about the quality of his
writing. Until that time, Hellenism knew essentially the ecclesiastics
and professors. But now, a new type of author becomes known in
Greece. Moisiodakas himself declared that he had "an almost invincible aversion" to the teaching profession. Elsewhere, he wrote
that he had "little interest in directing a school, but not in abandoning his talent as writer." The passion for study and research, as
well as for writing, characterized him. With Moisiodakas a disin-
terested intellectual begins to appear, a tendency to attribute to the
art of writing an end in itself, which, in a way, appears to touch
literary awareness. This image is reinforced by his profound self
awareness, an orientation we saw breaking through to a slight degree
in Dapontes, who was a real literary talent. We have pages, at any
rate lines, in his own handwriting that reveal a literary introspection which later will become one influence of romanticism. His
Apologia, with its characteristic title, its awareness of his own hard
fate, its sentimental elements, transport us to a psychological climate
similar to that of Rousseau. "Fatality," he wrote, "which always
takes pleasure in pursuing me relentlessly." And elsewhere, "my
destiny, my fierce destiny," or even, "persecuted by my unfavorable
destiny." "I asked," he relates in another place, "the advice of the
physicians present . . . and all told me that I was suffering from the
early stages of consumption, and that, if I wanted fame, I should die
a consumptive in my school; if I wanted life, I should resign." He is
one of the first after the preacher Joasaph Kornelios (1765) to have
sought to express in modern Greek the meaning of spiritual sensibility. This notion, so closely related to the spirit of preromanticism,
flourished during the last decade of the century. The meaning given
to the term αἰσθητικός (aesthetician) in his *Apologia* marks a stage
in the intellectual life of neo-Hellenism. Moisiodakas was barely
over fifty years old when he turned once more to events of his own
life and dreamed. This text gives a synopsis of his image as no other
lyrical confesson does. "If I have said that I had great talent in being usefully occupied, it was the truth." After what he had endured,
"my country has derived no benefit from me; as for me, I have
ended by becoming a vagabond in foreign places, often lacking my

daily bread, grown old before my time by tribulations, and, what is more terrible for a man of sensibility, constantly battling against the danger of becoming an outcast." As for his literary talent, it is perceptible in all his writing; sometimes he rises to sublimity.

A desolate glance on this celebrated school at Mount Athos, whose ruins, so to speak, are still misty before my eyes. Where is the great Eugene? Where are the countless choirs of students, who, to the joy of all Greece, formed the new Helicon of Muses and the disciples of the Muses? Banished is Voulgaris, banished are the students! The lightning of Nemesis has fallen and has dispersed the masters and students, and this establishment, about which everyone spoke in Constantinople and in the rest of Greece, has become, alas, a nest for crows.

However, let us not be deceived. If Moisiodakas had failed, it was not because he was persecuted by his colleagues or because the church had lost faith in him. His efforts, coming before their time, could not materialize, but neither were they crushed; the seed was to bear fruit later. Katartzis was not persecuted; he lived and died with honor as a Phanariot dignitary in Moldo-Vlachia. However, his action, derived from the same sensibility as that of Moisiodakas, remained equally unsuccessful during his lifetime. At the dawn of the Greek Renaissance, these two parallel personalities inspire respect, but also compassion for their martyred apostolic endeavor.

Katartzis

Demetrios Katartzis or Photiades was probably the same age as Moisiodakas, or slightly older, having been born between 1720 or 1725. He grew up in an affluent and esteemed family; he spent his childhood in Constantinople and was educated there. After occupying various offices around the provinces of Moldo-Vlachia, he achieved the rank of grand logothete in Vlachia. He died there in 1807. In the private texts of his time, he was cited as a "patron of scholars of Vlachia," the "venerable patriarch" of men of letters of his country. He was a type of enlightened nobleman, a disciple of the Encyclopedists and the French Enlightenment.

His writing career, except for some early poetic efforts written in archaic language and attributed to him, began later, in 1783. At this time, he systematized his linguistic convictions and created a scientific and philosophic system, whose fundamental ideas are known to us. The first of these works, according to his own listing, was subtitled: "About the Romaic Language, Written as It Is Spoken, Possesses Harmony in Prose and Rhythm in Poetry, and Passion and Persuasion in Rhetoric; Such that It Surpasses All Languages; and that the Study of Romaic and the Redaction of Works Constitute a General and Complete Education of the Greek Nation." Besides this essay, where he outlined his program, he composed in the following years a series of small treatises, among which was one entitled *Know Thyself*. Katartzis also did various translations, and as a jurist he composed a *Judicial Science*. He also wrote a *Neo-Hellenic Versification,* a *Grammar of Ancient Greek* in modern Greek, and a *Grammar of the Neo-Hellenic Language.* More of his works are cited below.

Language for Katartzis was not an end in itself. The harmonious charms and all the elegances of cultivated language should not obstruct the principal aim of language which is the propagation of knowledge. His linguistic arguments had a theoretic base in the evolution of language. We see something new, recently formed in the West. We should write "with eloquence of language that we speak in childhood, as do the English, the French, and all the other civilized people of Europe." Finally, we should use the forms of the folk language: no one "can modify a word when this is not in the mouths of the people." These practical arguments were not new. They are known to us: we should write in such a way that our texts "can be understood or learned by the rest of the Nation."

The language of Katartzis' preserved works presents a dryness, a rationalistic element that does not lack interest for the intellectual evolution of the new Greece. It should be observed, however, that his compositions had a didactic character. Also, we should praise his attempt to put together a language, popular in grammar, but enriched in vocabulary from different sources, and especially oriented ward abstraction and synthesis, toward philosophic thought:

> "But we, in order to distinguish our people, who have fallen into barbarism, have separated our language from that of the people and thus what we write, with the help of God, and what we say, are not accessible to all. Even more, we laugh at the people because they speak a natural language, with its ac-

cent, its inflection, its morphology, and its syntax. As for other matters, we boast about not corrupting our language by employing it in its natural form. And we write and speak in another language, of an ancient type, which we pretend to pronounce as ancient Greek, while we are ignorant of the exact pronunciation."

But Katartzis failed in his efforts. A dignitary of the court, heaped with honors, he was forced to abandon his linguistic doctrine after fighting eight years to impose it and to content himself with waiting for approval either from an assembly of scholars, from some other academy, or from time. Constrained to abandon the natural language, as he called the popular language, he used a mixed language, a simple *katharevousa,* as we would call it today. But he never renounced his principles.

> Therefore, I wish to say to the studious ones, all who do not study, or who do not write; I mean all who are gifted. Our scholars remain semi literate and sterile and leave the public in ignorance. From what we saw in the Greek people during their height, and in the Romans, and from what we see at this moment in Europe, or in our own country, we can conclude that, if we want to progress in the sciences and in all other fields, with profit but also facility, we must apply ourselves to the common culture, where this result is given admirably. If we wish to achieve this fundamantally, it is essential that we all join forces; it is essential that our scholars translate in concert ancient Greek and European languages into modern Greek, using its grammar and its natural eloquence. Even better, it is essential that they write books and that, analyzing all the branches of knowledge, they present them as lectures, thus contributing to their proper enrichment and to the improvement of the public.

Though he retreated from his former position, we should not take this as a failure. One should add, moreover, that Katartzis, who died at an advanced age, only left posthumous works of all he had written during his creative period.

Evidence assures us that nearly fifty years passed from the time that the French language predominated in Vlachia. Moisiodakas informs us that "all the young men of good families in Constantinople apply themselves in our day to the study of Italian and French."

During this period (c. 1780), the Italian language was also an agent for diffusion of French culture. In "The Consequences of Love" (1792), we read: "The young nobles of Constantinople understand French better than Greek." It is characteristic that books, propagators of culture, now took a French form; everyone sought to have small, elegantly bound books "for the pocket, as is the French custom." Characteristic was the publication which today can be considered the first expression of modern Greek creative prose. It survives in an untitled copy which was probably published in 1789. The author is called conventionally the Anonymous Author of 1789. The work is a personal libel in narrative form. The Anonymous Author imitates Lesage in *Diable Boiteux*. Indoctrinated with Voltaire's thought and technique and by the spirit of other French liberals, he alternates immodest erotic views of life with scenes in which the Christian religion is satirized vehemently. All this is done with a strong narrative talent; we know of no preparatory work that could have facilitated its creation. This work shows with precision that the new Hellenic prose owes to French culture. The moralists and professors of morality of the period, even those who admired the progressives and felt in accord with them, continually protested against this influence of the French spirit.

But matters changed. When in 1793 the church excommunicated a writer, Christodoulos Pamplikis (1733–1793), for his philosophic doctrines, he died without retracting them, and his disciples raised a monument to him in a public garden of Leipzig. When Rigas was persecuted for his ideas, and when later the Austrians delivered him to the Turks, the Greek intellectuals were aroused. Koraes published a pamphlet in which he defended the ideas of the national martyr. The circle of progressives in Jannina and Constantinople intervened to save him. Benjamin Lesbios and Stephen Doungas also encountered opposition from the official church which resulted in persecution. Both, however, finally triumphed and continued their activities. Pamphlets and books were circulated, whose content was not only progressive, but truly subversive.

It was thus with the *Greek Nomarchy* that came out in 1806: the nobles were "stupid and senseless men," the prelates were brigands of the Church," the Phanariots were "the bad men of Constantinople." It is worth noting that, with all the mettlesome libellous character of the pamphleteers, the book showed maturity of thought and doctrine. It gave useful information and statistics about Greece. The author endeavored to systematize a program for the elevation and emancipation of the nation. In its totality it was a humorous book which, despite the youthful imperfections, revealed an advanced degree of national conscience and social culture.

Around this same time, a satiric manuscript circulated, this one in verse, which attacked the nobles, the Phanariots, the merchants, and the higher clergy. It was called *The Russo-Anglo-Frank*. Here we see the metropolitan declaring: "Since I have put on this cloth, I am free of all fetters. I desire two things, I swear by the icons: much money and beautiful women." And the Phanariots replied: "The freedom of Greece is a distress [to us]." And the merchants said: "We, most merchants, want money, even if we do not have freedom."

The importance of this satire, whose author is unknown, is not literary, but rather informative. Shortly before the War of Independence, another brochure appeared in Paris under the title *Thoughts of Crito*. Here again we find a violent attack on the higher clergy. This small book was condemned and burned by the patriarchate. But a periodical which appeared in Paris at this time, *The Bee* (1820), did not hesitate to blame those who had taken the initiative in this condemnation.

The ideal of the progressive party was the neo-classical ideal of revolutionary France. From this time on, French influence dominated Greek culture with a force which has remained to our days. An important exception was the Italian influence in the development of the Ionian Islands.

Chapter 11

The New Morality

The Greek Problem

and Rigas

During periods of fermentation, such as the one we are studying here, the dominant influences are expressed more easily in translations. Indeed, one sees the Phanariots concerned particularly with the problem of translations from the beginning of the century. But it was Katartzis who systematized this movement and proclaimed its principles: it was essential to use translations of texts written in contemporary languages, "something actually considered very important in all kingdoms." Katartzis with his characteristic sensibility, proved the need for new dictionaries. The old dictionaries had already been condemned by Moisiodakas. Katartzis returned to the subject and developed it. But he did not limit himself to theoretical views; he undertook to compose a dictionary whose editing was ultimately interrupted. Moreover, scientific works of a more general scope, such as manuals or encyclopedic treatises, no longer satisfied the needs of new Hellenism; knowledge demanded differentiation of genres, specialization. Thus, books on physics were translated, which we have already discussed, and history books, with which we will be concerned here.

History Books

To this point we can classify the historical works into two distinct groups, neither of which belongs to scientific experimentation. There were, on the one hand, the ecclesiastical chronicles, narratives relating to ecclesiastical struggles which always continued to exist, and works written to fortify a religious sentiment. On the other hand, there were the works inspired by a growing curiosity about the external world and about fellow man, either in geographical terms or in historical time. In both cases, the accent was on what was most unusual in the world.

The orientation toward the conscious conquest of a new sector of knowledge, the interest in history, was illustrated in 1750 by the translation of Rollin's *Ancient History,* published by Alexander Kangellarios. The last volume of this work concerned letters and sciences. The work was dedicated to "the illustrious Romaic Nation" in order to make known to the *friends of History* "the glorious exploits of the proud children" of Greece.

From this point on, a pure historical awareness begins to develop, and an elaboration of a theory of history. Spiros Papadopoulos merits mention at the beginning of this new effort of Hellenism. We know that between 1767 and 1781 he was in Venice preparing editions and correcting prints of books. In 1770–1773, he published, in six volumes, a translation of the *History of the Actual War Between Russia and the Sublime Porte.* Just as the older authors of religious works had declared with pride that they were not relating the prodigious acts of heroes and generals, so now the editor of this *History* declared that he was offering "not a mythological work without utility," but something that could benefit his nation. In this work we also see the development of a theory of history; "the purpose of history," the "obligations of the historian," and the difficulties in editing a contemporary history are exposed. The translator added chapters borrowed from Voltaire. It is evident that he was aware of the unity of Hellenism and sought to discover points of contact between the ancient and the new Greeks. He noted that "the ancient grandeur of spirit" of the ancestors had not been lost on the Maniates. Papadopoulos himself had been charged with editing two volumes (the third and fourth) of a six-volume work called *Byzantine* (1767), which had been translated into simple language by John Stanos (c. 1768). The first two volumes, as well as the last two, had been edited by another scholar of the period, Agapios Loverdos. Loverdos and Papadopoulos characterize a particular moment in neo-Hellenic culture: the conscientious orientation toward history. In 1791, Lovedos published a *History of Two Years, 1787 and 1788,* in whose preface he exalted the benefits offered by the study of history. In the same years, other attempts were made at writing historical works, such as the *History of Cyprus* by the Archmandrite Kyprianos (1788), a *Short History of the Russian Empire* (1787), and others.

Zaviras

We thus see that historical interest extended to contemporary events, and furthermore, that these interests were not limited to political or religious history. The writing fever of the time added to the usual problems of publication, hindered the edition of a good number of important works, which remained unpublished. Among these was *New Greece* by George Zaviras (1744–1804). This author was a merchant from Macedonia, but he lived the greater part of his life in the West, principally in Hungary. As was characteristic of the times, this merchant was fond of letters. He wrote and translated many books, nearly all of which remained unpublished; some were even lost. Among those which survived was a work on his travels throughout Germany. In *New Greece* we have a long list of Greek scholars under the Turkish domination accompanied by biographical notes, a serious attempt at a history of literature. This work was not published until 1872, but it circulated in manuscript form, and many profited by it before its publication. Two other remarkable chronicle writers, whose work also remained unpublished, were Athanasios Komnenos Ypsilantis (c. 1807) and the Athenian John Benizelos Paleologos (1696–c. 1789).

What should be emphasized here is that most of the historical books of this period, particularly those whose spirit was differentiated from that of the old chronicles, were translations or variants, which, however, does not diminish from their importance, since they provide evidence of developing historical awareness.

Perhaps it was during these years of intense Western influences that the representatives of the Greek Enlightenment felt liberated from all inhibitions regarding the West, and specifically regarding the Catholic or reformed church. Foreign influences had never appeared in the history of letters, or even in the more general culture, as a foreign body brought in from the outside. A living influence was nothing more than a choice operating consciously or unconsciously among elements of foreign culture, and the choice responded to the needs of local life. The new orientation of spirits, the awakening of certain precise interests, were manifested first. Recourse to translations, the most direct means of giving satisfaction to new aspirations, did not come until later.

The development of historical sense principally expressed the new content of national awareness. That is to say, a relative independence from ecclesiastical tradition had an effect of giving value to elements of the ancient heritage. On the economic level at this time, there was a considerable increase in national wealth, which concentrated in the hands of merchants and mariners. A new class was being formed that felt the necessity to justify its position; the constant contact of this class with foreign worlds and certain other reasons already mentioned rendered religious doctrine—whose reactionary tendencies were being accentuated—inadequate for this endeavor. Finally, on the level of national life, the successive wars of Catherine the Great of Russia, the devastation these wars created throughout Hellenism, and their final fortunate consequences convinced the Greek people that Turkey was not invincible. The Napoleonic Wars reinforced this conviction. The new class sought a faith, an ethic, a knowledge to secure itself in its own world. New values came to the surface; they were expressed by neologisms, that is, new words or new meanings for words already in use.

The Ancestors

The development of historical awareness was transferred to those men of faith who needed it; they became proud of their ancestors, of their race. Throughout this entire period, references to the ancestors surge through the most diverse kinds of texts; this is even the case with works which have no historical character. Composite words derived from γένος, such as φιλογενής (friend of the nation), ὁμογενής (friend of the same nation), and others multiplied during this time. But the most revealing evidence is that the word γένος itself changed in meaning; it lost its former meanings and preserved only the one meaning imposed on it. It now became Γένος with a capital and without other qualifications. Under this new form, it was introduced and used everywhere: "printing office of the Nation," "master of the Nation," which formerly had meant a schoolmaster of a community, of a colony, now acquired a moral content which has been preserved to our time. It appears, as a sign of the times, that this word showed an enrichment exactly parallel to that offered earlier in France by the semantic evolution of the term "nation."

Toward the end of this period, there was such an abuse of the term that it provoked impatience: "Hilarion pleaded for the Printing Offices of the Nation, proposing that the middle class support and continually repeat the words Γένος, Γένος," wrote someone from Constantinople in 1820. In the periodical, *The Scholar Hermes* of 1821, we read a dialogue by an anonymous author, who was actually Koraes:

> Nik.: Do you know what I think?
> Ath.: About what?
> Nik.: About the abuse of the word Γένος, which characterizes all the demagogues.

It was essential, however, that the new Hellenism choose its ideal from the glories of the past. Comparison and criticism presented no difficulties. The neo-Hellenes were guided in their choice by the neoclassical wave that was breaking in the West. But the glory of classical Greece was not to be equalled by any other moment in world history. The new Greeks, then, must attain the level of their ancient ancestors. The method was easy; and they were taught by Greek classicism. It consisted of imitating the models which were offered. Mimesis constituted the base for the aesthetic teachings of classicism; with imitation one could achieve masterpieces. *Mimesis* would begin from the outside and advance gradually to the essence; vestments, names, language, one would imitate everything. "Even though we imitate phrases, we imitate the beauties of the language and we model ourselves on our ancestors. He who imitates these will arrive before long at an imitation of all the rest," wrote Doukas. Thus, the movement toward linguistic archaism, whose painful consequences appeared later, did not start from conservativism or from reactionary tendencies; a liberal spirit, a revolutionary spirit, was the origin of the movement. A comparison would be the *return to antiquity* of the French Revolution.

Morality

Morality now tended to replace catechism. Moral preoccupations prevailed during this period. Not only did works treating with morality multiply, but even the titles of theatrical works, books of verse, and novels took a moral turn, sometimes the most unexpected. The objective was no longer to attain the celestial felicity to which Christian faith led; what one sought now was the happiness offered by the present life on earth. A series of books appeared which promised true happiness to all who read them. The path was generally the same: happiness was attained through virtue. It became the condition of all human progress. Virtue was no longer that attached to ancient philosophy or to saintliness; virtue now became the supreme attribute of a citizen, the basis of ethics in human society. Timid and servile prudence had to be replaced by courageous and generous virtue. All sorts of moral questions were discussed in every literary form.

The Theater

One of these means was the theater. After the fall of Crete, the theater continued to exist as a literary genre utilized more often for satire than for pure enjoyment. Translation from French and Italian drama began with the Enlightenment. But what gave new life to the Greek theater was the moral turn of the new Hellenism. From about 1800 on, original plays were written and their production multiplied. The Phanariots, always pioneers, supported the movement in Bucharest, Jassy, and Odessa, and the scholars also supported the movement. Koraes believed that the new Greek theater warmed "the hearts of the Greeks for the resurrection of the homeland." C. Asopios, in a speech he made in 1817, said that the theater "proposed to correct the morals of men and to educate the people. It is the common school of men, which supplements the lack of schools." In the two decades before the War of Independence, these original theatrical works, nearly all tragedies, stimulated the strength of soul and virtue of Hellenism. Besides the names which recur often in this *History,* such as Christopoulos, Rizos Neroulos, Jacob Rizos Rangavis, J. Zambelios, we should mention two other authors of tragedies, performed before the War of Independence. Nicholas S. Pikolos (1792–1865) presented in Odessa in 1818 the tragedy *Death of Demosthenes.* He is also known for his various translations of Descartes (1824), of Bernardin de St. Pierre (1824, 1836), and for some verse. The second, George Lassanis (1793–1870), presented, also in Odessa in 1819, a patriotic drama called *Greece and the Foreigner* and a tragedy, *Harmodios and Aristogiton*. Tragedies translated from foreign authors, such as Metastasios, Alfieri, Voltaire, and others had the same didactic purpose.

Manners

However, morals did not suffice; one should study manners as well. Man acquired a unique importance, not as the receptacle of a soul, but as a social animal. One ought to know this social animal in order to understand how to conduct oneself with him. Original works, translations of ancient or foreign authors, would all be useful for this. From 1783 to 1818, two translations and two imitations of *Characters* by Theophrastus were published by the Greeks. The learned Demetrios Darvaris, author of a quantity of scholarly manuals, also published a translation of Theophrastus in 1795 to which he added some characters of his own invention. In 1818, Charisios Megdanis published his own *Characters*.

Certainly, the past understanding of man's nature and the analysis that had been made of his soul no longer sufficed; man himself had changed. He sought to be new in everything. Traditional teaching had been ruined by the critics; reason had replaced this teaching; each act, each opinion would no longer be based on a single teaching, but on *reason,* "a very powerful citadel." Moreover, men now discovered the world of emotions; they spoke to others with a certain vanity but in all cases with warm interest, about the sensibility of the soul; they were impressed by beauty, they were affected easily, their tears flowed readily. Koraes, writing to a friend, was overwhelmed *four times by tears.* Rigas cried while singing his patriotic songs; Koumas went twice to the theater to see *Themistocles* by Metastasios, "and twice my heart failed," he wrote, "and the torrent of tears gushed from my eyes."

Men took pleasure in the violent sensations of the soul that love provoked, the nuances of a new sentiment of *melancholy* heretofore unknown. They enjoyed and cultivated these: "It is a sweet sadness, a pleasant sorrow." Their passions inclined toward nature: "I caused the forests to resound with my cries,/with my laments, my pitiable laments." The passions that Mavrokordatos excluded from life now reentered triumphantly. "It is through the same means, through the same passions of the soul, that man falls into the depths of wickedness or rises to the summits of virtue," believed Koraes, who had read the French Encyclopedists and Rousseau, but not Katartzis, still unpublished in his time. When Koraes himself was accused by the conservatives of professing similar opinions, he wrote: "Not all the furies are bad. There is also a divine fury without which nothing can be accomplished."

The social change which man underwent was similar. It was at this time that we see *fashion* or *mode* appearing, as a word and as an interest. When it was deliberate, fashion expressed the existence of different social classes, but, simultaneously, desire of the lower classes to equal the upper classes. There were also the manners; the fate of man no longer depended on strange forces, worldly or otherworldly. It was his conduct, his deportment, associated with the soundness of his judgment, that determined his social career in large measure. It was the famous *politesse,* the *urbanity,* the good manners, as we would say today, the affability of the individual: "There is a new virtue; one calls it *politesse.*"

Theotokis defined *politesse* and the polite man excellently.

> Who in our days does not apply himself with ardor to practicing *politesse*? Who does not want to be considered polite? Nearly all the world agrees that *politesse* is a necessary art and a very useful science. Thus, she is encountered in our Courts, in the tribunals, in the streets, and alas! even in the Church. She is eulogized; she is admired, and she is considered as a great perfection and as being capable of realizing great things. And yet, the *politesse* of today is only a hypocrisy, and the polite man is only a hypocrite. At bottom, they are the same, only the words differ. Indeed, what else is the polite man but he who has one thing on his lips and something else in his heart?

"One deceives the other, it is the fashion of the times," wrote Polyzois Kontos in 1793.

It was a new world, new manners. The moralists were not content: "In our days, nearly all are young people," wrote Darbaris, "believe that they were born, not to labor as other reasonable beings, but to give themselves to debauchery and to pursue the passions of the flesh as beasts." And Kalfoglou ascertained with bitterness: "The furor for fashion and money to play at cards inflames their souls and ruins the poor." Perdikaris described the society of the day in the same manner.

It is a furious beast that preys on others,
And in his rage, devours friends and brothers.

A few years later, Epiphanios Dimitriades wrote: "Nothing has remained pure." In a poem he explained:

Aphrodite has departed and wanders like a pheasant.

The moralists were censors by definition. Was life at this time as corrupt as they pretended? Assuredly not. What appeared as corruption was the insatiable thirst of man for the new, the unknown. Efforts, experiences, sensations, and knowledge, all should be sampled, all should be enjoyed. It was a spirit full of health and vigor; the opposite of decadence. And that which prevailed was the aspiration for true knowledge, the ambition to open the great door leading to life. New faith, new morals, new knowledge. Naturally, it was new *Christoethics,* as the book on etiquette was called in the Greek language of the Turkish domination.

Periodicals

The slow rhythm of books no longer satisfied the effervescence of the new class. Men could no longer wait for the translation and editing of a foreign book. They were no longer content to quench their thirst by reading historical volumes, now that the world was on the move and the dawn of each day brought something new. The first Greek periodical we know appeared in Vienna in 1790. There is also mention of a weekly gazette, slightly older, which must have appeared for two months in 1784, also in Vienna. The capital of Austria had become an important commercial center for the Greeks. The Greek colony in Vienna was wealthy and enjoyed the protection of the Austrian authorities. In 1783, the Emperor Joseph II authorized the free printing of Greek books in Vienna. This permission, along with other causes, led a large part of the intellectual movement of Greek refugees to concentrate in Austria. Things changed radically with the French Revolution. Vienna, the "misochrist," to use a phrase coined by Koraes, cultivated good-neighbor relations with the Turks. But the spirit had been given, and it was precisely the close contact of the two countries that offered Hellenism the numerous possibilities which it did not fail to exploit for its own profit. Because of this, the first Greek periodicals saw the light of day in Vienna. The *Ephimeris* survived. Founded in 1790, it continued to be printed until 1797. The brothers Poulios, editors and printers, were persecuted for their association with Rigas and for having printed a certain number of his revolutionary works and the publication of the *Ephimeris* was suspended. In principle, the *Ephimeris* was a source of information; its objective was to inform the Greek people about Western politics by presenting events in such a manner that the Turks would not prohibit circulation among the subjugated Greek people. Besides this kind of information, there were also other matters of interest to the Greeks, but very few announcements and reviews of the new literature. This attempt to inform the Greek public as rapidly as possible was pursued in the Ionian Islands, where it took on a local character, and was recaptured later in Vienna by two other periodicals, the *Hellenic Telegraph* (1812–1829) and *The Scholar Hermes* (1811–1821). The history of the latter, which was the best means of communicating the neo-Hellenic revival, will be discussed in the chapter devoted to the activities of Koraes.

Rigas

The same reason for choosing Vienna as the center for publication of Greek periodicals also persuaded Rigas to lay his liberation plans in that country. Rigas was of a purely Greek temperament; he combined all the currents which at this time proceeded from Hellenism: the moral problems, the historical, the physical, the preoccupations with literature, the theater, and pedagogy. He treated all these subjects in his writings. His objective was to enlighten the Greek people on these various problems through original works or translations. A true dynamic personality, he exuded life and he applied himself to whatever life offered him. His contemporaries describe "his usual Greek glance, laughing and pleasing"; Perrevos characterized him as "gay, intelligent, lively, and quick to retort." Later testimony presents him as improvising a toast during a banquet:

> Having the glass of friendship full, the Greeks held festivities in the monastery; they ate and drank together with only the hope that they might charge, like lions, toward their beloved country.

Another time, he rolled a barrel in the snow to take it to Kalphog-lou, who was with his companions. On the way, Rigas improvised a quatrain:

> Even the good Lord realizes
> His Infinite designs,
> He suddenly sends Rigas
> With a barrel.

His detractors later said of him: "He was inclined toward pleasure." It was thus that the future national martyr lived. Submitting to the world of senses, he was full of imagination and was easily affected; he sensed more than he thought; he was inspired more by passion than by reason.

Rigas was born in Velestino, a village of Thessaly, perhaps in 1757. After his early childhood, his education was that typical of young Greeks avid for learning, spirited and ambitious. He began his education at Zagora, a neighboring village, which then had a fairly good school. Later, he went to Constantinople and managed to penetrate the Phanariot milieu. Then he went to the Danubian principalities around 1786, where he completed his studies while working in administrative and other governmental positions and busying himself with commercial enterprises.

Without doubt, it was at this time that he was initiated into free-masonry. Indeed, we encounter masonic lodges very early in Greece, around 1745. The movement at its beginning also animated the principles of liberty. This precocious masonic activity constituted additional proof of the intellectual and political maturity of Hellen-ism. Though freemasonry had been disapproved in a series of church-inspired publications, particularly around the end of the century; though much earlier the church itself had condemned it; it did not cease to prosper in Greece, and we find it appearing wherever we encounter patriotic unrest. (*Greek-Speaking Hotel* was a similar secret society established in Paris in 1814 and the *Society of Friends* was another.)

In 1797, Rigas went to Vienna where he became involved with publications connected with his liberation plans. From there, on his way to Greece, he stopped in Trieste, where a denunciation delivered him into the hands of the Austrian police. Since Austria was anxious at that time to appease the Ottoman Empire, the empress allowed his extradition and the Turks hastened to execute him in June 1798.

His first publication appeared in 1790, a translation called *The*

School for Delicate Lovers, "a moral work containing the curious adventures of the most beautiful women of Paris in that century." With one blow, Rigas brusquely stimulated Greek culture and particularly Greek literature. Until this time, attempts to compose and publish novels in modern Greek were awkward and without genuine interest. They were less literary works than edifying dissertations, presented under the form of novels, such as the *Minor Works of Philotheos,* a translation of Fénelon, *The Adventures of Telemachos* (1742), or even *The Voyage of Cyrus* (1783) by the Englishman Ramsay. What Rigas gave was something else; he offered short histories, full of love and passion, which told of a different time in Greek civilization.

The name of the author was not mentioned. Recent research, however, has established that these stories were taken from the work of the French writer Restif de la Bretonne. It is characteristic that Rigas attempted to give a moral content to these loose narratives, not only to avoid offending his readers, but especially to obey his own inclinations. The problems that absorbed Rigas were moral in the larger sense of the word. In his short preface, the translator revealed a somewhat belligerent attitude. He said, "Because detractors never cease to find pretexts to exercise their language, I think that they will reproach me for having chosen the subject of love . . . rather than some other subject. Hence, I will reply that the loves included in this book lead to marriage, which is a sacrament; then let them stop prating." This book was dedicated "to all the sensitive young men and women," who, it must be acknowledged, found there a rich supply of material for their disturbed souls. Paris, which was becoming for Hellenism what it continues to be today, the land of enchantment, was often praised in the text, as was only natural. Melancholy was encountered frequently. Preromaticism erupted abruptly in Greek literature; hence, a thought reminiscent of Young:

> One has the impression that under the cover of darkness, man recaptures his natural freedom, and he wishes to know nothing greater than himself. Everything appears to be permitted to him, everything is reasonable. This involuntary reserve which restrains us by day, when we see other men, is lost by night. From this, it follows that timidity and constraint also prevent young girls from accepting love. It is only at night that they also choose the moment to console those who shed tears and sighs for their charms.

The translation was crude, but a new note had enriched Greek letters.

A current of liberalism sometimes penetrated these romantic stories: "All men are naturally equal, but, as you yourself know, there are a certain number of prejudices. The entire world would be happy if these prejudices disappeared, and if they allowed reason to govern human affairs." Since this concerns a translation, we have no need to expand further on the text. However, the prose is interspersed, here and there, with some verses. I do not believe that they are those of Rigas. Rather, what we have is a production of the Phanariots, utilized by the translator.

Prose of the Imagination

The School for Delicate Lovers appears to have found an immediate response from the public, at least from the scholarly milieu. Two years later, another work entitled *Consequences of Love,* "a story of moral love accompanied by songs," appeared anonymously. The period which began with the Anonymous Author of 1789 had reached maturity. In 1797 some stories from Boccaccio, the most innocent ones, were translated. *Consequences of Love* was composed of three long novellas, "The First Story," narrating the passionate love of a young man from Constantinople; "The Second Story," narrating the pitiful love of an interpreter to the Venetian ambassador to Constantinople; and "The Third Story," narrating various adventures in love of a nobleman from Zagora. There is no question of character analysis; the various lovers, men or women, who pass through the pages can easily be interchanged in their personalities and actions. But the tendencies to which they all give evidence, those of the new generation coming alive, have verisimilitude and sincerity.

Elenitsa feels the birth of love in her heart. She is uneasy, she is hesitant, she is afraid: "What I feel must be love, and what I have read has been dictated by love and should not be doubted. Is love appropriate to a young girl? But what kind of love? A virtuous young girl, a young virgin, daughter of a respectable father, should not surrender to the charms of a young man. In this letter, I see only a compliment; however, that is of no help to me. . . ." As for the rest, we have exactly the same moral, social, and intellectual climate that we found in *The School for Delicate Lovers,* an intense feeling of nature's charm, a tendency toward innovation, a confusion between conservativism and superstition. Furthermore, because this work was original, some details relating to life in Constantinople and the world of the Phanariots should be mentioned. The work describes the small court of Alexander Mavrokordatos at Poltava. We learn that the secretaries, who have little work to occupy them, walk "around the walls of the chateau, as was the custom in the city." There, they meet with young girls of "great freedom and very worldly." Antonis, however, the youth from Zagora, has the good fortune to become acquainted with a young girl who "resembled the Greek girls in their modesty and seriousness." He goes with his companions to the public gardens and they sing. These novellas are full of Phanariot quatrains such as are found in *The School for Delicate Lovers.* We see the same verses in:

> I have uttered bitter sighs, my eyes fill up with tears.
> I find no consolation, my heart causes me to suffer.
> At night, I lie down with a sigh,
> In the morning I wake up with a sigh.

And in "Echo":

> Echo, tell me, what is this child who pierces
> Freely the flesh from every side?
> Tell me, is it truly the one the Greek myths
> Called divine and ranked among the gods?

It is extremely difficult at this distance to attribute each work to its true author, so here one must speak about super individual art, an expression of a society. We can attribute to George Kamarasis, father of Neroulos, another "Echo," and to Alexander Ypsilantis the following poem, which resembles that of Vilaras on the same subject:

> Strange little bird,
> So solitary,
> Where do you fly so fast?
> Where is your nest?

Another quatrain of the same genre is attributed to Thomas Danelakis from the Ionian Islands. The same uncertainty exists in the poetic production of Rigas; in fact, the difficulties here are augmented, because he died a martyr. His patriotic poems are numerous, though many, certainly, are only attributed to him. The confusion becomes greater in the manuscript and published anthologies which began to appear at this time; for example, that of Zeese Daoutis (1818) rarely mentions the names of poets.

During 1790 Rigas published *The Best of Physics*, "translated from French and German with the intention of giving intelligence to the Greek people and desirous of instructing them." This small book was written in the form of a dialogue between student and master, reminiscent of Fontenelle, though it also continued the tradition of "question-answer" manuals of Greek teachings. In the same year, Rigas announced the publication of *Esprit des Lois* by Montesquieu, a project that appears not to have been completed. It was also during this first period of his writing activity that the prose translation of *Olympiad* by Metastasios was written, but this work has remained unpublished to our time. This is probably the oldest work we have by Rigas and is interesting only for its curiosities. Otherwise, it consists of a youthful exercise, faithful but lacking spirit. Rigas returned to the work later and recast it in much warmer language, but it still showed little workmanship. As we have already seen, language was a means and not an end for him.

The second period of his literary production, when he went to Vienna in 1796, was the same. The remainder of his works were published in the following year. The *Moral Tripod* contains three translations: *The Olympiad* by Metastasios, *The Shepherdess of the Alps* by Marmontel, and *The First Navigator* by Gessner, translated by Anthony Koronis, collaborator of Rigas. *The Olympiad* had undergone amplifications which involved the development of the fifteen-syllable verse. With the exception of one or two words, the language was no longer that of the Phanariots; desire for refinement was obvious. A tendency toward archaism marks the second phase of Rigas's literary activity. It reveals, to my mind, a development of national awareness, fortified by the glory of the past. Whereas in the writings of 1790, at least in the printed ones, moral and pedagogical interests prevailed, the literary production of 1797 had, since physics also had a didactic purpose, a historical orientation.

He closed *The Olympiad* with a chorus in ancient Greek. *The Shepherdess of the Alps*, whose original was in prose, was translated into verse. Let us remember our observations on the subject of Voltaire's *Memnon*, which Voulgaris translated thirty years earlier. A few introductory remarks in *The Shepherdess* emphasized its moral character and cited an opinion by Marmontel, taken from one of his books, in which he said that "the sacred love of country is implanted in the heart and the heart never ages." The political verses have been replaced by the fifteen-syllable trochaic of the Phanariots, the Greek precursors to the strophe of Solomos in the *Hymn to Liberty* and the *Ode to Byron*. Either the poetic form he chose or the subject he treated led Rigas to use a more popular language. According to the laws of tragedy, language should be more elevated. But here we find again almost the same language used in *The School for Delicate Lovers.*

In this same year, Rigas collaborated with the brother Poulios and translated a large part of the fourth volume of the *Anacharsis* by Bartélémy. Besides these, he began in 1796 and completed in 1797 the edition of a series of geographical maps of the Greek world. This publication was obviously intended to exalt national sentiment in the Greeks. The maps were accompanied by ancient coins and portraits of great men from the history of antiquity. Rigas also published separately a portrait of Alexander the Great.

Until this time all Rigas's Vienna production had an indirect national purpose. But parallel with this, he carried on his insurrection activities through patriotic poems and proclamations; he planned a constitution, prepared a *Military Manual,* and apparently a new edition of *Agathangelos.*

This edition, which became known to us only in our time, does not show the influence of Rigas's ideas. Perhaps it simply expressed his desire to use printing to arouse the nation, for during that time Rigas had assumed such a character. His constitution, *New Political Administration,* and the Proclamation which accompanied it properly belong to the political history of Greece, but it should be noted that the various documents were based on the French Constitution of 1973, "which in many ways, constitute a translation." Rigas, however, was equally inspired by other French constitutional texts. His personal element appears principally in the definition he gave to a Greek citizen.

> One who speaks the modern or ancient Greek language and renders service to Greece, though he live at the antipodes (for Greek leavening has spread to both hemispheres), he is a Greek and a citizen. And finally, every foreigner who is considered as a worthy inhabitant of the homeland by the government, for example, a man who practices his art successfully, a good pro-

fessor, a good patriot, is assured a welcome in the homeland and can enjoy the same rights as the fellow citizens. A foreign philosopher or a European practicing an art, who leaves his country and comes to live in Greece with the purpose of transmitting his knowledge or his art, is not only considered a true citizen, but he also merits a marble statue, erected at the expense of the State, with the insignia of his service or his art, and the best Greek pen should write the history of his life.

Rigas was also concerned with personal instruction which, for him, was the duty of a citizen: "It is the duty of everyone, without exception, to know how to read and to write."

The differentiation between Rigas's verses and those attributed to him after his death has not been made to date. However, the *Song of War* is his work:

> Until when, brave youths, shall we live defiled,
> Alone as lions, on the crags, on the mountains.

It is difficult to make an aesthetic evaluation of this war song. What interests us is that the poetry of Rigas, "neglected, and urging the use of the proper term even to the prosaic," as Palamas said, responded to the needs of his time. The *Song of War* sent a shudder through Hellenism and nourished national aspirations of the Greek people during the years separating Rigas's efforts from the War of Independence. Scholars, illiterates, peasants, all knew his work, and they recited it with enthusiasm. Numerous copies circulated among the Greeks and it is believed that clandestine editions were made. This concordance between intention and effort leads us to concede that the work of Rigas had a certain literary quality.

The political and national activities of Rigas surpassed by far the limits of literature; indeed they expressed the rise of renascent Hellenism. His detractors were certainly not lacking; they were those who considered revolutionary aspirations for any kind of freedom premature or simply dangerous, men who had as yet to develop an autonomous political conscience. A monk called Cyril, who lived in Bucharest, expressed himself in severe terms against Rigas in an unpublished text: "Rigas, the man of the troubled spirit, perished miserably, as befits a miserable man." Something analogous could be said about one editor of the 1838 *Agathangelos;* he informs us about Rigas' edition, however, he speaks of Rigas with evident disdain.

Michael Perdikaris wrote a long book attacking Rigas entitled

Against Pseudo-Philhellenes. The title is indicative, as is the language; indeed, Perdikaris, who generally did not use archaisms, here used an extremely archaic language. The reactionary spirit, in fact, sought an adequate vestment.

Generally, however, we should emphasize that the liberation efforts of Rigas, tragically stamped as they were with his death, shocked Hellenism of the time. We have a written document, contemporary with his arrest, of exceptional importance, not only because it concerns his liberation efforts, but also because it was written by Koraes. In the preface to his last work, *Brotherly Instruction* (1798), Perdikaris mentions Rigas and his associates. "At the moment, perhaps, the martyrs of liberty are confined in chains before the tyrant. It may be that the sword of the executioner has already fallen on their sacred heads; the noble Greek blood may be flowing from their veins, and their blessed souls flying to live with all the illustrious souls of all those who died for liberty."

A few years later, a nobleman from Moreas sang Rigas's *Song of War*. A Turk passing by demanded from one of his compatriots the meaning of the song. "It is nothing," the man replied. "The Greeks are singing a hymn to their new Virgin, to Liberty."

Chapter 12

A Partial Synthesis of
Poetic Expression

Poetry to 1821

Alexander Mavrokordatos

The Phanariots continued their poetry in a more systematic manner. Alexander Soutsos later wrote:

> On the shores of the Bosporus, in the heart of feebleness,
> The poetry of modern Greece was born.

He meant poetry, or rather versification, which he himself represented in the Athenian circles, and about this he had a point to make: the poetry of the Phanariots, inspired by neoclassicism, was beginning to cultivate the purity of language. Whether their sympathies turned toward the popular language, or whether they turned toward archaism, they avoided falling into barbarisms. At this stage in the evolution of Phanariot poetry, Alexander Mavrokordatos, surnamed Firari, was considered the most representative figure of the new tendencies of his class. He was born in 1754, served as a prince of Moldavia from 1785 to 1786, but fled when he found himself in danger of being executed by the Turks. Having found refuge in Russia, he participated in the liberation movement and became a member of the *Hetairia or Society of Friends*. He died in Russia in 1819. Another Phanariot, George Nicholas Soutsos, who published some tasteless allegorical theatrical works in 1805, had written in his youth, in 1785, a comedy called *Alexander, The Prince Without Conscience*. Alexander was none other than Mavrokordatos.

In Moscow Mavrokordatos published anonymously in 1810 a collection of poetry under the title *Bosporus in Borysthenia*. This collection has no aesthetic value, but it offers us the intersection of the old progressive spirit with a more conservative tendency which henceforth will characterize the Phanariots. Since the new generation was evidently subversive, it was inevitable that the Phanariots should pass from conservativism to reaction. Forerunner in this reversal was

Bosporus in Borysthenia. Though this work adopted the new ideas and welcomed the hopes of the Greek nation and its liberation efforts with sympathy, it distrusted the new philosophic doctrines. The philosophers said about it:

> There are few rational men; the wicked are numerous,
> And all are inclined to bad manners.

The distrust began to extend even to learning:

> At present, I am an honest man; after having studied,
> Perhaps I will have lost my virtuous dispositions.

A long poem in political couplets entitled "Dream" merits our attention. The poet finds himself in a beautiful natural site where vestiges of classical times continue to exist. A fondness for long descriptions connect Mavrokordatos with the preceding century. Suddenly, a dreadful storm breaks out and destroys the place. The national allegory becomes evident after the first 120 verses:

> Nevertheless, I cannot say how the dolorous idea struck me that this catastrophe had taken place a number of years ago, and that all, victims of fear and anguish, had been tossed about miserably for more than three centuries.

In the general disorder one sees the Olympian gods rising and conducting a passionate discussion. They wish to destroy the people who inhabit this happy place:

> The cause of our wrath is, in the first place, the decadence of heroic morals: we see the children of illustrious men, the descendants of heroes, living in these centuries a life similar to that of beasts.

In vain, the anonymous people depend on foreigners to give them their freedom. Only Athena is favorable to them. She enumerates their virtues, not only their intellectual and moral qualities, but also their military capabilities. Athena convinces the gods, and they decide not to execute their threats. The place becomes tranquil once more, and in the general prosperity one sees a multitude of soldiers exercising assiduously. Two generals, one descended from Themistocles and the other from Xenophon, lead the troops. This vision of more than one hundred verses thus ends:

> I was dreaming, I quickly arose,
> I searched with astonishment
> For the meaning to this dream.

Another poem in the collection constitutes an apology for the use of the popular language in poetry. Mavrokordatos recognized the necessity of writing poetry in the folk language, but he wished that words of foreign origin could be banished from it: "It is unpardonable license, the result of a disordered will, for harmony of Greek pronunciation is disturbed."

These poems present a great variety of metrics and word play. It is worth noting that here we also encounter the strophe of *Hymn to Liberty* by Solomos.

Photinos

The poets to whom the rest of this chapter is devoted were not Phanariots, but they did belong to the Phanariot world; they were under the influence of the Phanariot poetry which predominated at this time and of the Phanariot spirit. Before passing to the most important figures, I should mention Denis Photinos, a writer originally from Patras who was born in 1769, and who lived in Constantinople and in Vlachia, where he died in 1821. His *History of Ancient Dacia* (1818–1819) is useful for the study of Hellenism in the Danubian principalities, but it is for his *New Erotokritos,* a work published in 1818, that he is mentioned here. This was a paraphrase of *Erotokritos* in the language and verse form of the period. The work reveals clearly the connection between Kornaros and neo-Hellenism, and simultaneously gives evidence of the neoclassical spirit which reigned at this time in Greek letters: "In the early legendary period of Greece,/When the Greek race gloriously occupied the first rank." Photinos, following the example of the first Greek prose writers in *School for Delicate Lovers* and in *Consequences of Love,* enriched his *Erotokritos* with songs from Constantinople. Along with Photinos, we can also mention the Macedonian George Rousiadis (1783–1854), who was apparently acquainted with Photinos. Among other works, Rousiadis also translated Homer. About this latter work, suffice it to repeat what his contemporaries thought:

Hades, seeing the blindness of Homer, asked him:
"Who has blinded you?"

—"It was George Rousiadis."

Perdikaris

All these scholars, Rousiadis, Perdikaris, Megdanis, Sakellarios, Christopoulos, were friends; they knew each other and felt reciprocal esteem for each other. The theoretician of the group was Charisios Megdanis (1769–1823). As a moralist, he left us the *Characters;* as an aesthetician, he gave us a poetics under the significant title *The Return of Calliope.* Michael Perdikaris (1766–1828), whose parents came from Cephalonia, was born and brought up in Kozani. He wrote a number of works, but was able to publish only his *Hermilos* or *Demokritheraklitos* (1817) and in the same year a prose work entitled *Preface to Hermilos.*

The term "Demokritheraklitos" was taken from Voulgaris's *Logic.* The poem forms a volume of 460 pages, which, in fact, appeared as the first volume of the work. It deserves attention as a violent satire against the society of the period. The essential parts of the work appear to have been written in 1806. The satire overpowers the theory. It is not easy to characterize the poet as a follower of the Enlightenment or as an adversary of it. He attacked the clergy and all important men with such vehemence that one would have difficulty citing all relevant passages, but simultaneously he also attacked the progressivists with equal vigor. He called the bishops of his day "janissaries." He disapproved of fasting and mocked the benedictions of the priests. But he called Voltaire "miserable votary of the flesh, unbeliever and blind." We must note, moreover, his unfair appraisals of Katartzis and his attitude toward Rigas. The subject of his poem was taken from *Lucius* by Lucian, who was even cited in the work: a scholar, having denied the impious love of the nun Parthenia, is transformed into a donkey through the magic potions she dispenses. From that point on, we follow the adventures of the hero through Constantinople and the Phanariot world. The work appears to have been enjoyed when it first circulated and was widely distributed, particularly in Macedonia. The church took umbrage and, if we are to believe certain sources, condemned it.

Sakellarios

A friend and compatriot of Perdikaris, George Sakellarios (1765–1838) was also a physician and poet. But Sakellarios was not a moralist who wrote in verse, nor a didactic, descriptive, or allegorical versifier. He was a true man of letters with literary ambitions. His interests place him at the crossroads of preromaticism and neoclassicism. Aside from his works on medicine, he translated *Anacharsis* (the translation that Rigas was to continue) and wrote a *Greek Anthology* and other historical works; he also possessed a collection of ancient coins. If our information is correct, it was he who introduced Shakespeare to Greece in 1789 by writing a five-act tragedy in prose of *Romeo and Juliet*.

His poetic work was collected in one volume and published in 1817 under the title *Short Poems*. Affliction gives the tone to the collection. He opens with two "lamentations" dedicated to the "death of his beloved wife," followed by two "night" poems where he evokes the vanity of worldly matters, and one poem to "Vanity."

> O dear wife, sweet dove, sincere turtledove!
> Alas! how you are in repose, and decked out as a bride.
> Have you no compassion for me?

Every so often his verses reveal a certain emotion, but it comes from the human suffering they express rather than from art. In "Nights," one distinguishes the intention to render Young's lamentations into Greek:

> Alone, I suffer cruelly and without respite;
> I cry the whole night through.

The patriotic inspiration can also be felt at various points of the collection, particularly in a poem called "The Passage of Thermoplyae." The poet passes through Thermoplyae and follows the path of Leonidas's traitor:

> The earth and sea are bloody red.

Then he salues the ancestors:

> A salute, hero Leonidas, a salute to you and to your comrades
> Who were sacrificed with you for the sweet homeland.

One can see a perceptible improvement in quality between this volume and earlier collections of poetry. Sakellarios knew Perdikaris, some of whose works are included in *Short Poems,* as well as a correspondence in verse with the poet. Sakellarios was also acquainted with Vilaras and Christopoulos, whom he admired greatly and considered "another Anacreon." However, strict in his convictions, inclined toward melancholy and toward a meditative life, he did not approve of the tone of Christopoulos. He wrote the *Anti-Bacchic Poems Against the Bacchic of Mr. Christopoulos,* where he sought "a library in place of a wine Cellar."

> Take away the pitchers, take away
> The bottle and the glasses!

He followed the poetry of Christopoulos closely and offered rejoinders, but he was influenced by him. By this time we can speak of a literary movement.

Christopoulos

Athanasios Christopoulos was considered the major poet of this generation. He was born in Kastoria in 1772 and lived the major part of his life in Bucharest, where he died in 1847. He was also a Phanariot by affinity, since the provincial Phanariots were generally warmer in spirit and most were tied to folk tradition. Of course, this greater warmth could be submerged at any moment in neoclassicism or be congealed in the cold cosmopolitan Phanariot spirit. But the passage of time and the enlightened teaching of Katartzis created more propitious conditions for a natural language. Thus, Christopoulos, who emerged from the circle of Katartzis, began his literary career with a *Grammar of the Aeolian-Doric Language* and a drama entitled *Achilles* (1805).

Achilles was inspired by the nationalistic spirit that characterized theatrical production at that time. The lack of unity throughout those years, which disturbed the neo-Hellenic conscience, was condemned here as well:

> When we are united, Greece flourishes;
> No enemy invasion can bring us harm.

The work betrayed all the awkwardness of a new genre in letters and ignorance of scenic art. The theme is the wrath of Achilles and his reconciliation with Agamemnon after the death of Patroklos. The language is the somewhat vigorous one of tragedy. The dialogue is relentless in its stichomythia. One could call it a bad translation. The long monologues exhaust the reader, who finds no image or formula to engage his attention. As for the *Grammar,* it exposed the linguistic theory Christopoulos admired; for him, the neo-Hellenic language was a product of two ancient dialects, the Aeolian and the Doric. Christopoulos adopted and systematized the ideas of Katartzis, but his application rendered them less subversive.

Lyrical Poems, attributed to Christopoulos, appeared in 1811. The work opened with a prose satire on linguistics called "Dream." It is representative of the Phanariot climate of those years. Koraes is attacked. The extremists of demoticism, who had a tendency to confuse archaism with the doctrine of Koraes, attacked the danger of "Koraism." We feel that the "Dream" and the *Korakistika* by Neroulos sprang from the same source. In a letter written in 1811, Christopoulos praised this comedy of Neroulos.

The rest of the poems are the essential lyric production of Christopoulos. The numerous later editions give us very few new elements worth mentioning. Christopoulos sought charm and lightness in his poems. Emulating Anacreon as closely as possible in form, he essentially continued the light-hearted French poetry of the past century. The subjects he preferred were those of love, wine, and pleasures of a carefree life. It was a poetry of the study, without doubt, but worked with all the attention that the calm of a study assures. As for language, he intended to write in a unified idiom, and from this point of view, the position he occupies in Greek letters is important.

> If I could become a mirror in which you could see me,
> I would want to look on you forever, you and your beauty.

We should not seek here a linguistic wealth, the flavor of the folk languages as it had been used in the folksing. The charm of composite words, the vivacity of images, the contributions of the folk spirit are lacking. We are here concerned with the elegant language of the drawing room, still rarely used in Greek literature at this time. Christopoulos's verses were intended to charm the Phanariot women, who in those years were accustomed to love poetry and to letter writing; they were even attempting versification. The position of women in the world of learning during this time is characteristic. Later, when Alexander Rizos Rangavis analyzed the contrast between the Phanariot progressive scholars and the linguistic theories of Koraes, he defined this contrast in a few words: "female attitudes." The Phanariots with their unaffected language could not accept the affected linguistic effort of Koraes; they turned against it, they mocked it, and they created the appropriate climate for such a work as the *Korakistika*.

In any case, the elegance sought by Christopoulos in literature did not exploit the tradition of the folksong. His verses were rather insipid. Around us hover petty loves and mythological symbols, domesticated animals and those of a lower order, the cock that disrupts the amorous night, the mosquito whose sting disfigures his beloved:

> Mosquito, insolent one and thief,
> How do you ever presume
> Each night to sting while on her bed,
> My beloved on the mouth.

All is in good order, slight, without exaggeration. Even when the poet takes an oath—"Let me not survive. Let me lose my life,/ If a day should pass without intoxication."—we can agree that his oath is a formula which binds no one.

When we succeed in recreating the times or looking through the anthologies of the period, we understand how much the new Anacreon, this poet covered with glory, must have charmed his contemporaries with his culture, his application, his search for simplicity, all of which contributed to the meaning of art. Perhaps Christopoulos was a born poet, perhaps he felt a nostalgia for the natural world he had known in childhood. He accomplished what his predecessors had not; he laid the foundations for lyricism. Others were to realize them. Furthermore, in addition to his poetic work, he wrote a good number of works in prose that give us a better knowledge of the genre which preoccupied him. He collaborated in works of law, of Phanariot inspiration, and published archeological studies, one of which carried the indicative title *The Name and Origin of the Greeks.* Further, he was concerned with linguistic subjects other than his *Grammar,* with history, ancient philosophy, and politics. Fragments of his translations of the *Iliad,* the works of Herodotus, and others have also come down to us.

Vilaras

It was John Vilaras who took one more courageous step toward synthesis. In comparing Vilaras to Christopoulos, Jacob Polylas said: "The former is a poet, the latter rather a clever versifier." From what we know about Christopoulos, we can discern in the contrast praise for Vilaras for the attention he paid to the folksong tradition. Christopoulos was a poet of free and light humor; Vilaras, a poet by profession, was concerned with cultivating technique in prose and verse as they had been fashioned by the Greek people. Vilaras had the good fortune to live far from the artifical Phanariot centers. He was born at Cythera in 1771 but grew up in Epirus, where his parents originated; and later, having completed his medical studies in Italy, he returned to Jannina where he served at the court of Ali Pasha. The outbreak of the War of Independence found him in Jannina, which he immediately left and found refuge in Zagora, where he died after having been ruined by the fire that destroyed Jannina in 1823. Thus he lived in constant contact with the purest manifestations of Greek folk civilization and with the living tradition of the Greek language. He published only one work during his lifetime, *The Romaic Language* (c. 1814).

This work was a succinct statement of his orthographic system and his linguistic theories and included a certain number of examples, original poems or translations. An ardent progressive, imbued by the enlightenment of the Encyclopedists, this rationalist not only taught a popular language expurgated of all compromises, but he simultaneously suppressed the historical orthography, the double consonants, and the different vowels that expressed the same sound. His strong personality stands out clearly from the other conventional scholars. One can compare his temperament with that of the dynamic and prolific Rigas.

The Romaic Language was dedicated to Psalidas in a short letter. The author's purpose was always to serve the interests of Hellenism. "What gives me the courage to put this small work of mine under your protection is your inclination for all that is useful to our Nation," he wrote. There followed a short notice, addressed to the reader, as was customary at the time. But a new element was the living and personal tone in which it was written. Vilaras related a short anecdote about a self-taught violinist who played his instrument with greater sweetness and sentiment than the professional teacher. Seeing this, one of the latter's students preferred the self-taught violinist and, abandoning the professional, followed the counsels of the self-taught musician. "From that day, he renounced the redundant erudition of the scholarly master and imitated the artistic manner of his neighbor. Shortly, he felt that his music had a sweetness and all who heard him felt the same." The allegory of the anecdote is revealed in a few verses that close the notice: "O prejudices of the world, tyrants of the soul!/Men adore you in order to be made miserable."

Six poems follow, some original and some translations. We note four titles: "A Hymn to Love," "Springtime," "The Bee," and "The Tiny Bird." In "Hymn to Love":

> Your powerful hand legislates and educates;
> It vitalizes the world and governs movements.
> It is you who makes resplendent
> The domes of the sky.

On first contact, we have the feeling that we are in the presence of something different. It is a new kind of love, common topic of this period, with the afflicted love of the Phanariots and the smiling love of Christopoulos. Suddenly, we find ourselves carried away by an elevated lyric breath. Love becomes the great cosmic force which regulates the procession of the world. Vilaras participates in this vast movement, he vibrates with the life of nature. His expression, whether weighty and imposing or light and gay, always contains the force and plenitude of natural beauty. The scholar has become one with tradition and has taken life from its sources. He sings of springtime with charm and solemnity; the first quiver which passes over the living world after the sleep of winter communicates with the spirit of the poet and finally acquires an impeccable form in Greek verse:

> Sweet Springtime,
> Ornamented with flowers,
> Crowned with roses,
> Look sweetly on earth.
> And earth covers herself with grass,
> The forests give their shade,
> Cold snows melt,
> And the sky laughs.

The language of Vilaras acquires a fullness which corresponds to that of the verses; the long composite words, in harmony with the creative power of the people in matters of language, confer a plastic flow to the verses. His adjectives are never random; they complete the noun or intensify its meaning, as is the case with the folksong: the rose is thorny and the heart is soft. His descriptions are given as results of action: forests give the shade, rather than trees which grow new foliage. In "The Bee," the poet does not chase the bee from the lips of his beloved, as Christopoulos did with the mosquito: ". . . the honey/is found in abundance on her red lips/. . . incomparably sweet." But the bee will not dare to approach the lips of the beloved; they are tender and his sting might do her harm. This indirect method of presenting beauty constitutes an absolute renewal after all the insipid descriptions of the Phanariots. The restrained expression of admiration brings us directly to the technique of the folksong, to the spirit of the people, expressed now through the mouth of a scholar. "The Tiny Bird," another poem in *Romaic Language*, has raised many controversies which have yet to be resolved. We know the poems attributed to Ypsilantis and Danelakis. The similarities presented by "The Tiny Bird" are not, of course, fortuitous, and perhaps they all had a common model. In any case, the fact remains that it was Vilaras who gave us "The Tiny Bird" in his collection. This long poem, with its rapid turn of rhyme, does not show great unity and provokes in the reader a certain feeling of satiety. The allegory of the bird is maintained to the end by the description as well as the narration. In the end, the bird is convinced he should return to the cage of his own free will, and this recalls the charming aspiration of Christopoulos, independent of the quality of language, certainly, which is always superior in the poet from Jannina. Moreover, the search for elegance, the anacreontics, and the bucolic poetry of the drawing room were not always absent from the work of Vilaras. He also translated Anacreon and his heroines have names like those in the equivalent eighteenth-century French literature; they are called Daphne, Chloe, or Phyllis. But all these affected conventions are grafted by Vilaras on a vigorous tree, itself planted on Greek soil.

The collection of Vilaras is completed with two prose translations. We have the *Crito* by Plato and the *Funeral Oration for Perikles* by Thucydides. The language of Vilaras in these translations is still awkward, but this also gives evidence of his abilities, and certain virtues of the neo-Hellenic language, which, had they been cultivated earlier, would have given excellent results. The translation of the *Funeral Oration* was meant to move a living audience. Vilaras brought the ancient text to life with the ardent patriotism it inspired. Ancestors, virtue, the familiar places of Hellenism are reborn, and all help give Thucydides's text the vigor of actuality.

Vilaras followed a strict linguistic orthodoxy in his poetry, his original works, and his translations. This led to a certain severity as one often finds in the early application of new ideas. Roidis saw a model for the demotic language in this translation of Plato: "We should acknowledge, in all justice, that, except for the translation of the text of Plato by Vilaras, we know of no other work which can compare with that of Mr. Psycharis with respect to the correct forms of the pure demotic language." This orthodoxy naturally prevented the poet from evaluating the efforts of Koraes with objectivity; indirectly and directly he attacked *koraism* in various posthumous works, as had Christopoulos and Neroulos before him. His theories continued to be associated with the Enlightenment of the circle of Katartzis; in fact, he pushed these theories to their extreme consequences. His poetry, however, became more and more natural. The contribution of the Phanariot spirit tended to associate itself with the spirit of the folksong; Vilaras lived the folksong and its form. From all evidences, he endeavored to associate himself conscientiously with folk tradition.

> Though I live in this world, do not consider me alive.
> I do not live for myself; I live only for you.

During his maturity, he approached the pure folk verse, and having rejected rhyme, he arrived at a simple, plastic versification, where the fifteen-syllable verse was enriched with the suggestive element of an elevated and generous thought. We are approaching Solomos:

> Imagine a long beach bordering a long river,
> And an endless sea, violently agitated.
>
> .   .   .   .   .   .
>
> I feel the sweetness of honey and the zephyr strikes me
> Gently in the face with its breath.
> I hear the murmur of the crystalline spring.

The poem from which the above excerpt was selected begins:

> I wish to play on the strings of a new lyre
> An original melody with new sound.

We have proof that he was aware of the new forms toward which he tended. His poetry was enriched, furthermore, by living currents coming from the West. This influence, so fas as we know, was not always direct, but the problem is not important; it stamps the prosaic versification of Sakellarios with the preromantic motif of nocturnal sadness, which Sakellarios borrowed from Young. But this second transmission operates favorably in a true poet; the poor expressions of Sakellarios and their heavy cadences take wing with the poet from Jannina. Sakellarios writes:

> Once again the brilliant torch quits
> Our hemisphere with serenity.
> The laughing moon advances in her place,
> The planets and the stars, with feeble gleam,
> To offer consolation to the sky and earth,
> For being deprived again of light of sun.

Vilaras writes:

> The sun has gone to bed, obscurity begins,
> And the day takes off its brilliant vestment.
> Dressed in black, face somber,
> Silent, the night goes softly.
> The pale moon diffuses an obscure light
> As on her silver chariot she advances slowly.

This poem once again supports the force of neo-Hellenic assimilation. It is considered one of the best works of Vilaras. However, we should point out as characteristic of Vilaras that his form is often more original than his theme; he borrows from La Fontaine, Parini, and perhaps Boccaccio, without acknowledging indebtedness.

He composed with ease. The Englishman Holland reports that Vilaras improvised in his translations of foreign poems, which echoes the improvisation evident in the oral tradition. Finally, among the many stories Vilaras left are those he paraphrased from the original French or Italian. The acrostics, an alphabet of love, different satires show us that versification was a game for him. But his satire also had a particular weight and requires separate investigation.

We identify as satires not only those of Vilaras's verses in which he derides through a play on words or stigmatizes a contemporary for one moral defect or another, but also those poems where the poet, as a moralist, disapproves of a flawed humanity in general. In the first instance, a jocose tone predominates and the poet often arrives at the greatest intemperance of language. These are easy verses, with every evidence of improvisation, written to provoke light laughter in the audience. Sometimes, the satiric sting is entirely lacking, as in the case of the "Aerostat," where he describes with humor an unsuccessful attempt made at Jannina to raise an aerostatic sphere. The tone differs in the pieces properly called satires; one finds the spirit, one finds the mockery, but through them runs an anger, an indignation against wickedness, against a false humility which is insolent, against incapacity which ignores its limits:

> That is how it is, young man,
> When you enjoyed a high station,
> because you were rich.

The man fallen into misfortune, who sees his old admirers abandoning him, should not take this as an indication that fate has also abandoned him "without a gold saddle." The *Friend of Ornaments* is justified in adorning himself:

> If you are without jewels and without glitter,
> Who would think to look on you?

The monks find no mercy in the eyes of the poet:

> You, the elder son of idleness,
> You pass your life in food and drink.

It has been correctly stated that some of these satires closely resemble the *Characters*. Though the description of the various defects does not follow all the particular rules of this genre, they possess in common with the *Characters* a tendency toward moral teaching. This is, indeed, what impelled Vilaras to write these stories. Interest in moral and social man has a large place in Vilaras, which contributes, as do his liberalism and progressive ideas, to associating the poet with the Greek Enlightenment.

Holland's description successfully summarizes, I think, the various aspects of the man: "He joins to these gifts the erudition and sensibility of the stoic character about which I have spoken already, and which sometimes raises him to the summits of pride, which would have been more expedient in ancient times of freedom than in the misery of our period." Vilaras, that is to say, is already the new man, full of courage. The image of the future champions of liberty can be distinguished in the background of this portrait. After a long, painful journey, Hellenism has at last been recognized; it gives birth to men endowed with high moral standards, who aspire to freedom, and who are worthy of reclaiming it. These elements appear at all levels and in all classes of the Greek world. One also encounters them in intellectual manifestations. The synthesis of forces which gave freedom to Greece were those which expressed awareness of this freedom. On the intellectual level, we must study Koraes, who concentrates all the living tendencies, though still diffused, of neo-Hellenism, as we already know them. On the literary level, we are in the presence of two parallel efforts: that of Kalvos and that of Solomos. Both tend toward a synthesis, but whereas the former based himself on a rational construction, the latter based himself on tradition. The following chapters investigate successively the Hellenic synthesis in Koraes, in Kalvos, and in Solomos, The end of these neo-Hellenic efforts coincide fatefully with the beginning of a new era.

Part Five
**Definitive Synthesis
of Expression**
The Decline

The Giants,
The War of Independence
and its Direct
Consequences

The final synthesis of expression takes place; Greek culture reaches its peak with Koraes, Kalvos, and Solomos. During the War of Independence, letters are cultivated, particularly far from Greek soil. Greek intellectual life is weakened during the years of the War of Independence. A new situation is created after the war: nostalgia for past sublimity and memory of ancient glory. The decline has started: Hellenism of the diaspora is weakened without comparable reinforcement from the now impoverished Greek nation. The tendency to escape from reality will become one of the characteristics of Greek romanticism.

Chapter 13

Koraes

"A Happy Medium"

The life of Adamantios Koraes spans nearly a century; born in 1748, he died in 1833. Thus, from a chronological point of view, he can be placed before and after the War of Independence. A more careful examination leads us to consider him primarily at the end of the Turkish occupation: Koraes matured late. His regular production began at age fifty; hence, the culmination of his activity should be placed in the later period. However, we should not ignore his participation in the War of Independence, during which he published the "exhortations which could be heard as far away as three hundred leagues."

The high point of his activity came late, and his influence and thought were quickly known over a wide area by his own name, Koraism. His exquisite sensibility and his constant attention throughout his life to keep informed about various matters make him a valuable witness in the development of Greek intellectual life, even to the early period following the War of Independence.

Early Years

Smyrna, where Adamantios Koraes was born and educated during his childhood, is not unknown to us from an intellectual point of view. The reactionary Hierotheos, who was his teacher, gave his young students "a very miserable instruction accompanied by numerous strokes of the stick." However, we should recognize that the Greek he taught them was good; Koraes early became familiar with ancient Greek texts and used the ancient language with ease. Furthermore, in the home of his parents, though it was not a scholarly environment, there was respect for culture. His father, John Koraes, was from Chios originally; he was a balanced and reasonable merchant, and he respected scholars. The home of Koraes also contained the library of his grandfather, Adamantios Rysios, who was one of the best intellectuals of his time. His daughter, Thomaï, mother of Koraes, possessed some education and she honored the memory of Adamantios Rysios, who had died a few months before the birth of Koraes (August 1746).

There were other scholars related to the family besides Rysios. Earlier, was Anthony Koraes, who composed archaic odes (1702–1703), which Adamantios Koraes was later to remember with pride. His own cousin was apparently a school master with progressive ideas. One of his uncles, Sophronios Veligradios, was a bishop, a friend of letters and scholars. Thus the environment was simultaneously intellectual and religious.

Issuing from such a line, Adamantios exhibited a strong inclination toward letters from childhood. He learned the foreign languages taught in Smyrna at the time. Here, he was greately aided by Bernard Keun, the priest of the Dutch consulate at Smyrna. Koraes later referred to him with gratitude. Keun was an enlightened man, and he was probably the one who oriented the youth toward the West.

When Koraes had exhausted the resources of knowledge in his birthplace, he dreamed of going to study in enlightened Europe. His father wanted him to become a merchant; however, Adamantios found a way to reconcile his own aspirations with his father's desires. He went to Amsterdam to take up commercial affairs, but once there nothing could stand in the way of his completing his education.

Amsterdam

The Amsterdam that Koraes knew in 1771 was not only a great commercial center but also the crossroads for all the ideas that circulated throughout Europe. A liberal state and tolerant in matters of religion, Holland served as a refuge for free thought. All books forbidden publication elsewhere were printed in Holland. The Greek colony in Amsterdam apparently had few members and was composed principally of merchants, but it followed the intellectual line of the land wherein it resided. An uncultured merchant, John Prin-

gos, lived there during those years and kept a journal. We read in it
that he hoped for the liberation of the Greek race. "Raise up, my
God, another Alexander." And at another point, he wrote: "See to
what superstitions Ignorance makes men stoop." He collected books
and sent them to his villagers, writing to them in the meantime,
"These are philosophical works, essential to the education of the
young, as they are taught in the schools of Europe."

Koraes suddenly went from a small village in the Near East to a
large cosmopolitan city. There, something surpassing the thirst for
knowledge appeared: a violent desire to experience life, an integral
primitive humanism. He wanted to know everything, to attempt
everything. At the recommendation of Keun, he studied sciences
and foreign languages. But he also learned many other things: he
pursued music, he learned to play the guitar, he learned fencing.
Beside him was an experienced man named Peter Stamatis, with little
learning but with a great sense of judgment, with great powers of
observation, and with ultraconservative tendencies. The conflict between the young inexperienced Koraes and Stamatis was inevitable.
For them it was a source of vexations and suffering; for us it is a
source of valuable information, which is contained in a long letter
Koraes wrote in 1774 and in a series of letters from Stamatis. The
latter described Koraes as given "to vanities and pleasures," paying
great attention to his personal appearance, his European attire, and
carrying a hat "as certain French comedians do, going sometimes to
the Opera and sometimes to the house of his mistress." Koraes himself, speaking later about those years, said that his youth was greatly
disturbed by storms of passion. The first shock of his life, that sudden light revealing all kinds of freedom, determined the line he
would follow. Although personal vicissitudes and family adversities
caused him early to abandon the happiness of worldly preoccupations, still that which would distinguish him from this time on was
his humanism, embracing all human manifestations and a profound
liberalism.

Stamatis wrote: "He is not made for commerce." And indeed, it
would seem that Adamantios's activities in commercial affairs contributed to the economic reverses which eventually ruined his family.
In 1777 he abandoned Amsterdam with great regret, after having
failed in his commercial enterprises despite his good intentions. He
went to Leipzig, Vienna, Trieste, Venice, and reached Smyrna at
the end of 1778. In Leipzig, he became acquainted with Mandakasis,
who undoubtedly introduced him to the thought of Voulgaris. At

this time Sophronios lived in Vienna; it is possible that Mandakasis also introduced him to Moisiodakas. Koraes had made a decision now. He would consecrate himself to letters and he would live in the Western atmosphere, which suited him. But before he could realize his plan, he went to Smyrna and lived there for four unhappy years, his only distraction being the care of his family, the companionship of Keun, and some books. In 1782, he succeeded in leaving for Montpellier where he would study medicine.

We possess some documents relating to his intellectual life before his final departure for the West. A letter in 1774 reveals a certain knowledge of antiquity and true literary capabilities; his style begins to break through; it is vivid and intelligent: "I would say to myself: how is it possible that the words of a man, which, as the saying goes, are being distributed like straw to two donkeys, cause the one to burst from satiety and the other from hunger?" The ancient authors, Aristophanes, Aristotle, Euripides, and others, Koraes utilized with ease. During this same period he wrote in ancient Greek, prose as well as poetry. In 1782 he sent a letter to Villoison. This scholar and exacting Hellenist concluded from this single letter that his unknown correspondent was versed in Greek literature. Religious questions treated with a progressive spirit concerned Koraes greatly and resulted in the publication of three catechisms. The progressive spirit of Koraes and the influence of Moisiodakas are apparent in the notes to the longer catechism, which is a translation. Dutch liberalism is visible everywhere. Koraes continued to write verses, which, however, remained unpublished. His philosophic meditations also were not published. He studied with pencil in hand, always ready to write, and was interested in Hume and Voltaire.

Montpellier and Paris

Montpellier was an intellectual center which nourished the interests and developed the virtues of Koraes. The University of Montpellier at which he studied was one of the best and most progressive in France. Koraes was there when both his mother and father died, leaving him nearly indigent. Poverty had its effect on him for the rest of his life, without ever altering his character. In 1788, doctor of medicine now, he went to Paris. Here he was nourished by the classical spirit of the times, the admiration for antiquity which served as a means to express liberalism and the dawn of the Greek insurrection as well as its course.

We possess, dating from the years of his studies and of his sojourn in revolutionary Paris, various medical works, or works written to earn a living, as well as a portion of his correspondence. His letters to his friend, Demetrios Lotos, first chanter, the protopsaltis of Smyrna, showed his early literary achievements. His style, though still tending toward the archaic language, had an inimitable charm, both when he adopted a familiar tone and when he soared to noble thoughts. His life in Paris at that time determined his future literary activities. Politics became his basic preoccupation: it was essential that the Greek race be liberated. In order to be liberated, it should first become enlightened. And the path toward enlightenment was knowledge of the classics. From this time, Koraes occupied himself with collating manuscripts for third parties to earn a livelihood. Thus, "abandoning the practice of his profession, which at that time would have gained him glory and wealth, he dedicated himself to all that could benefit his country." Already in 1796 he had procured an edition of the *Characters* by Theophrastus, which had been published two years earlier. This detail reveals the preoccupations of a moralist. But it was Hippocrates who formed the link between his medical studies and his literary vocation; it was the subject of one of his university dissertations, whose editing occupied him in 1800 *(On Air, Water, and Places)*. His image, as it comes to us from a German scholar in a personal letter (1800), is a good one. He was praised for his proud isolation, which Stamatis had already noted in some letters, but which was more obvious and more general in the German: "This noon I met the neo-Hellene Koraes, a sickly man around fifty, sitting in his room beside the stove . . . . He, too, is unknown in the city of Paris, and as much a stranger to it as I am."

Besides the edition on Theophrastus on which Koraes was working in 1796, he also was translating Beccaria's famous work, *Dei delitti e delle pene,* which was published later in 1802. It was precisely during these years that the French armies extended their enterprises toward the Orient and specifically toward Greek territory. This was the period when French propaganda was exerted on enslaved Greece; when Rigas was working toward the realization of his plan. Koraes moved in a more direct political area than Rigas.

His first political pamphlets appeared anonymously: *Brotherly Teaching* (1798), written against *Paternal Teaching*. *Song of War* (1800) in verse and *War Trumpet* (1801) in prose were written to inspire enthusiasm in the Greeks and confidence in the French guns. The last pamphlet of the period, which included a French *Memoir* on the Greek situation in 1803, was in the form of a dialogue; it was called *What the Greeks Should Do in Actual Circumstances: A Dialogue Between two Greeks When They Heard About the Brilliant Victories of the Emperor Napoleon* (1805). Salvation should no longer be anticipated from Russia but from France. However, the French drive toward the Greek Orient had already weakened; hopes for an early liberation were lost. Koraes continued on the other path, the indirect one.

The *Hellenic Library*

In 1804 Koraes published the *Ethiopica* of Heliodorus, and from 1805 he devoted himself to the *Hellenic Library*, which eventually constituted his most significant writing and editing activities. He was supported in this great effort by the Greek merchants, protectors of culture, and especially by the brothers Zosimas, who in many ways encouraged the diffusion of knowledge in Greece. Koraes presented the ancient authors in a carefully reviewed text, which was preceded by long introductions where the editor disclosed his linguistic, pedagogic, and political theories. Most of these texts are known under the title *Impromptu Thoughts*. Isocrates, Plutarch, Strabo, and others were the object of his critical commentaries. He also published other texts, either as supplementary works to those of the *Hellenic Library*, or as separate works, such as his *Aesop, Marcus Aurelius*, and the *Iliad*. During the War of Independence, he intensified his efforts by publishing *Characters* of a more directly moral or political nature: "If the nature of the enterprise, and if my financial situation permits, I will publish all the moral and political authors at the same time." He published Aristotle *(Politics* and *Ethics)*, Plutarch (sections of *Moral Works*), Xenophon *(Memorabilia)*, Plato *(Gorgias)*, Lycurgus, and others. It was characteristic that he also edited the writings of a tactician, Onisander. Before the Greek War of Independence, he had edited the work of another author, Polyenos. The editions of Koraes early acquired world authority. His name was mentioned with respect along with those of the greatest philologists. An exacting and severe critic, P. L. Courier, wrote about him: "Among those who have taken as the object of their studies the monuments of Greek antiquity, Koraes ranks first." Koraes was awarded a prize for his edition of Hippocrates and was offered a chair at the University of Paris.

The War of Independence

When the War of Independence erupted, Koraes resorted for a second time to direct political activity. He did not believe that Hellenism had matured; that is, that Hellenism was sufficiently enlightened to recover its independence. "It is not essential to be a great scholar to tear down the edifice, especially when this edifice has been shaky for a long time. The great and terrible difficulty is in reconstructing it" (1821). According to him, the War of Independence started "before the appropriate moment" (1825). But when he confronted reality, he put aside his objections and gave himself entirely to the new state of things. He fought as a volunteer: "If I were twenty years younger, neither gods nor demons could restrain me."

He was seventy-three years old when the War of Independence began. And yet, all who met him at that time thought they were dealing with a young man full of life and passion. Letters written by friends in 1820 show him as having ". . . the simplicity of infants and the vivacity of young men. He truly resembles the ancient sages of Greece. The benefactors of their people and their country, he considers as brothers and fathers and even more. Everything good for the Nation causes him to jump for joy; the triumph of evil causes him to die. He does not live for himself at all. He always thinks of his Country and breathes for her." The desire to inspire in others the enthusiasms which filled his heart brought him back to poetry; he translated Tyrtaios. The day the news finally broke about the victory of Navarino, the old man of seventy-eight requested a young man standing beside him to take down *Prometheus Bound* from his library. He selected a passage and returned the book to the young man, who read aloud the magnificent verses of Aeschylus:

> . . . . neither suddenly
> nor secretly your want of good sense
> has tangled you in the net of ruin. . . .

His correspondence, always vast and important, now acquired a directly political character; he wrote to Greeks and foreigners, exhorting the former to live in harmony and the latter to aid Greece. Furthermore, he was not a self-styled advisor; politicians and military men wrote him from insurgent Greece, seeking counsel or attempting to join him. Some indications of the esteem in which he was held are characteristic: a fortress in Missolonghi was named after him; in 1827 the National Assembly expressed the gratitude of the nation to him. Despite his advanced age, Koraes was a member of various committees with headquarters in Paris, which rendered great service to the insurrection. He was considered the official representative of Greece. But his principal activity, of course, was writing. His liberalism made him the guardian of the *Hellenic Library*, not only against the foreign enemy, but especially against the internal ones: "We have liberated the Greek land from the Turks. But who among us have liberated their spirits from the impure thoughts of the Turks?"

The End

Several years later, this attitude brought him fatefully in conflict with Kapodistrias. Among Koraes's numerous publications during those years, two dialogues, presented under a pseudonym, were directed against Kapodistrias. The first appeared while the governor was living, the second after his death. The assassination of Kapodistrias was attributed to Koraes. And yet from the first dialogue Koraes had indicated his position with perfect clarity: "No tyranny has ever been strangled by the murder of tyrants." As a young man, he had written: "I am a lover of Liberty, but, my friend, I also love Justice. Liberty without justice is pure highway robbery."

In the last years of his life, undeceived by the turn of events, he returned to his beloved literary compositions. He published his *Miscellany*, a collection of works devoted especially to the modern Greek language. He died in 1833 with his faculties intact, still lively and dedicated with the same passion to study, to meditation, and to politics. To the end of his life, he endeavored to keep up to date with intellectual and political actualities. He was perhaps the first to have discussed romanticism in Greek. The French newspapers that he read were the most progressive of his time.

Aspects of Character

The interest he exhibited for all real phenomena and his intellectual activity were Koraes's characteristic traits; both traits expressed the mature spirit of neo-Hellenism. The Greek forces, material and intellectual, had reached their height at Koraes's time and helped synthesize the new intellectual Hellenism. And this Hellenism, conscious of its increased force, could not renounce life and certainly could not renounce the heritage of its ancestors. In one of his first mature works, his *Memoirs* written in French in 1803, Koraes disclosed the mixed character of the Greek Renaissance with luminous clarity. And later, in 1815, observing the extension of culture, he wrote: "There is no doubt that good times have come for the Greeks as well, and they have come with such a force that no human power can henceforth resist us." We can also say that politics was central to his thought. The maturity of Greek nationalism tended to demand their reestablishment as a free people and to demand that education aid and justify these efforts.

The new classicism was the basis of thought for Koraes. His work revealed a desire for equilibrium and a harmonious synthesis of forces. Extremisms, reinforcing partiality in themselves, were judged inadmissable. The famous happy medium, applied to Koraes's linguistic concepts, was the general framework of his humanism. Greek dynamism and the new Hellenic spirit lived within this structure and gave it vitality. The young man who had abandoned himself to his passions without reserve maintained passion in all his activities to the end of his life. His character, his sentimental excess, reminds us that the Greek synthesis was not infertile for the seeds of a beginning romanticism. "With all his old age," we read in a letter dated 1818, "he is charming, humorous, calm, conciliatory, and indulgent of the weaknesses in others. Only the madness of many of our good compatriots' passions have distorted him into a melancholy old man, to say nothing of those who have turned him into a wild beast." This evidence notes specifically how his reactions fluctuated.

We find nothing of the methodical, pedantic philosopher in Koraes: "So long as my head is clear, I am not able to write a thing. It must first become excited and inflamed; then I can begin and complete my work in a single day." The desire to make his classical culture agree with his romantic state of soul led him to search for equilibrium. In him we constantly find the Aristotelian concept of justice: "J' idolâtre la Liberte," he wrote to Keun, "mais je voudrais la trouver toujours assise au milieu de la Justice et de l' Humanité." As for religion, he wrote that it should remain equally distant "from the impiety of Scylla and the superstition of Charybdis." With such premises, we can proceed to an analysis of his theories and the originality of his writing.

"Obtain Culture"

Koraes's theories naturally embraced all problems of the neo-Hellenic Enlightenment. His attitude toward religion was determined basically by his family origin; religious problems engrossed him. The solution he chose to give to this problem was influenced by the liberal concepts of the Dutch, by his philosophic readings, and by the revolutionary climate of France. But the traditional element always lived within him; change not by revolution, but by renewal. His theories concerning instruction bring us very close to the subject. A radical reform was long overdue in this area; the first efforts had been made, but, as we already know, the new ideas were persecuted more and more. A battle was needed to assure their triumph. In his correspondence, and particularly in his *Prologomena*, Koraes attacked the roots, the ancient educational system which tended to a purely grammatical instruction. For him, education should not look to grammar but to philosophy. It is philosophy which will aid man in life and make him a good citizen. Virtue is also instruction, if one believes in the principles of English empiricism and in French Enlightenment. "All our prejudices, all our wickednesses, and all our injustices originate from the hazy density of ignorance. Only education, liberating the spirit, teaches men the duties toward God and fellow man." The battle was an arduous one and it unfolded on two fronts, because it stimulated opposition from both the partisans of the ancient methods and from religious conservatives, who by now had learned the significance of philosophy. Insofar as instruction was concerned, Koraes did not hold to general principles, but was involved in establishing an educational program which was complete and incorporated the latest advances in Western education: Pestalozzi, mutual teaching, and so on. He insisted that the young Greeks go to the West so they could transport this progress to Greek schools. There was no need to seek original solutions; the West had undergone these experiences, which had led to positive results; consequently, the purpose of the Greeks should be to transport the lights shining in Europe to Greece. What was needed were translations, periodicals, schools. Koraes's correspondence and his *Prologomena* abound in suggestions on works which should be translated. The subject of periodicals concerned him no less, and it was through his advice that the periodical *The Scholar Hermes* saw the light of day.

The Scholar Hermes

The periodical began to circulate in Vienna in 1811. It was directed by Anthimos Gazis (1764–1828), a cleric and a prolific writer. He published a translation of a *Physics,* a dictionary of ancient authors *(The Hellenic Library),* and another large dictionary on ancient Greek. Gazis was also working on various editions of both older and contemporary Greek writers. He was influenced greatly by Koraes, but he was not disposed to admit it. Furthermore, his concepts were not as progressive as the theories professed by Koraes. As an affiliate of the *Society of Friends,* he became one of its leaders and there found the best method to channel his activity. So long as he edited *The Scholar Hermes,* the periodical failed to defend Koraes. The publication went through a period of difficuties, then began to appear regularly in 1816, by which time, two disciples of Koraes, C. Kokkinakis and Theoclitos Pharmakides, directed it. Both men were combative and inspired. *The Scholar Hermes* became the outlet of Koraes and continued to appear without interruption until the Greek insurrection. Then the Austrian authorities demanded that the publication insert the excommunication pronounced by the Patriarch Gregory V against the insurgents. The excommunication was published in a supplement, but the periodical ceased to appear. Kokkinakis and Pharmakides returned to Greece. During all these years, *The Scholar Hermes* had followed the intellectual affairs of the West, had transmitted the scientific knowledge of the West to Greece, and had served as a model for publications of the same order during the prerevolutionary period. It is difficult to assess the importance of its direct contributions to the neo-Hellenic Renaissance, because there are certain indications that its diffusion was extremely limited. In any case, thanks to the questions it raised, when *The Scholar Hermes* fell into the hands of professional scholars, it offered immense services to the new Hellenism.

The Language Problem

The interest of Koraes in the schools also proved helpful to the problem of teaching in Greece. His admirers and followers cooperated in establishing new schools; they themselves returned to Greece, once they had completed their studies in the West, to teach the new science by means of new methods. Aside from this and always under the direct supervision of Koraes, an interest was developed in experimental teaching, in libraries, in printing shops, in scholarships. But Koraes was principally concerned with the problem of language in educational matters, as evidenced in the synthetic manner with which he always confronted related problems. Liberalism and the happy medium were also found here: "Language is one of the most inalienable possessions of the nation. All members of the nation play their part with democratic equality, I would say." And again: "Neither tyrants of the vulgar, nor slaves of its vulgarity." Here, we also find a battle on two fronts; the two extremes were equally opposed to Koraes. To this time, we have noted the coexistence of two linguistic tendencies, neither of which had a conservative character. The partisans of the folk language sought the enlightenment of the people and for this reason they supported the view that scholars should use its language. Those who favored archaism, on the other hand, believed that the ancient language would revive the ancient and glorious race of the Greeks. In other words, both sides had a positive movement toward an end which was neither conservative nor reactionary. Koraes had a position much closer to the partisans of the folk language, but his classical culture did not permit him to go to the extreme conclusions held by the linguistic movement that already existed. According to him, the language of the scholars should be corrected and enriched.

We will see that his corrections were inspired by the French philosophy of his time. The nature of language should be respected and reform should be based on *reason*. Koraes demanded that one begin by knowing the nature of the Greek language. Hence, a need for a systematic study of modern Greek was created; the editing of a modern Greek dictionary and a grammar became necessary. Toward this end, it was indispensable to study the language as it survived in popular spoken form and as it appeared in recent literary works of importance. Later, one could compare the new language with the ancient in order to verify the new elements and the right of each to survive: "I call amendment of language not only the transformation of the various words and barbarous constructions, but also the preservation of many others, as those who have not studied the nature of language carefully endeavor to banish as barbarous." The comparison between the two languages would also have another result: a better knowledge of ancient Greek. The notes of Koraes abound in such parallelisms, which aid in a better comprehension of the ancient language and thereby of the current language. The comparative method was not one Koraes invented; it was an aspect of his time. But we owe to Koraes the application of this method on such a vast scale in the modern Greek language. It was called the *method of Koraes*. Be that as it may, the language that the Greek nation would speak would be based on the new language. "The bad and perverse practice of being contemptuous of the new language, which is the only one we can carry to perfection" was condemned. The purified term was closer to ancient Greek.

Also characteristic of this period was the notion of evolution: "Only time is able to transform the languages of the people." Finally, *reason* demanded that language should not be separated from common usage, from the *koine;* in the matter of words, forms, syntax, it was more comprehensible when those of the *koine* were given preference. And even if all these linguistic theories should be erroneous, then, Koraes wrote: "One could do no better in giving counsel to the nation than to hold to the doctrine of vulgarism, that is to say, to write as one speaks and not to seek to rearrange the language he has received from his parents." Thus, Koraes passed a theory of linguistic usage which approximated the spoken language. It was a *koine* refined within measure. D. Vernardakis made a most fortunate definition when he wrote that the language of Koraes was "an imitation of the demotic." Throughout the long life of Koraes, we observe a continuous evolution toward simplicity, toward the spoken language.

Doukas

Such a position could not satisfy either faction. Certain excesses, awkwardnesses and errors in the language corrections offered an opening for criticism. On the side of the archaists, the most significant adversary was Neophytos Doukas (c. 1760–1845). Doukas was not considered an important literary figure and no one today would presume to compare him with Koraes. Nonetheless, from a certain point of view, their careers were parallel; both were dedicated to the rebirth of Hellenism and they based their efforts on the ancient authors. Doukas edited a great number of ancient texts. In his original works, he used the archaic language almost exclusively. But he was a man full of life and quick spirit. What was evident from the moment he engaged in the battle against *koraism* were his critical and comparative capacities. If Doukas was awkward when he attacked theories for which his culture had not really prepared him, his criticism, at any rate, as he exercised it against the language of Koraes and his followers, was intelligent and convincing. From certain standpoints in the history of Greek literature, he can be given first place in criticism of modern Greek prose. His case confirms a general rule. His archaism did not derive from a conservative spirit, but was an expression of the neoclassical spirit which had been spread during the French Revolution. He turned toward ancient Greek in order to approach the perfection of antiquity. As for the rest, his thought was courageous, and in religious matter, he sometimes even aroused uneasiness in the conservative element of the church. The monk Cyril, who disapproved of Rigas, also condemned "the atheists, such as Voltaire and Doukas Neophytos." It is unfortunate that Doukas's other activities were neglected because of his linguistic exaggerations.

The Korakistika

This linguistic battle, though often distinguished by an ethical bearing and a responsible spirit, shows the defenders of demoticism as lacking in brilliance. In 1813 a comedy entitled *The Korakistika* by the Phanariot Jacob Rizos Neroulos appeared. It was a satire against the linguistic theories of Koraes and his followers. Plot, naturally, was lacking; the entire comedy rested on a parody of language. Neroulos also used other comic devices, such as presenting on stage people who spoke in a dialect. He also attempted to ridicule the representatives of *koraism* by showing them in humiliating scenes. The Phanariots were never reluctant to be spirited or intemperate of language. So it is with Neroulos. Laughter is provoked by indecent implications or by an easy play on words.

An epigram dedicated to Doukas by Alexander Mavrokordatos, the brilliant diplomat and later prime minister of Greece (1791–1865), is characteristic:

> Racine, the most tragic French poet, has excelled in all his tragedies. However, when he attempted to write a comedy, he failed and directly lost his courage. But you, you are successful in both genres; you have been both comic and tragic.

Satire was not the only weapon of Phanariot demoticism. Around this same time Neophytos Doukas was found beaten one morning on the streets of Bucharest. The attack was organized by the demoticists. In fact, Doukas considered the moral perpetrator to have been Alexander Mavrokordatos himself.

Parios

But different weapons used by other adversaries of Koraes were more painful, because his endeavors also embraced aspects of both religious and social life; Koraes denounced the clergy and the governing class (nobles, Phanariots), and his theories, to a degree, were directed against them. Freedom, democratic spirit, renovative tendencies were all matters bound to provoke discontent in certain circles. The church reaction took concrete form in the attacks Parios made against Koraes. The aristocrats' violent polemic was written by Kodrikas. Athanasios Parios (c. 1725–1813) had been educated in Smyrna under Hierothios. Remaining faithful to his teaching, Parios refused to go to the West to complete his studies. He went to the academy at Mount Athos and there became a student of Voulgaris, whose political orientation he approved but not his renovating spirit. From 1786 until his death, Parios lived in Chios, where he served as director of the school.

He wrote much, always in a reactionary spirit. He was fond of controversy, particularly over all that concerned religion. It was natural that he should come in conflict with Koraes, the most eminent progressive spirit in Greece. These ideological conflicts began early, when Parios obtained a letter in which Koraes disapproved of fasting (1791). Parios replied with a dissertation in the form of a letter, which apparently circulated widely. In 1798 came a new work by Parios against Koraes's *Brotherly Teaching*. This work remained unpublished, thanks to the intervention behind the scenes of Koraes's friends. However in 1802 Parios succeeded in publishing his *Response,* where all Greeks studying in the West were accused of immoral conduct. Koraes produced a violent reply to *Response,* but Parios continued the attacks, either in works he left unpublished or in verbal attacks which sought to compromise Koraes in public opinion and present him as an atheist. We know that during this time such an accusation was not negligible, particularly when it concerned a man who depended on the circulation of his books among the enslaved Greeks.

Kodrikas

Panayotis Kordikas (1762–1827) also attacked Koraes on religious grounds. He was born in Athens, but he lived in Phanariot circles at Constantinople and Bucharest until 1797, at which time he went to settle in Paris and lived there to the end of his life. He published little: a translation of Fontanelle in 1794, a *Study of the Greek Dialect* in 1818, and some polemic or patriotic pamphlets. His conflict with Koraes, which came to public attention two years before the publication of *Study,* used the linguistic theories as a pretext; Kodrikas supported something which today we call the *katharevousa.* He believed that a certain language had been formed in the writings of the patriarchate or in those of the princes of Moldo-Vlachia, and that this language should be adopted for official purposes, as the language of Versailles had been imposed in France. He was an enthusiastic partisan of the nobility's language. He became lyrical and interspersed verse translations in his prose.

Our language is simple, versatile, and rich. The phrase is sweet,
rhythmic and authentic. Only the wise seek to find fault with it.
For them, it is a poor language since they do not know how to
use it.

In reality, however, the battle was of another nature, as he admitted: "In truth, it concerns the fundamental traditions of our
nation, and not simply two or three barbarous Greek words." For
him, Koraes was a revolutionary, a *Jacobite* because he attacked
religion, the nobles, and he constituted a threat to the Greek nation.

Kodrikas had knowledge, freshness of mind, a desire to seek the
good. A description of him from a French source of the period said:
"Il a beaucoup d'esprit, est très instruit, il parle français avec faci-
lité, avec grâce, il fait de jolis vers." One of his recently published
journals, which extends over a ten-year period, until 1797, reveals
both the period and the man. He knew how to perceive, how to
evaluate. He was not lacking in the virtues of composition and perhaps possessed some spiritual virtues. His attacks on Koraes injured
only his own memory. He was worthy of having left something
more to the history of literature than the memory of a strictly libel-
ous writer.

Koumas

But these attacks only express certain sides of Hellenism, and they
are neither the principal ones nor the more dynamic. Even demoticism, though it had depended in great measure on the Phanariot intellectuals, followed the renewal efforts of Koraes with faith
and perseverence. Hellenism had need of new values and these were
offered by *koraism*. The followers of Koraes, spread throughout
Greece, introduced the new sciences, the new ideas. Neophytos
Vambas replaced Parios. Koumas and the brothers Ekonomos, Constantine and Stephen, taught in Smyrna. It was thus that the bastions
of the conservative spirit were shattered. Even Constantinople came
alive at certain moments of tentative renewal. The new spirit blowing through the other schools was not unlike that advocated by
Koraes; in Kydonies, we have Kaïris, in Jannina, Psalidas, in
Trieste, C. Asopios, all attempting the same thing.

Constantine Koumas remained the most faithful and most important follower of Koraes. He wrote of himself in relation to Koraes: "No one perhaps respected the ideas of Koraes more than Koumas." He was born in Larissa in 1777 and studied in many schools in Greece, then managed to finish his studies in the West. He remained in Vienna, where he studied, taught, and wrote. Later, he accepted the theories Koraes professed and continued his prolific career under this inspiration.

His work, on the whole, was not original; it was mostly compilations and translations. This fact, as well as the variety of subjects that concerned him, put Koumas slightly out of tune with his period, which saw specialization in the development of Greek culture. But the quality of Koumas's work represented an important contribution to the rebirth of Greek letters. All the branches of mathematical and natural sciences, philosophy, history, geography, lexicography, and grammar became objects for his attention. It is worth observing that Koumas especially presented the new tendency of neo-Hellenism toward German thought. Of all his works, a long history in twelve volumes (1830–1832) called *Histories of the Deeds of Men* was of special significance. The greater part of this work was composed of borrowings, but the numerous pages devoted to contemporary Greek affairs make this a reference book, though facts are sometimes obscured because he writes from memory. All in all the work is valuable, not only for what the author knows, but also for his precise evaluation and attention to expression. The educational activity Koumas confronted in Smyrna merits mention. He faced the reactionary works of the old professors with courage and success. The War of Independence marked a definitive end to his educational efforts in the Near East. He went to Austria, where he finally was appointed director of the Greek school in Trieste in 1835. There he died the following year.

Vardalachos, Psalidas, and Kaïris

Another meritorious writer, Constantine Vardalachos (1755–1830), also remained faithful to *koraism,* faithful to the spirit, liberal and progressive, faithful to the letter, even perhaps excessively: "Then I left the laboratory of my uncle and came to the home of my father, with constant sighs and with tears in my eyes, and complained of the beatings he had inflicted on me. . . ." So he translated Lucian. Besides the translation of the ancients, which he left unpublished, two books in particular must be mentioned: his *Physics* (1812) and his *Rhetoric* (1815). "Let us take care," he wrote in the second book, "not to pay blind respect to all that the ancients wrote." And further: "Antiquity is without value to a system of philosophy."

Perhaps it would be appropriate here to mention two other scholars who were influenced by Koraes, without subscribing to his movement. We already know Athanasios Psalidas (1764–1829) from his contacts with Voulgaris and Vilaras. As a young man, he published in Vienna some pamphlets, several translations (1791), and a philosophical treatise which was without consequence. Later, he went to Jannina as director of a new school called *Kaplanaias,* which had been founded by a national benefactor named Zoïs Kaplanis. His heavy professional duties, the financial difficulties against which he had to struggle, left him no time to pursue a literary career. He left a certain number of unpublished educational works. A partisan of the spoken language, he maintained contact with Koraes and, though with some impatience, in many ways he followed the path Koraes had carved. His educational activities were enlightened and progressive, as opposed to the conservative teaching he found in Jannina under the Balanians of the Balanian School: "The Balanians generally are contemptuous of the students of Psalidas, and the latter are contemptuous of the Balanians."

The case of Theophilos Kaïris (1784–1853) is even more complex. He also was influenced by Koraes, in fact, to a much greater degree. We first meet him among the followers of Koraes in Paris and later in Kydonies, where he taught. He participated in the War of Independence by following in intellectual matters the line traced by Koraes. The speech he made at the reception of Kapodistrias in Aegina is famous and significant: "Long live! but by holding the sacred emblem with which God and Justice rule Greece. Long live! but govern in such a way that the country will feel, that we will also be aware, how impartial history repeats itself, how the centuries proclaim that neither you, nor your son, nor your friend, nor an emanating spirit, but the Divine Law itself, but Justice itself, but the institutions of Greece themselves, will govern Greece through your intermediary." He proclaimed this same liberal attitude toward King Othon. He did not accept the public offices offered him, but he founded an orphanage in Andros, his birthplace, in 1835 and there he lived a virtuous and honored life, teaching his beloved students with a liberal spirit. What did he teach? Rumors were not long in circulating about the unorthodoxy of the teachings of Kaïris. In 1839 the persecutions which were to victimize him until his death began. The orphanage was closed. He was arrested for his ideas and died in prison.

He admitted that he had his own faith, his own revealed religion, and that the cult had its own particular hymns and prayers. These texts were written in an archaic style and language, as were the few educational works in philosophy that he published during the second period of his life. The influence of Koraes, the sense of measure, of equilibrium, the feeling of reality had been extinguished in an inflamed mysticism. But the unjust treatment inflicted on him and his subsequent death outraged liberal spirits. Their indignation was like a long echo of Koraes's teachings.

Kaïris had a sister named Evanthia to whom he was attached and who was also his student. Following her brother's example, she also began to correspond with Koraes and to consult him about translating some good book from French into Greek. This was another sign of the times. The name of the first woman of letters is authenticated in the *History of Modern Greek Literature*. Later, Evanthia Kaïris wrote a tragedy in prose, which is no better and no worse than the tragedies of the period. She called it *Nikiratos* (publ. 1826). The life and correspondence of Koraes are full of such requests and recommendations, for his friends applied themselves to translations of foreign scholarly or classical works.

Generally, the period at Koraes's height showed, as was natural, a great activity in translations, a consequence of the flights of Hellenism, but also a result of the efforts of Koraes himself. We have a strong and conscientious effort to advance in all branches of science; a more lively interest is manifested in foreign literataures. The various periodicals, and particularly *The Scholar Hermes,* contributed to this awakening. In addition a certain number of intellectual centers formed, which exhibited influences other than the French. Vienna was under German influences; the Ionian Islands showed English influences. During the first twenty years of the century, aside from various classics, more recent texts expressing newer orientations were translated: Chateaubriand, Thomson, and Goethe, among others. The translators considered it a point of honor to imitate the style of Koraes in their prefaces or in their translations. But it was his language they imitated and perhaps above all his weaknesses.

Koraes, the Writer

Koraes actually possessed great literary talents. Educated in the school of the ancients and in eighteenth century France, he sought clarity and elegance in his expression. His vivacious temperament and his humor assure against dryness. His apparent simplicity was the result of reflection and attention to everything he undertook. This becomes evident from the frequent observations he made on style. Yet, without interrupting the balance of his style, he passes with ease from the gracious to the sublime. Here, as well, the sense of measure, of equilibrium, preserve him from extremes. "Sweet *koraism*" is the term Palamas used to characterize the language of Koraes. In his abundant production, the works which are distinguished for their literary quality are his correspondences, the famous *Papatrechas,* and his autobiography. Nonetheless, it is useful to observe that, throughout his long career, Koraes cultivated the literary form of the dialogue. Without doubt, we find here the French eighteenth century influence, the spirit which dominated a Fontanelle or a Voltaire. But we must not forget that the dialogue expressed simultaneously the tendencies toward renewal and a certain inclination toward equivocation, as we found it in the Renaissance, and as it was expedient to one or another intellectual interest of Koraes's group. Finally, it appears that the dialogue form was an expression of Koraes's personality, a desire for justice and equity, a didacticism. One would expect mention of his poetic inclinations as well. But the didactic intention found at the base of his endeavors, the literary climate of eighteenth century France in which he matured, necessarily restrained him from lyricism. For him, poetry was a servant of rhetoric; it served as an auxiliary element for persuasion. Prose was the medium that best suited him.

His correspondence was voluminous. More than one thousand letters have survived. Many of his letters intentionally have the character of a circular, such as when he wrote in his youth of Protopsaltis, or later when he made recommendations in connection with education, or when in old age he counselled the fighters of the War of Independence. His letters circulated from hand to hand, copies multiplied. Their essential characteristic is direct contact with life; whatever he wrote surged from life and its concerns. Certain of his descriptions, his impressions of revolutionary Paris have the tone of excellent journalistic reports. At other times, he remembered the old storytellers, his ancestors. He wrote with good humor, he possessed the qualities of a born narrator, the ability to observe and make the reader observe as well. He used the unexpected and the picturesque artistically. When he judged well, he inserted popular aphorisms, gnomic verses, sayings and anecdotes into his narratives. His famous "Dream" was written as a letter to Protopsaltis; it is a long narrative of a dream, vibrating with life from beginning to end, full of freshness and humor, without superfluity or pedantic didacticism. It was a genuine literary success.

Papatrechas was taken from his Prolegomena to the *Iliad*. There he sought to stress how much an enlightened clergy could offer to the rebirth of culture, but he also satirized the bad clergy. His art was so great, his ability to praise certain individual characteristics, to isolate the ridiculous, to sketch the form and thought of an individual in a few words, that he succeeded in drawing one of the most lively characters in modern Greek literature in a few pages. He was the first to create a human type which remains alive even today: it is Papatrechas. Modern Greek narrative prose began with the work of a scholar. What is characteristic is that Koraes did not invent Papatrechas; this time, as well, he drew from life. In his old age, he used memories of his early youth for his writings.

He wrote his *Autobiography* when he was around eighty years old. We should not seek youthful virtues in this short work. What prevails here is a quasi-formal tone, without being cumbersome, a style free of every rhetorical device. The seasons of flowers had passed; now it was time to harvest the fruit. Each phrase was carefully weighed, prudent, sober, and expressed the experience of life. "I have been attacked violently as an innovator, not only in matters pertaining to education, but even in those pertaining to religion. I regret now that I have countered these attacks. It would have been wiser to follow the precepts of Epictetus: ἔδοξεν αὐτῷ. A philosophic tone is imprinted in these words. While he still lived, it was remarked that Koraes's thought had an essentially philosophic turn and that his patriotism caused him to turn from philosophy to literature. His memoirs in 1803 are a sample of profound philosophic thought, but in all his works, the philosophic ideology of eighteenth century France is evident. The comparative method, the historical awareness, the theory of environment, as well as the contemporary acquisitions that stamp his thought so strongly serve his tendency to remain in contact with reality and place him securely in his period. The path followed by Voulgaris and Koraes is parallel, but we observe some subtle differences between them. Koraes never sought to withdraw from the spirit of his time, nor did he dream of resurrecting dead forms. The difference between these two intellectual leaders, in fact, permits us to measure the intellectual progress of Hellenism from the period of the former to that of the latter.

Koraes as Philosopher

With the resources and spirit we have examined in this chapter, Koraes expressed the Hellenic synthesis that was realized in his time. But his efforts were based on classicism, on the values of the past. In order to complete the intellectual evidence of the new Hellenic life, it is essential to appraise work based on this new Hellenism. It is that which Solomos sought and succeeded in accomplishing. But before discussing Solomos, we should mention an intermediary effort; this is the attempt Kalvos made to give form to the spirit of the times by associating the ancient with the new in an original manner. In the following chapter, the work of Kalvos is examined basically, along with various manifestations that parallel his work.

Chapter 14

Kalvos

"As an Idea of Joy"

Everything contributed at this time to the immense prestige that Koraes enjoyed. Hellenism, conscious of its cultural unity, needed an inellectual leader. And Koraes was infinitely greater and more illustrious than the other intellectuals of his period. He also had an imposing body of work which incorporated the ancient Hellenic glory; he had his friends, his followers, the periodicals, the various cultural movements of which he was the animator. Rare were the young scholars, contemporaries of Koraes, who did not benefit from his radiance; the simple manners of the period permitted them, for the most part, to seek contact with him. A letter of recommendation, a more or less fortuitous opportunity permitted entrance into a correspondence or a visit with him to seek his counsel. Whether they wrote essays, tragedies, or poetry, the young men sought Koraes's approbation. The two brothers Soutsos and John Zambelios went to see him with a letter of introduction; C. Kokkinakis sent him the translation of Moliere's *Tartuffe* and asked his advice. To each writer Koraes gave advice which concerned language alone, but also at times touched on matters of style and technique. Replying to Kokkinakis he pointed out to him the faults of his translations and indicated their causes: "In the first place, the difficulties are presented in your exact translation: the barbarous rhyme that has invaded us resembles a mange" (1816).

John Zambelios

In 1809, Koraes was visited by John Zambelios. The latter was born in Leukas in 1787 and had studied in Italy since 1804. It was there that he came to know Foscolo. His encounter with Foscolo, and much later with Koraes, determined the orientation of his literary career. In the interesting autobiography he wrote much later and left unpublished, he said, speaking of himself in the third person: "Foscolo and Koraes were the two great men who inspired in Zambelios the love of country and the glory and encouragement to write." Zambelios knew and admired Italian tragedy; he had the occasion to hear Foscolo's opinions and theories, which, precisely at this moment, agreed with the new verse of the theater. The classical teaching of Koraes was added to the neoclassicism of Foscolo. But after a brief sojourn in Paris, Zambelios returned to his country. In 1817 he published some verses under the title of *Anacreontics*. We note here something reminiscent of Goethe's *Faust:*

> I have studied Law, subtle Philosophy,
> Politics and foreign languages.
> What have I gained? Nothing!
> What does Law teach?

His relations with Koraes were not interrupted; Zambelios wrote to him asking his advice. He dreamed of becoming a tragic poet, and when he wrote his first tragedy, *Timoleon* (1818), he sent the manuscript to Koraes for his advice. Koraes advised him as expected: "I congratulate you on being contemptuous of rhyme." In his autobiography, Zambelios noted other recommendations Koraes gave him, such as saying that the iambic trimeter could help him, "in order to relieve you of the monotony of political verses."

Zambelios had no sympathy for romanticism. His tragedies tended to remain on classical lines; but his period is reflected in his work despite himself. Hence, numerous romantic elements are found in his tragedies; reminiscences of Schiller and Byron, melodramatic choruses, and the rest. Moreover, the didactic character which he attributed to tragedy oriented him, from the time of the War of Independence on, to a composition of works with a contemporary subject. What was an exception for classicism became almost a rule for Zambelios. The classic intention was manifested in an absolute manner only in verse and language. The verse tended to revive the iambic of tragedies. His effort in metrics, especially for the theater, should be appreciated for its true value; the iambic trimeter, as the versifier understood it, presented great variety and approached the natural course of prose by avoiding monotony, while continuing to remain within the limits of meter. His linguistics were inspired by the neoclassicism of Foscolo. These were the theories of the poet from Zakynthos—who spoke Italian—as they appeared when he wrote: "The literary language should borrow from the ancient language when it is necessary, and it should select and use phrases and idioms of the people." Thus, he settled for a bizarre linguistic mixture, where the ancient elements were mixed with contemporary, purely popular elements. But this manner of mixture neither elevated the demotic language to the level of the tragic nor did it invigorate the classical language. His idiom was cold and insipid, and when he surprises us, our amazement is not accompanied by any aesthetic pleasure.

A cerebral writer, who had no need to write or inspire or excite, Zambelios continued to the end of his life (1856) to write tragedies or to revise those he had written. However, because he refused to relinquish certain theoretical principles, he failed to develop. His last tragedies represent the survival of this genre as it had existed before the War of Independence.

There is a natural passage from Zambelios to Kalvos. The resemblances are not only external; they extend even to the meaning of their art. The same desire for elevation is found in both, even if their effort to exclude romantic elements. Their efforts are also parallel on two essential points, language and metrics. In language, they both sought a discriminating mixture of archaic elements with folk elements; in metrics, they both endeavored to eliminate the fifteen-syllable verse or to ignore rhyme. The resemblance between the two is evident: the same language, the same prosody; it often suffices to combine two verses of Kalvos to obtain the meter of Zambelios, as it is enough to separate the verses of Zambelios in order to obtain the verse of Kalvos. The difference between the two is that one remained mediocre, while Kalvos, the poet of the *Odes,* scorched his wings in approaching the flame of art.

Elizabeth Moutzan-Martinengo

Before discussing Kalvos, however, we must stop on another literary figure, Elizabeth Moutzan-Martinengo. The work of this young woman from Zakynthos is slight and remains unpublished for the most part. It was only in 1881 that her autobiography saw the light of day. She prefigures the Zakynthian mothers of Kalvos and Solomos, both of whom left a profound imprint in the souls of their literary sons. Evocation of Elizabeth Martinengo will help us revive the spirit of the times. She was born in 1801 and died in 1832. Her autobiography, written a short time before her death, is not only informative, but it is also a literary text of rare quality, one of the pure ornaments of modern Greek literature.

Her pages are characterized by a simplicity which arises from love of beauty, elevation, and spirituality. Sensibility, nobility, love of culture are the qualities which distinguish the spirit of this candid woman. The expression of her thought is also simple, pure, serene:

> This venerable priest, knowing that he could no longer instruct me more than he had already done, many times remarked to father that he should find an expert teacher to instruct me. But my father paid no attention to him, because he had in mind the old barbarian notion that women should be prevented from obtaining too much education. In Constantinople, the women were locked in their homes. It is only in the country that they are able to find the joy of life. . . .
>
> I accompanied my parents to the church. I had been going to mass since I was eight years old. I went out, I walked around, I sat beside the door of my home, I went to the window. All this was of little interest to others, but for me, always locked in the house, it was a great deal. . . .
>
> The ardent desire that I have known from instruction has only rendered me so sensitive that at every obstacle, even at one, I would wish myself dead."

So she grew up, so she lived, this noblewoman of Zakynthos at the beginning of the nineteenth century.

Kalvos

Andrew Kalvos was born to a noblewoman in Zakynthos in 1792. His father appears to have been an adventurer; from time to time a soldier, a mariner, a merchant, he abandoned his wife. In any case, after 1802 we find him definitely established in Italy with his children, that is to say, with Andrew and another son, much younger. Andrew lived approximately ten years with his mother; later, when he remembered her, he wept and often dreamed of her. The mother is the only feminine figure to occur in the poetry of Kalvos:

> O voice, O mother, firm consolation of my early years;
> Eyes which dampened my tender fears!

He retained certain childhood memories of his disturbed life in the country where he was born. We can imagine him with his deep, troubled eyes, observing the democratic holidays organized by the French, observing the popular enthusiasm, hearing the improvisations of orators and poets proclaiming their liberal convictions in a single voice. All this was done with a spiritual intensity and must have been engraved in his memory:

> I have never been dazzled by wealth and glorious titles.
> I have never been dazzled by the brilliance of sceptres.

The beauty of his island also remained vivid in his memory:

> Your climate is like perfume, O dear country,
> It enriches the sea with scents of golden cedars.

Later he left his birthplace. Installed in Livorno with his father, he lived in the rich Greek colony; he studied and became, in all probability, secretary to one of the brothers Zosimas. In any case, he had the opportunity in Livorno of following the new Greek publications, full of hymns on virtue and animated by pride in ancestral glory. But it was the acquaintance with Foscolo that finally oriented him toward a literary career. He was twenty years old when he met Foscolo. His illustrious compatriot, who was approaching thirty-five, advised him and inspired him into following his example. We have letters in which Foscolo advised Kalvos never to cease studying the classics. Following Foscolo, young Kalvos, who had already written verses in Italian, dreamed of becoming an Italian poet. He wrote odes, tragedies, essays, all in Italian. The small circle of merchants of the Greek colony at Livorno was effaced in his eyes by its mediocre knowledge of Greek literature. The popular element, which honored Foscolo, appeared to him a very poor substitute for his own high aspirations. In his remarks on meter, written in 1824, he spoke about "the monotony of Cretan verse." These are almost the same words that Zambelios used.

Art should aspire to greater heights, with a grandeur inspired by the ancient models and by important subjects; the language of literature should be based on the current language in order to give dignity to poetry. We should enrich "the ancient words," as Foscolo desired. Moreover, conforming to the same principles, we should exclude "the barbarous elements of rhyme," wrote Kalvos. We have no way of knowing if Koraes influenced this kind of thinking; the influence of Foscolo is indisputable.

In the meantime, we follow the life of Kalvos. His sorrow at separation from his mother was followed by other griefs. She died in 1815 without having seen her beloved son Andrew. We lose trace of his father after 1812. The young poet lived in poverty after his separation from his mother and saw the dissipation of his hope to study systematically. In England, he broke off with Foscolo; he earned a living by translations and private tutoring. He gave lectures on modern Greek subjects. His love life appears to have been intense. Finally, he married in England and had a daughter by this marriage. But sometime before 1821, Kalvos lost both his wife and child. It seems that he then contemplated suicide.

The poet appears to have been extremely sensitive from early youth. We recall the tears he had shed for his mother. He shed tears when he thought of Foscolo, who was separated from him; he shed tears when he was informed that a young man who was not even a friend of his had fallen ill; he shed tears when Foscolo criticized him for carelessness. His break with Foscolo revealed that both were irascible characters; their loves inflamed them and were extinguished over nothing. All this agrees with what we know of Kalvos's later character; that he was haughty, somber, irritable, serious, anxious, always ready to consider matters pessimistically insofar as his own existence was concerned. He lived a solitary life, he always dressed in black, and he even dyed his furniture black. He was also in ill health and he suffered from bad eyesight.

From 1821 we find him in Switzerland, where he published his first collection of poetry in 1824 under the title, *The Lyre*, a composition of ten odes. He published another volume of ten odes two years later in Paris, where he stayed for a time. It was from there, in fact, that all his production in the Greek language came, except for the metrical preface to *The Lyre*, and his remarks on metrics attached to his translation of the *Iliad*, published at the same time as his poetry. In 1830, there circulated in Kerkyra, where the poet was living at the time, a *Hymn to the Olive Tree*, written in the particular meter of the Kalvic ode; we cannot exclude that this was his work. As for other writings, nearly all we have of Kalvos after 1826 is in prose and in the Italian language.

In 1826 he returned to insurgent Greece, but he did not remain there. This same year he went to Kerkyra. He was to remain there until 1852, either as a private tutor or as a professor in higher education and even in the Ionian Academy. We note that for twenty-five years or more he lived in the same city with Solomos, but we find no evidence of direct contact between these two, even though they had common friends, such as Braïlas-Armenis. Much later, when time and death had effaced their personal oppositions, De Viazis thought to bring out a new edition of the writings of Kalvos. Polylas dissuaded him. In 1852 Kalvos left for England where he lived until his death in 1869.

Thus the aggregate of Kalvos's work in Greek that we have to examine here is composed of two small collections of poetry, published two years apart in 1824 and 1826. If we consider that almost all his *Odes* were inspired by the War of Independence, we ascertain that the lyrical production of Kalvos in the Greek language is contained between 1821 and 1826, a period when the poet was between twenty-nine and thirty-four years old. It was juvenilia, typically romantic, let us not forget.

Judging from the dates, we can say that the War of Independence gave us the poetry of Kalvos. It remains for us to reconstruct the moral and intellectual world of the poet around 1821. He was an unfortunate man. At an age when others still lived under family solicitude, Kalvos grew up far from his native land, far from his beloved mother. He lost both mother and father; the death of his wife and daughter destroyed the dream of a new hearth. He was separated from his great friend Foscolo under circumstances that could only have wounded him. He was melancholic, a recluse, erotically inclined, but inconstant. We must further bear in mind that these years, whether he was in Italy or England, or toward the end in France, the poet breathed romanticism. One of his odes is dedicated to the death of Byron. However, the vision of Kalvos's particular time would not be complete if we failed to consider how he incorporated neoclassical elements with the romantic.

We can approach the work of Kalvos in this manner. His education—all he could receive, or, in fact, all that he had received—was neoclassical. His poems often contain elements of the neo-Hellenic culture of the period, the virtue, the ancestors, and their glory. Contact with Foscolo came at a later, a critical and decisive stage. Foscolo taught him the principles governing poetry, the rules of versification, and the linguistic system. All this was inspired by neoclassicism which at that time constituted the theoretical world of the poet of *Graves;* in other words, borrowings from the ancients, imitation of their ways. Thus, the Greek and Italian formation of Kalvos were in accord: archaism, ancestors, virtue.

But this aggregate was not suited to the milieu in which he lived. Nor was it suited to Foscolo's earlier works, those of the preromantic period with which Kalvos had naturally become acquainted when he met Foscolo and became attached to him. Later, after the brusque and unpleasant rupture wtih Foscolo, a young man as sensitive as Kalvos could only turn against Foscolo's teachings, and conversely be attracted to the romantic mood, of which we find many traces in the *Odes,* as well as in the life and character of the poet.

Be that as it may, this was the intellectual world from which he derived his theories when he undertook to write in Greek. Now, he moved in a world clearly opposed to his spiritual world and to the atmosphere of his time. At the age of thirty-two, he was confronted with the inspiring experience of the War of Independence. His poetic spirit, his poetic temperament, his enthusiasm moved him to become the poet of insurgent Greece. At this time, he considered the problems of the Greek language (which do not appear to have concerned him earlier) in a more or less practical manner. What solutions did he have for these problems? They were almost the same problems which Solomos faced at this same period. Different points of departure lead to different solutions. Kalvos applied what he had been taught.

It was the popular verse that he took as a point of departure, the fifteen-syllable, but he had to be archaic. Kalvos broke the fifteen-syllable into two hemistichs, working independently of one another; he abolished rhyme and created a type of ancient verse, which recalled the Italian neoclassical metric groups but often revealed their neo-Hellenic origin. It is not rare that the hemistichs of Kalvos follow an absolutely regular form of the fifteen-syllable verses when placed together:

> Great and savage roll the mountains to the sea . . .
> It appears in the horizon as an idea of joy.

What saves the language and verse of Kalvos is that, under an elaborate scholarly garment, one senses the warmth of language and versification of the Greek people. The medley does not operate in an organic manner, which makes the "heteroclita" elements retain their independence. But this is not his only charm.

The Drama of the Poet

Another of his attractions comes from the personal drama which harassed the poet and which is reflected in his work. From his desparate personal life, to which was added a strong dose of romanticism, tears, melancholy, despair, ruin, and cloudy skies, Kalvos undertook to exalt the heroic deeds of people who were just emerging into the light of freedom, palpitating with life. He sought to make this contrast by using the teachings of neoclassicism, which had enriched his thought throughout his entire youth. The impact between this internal sadness and the classical form gives a dramatic tone to all his work, and this is one source of our emotion. In the austere and cold form of Kalvos's *Odes*, one easily distinguishes the pathetic voice of an Ossian or a Young, the voice of the poetry nourished by romanticism. As could have been foreseen, moreover, the poet exploits his desperation and utilizes the matter even in his poetry; a play of oppositions passes constantly before the reader. The teachings of romanticism agreed with the needs of the poet. The structure of the odes often obeys the law of opposition, as do the succession of images and the reconciliation of ideas:

> Thus, in the camp of the barbarians, one hears the cries, the drums and blows. But death in harness, they regard without fear.

And elsewhere:

> Fate has ravished the laurel of victory as it has been woven with myrtles and branches of the funereal cypress, another crown.

Technique

Antithesis and accumulation were the common ways in which the world habitually presented itself to Kalvos. With art, he succeeded in combining his classical culture with the romantic atmosphere of the period and with his own romantic sentiments. His comparisons showed the full range that unite these two tendencies. At times, he began in a Pindaric manner.

We have now arrived at his technique. The arrangement of the *Odes* is simple and rational. He follows a syllogism: a general idea, a particular application, a conclusion. This plan is elaborated by descriptions, flights, prayers; in a word, all the elements of lyricism. Thus classical thought and romantic sentimentality are combined on the first level. Likewise, the general idea is elevated, the application is passionate, the conclusion is noble. The alternation of images, which are always on a grand scale, whatever the origin, and that of emotions, which are always forceful, hold us in perpetual tension, without an annoying feeling of letdown. The rare lowering of tone, when it is not owing to an awkward use of a term, or, more rarely, of an image, is caused by the prosaic elements classicism introduces into the verses.

The language of Kalvos is considered antipoetic, which is the cause of most drops in his tone. It is certainly an antipoetic language, an artificial elaboration, deprived of the indispensable natural association with tradition. However, first of all, we see that the language is not entirely dissociated from its roots. Then this impotent instrument permits us to distinguish better the poet's personal part in the creation of his poetry; the charm of the popular language, which later contributed so often to masking mediocrity, is entirely missing in Kalvos. Whatever we receive is given by the poet. And he gives us a great deal.

His verse of seven syllables is dense and supports with difficulty the excessive elaboration which, furthermore, is contrary to the poet's theories. Each word is detached and imposes itself on our awareness, powerful and autonomous:

> Ἔσφαλεν ὁ τὴν δόξαν
> ὀνομάσας ματαίαν,
> He is deceived who considers glory futile;

or:

> Ἔφθασ᾽ ἡ ὥρα· φύγε.
> The moment has arrived, now depart.

Or even:

> Τὴν ἐκλογὴν ἐλεύθερον
> δίδει τὸ θεῖον.
> Divinity gives us freedom of choice.

Not only is elaboration unnecessary; it is not even tolerable. The adjective exists everywhere; it completes the noun and creates an entirely new irreducible unity. I should further mention about words his search for etymological precision: τὸ πνεῦμα τῶν ἀνέμων, with *pneuma* used in the sense of blast of wind. It is certainly a scholarly poetry, one that presupposes a very long preparation for its enjoyment. The abuse of mythological elements accentuates its scholarly character dangerously, because these elements are a contribution of classicism, as well as a love for periphrasis.

But lyricism gushes through all this. Force is associated with grace, elevation with tenderness.

> As a proud myrtle, full of flowers and dew,
> When the dawn girdled by gold salutes it. . . .

I mention the ode he dedicated to Zakynthos, in which the verse is softened by means of synizesis or else acquires the sonority and resonances of oratory. Great visions and epic images pass through the *Odes* without surprising us; this poetry is in a state of perpetual exaltation: the torrents, the lions, the blinding light of the sun. And alongside, warmer, more subjective, is the wealth of romanticism.

> All the Earth is covered by large somber wings,
> Calm and chill of the profound night. . . .
> The sky with clouds arrayed in black wings,
> The moon in its cold obole. . . .

Ideas

The ideas of the poet, the ideas of his time which nourished the reborn Hellenism, were these: national pride, liberalism, moral preoccupations, tendencies for renewal. On this level, synthesis is realized, but it is not realized on the level of art; the elements of tradition are all brought up here, but they are not unified. The poet knew the importance of these elements, as he had known the importance of synthesis, but he was unable to accomplish the latter. Thus, all this universe, all this richness, could not become organic, could not become fertile. The poet himself stopped before this impasse. Succeeding generations have often paused with admiration on

the *Odes,* but they refused to continue on this unrewarding path.
The work of Kalvos remained without heirs. Years were to pass before his work became an element of tradition, before it could be
evaluated properly, when the entire tradition spoke again in the
souls of the Greeks, following the purification securied by demoticism. At the beginning of the new evaluation of Kalvos, we find
Palamas. He brought Kalvos to scholars' attention at a conference
held in 1889. A few years later, in 1897, the *Iambs and Anapaests* of
Palamas would have their metrical source in Kalvos. It was the beginning of a restoration which was finally achieved in our own days.

What Kalvos did not accomplish, Solomos did: the essential synthesis of traditional elements in a new art. The following chapter
examines the success of Solomos. We are at the peak of our modern
Greek *History.*

Chapter 15

Solomos

"A Mixed Genre,
but Legitimate"

We find in Solomos the same struggle which characterized Kalvos's attempt to achieve art, although Solomos was victorious in this attempt. He succeeded in subduing and unifying the elements of romanticism and classicism, which remained unreconciled in the work of Kalvos. In a note addressed to himself, Solomos wrote: "Consider well if this is to be in the romantic genre, or, if possible, classical, or in a mixed genre, but legitimate. A perfect example of the second kind is Homer; of the first, is Shakespeare. I know of no example for the third." The third kind was the ideal goal which Solomos sought and found. Kalvos sought this goal, but he was unable to attain it.

However, in passing from Kalvos to Solomos, one tends to consider their parallelism; to the last details one finds enlightening comparisons and contrasts. They share the same island, the same period, expatriation; there are resemblances and differences. Kalvos began with the limited culture which contemporary Greece offered him; contact with the foreign intellectual world followed, and he was dazzled by his acquaintance with it. The aristocratic Solomos started out with Italian culture and discovered, at an opportune moment, the new Hellenism as the foreign force, admirable and fertile. And even closer spiritually, we should remember the aristocratic mother of Kalvos, the plebeian mother of Solomos. The maternal influence so fundamental to personality formation was equally stamped on both poets, but it was exercised in an inverse manner.

Early Years

Dionysios Solomos was born in Zakynthos in 1798 of an aged father, the Count Nicholas, and a very young mother, Angeliki Niklis, who was a servant in the house. Shortly before his death in

1807, Nicholas legalized his relationship with Angeliki making their two children legitimate. The guardians of Dionysios, undoubtedly wishing to remove him from the influence of his plebeian mother, hastened to send him to Italy, first to Italian teachers at Italian schools and later to the University of Padua, where he studied law. Even in Zakynthos, the language of the nobility was Italian. The sons of better families spoke Italian and were taught that language in their homes.

"The instruction of children begins with Italian," wrote Polylas. "The first teacher of Solomos was also Italian." His few letters, then, the few readings and conversations which occurred in his paternal environment were all in Italian. Solomos unquestionably had a thorough knowledge of the Greek language, first by reason of his age, but also because of conditions in childhood. It has been correctly observed that, when he later wrote in Greek, his handwriting was not Greek; he did not form his letters as did men of his time who had been taught from childhood to write in Greek; he formed them in the manner of foreigners.

This, however, does not signify that the Greek language was unknown to him. His mother, with her different social background, must have spoken to him in Greek, must have sung lullabies and other songs in Greek. Indicative is the phrase which Solomos noted about *The Shepherdess* a few years after his return to Zakynthos. He said: "There is no woman in Zakynthos" who does not know the work. We know the Greek spoken by his mother. She was illiterate, and whenever she dictated her letters, she used a warm, folk idiom, picturesque and charming. Thus, Greek not only lived in his consciousness, but Solomos had the affection for it of part of his childhood. And this childhood universe was apparently highly developed; the few evidences we possess on Solomos during his childhood years, before his departure for Italy, show him extremely sensitive to the beauties of nature and endowed with a precocious tendency toward dreaming and toward religiosity.

Italy

These dispositions were accentuated when he separated from his mother; his intellectual world began to be enriched by the intense intellectual movement taking place at that time in Italy. In Italy,

Solomos early exhibited his inclination toward letters; he wrote verses in Latin and Italian which stirred the admiration of his professors. He became a part of Italian literary circles, became acquainted with Monti, who was the most famous Italian poet of the time. Already, his personality had begun to take form. One day he said to Monti: "The mind must first conceive and then the heart must feel warmly what the mind has conceived." He was influenced by Manzoni, in particular by his collection *Inni Sacri* (1815), as his first Italian poems show. He also admired Foscolo, and it appears that he was early interested in his life, work, and ideas. In 1827 when he learned of the death of the poet of *Graves,* Solomos, twenty years old at the time, pronounced a very beautiful memorial eulogy in Italian. The intense controversy taking place in Italy between romanticism and neoclassicism did not leave him indifferent. He sought a personal solution. However, these literary preoccupations did not absorb all his attention; he was interested in other intellectual questions; the problem of language so closely allied in Italy to the conflict of ideas could not leave him indifferent. On this point, he appears to have been especially influenced by the ideas of the French Enlightenment; culture for all based on a national language. These theories concerning the importance of primitive, popular creation, which would include the folksong, became his preoccupation at the same time. In his *Dialogue,* Solomos used evidence from classical and later literatures: Italian, English, German, and French. But his scientific arguments were based on the thoughts of French Enlightenment. He mentions the precursors, Bacon and Locke, and among the most important representatives of the Enlightenment in France, d'Alembert and Condillac.

Zakynthos

Such was the world that Solomos took with him when, at the age of twenty in 1818, he returned home from Italy. His theoretical formations were removed from every Greek intellectual tradition, but rich in aesthetic experiences. He believed in the value of national traditions; he believed in folk art and folk language. These convictions were in harmony with his feelings, which were a mixture of religious tradition, folksong, and the maternal tongue. Greece did not appear to him as a common ground for scholarly teaching, but as a living reality, which one must come to know as an ideal, which one must conquer. The conquest of the idea of Hellenism constituted the central theme of his life. With the same fervor in everything that he believed, he began to study the living elements of his country. We know that in Zakynthos he busied himself collecting folksongs that the people had preserved. Returning to his island, with such preparation and such a disposition, Solomos found fertile soil on which to work, for the Cretan tradition that had passed over to the Ionian Islands had, as we have seen, been cultivated in Zakynthos in a particularly fortunate manner. We know from Solomos himself and from other sources that works like *The Shepherdess* or *Erotokritos* lived in the popular memory on Zakynthos. Original literary production was associated on one hand with the Cretan tradition and on the other hand with direct Venetian influence. Here we can cite the poets of the eighteenth century, who wrote in the popular language and whose technique derived from the Cretan tradition.

These poets are such men as Katiphoros, Danelakis, John Kantounis (1731–1817), and Kokondris. The last continued the tradition of the Cretan rhymed ballad, with all the richness of the Cretan technique. Danelakis wrote not only lyric poems, which exhibit a remarkable lyric gift and an advanced technique of Western inspiration, but he also wrote satiric verses. Let us remember that satire had been cultivated in the Ionian Islands, and that the satires of Katiphoros were mentioned in this *History* as manifestations of a precocious new lyricism in the Ionian Islands. Let us remember further that we also found in Zakynthos the rhymed ballads, with meters and metrical constructions that show a long familiarity with the difficulties of versification. Stephen Xanthopoulos was the oldest poet of this group mentioned here. His best period should be considered the middle of the eighteenth century. He was a mediocre lyric poet, lacking originality, but one who understood how to associate reminiscences of the Cretan tradition with Italian influences in his work. His language also indicated that the language had been artistically elaborated by writers who had preceded him.

The creation of verses, especially satiric ones, appears to have been a characteristic practice of the Ionian Islands. Nicholas Koutouzis (1741–1813), a painter, left some satiric poetry. Nicholas Logothetis used satire in his political campaigns. Of all these scholars, however, Anthony Martelaos and Demetrios Gouzelis have the greatest importance. They interest us particularly because they introduced elements of French culture into the Italian milieu of the Ionian Islands.

Anthony Martelaos (1754–1818) was a professor, an ecclesiastical orator, and a poet. He wrote patriotic verses in the folk language. It is a well-known fact that one of his works, "Hymn to Glorious France, to the Commander-in-Chief Bonaparte and to General Gentilly," would provide inspiration for Solomos:

> Ὅθεν εἰσθε τῶν Ἑλλήνων
> παλαιὰ ἀνδρειωμένα
> κόκκαλα ἐσκορπισμένα
> λάβετε τώρα πνοήν.

> You scattered bones
> Valiant as of old
> You belong to the Greeks
> Come now take new life.

Martelaos attacked the aristocracy of his island:

> How can human speech relate
> Misfortunes raised by nobles,
> The pillagings
> And the injustices.

To complete the picture of this period's intellectual currents, as they appear even in Martelaos, we should point out that, along with the demotic, this revolutionary man also used the archaic language, and he defended it theoretically: "Lightning and thunder . . . how Koraes has ruined his language." However, it seems possible that in his maturity, his ideas generally became more conservative. His popular poems circulated widely, even beyond the Ionian Islands.

Demetrios Gouzelis (1774–1848) was a nephew of Martelaos and his student. He followed the same liberal path of his teacher. Gouzelis continued the Zakynthian comedy, whose oldest representative was Savogias Soumerlis (or Rousmelis). It appears that comedy had passed without interruption from Crete to Zakynthos where we encounter theatrical performances which showed great interest in Cretan comedy. Moreover, since the Ionian Islands revealed themselves to be a region amenable to the development of satire, a fundamental element of ancient comedy, it was also a favorable place for the development of comedy. Gouzelis's inclination for literature was manifested early with surprising maturity. In 1790 he wrote a comedy entitled *Hasis,* which has remained, even to our days, one of the most remarkable accomplishments of the modern Greek theater. This work was written in the meter of Cretan comedy, in political couplets. Gouzelis broke the monotony of the couplets with other meters, which we will find later in Solomos. His language was idiomatic, that of Zakynthos, and it contained all the vigor of the natural language. The poet was a lively observer, amusing in his flippant language:

> He's gone, but he is late, he is a lazy dawdler,
> He goes on an errand as a child, returns as an old man.

His dialogue often took the form of stichomythia, which gave a rapid rhythm to the comedy. Monologues were short. This was no comedy of manners. Gouzelis painted a human type, a quarrelsome braggart not lacking in courage and abilities:

> Am I not he who played this joke on the Jew?
> That makes me famous when I tell it, and I shudder?
> O, how I remember!

Hasis was published very late, after the War of Independence. But it circulated widely in manuscript form throughout the Ionian Islands, where it was also performed, despite the lack of scenery which characterized comedy. In 1800 Gouzelis published a short satire, *The Brawl of Saint Roch,* translated from the French *L' echauffourée de Saint Roch.* This work is mentioned only for its liberal and progressive character. Gouzelis himself has been mentioned here only because his early works belong to this period, and this helps familiarize us with the milieu which Solomos knew in 1818. The poet of *Hasis* later took an entirely different path; he became prudent, and we find him profoundly changed during the years of the War of Independence.

The Circle of Zakynthos

But in addition to tradition and the more general climate of Zakynthos in 1818, we find at this same period a circle of friends who assisted Solomos on the difficult path that he will learn to follow. I mention three of these friends: Anthony Matesis, Dionysios Tagliapieras, and Spiros Trikoupis. All three have their own place in a history of Greek letters, but they must be mentioned here as well.

Matesis was an ardent demoticist during his early years; Tagliapieras acquainted Solomos with Vilaras. Tagliapieras was a man of wide, general culture, who lived at the court of Ali Pasha after a long period spent in Paris. Thus Solomos had occasion to learn the partial language synthesis which Vilaras had achieved. Finally, there was Spiros Trikoupis (1788–1873). Having completed his studies in the West, he returned to Greece as one of the first to fight for his country. In 1821, he published a poem under the title, "The People, A Klephtic Poem." In a prefatory note, the poet explained that, because he was writing "for the people," he used the meter and language of the people. The following year, he was in Zakynthos where he became acquainted with Solomos, who expressed regrets that he did not know the Greek language sufficiently well to write in it. Trikoupis offered to assist him and they began by studyng the *Lyrical Works* by Christopoulos. Solomos was to profit from his knowledge of both Vilaras and Christopoulos. Their roots extended deeper and deeper into Hellenism. During this same period, Solomos asked for and read other metrical works dating from the end of the Turkish Occupation.

Early Works

In Zakynthos, Solomos wrote verses in Italian; he also wrote his first verses in Greek, either in the metrical tradition of Crete, or in that of Zakynthos, or even according to his knowledge of Italian metrics. When he wrote in Greek, he sought the Hellenicity of his themes, though his inspiration was profoundly influenced by romanticism and the romantic meditation on death and the grave:

> Ocean, when will I see the fair Eurycome?
> A long time has passed and she has not yet come.
> How often stooping on the rock anxiously and pale
> Mistook the foam of the sea for her white sail!
> Bring her back, bring her at last! So Thyrses exclaims,
> And takes water from the sea, kisses it, and complains;
> And he doesn't know, the miserable, that he is kissing the wave
> The same that has given her death as well as a grave.
>
> (taken from *Eurycome*, trans. by M. Byron Raizis)

As for everything else, his world was simple, his inspiration usually took him to nature. He developed a tendency toward idealism. An elegiac tone predominated. His language was simple, without grandiloquence and great embellishment. Some awkwardness is visible in his versification.

In the meantime, the War of Independence had erupted. This great experience embraced the poet's soul. Within a few weeks, in the spring of 1823, he composed the *Hymn to Liberty*, which remained unpublished until 1825. This *Hymn*, as well as *For the Death of Lord Byron* (1824), shows certain weaknesses that have been pointed out in the early Greek poems of Solomos. He himself left us most severe criticism in notes to the manuscript of the second poem. Moreover, in these pieces, where he attempted long poems (158 and 166 strophes of four-verse stanzas), we find certain weaknesses in composition which contain a number of prose or rhetorical elements. Nonetheless, we already sense that we are concerned with a poet who goes beyond all that he had found in his native land and all that he himself had created before this time. The long epic conceptions, the rich visions of imagination, the idealism which will always constitute one objective for Solomos enlighten his creations from this point on. His accents were added to his range without loss of soft tones. In the poem on Byron, he artistically played with antitheses and emphasized the importance of words of association. His poetic awareness was mature. "The difficulty which the writer feels (I refer to the great writer) is not found in the expression of his imagination or of passion, but in the subordination of these two elements, which takes much time and much work, for the meaning of Art." Images of horror alternate with idyllic images:

> Σὰν ποτάμι τὸ αἷμα ἐγίνη
> καὶ κυλάει στὴ λαγκαδιά,
> καὶ τὸ ἀθῶο χόρτο πίνει
> αἷμα ἀντὶς γιὰ τὴ δροσιά.
>
> .   .   .   .
>
> Στὸ χορὸ γλυκογυρίζουν
> ὡραῖα μάτια ἐρωτικά,
> καὶ εἰς τὴν αὔρα κυματίζουν
> μαῦρα, ὁλόχρυσα μαλλιά.

At this same period, he shows perfection of technique in his epigram on the destruction of the island of Psara (1825) and mature idealism in the poem "The Poisoned One" (1826). Harmony, sense of language, sense of sobriety, imagination, elevation of thought, he possesses all of these. The way to his great creation has opened for him.

Dialogue

Parallel evidence of his success during these years is given by his prose *Dialogue,* presumed to have been composed between 1823 and 1825. This concerns a fervent defense of the popular language, directed without discrimination against archaism and Koraes. The dialogue unfolds between three people: the pedant, the poet, and the friend. As appears from an autographed outline, the friend was Spiros Trikoupis. We have no definite name for the pedant, but at that time, Hermanos Loundzis (1806–1866), later a historian of the Ionian Islands, was studying in Zakynthos. In his unpublished autobiography, Loundzis remembered with horror his Greek professor. "I had as professor in Greek, Anastasios Karavias, the most pedantic of pedants, who was repulsive to look on. I remember the offensive sore he had on his neck at the time, from which pus dripped. The ugly face, the shaggy hair, which knew no other comb except his fingernails, the tiny bleary eyes with the eyelids destroyed by smallpox, which had also marked his face, the absurdity of his teaching, the hell of his grammar, the vulgarity of his character, the coarseness of manners of this professor; all these contributed to inspire me with an invincible distaste for Greek letters." His experience occurred shortly after 1818. The pedant in the dialogue shows similar characteristics. Karavias was among the acquaintances of Solomos.

Solomos resorted to arguments of recent demoticism; he knew the letters of Katartzis, the parts which treated of language in the books of Christopoulos, the *Grammar* and the *Dream,* and perhaps those of Vilaras. As we observed above, he was equally in contact with comparable French texts. But the passage from the Greek Enlightenment to Solomos is felt. I do not mean only the fervor and the spirit pulsing through the *Dialogue,* but more particularly the extension of critical thought into the world of the soul. If we find in Solomos also the ascendancy of reason, the awareness of history, the meaning of popular education, certain other thoughts we encounter are new: "Go, then, make a tour of Greece, go find the young girl, ask with what words she can say that the supreme beauty of her body is her honor. Go seek the captains, feel their wounds, and tell them that they ought to be called 'lesions.' Go find the white-haired man who remembers how much blood Ali Pasha has cost us, and ask him the words that should evoke the cruelly slaughtered children, young girls, old men, some sixty thousand in all. . . ."

The sentimental elements, particularly the emotional burden of language, is recognizable here for the first time, and this turns a new page in Hellenic intellectual history: we see the end of the intellectualism, which has characterized Greek culture since the first manifestations of the Phanariots. The timid thrill of Greek pre-romanticism now becomes an imperious awareness; the theoretical manifestations of Koraes become an element of life in Solomos. We expect something new in his art.

The Woman of Zakynthos

Besides the prose writing of *Dialogue,* we should mention the other Greek prose work of Solomos, *The Woman of Zakynthos,* which dates around the same period of 1826. The work is a satire whose content, however, is not entirely clear from the poor manuscript we have today. It is a satire full of imagination, vigor, and passion, written in the vocabulary and syntax of a pure demotic language, enriched in expression and images by the intellectual and spiritual treasures of the past.

At the beginning of the work, a monk speaks. He is leaning against the mouth of a well and says:

> And the Just, according to the Scriptures, how many are there? Reflecting thus, my eyes glanced at my hands which were resting of the well. Wishing to count the Just men on my fingers, I raised my left hand from the well, and looking at the fingers on my right hand, I said: Are there perhaps too many fingers? And I began to enumerate the number of Just men I knew on those five fingers. Finding that these were more than enough fingers, I removed the little one, concealing it between the well and my palm. And I stood looking at the four fingers for a long time, feeling a strong emotion, because I saw that I should remove yet another finger; so I placed the next finger beside the little one. There remained only three fingers under my gaze. I struck restlessly on the well to aid my spirit in finding at least three Just

men. But because my entrails began to quiver like the sea, which is ever in motion, I raised my three fingers and I made the sign of the Cross.

Elsewhere, the "Women of Missolonghi" must have passed as refugees to Zakynthos: "At the beginning, they were ashamed to come out and they waited for darkness to extend a hand; they were not accustomed to begging, for they had had servants and they had had many goats and sheep and cattle on many plains. They waited impatiently, often looking out the window at the sunset, at which time they could emerge. But when needs were pressing, they lost all embarrassment and they ran about all day long. When they became exhausted, they sat by the seashore and listened, because they were afraid that Missolonghi might capitulate." The juxtaposition of phrases confers to the text a Biblical simplicity, which, while remaining in the spirit of the Greek popular language, harmonized with the prophetic spirit the poet possessed.

"The fact that Solomos had not been touched by scholarly tradition was, in this instance, a blessing," writes Linos Politis, editor of his works. "It is thus that his contact with the popular element remained so spontaneous and fruitful." Similar observations are made in another chapter of this *History* concerning Makriyannis. But what distinguishes Solomos is his scholarly intention to transform the popular language into an instrument of art.

The Woman of Zakynthos remained unpublished until our times. Other metrical satires, which Solomos wrote when he was living in Zakynthos, appear to have circulated in manuscript form throughout a very wide circle. In *Dream,* we find the vigor of passion, indignation, faith in virtue, satiric elements which, though inferior linguistically and technically to his later metrical work, relates directly to *The Woman of Zakynthos.* Two other youthful satires of Solomos have survived; they are light, facetious, obviously intended not to censure evil but to entertain a circle of friends. One observes in these also the influence from works of the same genre by Vilaras. In the later satires, however, we find the vigorous works showing the lyrical elevation which characterized the later production of Solomos.

Furthermore, life on Zakynthos, as portrayed in Solomos's satires or the youthful satiric verses of Matesis, revealed a social climate that was not conducive to intense intellectual activity. This was a life turned outward toward the world, where friends encroach on the hour reserved for isolation and meditation. The poet, ascending toward the summits of artistic awareness, reached a level of work irreconciliable with such an existence. He conceived a plan of vast epic-lyric compositions whose realization would require intense and exclusive concentration on his part. In 1823 a real incident gave him the first idea for *Lambros*. It was to be a long poem, divided into Byronic episodes, which would illustrate the poet's patriotic interests. In 1826 the capitulation of Missolonghi inspired another long poem of similar character, *Duty,* which later was called *Missolonghi* or *The Free Besieged.* In 1828 at the age of thirty, the poet decided to leave his native island and he went to Kerkyra where he hoped to find the peace he needed for his great compositions.

In Kerkyra

Indeed, during the first years, his letters from Kerkyra overflowed with the joy of productive isolation that he had created around himself: "It is truly sweet to be able to express what the heart dictates in the peace of a small room." Elsewhere, he wrote that he lived "the existence of a hermit." Or even that "no one lives well except when he is alone." The works of these years were, of course, an extension of his period in Zakynthos and were stamped by maturity. Solomos polished his popular language, fashioned a new fifteen-syllable verse, elaborated on *The Woman from Zakynthos, Lambros,* and *The Free Besieged.* Short meters always concerned him. *Lambros* was written in ottava rima. In 1834 the publication of a poem fragment gave him an idea for the perfection of the technique which he had now achieved.

> And Maria comes forth seeking the solace
> Of coolness for her hope-forsaken breast;
> The night is sweet, and the full-moon's face
> Has not emerged any star's glow to contest;
> Multitudes, myriads, they glimmer in all their grace
> Some solitarily, some others abreast;
> They too are celebrating the Resurrection
> That is mirrored on the calm sea's reflection.
> (taken from *Lambros,* trans. by M. Byron Raizis)

Absolute mastery of verses, a wise use of synthesis, and the other musical elements of language, such as alternating consonants with vowels, a developed linguistic culture, clarity of images, richness of imagination characterize the eleven-syllable verses of *Lambros.* The promise Solomos had showed in Zakynthos are realized here: this synthesis of romantic inspiration and classical technique show that it was the "mixed genre" which Solomos sought to create. Even if this were his only work left us, Greece would still have had a great poet in Solomos.

Some of his older poems in short meters found in the *The Two Brothers* and *The Mad Mother* are incorporated in *Lambros*. The rapid rhythm of his verses, with its frequent repetition of rhyme, no longer fits with the tragic subject in each of these poems. We get the same impression from the first draft of *The Free Besieged*. The work would have represented a synthesis, through the sacrifice at Missolonghi, of the spirit of the revolution and the spirit of the fighters. Here, as well, the poet uses meters that better accord with the laws of harmony, as they were taught by Italian verse.

> Apart stands the warrior
> With tears in his eyes
> Then slowly lifting
> His rifle, he cries:
> "What use are you, musket,
> In this hand so shaken?
> My enemy knows it:
> To me you are a burden."
> (taken from *The Free Besieged,*
> Draft I, trans. by M. Byron Raizis)

There is an obvious contrast between the elevation, the seriousness of inspiration, and the verse to which the poet resorts.

Idealism

During his first five years in Kerkyra, however, Solomos had other preoccupations, which would fortify even more his high awareness of the poet's duties. We know that already in 1830 he was interested in German thought; he studied the German philosophers and poets in translation. We possess precise evidence concerning Schiller and Schlegel. Later, he was assisted to a better understanding of these two by Nicholas Lountzis, brother of Hermanos, who had been educated in Germany, perhaps also by the educator John Menagias, who contributed to the development of idealism in the Ionian Islands, and by Spiros Zambelios, son of John, who was also deeply influenced by German idealism. Schelling and Hegel aided the poet in his natural movement toward grasping the concept of an ideal world. Parallel with his, he studied Cretan poetry, enriched his vocabulary, expanded the potential offered by the fifteen-syllable couplet. Idealism and linguistic versification experience multiplied his requirements. He returned, matured by work and fully aware of his responsibilities, to the simple attempts of his youth. But his efforts acquired a new meaning. He wrote Tertsetis in Italian in 1833: "I rejoice that folksongs are taken as a point of departure; I would wish, however, that whoever uses the language of the klephtes do so in its substance and not in its form. . . . It is good that one should set his roots in such a model, but it is also bad to stop there. He should rise vertically. . . . The klephtic poetry is beautiful and interesting, because it was used by the klephtes to describe their lives, their ideas, and their sentiments. But it was not the same interest in our mouths. The nation expects us to carry the treasures of our own thoughts, dressed in a national costume."

The distichs of *The Cretan* (1833–1834) results from these rewritings. The melody emanating from these verses was the echo of a soul confronted by the ideal and aspiring to attain the absolute. Remaining strictly attached to the poetic tradition of Crete, the new manner of Solomos was ethereal; the harsh consonants were missing from the language, a magical charm envelopes the verses with a mysterious veil. Inspiration was also of an ideal nature. The vision of *The Cretan* constituted the most precise expression in the poetry of Solomos during this period; clear images confer on the verses an absolute clarity, the clarity of spirit.

Κι ἀπὸ τὸ πέλαο, ποὺ πατεῖ χωρὶς νὰ τὸ σουφρώνει,
κυπαρισσένιο ἀνάερα τ' ἀνάστημα σηκώνει,
κι ἀνεῖ τς ἀγκάλες μ' ἔρωτα καὶ μὲ ταπεινοσύνη,
κι ἔδειξε πᾶσαν ὀμορφιὰ καὶ πᾶσαν καλοσύνη.

.   .   .   .   .   .

῎Ελεγα πὼς τὴν εἶχα ἰδεῖ πολὺν καιρὸν ὀπίσω,
κὰν σὲ ναὸ ζωγραφιστὴ μὲ θαυμασμὸ περίσσο,
κάνε τὴν εἶχε ἐρωτικὰ ποιήσει ὁ λογισμός μου,
κὰν τ' ὄνειρο, ὅταν μ' ἔθρεφε τὸ γάλα τῆς μητρός μου·
ἤτανε μνήμη παλαιή, γλυκιὰ κι ἀστοχισμένη,
ποὺ ὀμπρός μου τώρα μ' ὅλη της τὴ δύναμη προβαίνει.

And on the surface of the sea that does not ripple
as she walks, she stands stately as a cypress, and
opens her arms in a gesture of love and humility;

she is all beauty, all goodness. . . . It seemed to me
that I had seen her long ago, or else I had admired
her desperately, painted in a temple; or else my
spirit had imagined her amorously, or else I had
dreamed of her when I was still suckling on my
mother's breast; it was an old memory, sweet and
hazy, that now appeared before me in all its force.

In such poetry, form is inseparable from substance. It is the culmination of the happiest period in Solomos's life, that is, the first
five years after his departure from Zakynthos.

His poetic world tends to the sublime: the poet demands much
from his art. Facile improvisation is condemned. Poetry should be
the result of spiritual maturity, security and equilibrium, the
serenity and elevation of the poet's meditation, and the full possession of technique. Euphoria characterizes this period: a euphoria
stimulated by the creative desire and creative spirit. Animated by
the ideal of what art should be, Solomos again took up *The Free
Besieged*. It resulted in a new poetic pattern; the old inspiration was
subdued by the new aesthetic will.

The good Souliot stands apart and cries:
"My poor musket, why do I hold you in my hand?
You have become a burden to me and the Turk knows it."

The poet devoted himself henceforth to this work; he put all his
energies into completing it. Greece and the Great Idea were one in
his spirit. In a note written in Italian, he says: "Enclose Greece in
your soul, and you will feel all forms of grandeur." Of this long effort, which continued for some ten years, until 1844, a number of
verses, fragments, and improved units exist as evidence.

Turning Point in 1833

But the happy period had passed; a sad family affair, which obliged
Solomos to appear in court against his mother, deeply affected him.
The peace to which he had aspired, and which had offered him so
many benefactions, abandoned him forever. The trial against his
mother lasted from 1833 to 1838. "If his spirit emerged from the
battle, and was perhaps even fortified, the mode of his life, however,
changed. . . . His heart remained mortally wounded," wrote Polylas. The poet became more and more withdrawn, but there, before
the sanctuary of his tragic and shattered soul the world awaited him.

Aside from reworking *The Free Besieged,* which Polylas mentions, we know of no other work he did during this period. Time to work intensively on material already conceived were there, but these years were unfavorable for new creations. He lacked the necessary calm and concentration. His work was done in an irregular and spasmodic fashion; creative effort required another manner.

We do not know at what moment Solomos was liberated from these fetters. At some moment, which should not be placed after 1844, he again found serenity. But the old joy and euphoria had left him forever. The worlds of imagination that had been familiar to him for years, now became his only refuge from the ugliness of life. His new artistic ideal would correspond to this last creative period: more austere, more sombre, more hermetic. The elements of melody and sensual pleasure no longer agree with the poet's mood. If the formal and imposing fifteen-syllable verse was always the verse appropriate to his poetic inspiration, the charm of rhyme, the soft cadences offered by synizesis, disappeared from his work. The harsh ideal of a man who has known the tragic aspect of life found an appropriate form in the fifteen-syllable verse; it was robust, plastic, colorless, something approaching the work of a marble sculptor. "The higher he climbed to the light of *Idea,* the more seriously he felt about the dignity of his art," wrote Polylas.

For the third time, in 1844, he took up *The Free Besieged* and remodeled it in accordance with these new, more secure, laws. The verse is slow, sonorous; the long words are full of resonances. A sobriety associated with charm offers us once more the mixed character that remained the poet's persistent ideal:

> Water clear and sweet, full of charm and magic
> Flows and pours into an abyss of fragrance,
> Taking the perfume with it, leaving coolness behind.
> > (taken from *The Free Besieged,*
> > trans. by M. Byron Raizis)

Three years later, an accident in the waters of Kerkyra inspired him with a subject for a new poem. A shark had torn a British soldier to shreds. The poet described the beauty of the victim, his intimate association with the beauty of nature:

> Nature, you shone in a smile, and became one with him;
> Hope, you tied up his mind with all the charms you master;
> A young, all-beautiful world full of joy and goodness.
> > (trans. by M. Byron Raizis)

But this poem, like the others whose inspiration came to him during the last period of his life, remained unfinished. So it was with *Carmen Seculare*, as he called a poem (1842) where he described the situation of Hellenism and predicted the future reserved for the Greek nation. Another poem, inspired by the Crimean War, was also destined to remain unfinished.

During the same time, obeying an impulse that is difficult to explain, he turned with nostalgia to the happy years of the past. He regained his religious faith intact; he retrieved the old modes of expression, the spiritual harmony and techniques enclosed within him. He again wrote verses in Italian. He wrote short poems inspired by his immediate experiences; he returned to rapid rhythm:

> Thrice she glanced at the high mirror
> That reflected her graceful nuptial gown
> That her image wore, and the crown;
> The maiden solemn and speechless
> Looked around her thrice, not less.
>
> (trans. by M. Byron Raizis)

He was approaching the end of his life. His glory surpassed a small circle of immediate admirers; it surpassed the boundaries of the Ionian Islands and touched all of Greece. But the poet had not sought such renown, nor was he pleased about it. Internal and external peace announced the approaching end of his life. His fondness for solitude had become a fear of society. His fondness for perfection rendered his criticism sharp and quarrelsome. Escape to an ideal world was achieved by artificial means. One of his last verses expresses exactly the state of his soul during these years:

> Ah! Where is the sweet sleep with its beautiful dreams?

Characterization

In February 1857 Solomos found peace in the arms of his creator. As a good servant, he had brought his talents to fruition and left much more than he had found. The achievements of his predecessors appear as simple essays compared to the accomplishments of Solomos. Where Kalvos stopped, Solomos persisted and arrived at his goal. He bequeathed a legacy to the poetry of Greece; he gave a voice to his country that dignified it. Thanks to him, the Hellenic poetic tradition was unified for the first time.

But another contribution Solomos made to Hellenic culture, one of a more general character, should be mentioned. It concerns criticism. The Solomos of *Dialogue,* and later of his own thoughts as the author noted them in the course of elaborating his poetic compositions, offers us a sample of a critical mind exercising itself in the evaluation of works of art, therefore of fundamental aesthetic ideas. Finally, we should point out his prose contributions of *Dialogue* and *The Woman of Zakynthos.*

Since we find here a complete model of literary creation, it is worth drawing certain conclusions. What prevails in Solomos is an inspiration constantly supplied by the experience of life, an unceasing exaltation from the time of his maturity, but one always founded on reality. A second observation is obvious; this concerns the persistent attachment of the poet to the ideal of his art. His entire life was an uninterrupted effort to perfect his art, as the successive recastings he made, either in isolated verses, in important units, or even in entire compositions, testify. His evolution is the third important point when attempting to evaluate Solomos. The parallel journey of his form and content toward an ideal perfection, an image of the organic world, was constantly developing in the poet's consciousness.

Certainly, the maturity of Solomos, though prepared for, surges brusquely into Hellenic culture. Hellenism was incapable of assimilating such a heritage integrally. For this reason, we see this heritage displaced in space and time. In the Ionian Islands, his immediate disciples, the representatives of the Ionian Island school, shared the wealth of his criticism, harmony, idealism, sweetness, and elevation. But no one was able to present all these elements simultaneously and each of his followers expressed only one aspect of the master's work or one instant in his creative evolution. In the rest of Greece, before the union with the Ionian Islands and even afterward, it was by stages that people came to know the work of Solomos. Even in our own time, research and discoveries relating to the quality of his work continue. Furthermore, before coming to the generation of 1880 which was finally able to use the poetic inheritance of Solomos, intellectual Greece had to undergo numerous experiences; the ideal of ancient glory and romanticism, both unadaptable to reality, set the tone for a long period. This phase of Greek culture will be the subject of the following chapters.

Chapter 16

The War of Independence

"Take Up Arms"

The period under examination here embraces the years of the War of Independence. It was a time for direct action, thus letters were relegated to a secondary position. Nonetheless, intellectual activity continued to exist, and we shall see the forms that national literary activity took during the few years marking the turning point of modern Greek history. The poets, playwrights, and orators, when they did not actually participate in the war, attempted to instill enthusiasm, to elevate spirits. Inspired by Koraes, some wrote exhortations. Contact with the folk was limited, because the language created an increasingly greater barrier between the intellectuals and the common people. For this reason, we encounter the popular manifestations of a spontaneous character which took the form of improvised poetry and improvised theater.

Insurgent Greece was a true rallying point for intellectuals. After 1820 recipients of scholarships from the *Cultural Society,* established in 1813 for the development of Greek culture, were ordered to abandon their studies and return to Greece. And later, so long as the War of Independence continued, we observe more and more men, young and old, arriving on Greek soil. Many of these men pursued politics, but more were interested in educational matters. Among the latter were Spiros Trikoupis, Anthinos Gazis, Kaïris, Benjamin Lesvios Pharmakidis, and Gennadios. The movement of return continued, naturally, during the time of Kapodistrias, when Vardalachos and Doukas arrived. Some intellectuals died during these years, such as Gazis, Lesvios, and Vardalachos. Others were in advanced old age, such as Doukas and Koustandas, and were no longer able to render services corresponding to their abilities. Among the scholars we have not encountered before, George Gennadios (1786–1854) merits special attention. His literary work clearly belongs to the history of education, but during the War of Independence he was a great influence through his discourses and his liberal activity. Among the orators of this time, we should also mention

Vambas and Kaïris, who are encountered elsewhere, and especially Trikoupis, who was restrained for a long time by declining archaism. His funeral oration to Byron also has direct literary interest, because he took a position, without mentioning it specifically, on the question of romanticism: "He, for whose death we weep inconsolably, was the man who (in his country) gave his name to our century. The breadth of his spirit and the sublimity of his imagination could not allow him to walk on the brilliant but common traces of the literary glory of the ancients; he was engaged on a new path, which senile prejudices endeavored, and still are endeavoring, to bar from intellectual Europe. But so long as his writings continue to live, and they will live so long as the world lives, this path will always remain open."

Exhortations

Rhetoric was closely affiliated with exhortations of the time. Gregory Zalikoglou (1777–1827), who had distinguished himself in Paris with his patrotic and literary activity before the War of Independence, left a long dialogue, *The Greek Revolution*, published later in 1828. He is mentioned specifically because he translated Rousseau and was editor of a French-Greek dictionary which became a great publishing success. Constantine Nikolopoulos (1786–1841), who also lived in Paris and was an admirer of Koraes and a friend of Kalvos, published various exhortations during the War of Independence: *Exhortations of Encouragement* (1821), *The Salutary Trumpet of the Greeks* (in the same year), and others. The style of Zalikoglou and Nikolopoulos is cold. Their patriotic enthusiasm tends to graceless bombast, particularly in the latter. After his early success, D. Gouzelis was influenced by neoclassicism. In 1807 he published a very bad translation of *Jerusalem Delivered* by Tasso. Ten years later he appeared with a long metrical work, *The Judgment of Paris, A Mythological Poem of Love and Morals*. His annotations were very interesting for their liberal spirit, but the work was not read. In 1827 he published a metrical work called *Martial Trumpet* and later continued with exhortations, gnomic works, and a play, *The Great Friendship of Damon and Pythias, or Dionysus, Tyrant of Syracuse* (1835).

A great and faithful friendship immortalizes men;
Consider the tyrant whose atrocities dehumanizes them.

War Songs

Patriotic poetry flourished during the War of Independence. Men
sang some of the old songs, the *War Song* of Rigas, and others.
Alexander Ypsilantis, who we know wrote verses before the insurrection, is also mentioned as the poet of a war song called *Greeks,
Greeks, Greeks,* which was popular during the revolution. The
efforts of J. R. Neroulos in the same area are mentioned in the following chapters. Among the scholars who prepared the way for the
revolution or fought in the war, some composed war songs which are
still well known, such as

> Oh my children,
> My orphan children,

written by Panayotis Andronikos (c. 1820) shortly before the revolution. Stephen Kanellos (1792–1823), who died before his literary
personality could be realized, also composed poems in this genre:

> Sons of Greeks, why do you wait?
> Take up arms, the time has come.

And:

> The true *pallikaria* do not fly,
> Nor do they ever plunder.

Kanellos was a friend and collaborator of Kokkinakis on *The
Scholar Hermes.* Kokkinakis (1871–1831) had returned to die in
Greece. The famous war song, "O pliant and trenchant sword,/And
you, my flaming gun, my bird. . . ," is attributed to him, as is the
Call to Arms, "Come, children of the Greeks." Finally, a war song
in rapid rhythm, "Brothers, the moment of Liberty has arrived," is
attributed to Spiros Trikoupis. We can place George Kleanthis
(1801–1839) in the same category; he left such verses inspired by the
War of Independence as, "Young patriots, let victory or death be
your only desire."

However, the quality of the latter's verses is clearly inferior. He
takes us to another circle of fighters who composed works of contemporary significance. Zoïs Panos was one such fighter. In his

poems, published later (1842), he related the reasons which had inspired him to write each poem. One of these, "he sings on the table in order to enrapture the Greeks," was written in 1822. Another was written to slander the inhabitants of Moreas:

> One knows that, in Moreas, he must kill the Turks. . . .
> Bear in mind, people of Moreas, the children of the heroes.

The Athenian Spiros Bouyouklis, a violinist, singer, and poet, whose later production we will examine elsewhere, greeted Androutsos in Athens in 1822:

> Like a new Leonidas
> He appears at Thermopylae
> Odysseus, the valiant.
> He fires like lightning
> The guns of the Greeks
> At the hearts of tyrants.

The most typical representative of folk poetry during the War of Independence was Panayotis Kallas (c. 1789–1825), who was known under the name Tsopanakos. He sang his own poetry as he accompanied the insurgents to battle:

> Until when will we remain in caverns, slaves of Turks?
> Until when will we endure tyranny? Long live Liberty!

Folksongs

We already know that the leaders of the klephtes enjoyed having verse makers accompany them in battle in order to praise their exploits. If this custom brought us, on the one hand, to the rhymed ballads which were always popular, on the other hand, it brings us to the folksongs, which continued to flourish. Some of these folksongs were snatched by anonymity. Kolokotronis, Makriyannis, and Thodorakis Grivas all composed folksongs; other folksongs belong to less famous fighters. Well-known rhymed ballads of the period were written by Stasinos Mikroulis, George Gazis, who also appears in the following chapter, the Albanian, Hatzis Sechretis, and by still others.

Karaghiozis

But the folk inspiration in these years already begins to take on new dimensions with a more obvious urban element. Such was the Karaghiozis, the shadow theater. The history of Karaghiozis in Greece is imperfectly known. Certain researchers assert that it penetrated the Greek countryside only in recent times, but this is not correct. Karaghiozis was known in Greece even before the War of Independence. Whatever its ancient, probably oriental, origins, the immediate origin of Karaghiozis was Turkish. This is one more instance pointing to the assimilating power of Hellenism. Thus, while the Turkish Karaghiozis was developed by shadows and used obscene language, the Hellenized Karaghiozis was elevated to a new form of art and perfected to a type essentially symbolic and rich in human content. Moreover, Karaghiozis is not the only human type represented; all the characters circulating around him participate in life and represent permanent types in Greek society. Karaghiozis has a complex personality which is not easy to define; in true satiric spirit, he loves to present himself as a stupid or immoral man. And yet, at moments when one can truly judge a man, we suddenly see Karaghiozis revealing himself in rich sentiments, courageous, generous. The first of these aspects provokes spontaneous laughter and gives the audience a feeling of superiority, which constitutes one element of the comic genre. But the second aspect leads us to aesthetic sympathy and composes a complete human type. Thus, in this character, we sense that we have approximated the Greek spirit, which is prepared to rise from pettiness, but which is equally about to succumb under the burden of daily obligations. Certainly, the intelligence of Karaghiozis is what strikes us first; an incessant sparkling where we equally admire the self-evaluation and the active clairvoyance. But afterward, everything else follows: the human accent, the Greek home, Greek society, the relations of Karaghiozis with Kolitiri and later with his brothers, the unobtrusive presence of woman. More specialized types circulate around the central figure: Hadziavatis, the middle-class man with the large inheritance from the rayah, lacking great faults, but also lacking capacity for elevation. Then there is the candid man from Roumeli, Barbagiorgos, brave, straightforward, naive, but lacking intellectual faculties. It is clear that we have here a man from Roumeli as seen by one from

Moreas. And further, there is Nionios, originally from the Ionian Islands, with all the marks of Western influences, which always appear foreign to the Greek character. The theater of Karaghiozis, as we know from actual experience today, was constantly enriched and brought up to date by the introduction of secondary characters corresponding to new social types. In generalizing this observation, we would observe that the characters were not the only ones to be renewed in each period; so were the subjects, thus proving the vitality of the genre in its capacity for adaptation. Uniting in himself various elements of Greek folk tradition, such as song, Alexander the Great, the heroes of 1821, Karaghiozis is presented to newer Hellenism as an example of the creative abilities of the Greek people adapted to the urban character of modern Greek society.

Tower of Babel

The works of the neoclasssical theater which sought to teach a moral lesson to the public were far removed from every kind of reality. Though the patriotic exaltation characterizing the period could satisfy the people, today, neither the aesthetician nor the historian can profit by reading these works. The only work which truly can be considered an authentic product of the period is the famous *Tower of Babel* by Byzantios, first published in 1836, which describes Nauplion as it was at the end of the War of Independence in 1827. Demetrios Hadjiaslanis, known under the name Byzantios, was born, as his surname indicates, in Constantinople and came to Greece during the War of Independence. His various activities during the war years acquainted him with the many aspects of the society being constituted at that time. This society was composed of all kinds of people, coming from every region of Greece, each with his own local ideas, his own morals, and his own idiomatic expressions of language—a subject particularly suited to comedy. These diverse types tended toward some kind of synthesis and as a consequence were to attain later a unified form of life by the awareness of their unity. But the process was still incomplete. Byzantios chose this moment to describe the Greek world in his comedy. The *Tower of Babel* is lacking in plot. We are in Nauplion on the day news arrives of the battle of Navarino, in a hostelry where victory is being celebrated. The comic element is sought in the variety of idioms and in the misunderstandings which result from these idioms. Byzantios, who was a painter, knew how to observe, how to distinguish the characteristic traits, and thus his comedy animates typical Greek figures. The success of this comedy is certainly not owing to its linguistic content; what charms is how the author renders a particular character from each Greek region, as Roidis, in fact, had already observed.

Greek society, as Byzantios portrays it in the *Tower of Babel,* was not yet so constituted as to be able to create great literary works. Lacking maturity and unity, it presented a common awareness, a presupposition to group action, but it had yet to arrive at a synthesis. Into such a social milieu, the heavy and disintegrating forms of Western life fell; Hellenism was not in a state to assimilate them, because it had lost its organic equilibrium. On the other hand, neoclassicism, which was increasingly reinforced for various reasons, created new conditions, posed new problems to thought and expression. Thus, the years of the War of Independence with their strong emphasis on action constituted a period of expectation for letters, or at best, a period of fermentation. In the next chapter, we will see how action itself gave rise to original intellectual forms, while the general cultural conditions led Greek literature toward its new destiny.

Chapter 17

Memoirs

"Later, We

Dropped Anchor"

Introduction

The War of Independence caused a rupture in intellectual life, but also an awareness of change. Until this time Hellenism had lived under an uninterrupted tradition; cultural values were transmitted organically and were enriched normally by foreign contributions. Now suddenly in the regions that had been deprived of all life by a long, exhausting war, by the interruption of education, by the death of older professors and even of the younger disciples, and by the scarcity of publications, one sees the rebirth of intellectual life. This renewal was based on contributions of scholars who either came from abroad or who no longer represented a continuation of a now enfeebled tradition. The spirit of the times was best expressed by Gregory Papadopoulos, who wrote: "The history of our fathers is already ancient history on many points." Today, we would say that tradition is transmitted through history. The War of Independence, with its admirable results, but also with its pettinesses of human nature inseparable from life under abnormal conditions, had need of exaltation and justification for those who had participated in the struggle. The fighters, whether political or military men, were absolutely aware they had witnessed and participated in a great work. Glorious deeds should be related, reputations defamed by civil strife and political battle should be defended. Eye witnesses and historians were invited to write their accounts. Many men at that time, both members of the *Society of Friends* and those who had fought, felt the need to say what they knew, to transmit the truth to later generations. The erudite scholars, the instructed, and even the illiterate took up the pen to relate events in which they had participated. The printed materials, which abound, are stimulating. Karaïskakis claimed that his historian Markiyannis learned to write only so much as sufficed to compose his memoirs. Without doubt, even in earlier times we encountered some memoirs which were closer to chronicles. Now, it becomes another matter; we have the literary effervescence of a particular genre, new in many ways. Aside from the fighters, several younger men also participated in this movement.

At the dawn of the new free Greek state, we should mention, first of all, the historical and autobiographical texts, which simultaneously expressed an association with the past and an awareness of the rupture of the past and the present.

Perrevos

Certain writers had participated in earlier liberation attempts; Perrevos shared in the activity of Rigas; Zanthos, Sekeris, and Anagnostopoulos in that of the *Society of Friends*. Before the War of Independence, Perrevos (c. 1773–1863) had published a *History of Souli and Parga*. Later, among other writings, he published a biography of Rigas. He had known Rigas in Bucharest, as we already know; he was with him in Vienna and later in Trieste when Rigas was arrested. In his earlier works, Perrevos expressed himself unaffectedly in a simple language, and his direct contact with life gave a certain charm to his style. Later, his language, conforming to the tendencies described below, became more archaic, and his style was inflated, charged with rhetoric and elegance. His testimony, as it proceeds, becomes more suspect to modern historians. Nonetheless, it remains a valuable source, and given the extreme length of his writing career (1803–1860), he presents us with a remarkable document of evolving literary concepts in his time.

Xanthos

Many of the founders of the *Society of Friends* survived the War of Independence and, finding themselves neglected by the state, they desired both justice and some kind of historical rehabilitation. A secret society whose origin and organization remained concealed could easily provoke accusations and, indeed, it did. Some of the members are mentioned below. Here, I want to note Emmanuel Xanthos (1772–1852), who published the *Memoirs in Connection with the Society of Friends* (1845). It was a well organized composition whose purpose, certainly, was to exalt the role of Xanthos, but which simultaneously possessed all the characteristics of an autobiography. Xanthos attempted to purify his language and hence his true inner spirit was suppressed, but his work remained full of feeling. The description of his meeting in Petropolis, in 1820, first with Kapodistrias and later with Alexander Ypsilantis, had a dramatic rhythm, a style.

Skouzes

The prerevolutionary years in Athens were clearly described by Panayis Skouzes. About the War of Independence itself in Athens, we have a short chronicle by Angelos Gerontas. Both men extended the work of John Benizelos, but they were animated by a more natural, more spontaneous, more popular spirit. Benizelos was a professor; Skouzes and Gerontas were men of action who believed that it was desirable to recount all they had seen and suffered. Skouzes (1776–1847) left us two works; both were memoirs, quite similar, and we have been led to believe that the second memoir was written because the author supposed the first to have been lost. The first work, written in 1841, is a fuller account, Skouzes relates the historical events which unfold in Athens from the time of the tyranny of Hassekis and ends with his own autobiography. The same personal tone animates the work from beginning to end, the same compassion for the sufferings of Athens, and generally for the rayahs. Skouzes's style is marked with imperfections inherent in the popular language of his period; it reveals, however, a true literary personality. It is an expressive style, rapid and ingenious. The articulation of phrase and composition obey neither rules of art nor laws of logic but depend entirely on psychological associations; hence, he often presents a perambulatory form of composition in which the main narrative is completed in successive stages.

Persecuted in Athens by the tyranny of Hassekis, the Skouzes family went to Euboea in 1790. Panayis, still a child, was forced to go to work. He became an apprentice to a shoemaker. In the same village, he found a religious man from Mount Sinai who collected alms for the monastery. The charm of the spoken language is found in Skouzes's account of how he entered the monk's service: "There, by Divine Grace, my stomach was always full of everything. Daily, we would go to bless the homes, because the people feared the plague which was spreading or because they were superstitious of ghosts. Every day, men came to solicite us. As for me, I put on the cap of a monk and served as a monk beside the old priest. . . ." But Skouzes knew that he was an Athenian; he knew what it meant to be an Athenian. The ancient glory of Athens lived within him, even though his education was slight. It is thus that he recounted the cooperation between the Athenians and Hadji Ali Hassakis in attacking the Albanians: "They deliberated and counselled Hadji Ali that the operation they proposed, which would permit them to repulse the enemy, resembled that which had come to pass when the barbarians had debarked at Marathon to subjugate the Athenians. They related the story to him; they also told him that after the battle, the Athenians had reconstructed their walls. They added also that the menace from the Albanians recalled the menace of Xerxes." Thought and expression without flourish; all was content here. Juxtaposition is frequent, and he often gives an elliptical character to his narration. The simplicity of his composition has its own artistic limits. But one is free to express admiration for such talents as those of Skouzes and Makriyannis, and one wonders how many great writers Greece could have offered if men had been educated generally and still participated in life.

Gerontas

Similar comments are suggested by Angelos Gerontas (1785–1862). We have nothing but a few simple, inspiring pages. The elders of Athens were called by the Turks to serve as hostages in case the Athenians revolted. "Despite knowing the reason we were held as hostages, we thought it better to perish than to allow three or four thousand Christians to perish. And we thus decided to accept this warranty." An adventurous escape from the enemy follows. Finally came disillusionment, the end of the war, the beautiful dreams that faded. "Later, we dropped anchor. I remained grieved. . . ."

Vambas

Understandably, there were many who wrote memoirs about the war years and the immediate postrevolutionary period: scholars, such as Psyllas and Vambas, fighters and politicians such as Germanos, Bishop of Patras, Makriyannis, Constantine Metaxas, Photakos, Kasomoulis, and Spiliades. Neophytos Vambas (1776–1866), a prolific writer with an obvious preference for educational manuals and a compliant orator at school festivals and other holidays, appears to have only partially completed his memoirs. He could have told us much about his long intimacy with Koraes, about the school at Chios, his own participation in the war, his teachings at the Ionian School, his teachings in Athens and elsewhere. But neither his expression nor his spirit are warm. He wrote in his maturity when he had abandoned the influence of Koraes as well as his old progressive principles, "if he ever had principles," writes Pharmakides in 1852. Linguistically, he inclined toward archaism, conforming to the spirit of his time, though in a somewhat more reserved fashion than other contemporary writers. He has given us an account of how the insurrection was proclaimed at Hydra. He said to Lazaros Kountouriotes that the island should be the one to set an example. "And Lazaros replied that the reason for the delay lay in differences of opinion and he begged me to speak on peaceful agreement on the next day, which was the Sunday of Saint Thomas. As soon as I was alone, I reflected on my speech. And then, when Lazaros returned from the meeting that had taken place at the monastery, he said to me, 'Vambas, tomorrow the flag will be raised as you desire. Thus, your speech will be on Freedom.' "

Dragoumis

Before passing to more military personalities, we should mention two authors of memoirs who performed significant political activity, but who distinguished themselves, above all, by their literary awareness. They are Nicholas Dragoumis and Alexander Rizos Rangavis. Nicholas Dragoumis published his memoirs in 1874; Rangavis com-

posed and published his at an advanced age after 1890. Both men
have Phanariot roots, with a greater Phanariot awareness in the latter. Dragoumis (1809–1879) gave us reminiscences which began with
the War of Independence. His language was that of a purist, but he
was a spirited man, endowed with an artistic sense, with a good intellectual orientation. Because he had literary ambitions, he managed
to enliven his expression. His descriptions, particularly those of
Kapodistrias's in Nauplion, are models of this genre. He knew how
to select objects, persons, and actions which would be of interest.
The new social life at Nauplion, the conflicts between the ancient
traditions and the new society beginning to take shape, are rendered
with a remarkable penetration. The author's artistic sense dictates
that he portray characters in an episode or act which reveals their
nature. With this same direct method he describes situations and periods, a class, or a social entity. He often interrupts his narrative
with skillful elegance to slip in a more general idea, which will
serve as a point of departure for what is to follow.

In general, the *Memoirs* of Dragoumis were carefully composed
and their diverse parts were well arranged. He wrote with care and
loathed all forms of improvisation. Certain of his remarks indicate
that he was an aesthetically cultured scholar with ideas too advanced
for his time. He said of Vilaras that some of his works were masterpieces and that *Springtime* "surpasses even that of Christopoulos.
His judgment of a poem, in which Vilaras imitated Sakellarios,
merits consideration as a successful piece of contemporary criticism:
"He imitates so well, through poetic images and arrangement of
words, the setting of the sun, the rising of the moon, the fatigue
of the workers and their animals, the calm of night and constancy of
love, that one can see nature acting or suffering, that one can believe
he is experiencing everything himself, that he is himself returning,
in fatigue, to his hut."

However, where he excels and where he offers us the Greek model
of the genre is in the retrospective account of social and political
affairs. He alone among the Greek memoir writers had sensed this
special genre. An entire world is created in a few lines, as when he
describes, for example, the consequences of the War of Independence on Greek letters in Turkish-dominated Greece. "Among those
who dispensed education, either oral or written, either for free or
for money, some were crowned with martyrdom, others were dispersed, suffering famine, or even perishing from their ordeals.
Among the scholars, some were reduced to silence, others, breaking

their pens, sought refuge in aroused Greece and undertook to preach freedom, harmony, and public order."

A reception took place at the home of Spiros Trikoupis. The governor, foreigners, and Greeks in various kinds of dress were present. ". . . at the entrance stood the Governor, the foreigners, and many others. Among these others was a prince of Greek origin, recently arrived from Paris, accompanied by his delicate spouse, wearing 'a beautiful coat of purple and a robe descending to her feet.' Her hair was piled as high on her head as is the tower of Cybele. Glancing often around the room, this greasy princess appeared to be deploring the attire and manners of those present. She mocked the people and burst into laughter, and as the deceased Klonaris would say, she chattered in French like a magpie."

Rangavis

Alexander Rangavis wrote four large volumes to praise the Phanariots, but specifically to praise his own home and especially himself. This remarkable, intelligent, and above all curious man, whose career was rich and varied, could have covered a century of Greek history in his memoirs. Instead, this prolific and rapid writer poured forth a torrent of personal impressions and episodes, about which he neither tried to generalize nor could have if he had so wanted. His wit, which sparkled in social gatherings, scarcely pierced through his writings. He saw only the external aspects of life, and this only as they touched him directly; he needed a cosmopolitan audience, amiably disposed to his sort of chatter, in order to shine. When this was lacking, his expression became dry and indifferent. He was interested only in those who were amused by scandals from the past or who were fascinated by the offensive taste of petty personal passions. At rare intervals among his hundreds of pages he makes token mention of his period, particularly of his class. He does this unconsciously when he has a typical Phanariot reveal some detail in the composition of his class. His purist style was cold, a long account of uninteresting matters. We must not forget, however, that this was the work of an old man. In any case, other witnesses to the War of Independence will be of greater interest to us.

Germanos, Bishop of Patras, and Kasomoulis

Germanos, bishop of Patras (1771–1826), left memoirs of no literary pretensions, which lack the kind of brilliance that is associated with his eminent name. This prelate gives us a dry narration of events in which he participated, written, while internal strife was impairing the progress of the War of Independence, to justify the narrator's point of view. His great education did not prove useful for evoking the fighting spirit. His attention to precise expression, in contrast to the fighters' spontaneous efforts, deprive his text of all life and make its faults more apparent. It is the same with Kasomoulis (1795–1871) in his long three-volume memoirs, published much later under the title of *Military Memoirs*. With a negligible education, he labored to corrupt his language in order to render it more noble. Had he written naturally, perhaps he would have been a great writer. As it is, his linguistic efforts are very superficial, and he allows a supple, popular language to show through. He has a direct style, a tendency to avoid casual constructions, and a narration composed of coordinated propositions; these are the principal elements giving vivacity to his language.

The author's animation surges aurally and visually out of his rapid descriptions; he is a perfect reporter. He sees everything, hears everything, understands everything; he allows nothing to elude him, nothing to be lost. He seeks to tell everything exactly as he heard it or saw it. He rushes to expose facts for fear of disrupting the rapid rhythm of events; if words can be omitted, they are. Those he does use acquire a dramatic elliptical turn, infinitely more suggestive in form than any carefully constructed narration. This passion for precision and the desire to omit nothing sometimes gives his *Memoirs* a realism which exposes the indiscretions of the simple combatants of 1821. Characters and actions are one in the simple narration. What Karaïskakis demanded of Soutsos, he obtained from Kasomoulis: the description of a general from Roumeli, for instance, was presented with admirable clarity and true theatrical accent.

Without any attempt at idealization, we are shown the daily life of the fighting men, a life full of heroism and a high spirit of self-sacrifice. But what is significant is that, contrary to the pioneer memoir writers of the War of Independence, the unassuming Kasomoulis, thanks to the modest station he occupied, presented the war

from a close view, from within. The great men, such as the remarkable diplomat and patriot, Mavrokordatos, pass through his narrative, but more specifically the procession consists of the large
anonymous masses. Sometimes Kasomoulis becomes severe, but his
severity does not arise from personal passions; he judges and con-
demns, always seeking to arrive at the truth. It would be an injustice, from a literary viewpoint, to look on him only as a good
and intelligent war correspondent; Kasomoulis possessed historical
awareness. He attempted to weigh the evidence and he knew the
value of an eye-witness account. His great experience with men permitted him to penetrate motives and causes. His judgment was
sound, and whenever he was limited by imperfect knowledge of circumstances, he consulted written sources to supplement his information. And finally, he was animated by the great desire for objectivity; he had a scrupulous conscience. The work of Kasomoulis
provides ideal access to the soul of the fighting men of 1821 and to
their high accomplishments.

Makriyannis

Makriyannis (1797–1864) was not objective. His work was not objective evidence but an impassioned personally biased account. He
participated with all his soul in the War of Independence, as
Kasomoulis did, but his memoirs vibrate with the passions aroused
by civil strife. We have here a man of parts; his language is itself
a slice in the life of the fighting men. He does not narrate, he does
not describe, he fights. His patriotic passion and his animating political fanaticism confer a unique character on his memoirs. Furthermore, he was uneducated; no scholarly element troubles the expression of his emotional world. And when he meditates, his thought is
inspired by experience and by the wisdom of the masses. Liberated
from cumbersome linguistic shackles which more or less burden the
prose of other memoir writers, he was able to create a perfect literary work. His language was nearly unadulterated; only here and
there do we encounter a scholarly word, taken from newspaper or
from the official oratorical contests of his time.

Hence, his style remains close to his spirit. The dramatic element
predominates, the dialogue surges out of the narration without in-

terrupting a purely psychological unity, which augments the expression and renders it more imposing. He appears before Ibraham as an envoy along with some companions: "He asked us where we came from. One said he came from the Peloponnesus, the other from Sparta and I, 'from Roumeli,' I said. 'What part?' I told him . . . . 'What do you want?' (He said to me: 'Leave the men from Moreas; in a few days, I will talk with them,') 'We are seeking European boats . . . ?" His stichomythia is always rapid and its rhythm terse: "He came, he saw me. 'What do you want?' he said to me.—'The Governor of my country.'—'I don't have time,' he said.—'Neither do I have time to see you again.'—(At that moment they were searching for me to take me back to the fort of Palamidi.) 'Go,' he said to me. 'I have no time.'—'I wish not go anywhere?'"

His evaluations of other people gush forth in this same manner. Judgments are not weighed on the scale of justice; they are made by the sword of fighting men. One-sided, direct judgment: "A guttersnipe with a bad reputation," says the one, and the other says, "Crafty and bloodthirsty." Sometimes he was almost epigrammatic: "He was a louse-ridden count, and he became one in fact." The same spirit is also found in his reflections; they were the fruit of fundamental experience, whose expression preserved something of the flavor of the ancients. "The country belongs to all, and as the work of the effort of the youngest and the poorest citizen, he also has an interest in this country." Thus, this spontaneous and impetuous man from Roumeli found his equilibrium through the folk tradition, through intuition, which is an unconscious knowledge. His actions were apparently based on psychology and history, which he always remembered with pride: ". . . from beginning to end, from ancient times to the present, all the wild beasts seek to devour us but cannot. They eat a few of us, but some leavening remains. And the few decide to die. When they make this decision, they sometimes lose, but often, they win. This is our actual situation today. And we will see what your fate will be, the weak against the strong."

As one of the people, he carried within him the treasure of tradition. From this tradition he derived the creative force of language and the capacity to grasp an expression in the early freshness of its genesis. Whatever, for us, is only a conventional expression, a metaphor, in Makriyannis retains its original value: "The Turk, enormous beast, expects to see me give up my soul; he does not know how deeply lodged it is." This overworked expression, "give up my soul," assumed the freshness of the proper term under the pen of Makriyannis. His particular world is constructed entirely in this way; he relates his dreams, he has a pictorial concept of the universe, he sings, he improvises folk poems. Thus, he can be seen as a symbol of modern Greece, with the faults and virtues which characterize the race; he was simultaneously spontaneous and calculating, violent and conciliatory.

His style also constituted an ideal synthesis of folk linguistic elements as oral tradition had shaped and transmitted them. Just when the creation of a state and the introduction of a Greek administrative machine allows the scholarly element to predominate in Greece, Makriyannis safeguarded and gave value to popular tradition in a most definite form. Even more than content alone, his *Memoirs* revive the memory of the still unaltered Greek culture in its ultimate phase.

Photakos

In the same group with Makriyannis, but less prominently, we should place Photakos (1798–1878). He was a simple man as well, with an unaffected style using simple terms, he attempted to narrate the events of the War of Independence as he knew them from personal observation. Originally from Moreas, quiet and always smiling, he was soft-spoken, without exaltation, without passion. He knew how to describe and narrate: "The commander and all the soldiers laughed when they heard about their simplicity. He reprimanded them, without severity, not to waste gunpowder because we had none, and he left them." Such a passage reveals the spirit of the author; he underscored the words, laughter and simplicity, emphasizing the mildness of the reprimand. He never raised his voice in either exaltation or generalization. His attempt to furnish positive evidence was characteristic: frequent use of dates and numbers, citation of authentic texts. His purpose was help, with his personal testimony, in reestablishing the truth and controlling the historians, who at this time (1858) had begun composing their works: "It is a shame, my friend, that the Peloponnesian, the Roumeliot, the islanders, the Greek of whichever place, does not really know the exploits of his fathers, but reads inept histories instead." A tranquil tone predominated throughout his work, even when he corrected the inexactitudes of others.

Tertsetis and Kolokotronis

Photakos dedicated his book to George Tertsetis, to whom he also dedicated a biography of Papeflessas (1868). Tertsetis was the only scholar who systematically and with perseverance attempted to collect testimony from the fighting men and who assumed the responsibility of writing it down. Photakos wrote in his dedication: "Each time you see me, you ask only one thing of me, to reveal what I know about the Greek Revolution, and especially what I saw with my own eyes. You even demand the same thing in your letters." No one but Tertsetis felt so urgently the duty of his generation to preserve every recollection possible of this great period of Greece. "The centuries will proclaim to the centuries that never has there been a war more justified, more pure, and more sacred than ours to honor the human race." It is in this spirit that he succeeded in getting several memoirs written. In certain cases, he wrote down memoirs which were dictated to him.

Such was the case with Kolokotronis. They become acquainted during the famous trial of 1833. Three years later, Tertsetis convinced Kolokotronis: "I understand that audacity and persuasion were needed to make him decide to work. The third time, I said to him: 'General, the Greeks resemble a musical instrument which emits harmonious sounds; men perceive this, but those instruments are unaware of their function. What have you done? I know you cannot relate your deeds; they are as games of chance, and not deeds of conscience and reason. And if you are the only one who knows what you have done, or where you have gone, you are in error. Your deeds are as leaves in autumn, which the storm scatters.' "

The History of the Greek People, that is, the memoirs of Kolokotronis (1770–1843), was a work written in collaboration with Tertsetis. But it is evident throughout the work that Tertsetis had no desire to edit but only to transmit the voice of Kolokotronis with the fidelity of a phonograph. The work contains a marked apologetic character which tended to excuse and exalt the exploits of Kolokotronis. He was versatile and prudent. The narration of his exploits was intelligent and convincing; it was animated by dialogue and embellished by aphorisms which were dear to Kolokotronis. The author ornaments his prose with myths and parables. "On the first day, I greeted Mavromichalis and the others. Petrobeys asked me: 'How long will you dance, Kolokotronis?' And I replied, 'So long as you sing, I will dance. Stop your songs and I will stop dancing.' "

Epigram also pleased Kolokotronis. But his purpose was more to describe than to pass judgment. His style was an oral one; however, since this was a dictated text, it was less elliptical than that of Kasomoulis or of Makriyannis. There is no doubt that Tertsetis unconsciously gave a literary turn to the narrative.

Historians

We move away from memoirs toward history. The boundary between the two genres is difficult to trace exactly when it comes to the battles of the War of Independence and such early historians as Anagnostopoulos, Philimon, who wrote about the *Society of Friends,* M. Ekonomos, Phrantzes, Trikoupis, and others who wrote about the insurrection; that is, they attempted to compose something surpassing a chronicle, even though they were contemporary with the events they related, even though they were eye-witnesses or participants in the events. Kanellos Deliyannis wrote his memoirs in order to refute the historians of the War of Independence. This same mixed character also appears in the early biographies of such fighting men as Botsaris and Karaïskakis by George Gazis (1795–1855, or Karaïskakis by Demetrios Ainianas (1800–1881).

Spiros Trikoupis, though he was also accused of partiality, not always unjustly, has given us a scholarly and coordinated verbal construction, a balanced composition. His history (1853–1857) is one of the most complete monuments for language of the time, despite the tendency toward accentuated purism which begins to appear. His definite political thought, influenced by the diplomatic clairvoyance of Mavrokordatos, gives his work exceptional weight and prestige. Equal importance should be attributed to his criticism when he discusses texts or actions.

We can say nearly the same for Kanellos Deliyannis (1780–1862). His *Memoirs,* published recently, were written late, when the Greek language had evolved in a direction that was not propitious to the progress of literary form generally (1854–1858). But the vivacity of his spirit and the force of his passions were such that they brought him to compose an apology to the nobles, which vibrates with honesty and persuasiveness. Thanks to him we now have, in a style lacking charm but full of force, the other side's opinion of events and men in the War of Independence and the years preceding it. He was the lion of the fable, but a lion who knew how to paint.

John Philimon (1798–1873) published an *Historical Essay on the Society of Friends* in 1834. From 1859 on, he published the *Historical Essay on the Greek Revolution* in four successive volumes. A meticulous chronicler, he attempted to neglect no detail of the events he related; despite his fondness for general considerations, he did not succeed in a synthesis of the particular facts. In details, he was conscientious and critical. He cited and utilized abundant documentation. Events were still too recent to become the object of an historical work, but in many ways Philimon gave us personal testimony which lacks neither sincerity nor value.

Movement toward Antiquity

It was easier to write history about periods long past. And, indeed, the years following the War of Independence offered a favorable climate for the development of historical science. Many reasons contributed to this. The new Greek nation needed to strengthen its position in world opinion. It would now orient itself toward its origins and resurrect the glory of its ancestors. Philhellenism disappeared immediately following the liberation. The Greeks preserved order and exalted the brillance of antiquity in the miserable framework of the new state. The limited frontiers conceded to Greece stimulated desire for the revival of a great Hellenic empire. Even the neoclassicism of the Bavarians contributed in inflaming ancestor worship and in nurturing it with architectural monuments and other offerings. The spirit which presided at the establishment of the University of Athens (1837) should also be mentioned here. The thought of new Hellenism, at this point, was oriented toward history, so there also appears a systematic effort to develop a philosophy of history: from G. Kozakis-Typaldos, we have the *Philosophical Essay on the Grandeur and Decadence of Ancient Greece* (1839) and from M. Renieris, the *Essay of Philosophy of History* (1841). The latter also wrote various historical studies.

In this nostalgic mood, another event provided a definitive orien-

tation. This was the series of works by Fallmerayer, who supported
the theory that new Hellenism had no racial connection with the
ancient. Such a slap in the face, at so critical a moment, could not
remain unanswered; in the difficult years following the liberation, all
intellectual Hellenism had only its classical heritage as support. The
Greek scholars resented the affront profoundly and they responded
to it.

Within a short time a number of works were published contradict-
ing the theories of the German scholar. In 1842, both the *History of
Athens* by D. Sourmelis and the *Essay on the Study of History* by
George Pentadios Darvaris appeared. In the following year, we have
two more significant contributions: a study by Paparrigopoulos,
based on history, and another by Georgiadis Lefkias (1773–1853),
written in ancient Greek with a Latin translation. Georgiadis was
the first to use linguistic arguments in the controversy with Fallmerayer.

The purpose was the same, but the means varied; we know that
awareness of the connection between the new and the ancient Hellenism had never ceased to flourish during the years of the Turkish
domination. After the liberation of Greece, this awareness was reinforced and was more powerfully armed to give battle. Thus his-
toriography was developed. But another means to prove this connection between the old and new consisted in establishing a parallel
between the life of the ancient Greeks and that of the modern
Greeks. Even before the science of folklore had been constituted in
the West, the Greeks had begun a systematic study of modern Greek
customs, comparing them with the ancient ones. Thus it was that
Greek folk literature was born. Finally, to limit ourselves to the most
important facts, the continuity could also be proved by the linguistic
unity. But the Greek language had evolved and showed perceptible
differences from the ancient language. A considerable effort would
be needed to reconcile the two. Thus we enter into a new phase of
the linguistic battle.

Zambelios

The unity of Greek history was defended in this period by a number
of writers. Spiros Zambelios was among the first to publish a small
collection of folksongs in 1852, to which he added about six hundred

pages as an introduction. There he used the term Helleno-Christian, which he apparently coined himself. In 1857, under the title *Byzantine Studies, about the Sources Concerning the Modern Greek Folk from the Eighth to the Tenth Centuries, A.D.*, he traces this historical period from a philosophic and theoretical point of view. In both works he maintained the connection between each successive period of Greek history. Later, in 1860, he discerned two parallel traditions in modern Greek culture: one scholarly, the other folk. The thesis he defended and the manner in which this was developed were original for his period and revealed an awareness of the times and a remarkable desire for unity. Indeed, so long as the new Hellenism was disposed to seek its roots in antiquity, a connection with Byzantium was held in contempt and repugnance. Spiros Zambelios merits praise for having attempted to reinstate the Byzantine period.

Paparrigopoulos

But we already have Constantine Paparrigopoulos and his efforts at a synthesis (1851–1891). His small volume, published in 1853, is titled *History of the Greek People from Antiquity to the Present*. It is the same title, the same spirit, which we will find again in his large historical work. He was born in Constantinople of a father originally from the Peloponnessus. His writing career began early with historical monographs and translations of history manuals to be used in education. His large historical work was published in five volumes between the years 1860 and 1872. Later, his contributions to history were followed by monographs and also by more composite works.

It would not be precise to say that he gave the Greek people the awareness of their historical unity or that he was the first to grasp the idea of writing a history to illustrate this unity. The contribution of Paparrigopoulos lies elsewhere, in the form that his Greek history takes, in its admirably balanced composition, its brilliant style, and its wise and harmonious arrangement of the successive periods of Greek history. A romantic historian, he never hesitated to elevate the tone or to meditate on the phenomena he related. Excessively sensitive to history, he adapted to the particularity of each period in such a manner that the passage of time became perceptible even in his language.

Aside from these great qualities, he never lacked the essential application in examining details. In drafting a composition, he often used secondary sources for the details; nonetheless, incessant recourse to primary sources was a fundamental principle directing his research and characterizing his writings. Indicative of the incontestable creative value of his work is that, while in time much of what he wrote has been rectified by later research, the aggregate of his work remains unaltered to this day. It is not a simple assemblage of facts; the information has passed through the creative spirit of a courageous intellect and has taken a body.

In his own time, he was accused of pettiness because of certain secondary matters. Even in our times, he has been reproached for not giving all his attention to the recent upheavals of 1821. Leaving aside this criticism of pettiness, we should observe that his ambition was infinitely more elevated than the demands of his detractors. Even though he had lived during the period of the revolution, this historian of the nation did not propose to write only a simple chronicle or a diary of the revolution. He sought to write the biography of the Greek race throughout the centuries and to grasp and render the unity of the spirit of Hellenism in the military exploits of antiquity as well as in the contemporary exploits and in the cultural efforts which characterized the successive Greek Renaissances. In this, he attained his end. To be able to express oneself thus on an intellectual subject is already great praise. But to be able in addition to praise the purpose he pursued is to praise without reserve. Such is the praise due Paparrigopoulos.

Studies of Customs

Establishing a correlation between the customs of modern Greeks with those of Hellenic antiquity was nothing new; during the Turkish domination, the foreigners who were drawn to Greece by the vision of classical beauty tended to discover a resemblance between the manners of the past and those of the present. The maturity of Hellenic consciousness developed a similar interest among the Greeks. Just as Koraes taught the need for a comparative study of the two languages, extending his research even to matters that today belong to folklore, so younger scholars made various comparisons with a visible national pride. In 1815, Gregory Paliorites compared ancient with contemporary customs in his *Archeology*. In 1816, S. Karatheodoris mentions the *Songs of the Swallows,* and he treats the subject of these folksongs more fully. Proverbs, the great concern of Koraes, became the habitual subject of comparisons. The folksongs, especially those published with the famous introduction by Fauriel (1824), constituted one of the more impressive arguments in favor of the ancient origin of modern Hellenism. After the revolution and in fact after Fallmerayer, the movement gained intensity. From 1850 on, it was characteristic that works from continental writers appeared refuting Fallmerayer more directly, while simultaneously the researchers exalted the Greek folksong. Collections of Greek folksongs and studies relating to these songs were published in rapid succession. Toward the end of the same period, from 1870, we have the imposing figure of Nicholas Politis. He undertook to reclassify the successive currents into a unique science, that of folklore. It appears from this that, contrary to what occurred in most other cases, the demand for folklore did not arrive in Greece through a foreign influence, but proceeded from a native need.

The Language Problem

It was also out of a real need that still another phase of the Greek language problem, the return to archaism, arose. This new phrase showed a lack of historical awareness, which characterized these years when linguistic purification dominated.

Koraes was dead, and we now are in a well-known stage of intellectual history when the death of the great creator is followed by a period of criticism and neglect. Parallel with this, the scholars pushed the intellectuals toward a massive purification of the language which tended to identify the new Greek language with the ancient. Finally, the Phanariots, who even before the revolution had started to manifest reactionary tendencies, now turned with hostility away from the Enlightenment and tended, more and more, by reason of the antipathy they had created among liberated Hellenism, toward an aristocratic isolation.

Signs of this change were discernable even before the death of Koraes. Though Neroulos wrote his *Korakistika* in order to defend

demoticism by attacking Koraes, several years later, when the revolution broke out, he was already much more conservative than
Koraes had been. Matesis wrote around 1824: "See the amusing
comedy by Rizos, *The Korakistiki Language*. I cannot understand
how the same man who wrote this comedy could recently write an
Ode, published in the Journal of Missolonghi, which appears to have
been written by Beelzebub!" Such a change toward archaism was
naturally much easier for the old disciples of Koraes, who had found
the same principle in the teachings of their master. Even in this case,
the tendency toward archaism was not presented as an isolated fact
but as a manifestation of a more general change.

Such was the case with Constantine Ekonomos; as a cleric in
1817, he was a partisan of Koraes without reservation. He wrote in
the language of Koraes and his teaching contained all the Enlightenment elements extolled by Koraes, Around 1820, when in the en-
tourage of Gregory in Constantinople, he made obvious concessions
both to conservative theories and to linguistic archaism. He followed
this path with perseverance and finally arrived at a language charged
with all the characteristics of a most severe archaism. In later editions of his previously published works, he improved, in his own
way, and purified the language he had used earlier. Simultaneously
we find him withdrawing from the spirit of Koraes, until he disavowed him completely.

The phenonemon was more apparent in the younger writers.
Panayotis Soutsos, who had known and respected Koraes, became
enthusiastic over the new Hellenic ideal; he published the *New
School of Written Language* in 1853. The subtitle of the book was
*Resurrection of the Ancient Greek Language Understood by All the
World*. He labelled the attempt of Koraes as "Frankish." "Insolent
pioneers, today, we overturn this miserable Frankish edifice, and
elevate the Greek language of our ancestors, formerly called the
koine, and make it easy for all the world to understand." In the *General Rules,* which serve as an introduction, we read first of all: "The
language of the ancient Greeks and that of our contemporaries is
one and the same. Their Grammar and ours is one and the same."
Future and simple pluperfect, infinitive, dative, all these should be
returned to the Greek language. Soutsos was ridiculed for this book,
because the regular critics were among the last followers of Koraes
and they published anonymously a *Critique of Soutsos* in the following year. The line he traced was truly that of other scholars of the
period; but from this point on, one no longer finds all the disap-

probation which used to flood discourses and prefaces concerning the folk language or *Koraism*. Gregory Papadopoulos (1857) informed his audiences that language "had advanced to such an extent that Koraes himself had been surpassed long ago." That same year, a scholar from Chios, Argyrios Karavas, termed the popular literary production as "disgustingly vulgar." A little later, around 1860, the Graeco-French scholar E. Yemeniz was convinced that the Greek language had changed greatly in the preceding thirty years, that it had been purified, and that the form of more recent works was "almost classical."

A national effervescence animated scholarly Hellenism; nothing was extreme, all aspirations could be realized, if the Greeks would cultivate their national character, if they would remain faithful to the Greek vision. The foreign element which had nourished the Greeks and which Koraes dreamed of grafting to the Greek tree was rejected suddenly with hostility; Greece would live, if she based herself on her proper forces, if she cultivated a return to herself. Moreover, these years coincided with the Crimean War and with the new hopes that the war awakened. Prophets and apostles are at their height again; they circulated throughout the Greek lands and stirred the population. Zaloskostas wrote:

> The battle is not over
> Do not accept the customs of the foreigners.

To this general movement, to this unanimous effervescence, the most typical Greek politician of the time, John Kolettis, was able to give form and awareness. It was the hour of the *Grand Idea,* with all the dangers and all the hopes it included.

Part Six
Greek Romanticism
Romantic Phenomena
1830-1880

In the new Hellenism as it emerges after the War of Independence, only two organized forces survive: the Phanariots and the Heptanesians. The literary climate clearly becomes more romantic; it is colored by neoclassicism among the Phanariots and by idealism among the Heptanesians. The Athenian scholars, carried along by the spirit of it, give themselves without reservation to romantic excess, which responds, moreover, to certain essential tendencies of Hellenism. Kostes Palamas considers that Greek romanticism begins "with the Voyager *of Panayotis Soutsos . . . and ends with the 'Ode to Byron' which Achilles Paraschos recited at Missolonghi in 1880." In other words, the movement lasted from around 1830 to 1880. We should add that three translations of Edward Young's* Night Thoughts *(1835, 1852, 1881) mark this period.*

Chapter 18

A World Ends

The Phanariots in Athens
and in Constantinople

A number of the subjects we examined in the preceding chapter could have been titled "romantic classicism," because actually one must observe that first of all in the nostalgic return to antiquity there were many purely romantic elements. Furthermore, the nationalistic spirit that characterized the scholarly tendencies of the period was also interwoven with many romantic elements. In a way, this created an opposition between theoretical orientation, whose ambition it was to exalt Hellenism under all forms, and literary activity, and even profoundly, the state of the soul, which was clearly romantic. In no other period do we encounter Western influences, or more precisely, French influences, as direct as those of this period, where national awareness exhibited itself in so exalted a form.

French influences, already noted in a much earlier period, are now fully developed. We know that the Phanariots, the more educated social element of the new nation, represented only French culture. Their poetry derived from French poetry. (Panayotis Soutsos criticized Solomos for the poverty of his rhyme and his hypermetric fifteen-syllable verses.) Classical while French classicism predominated, they followed the movement toward romanticism as soon as it began. We arrive at the height of French romanticism, that is to say, at the period which, though it did not produce the most important works in French literature, nonetheless created the greatest disturbance in European letters. It was natural that intellectual Hellenism, which always turned so actively toward France, should be moved by the spirit of the new times. If we look at the situation more closely, however, we ascertain that the romantic effervescence characterizing Greek scholars of the time was not as new to Greek psychology as classical criticism had indicated earlier and as the history of Greek letters maintained later. We are justified in thinking that the seeds came from outside, but they found Greece a favorable terrain in which to grow. Nostalgia for the past, melancholy disposition, and exaltation of liberty are the essential elements of romanticism and, simultaneously, traits attractive to the Greek spirit. All other interpretations of the romantic phenomenon that dominated Greek letters for fifty years (1830–1880) are very poor: imitation or influences can be fruitful in a literature only if they respond to some inner requirement of this literature; otherwise, the are extinguished. And we know that Hellenic romanticism, whether we honor or condemn it, flourished in a fruitful manner as part of the new Greek literature.

We encounter the first romantic experiments early in Greek letters. And we also find them early in Athens under the form of folk creation. Even before the War of Independence, Spiros Vouyouklis, influenced by the old Phanariot poetry, produced a series of poems expressing the romantic spirit and the sadness of love. His most representative works remained unpublished, but they show that a literary production had begun in Athens which was halfway between the folksong and the scholarly poem. It was precisely that which in later years, starting from the same city, replaced folk poetry for the most part.

Neroulos

With the liberation, most Phanariot scholars went to Greece. The most representative figures were Jacob Rizos Neroulos, Jacob Rizos Rangavis, his son, the famous Alexander Rizos Rangavis, and the two brothers, Panayotis and Alexander Soutsos, all of whom were related to one another. Neroulos (1778–1850) had published the well-known *Korakistika* before the revolution and the two tragedies, *Aspasia* (1813) and *Polyxena* (1814). Both were inspired by the classicism of the period and were written in a French classical style, deprived of all aesthetic value. However, *Polyxena,* which is written in a most homogeneous demotic language, reveals a certain charm in spots.

Another imitation of French classicism was *The Elopement of the Turkey* (1816). Neroulos used the *Lutrin* by Boileau as a model for his satiric poem. His kinsman, Alexander Rizos Rangavis, assures us in the French edition of his history of literature that the imitation surpassed the original. Since we are concerned with modern Greek literature, it perhaps suffices to note that this work ridicules the

Phanariot class, but critics were rarely able to stop at satire. During the period of the War of Independence, Neroulos published his *Literature* and his modern Greek *History* in French; both were written to illustrate the participation of the Phanariots in the neo-Hellenic Renaissance. He also published various poems which are distinguished by coldness and the absence of inspiration. His language, as was noted in the preceding chapter, is characterized by a return to archaism.

Neroulos received various important posts in the new Greek state; he was named repeatedly as minister of public instruction, and he died as ambassador to Constantinople, where he was born. At times, when he withdrew from public affairs, he devoted himself to intellectual matters; he was one of the founders of the Archeological Society. We should not forget his literary interests. In 1837 he published two comedies anonymously. In both works the author's sole aim was a personal attack, and he smothered, with his aggressive humor, all general or aesthetic effort. This, moreover, was the way these works were judged, not only by those he sought to attack, but even by the Phanariots: "Rizo n'a pas su renoncer à la Muse avant qu'elle ne renonçât a lie."

And yet, the Phanariots continued to compliment one another. According to Alexander Mavrokordatos, Neroulos was superior to Racine, for Alexander Rangavis, he was superior to Boileau, while Neroulos found Jacob Rizos Rangavis superior to Racine.

> Jacob Rizos has translated Racine. Is it Racine who has translated him, or is it he who has translated Racine?

Jacob Rizos Rangavis

Jacob Rizos Rangavis, a cousin of Jacob Rizos Neroulos, was also born in Constantinople in 1779. He attained high positions in Vlachia before the War of Independence and was able thus to contribute to the development of a theater movement at Bucharest. It was at this time that he translated the *Orestes* by Alfieri anonymously. After the insurrection, he established himself in Greece where he published poetry, original tragedies, and translations. He translated Corneille, Racine, and Voltaire. His original tragedies conformed to classical rules, but this did not bring him any closer to poetry. In his lyrical works, which often show the influence of Christopoulos, we encounter certain preromantic attempts; he was able to live far from the social tumult; he was able to live in freedom. He was attracted by the theme of parting, by the bitterness of love, and by the feeling of injustice which rules the world:

> Where are you, sweet light of my unhappy eyes?
> Where are you hiding, brilliant flame of my days?

The Phanariot theme of sadness acquired less conventional accents in Rangavis:

> Where am I? Where are they taking me? What solitude!
> Insupportable exile, frightful!
> How I am deprived of everything. . . .

The play of opposites, typically romantic, attracted him:

> When I amuse myself with my friends and when I am surrounded by delicacies, I dine and I fill up with wine, I laugh. But when I think that while I am of great cheer, others, strangers, half-naked, suffer privations, cry with hunger, I mourn.

His language, purified of foreign words, simultaneously lost much of the charm of the older Phanariot poetry. Sometimes, he attempted to write in the popular language, but we see that this language had become foreign to him and what he wrote were mere exercises. He died in Athens in 1855 leaving his son, Alexander, heir to his literary interests.

Alexander Rizos Rangavis

Alexander Rizos Rangavis continued his father's career, but with the difference which separates two successive generations, especially when a movement such as that described in the preceding chapters, intervened. We must also stress that the son presented an extraordinary force, an excessive activity, which was manifested both in his life and in his work. He was born on the shores of the Bosporus in 1809. He accompanied his father to the Danubian principalities and to Odessa and finally to Munich where he entered a military school founded by Louis of Bavaria. He went to Greece as an officer, but before long he moved on to administrative positions. In 1844 we find him a professor of archeology at the university; in 1856, minister of the exterior; in 1867, an ambassador. Twenty years later, he retired and died in 1892. During all these years, his many occupations did not keep him from incessant literary activity. He began by writing verses around 1830; he continued with plays, short stories, criticism, and simultaneously translated and wrote works in mathematics, military art, and archeology. He wrote histories of literature, scholarly manuals, a dictionary of code, and a great variety of works. His production came to dozens of volumes. A prolific and rapid writer, ever hasty and careless, he had no time to edit his work; thus his scientific writings, his histories of literature, and his memoirs are all an inexhaustible source of errors for anyone who trusts them without submitting them to critical appraisal. Furthermore, his criticism was awkward and hurried; it abounded in prejudices and in borrowed formulas. Nonetheless, despite the burden of his many occupations, he did apply himself to the purity and elegance of expression, to charm and wit, which can be appreciated all the more when the work is analyzed. His concern with style was such that he did not hesitate, despite his prolixity, to revise his works when he was about to reprint them.

This revision, conforming to the tendencies of the times, always consisted of an increased archaism. He began with romanticism, with which he had been profoundly imbued in Bavaria. His intention, in his earlier works, was to honor the national language and to rehabilitate the popular literature. Thus, his long poem *Demos and Helen*, published in 1831, was directly inspired by Greek tradition in subject, form, and language. In order to express himself, the sensitive young Phanariot found a form infinitely superior to that used at the time either by Phanar or by the rising School of Athens. We should not forget that a few years earlier Spiros Trikoupis had given us a similar attempt with his *Demos*. But in Rangavis treatment of verse and rhyme was more buoyant and much more effective. Rangavis triumphed over the difficulties and succeeded in retrieving from the thorns of scholarly production what he had come to know in his social environment, the royal road to the new Greek poetry: "Prairies strewn with flowers,/Ornamented with charm. . . ."

His verse was everywhere the fifteen-syllable with interlacing rhymes. His language, to the extent that the poet was able to liberate himself from Phanariot teaching, was the demotic.

See that white form among the flowers in the garden?
Tell me, is it a cloud come from the West to sprinkle
The imperishable flowers of the palace?

In these verses, Rangavis did not require the easy synizesis, particularly from one word to another. Thus, a hiatus resulted, although he did not seek it. He often resorted to elision, which gave a tight plastic character to his verse. All his verses did not show the quality of the examples presented here, but the fact that he sometimes achieved that level is something which should not pass unobserved:

'Αγγέλων χαμογέλασμα στὰ χείλια της πεθαίνει,
τὸ στῆθος της ἐνθύμισις κρυφὴ ἀνασηκώνει
καθὼς ἂν ἀπὸ θύελλα ἐχθεσινὴ δαρμένη
ἡ ζαφειρένια θάλασσα τὸν κόλπο της φουσκώνει.

A smile of angels dies on her lips,
A secret memory swells her breast
As though yesterday a storm had lashed her,
The sapphire sea inflates her breast.

We have other poems written in the demotic language, both original creations and imitations. Among these, the "Klephtes" was outstanding; put to music, it has served as a military march to our day:

Black is the night on every hill
The snow falls on the crags,
On the savage, somber ground,
On the crags, in the marshes,
The klephtes draw their swords.

In 1836, when Christopoulos spent a few weeks in Piraeus, Rangavis wrote him:

The winter is over,
The snow has melted;
To blossoming old gardens
You returned, nightingale,
Bird of Parnassus.

Polylas testifies that "even Solomos praised this ode." A little later, in 1837, the first volume of Rangavis's *Various Poems* appeared. His drama, *Phrosyne,* which was included in this volume, was preceded by an interesting introduction in the form of a dia-

logue between ME and HIM. HIM comments on and criticizes the
drama, which he has read in manuscript form, but actually this introduction is a manifesto in favor of romanticism.

> HIM: Are you a romantic?
> ME: What are you saying?
> HIM: You are a romantic . . . . Either you have never read any
> rules of the art of drama, or you are a romantic, as I am.

In a way, the poet took his occasion to reveal the romantic credo,
which contained all the key words of the new French romanticism.
And he concluded: "Rules neither introduce, nor do they trail after
Genius: they observe it from a distance, marking its path, as the
compass does not drag a comet behind it, but measures its heavenly
trajectory." We also find this same withdrawal from classical aesthetics in a letter that Rangavis addressed two years later to the
young Karasoutsas; he recommended the cultivation of personality
and nonconformity to the old rules: "Reject the enslavement of imitation. Support yourself only on your own poetic sense, on your
sensibility, which, for the poet, should be true and not feigned." It
is evident that Rangavis belonged to a new climate. A typical illustration is *Phrosini,* with its clearly romantic tendencies. The drama
was written in the demotic language, but its gaps, both scenic and
technical, are so numerous that his language is insufficient to bring it
to life. The romantic influence, particularly the Byronic influence, is
visible here. However, the latter is still more apparent in *The Deceiver of the People,* which is included in the second volume of
Various Poems (1840). *The Deceiver of the People* is a long metrical
narrative with a theme borrowed from the revolutionary period of
Orloff. In the short space of time separating *Demos* from this poem,
we already ascertain in Rangavis the beginning of a change toward
archaism.

In the 1837 volume among other writings, we find a short story
called "The Prison or Capital Punishment," which places Rangavis
at the beginning of Greek short-story writing. Later, his production
extended to all genres. The author's development is evident not only
in the change of language, but also in a more conspicuous tendency
toward classicism. We can say that Rangavis disavowed his early
convictions. In the theater, his *The Wedding of Koutroulis* (1845)
was archaic in language and in meter. Rangavis had always exhibited a vivid interest in metrics. The most well-known of his stories
are "The Notary Public," "The Horse-whip," and a novella, *The*

Prince of Moreas (1850). Rangavis sought to knit a plot, to create a myth. His dialogues possessed a certain life; they would have been more lively and of greater consequence if he had used the popular language more systematically. But, on the whole, once the boredom caused by language has been surmounted, we are confronted by spirited, substantial, well-composed works, perceptibly superior to the studies of manners which were to flood Greek literature much later. Greatly influenced by Sir Walter Scott, *The Prince of Moreas* even today is certainly lacking in depth, but is agreeable in the different foreign languages into which it has been translated. The development of Rangavis is especially discernible in poetry. His later works are marked with a cold archaism, often manifested in choice of subjects and always in the manner in which those subjects are treated. The best known of these later works are: *The Voyage of Dionysos* (1864) and *The Quick-Flying Falcon* (1871):

> The wide expanse of the Aegean sea was sleeping.
> And we observed two skies: the one above, azure.
> The other, below, the color of turquoise.
> (taken from *Voyage of Dionysos*)

Both works mentioned above are long narratives with a very carefully worked form, attempting to attain a continuous classical line, either by the wealth of images or by the exaggerations of language. In his poem "She" (1863) we again encounter this commonplace of Athenian romanticism, but formulated with somberness and with remarkable discretion:

> Renouncing life, an impassive voyager,
> I wandered endlessly searching for repose,
> Then I saw her beauty glowing before my eyes.
> She was full of sympathy, full of sweetness,
> The beautiful sister of the angels.

Longevity permitted Rangavis not only to be the precursor of romanticism but also to observe the evolution of romanticism to a certain degree, then to disavow the movement and to assist in its inglorious end. Always curious, interested in a variety of matters, he was in time to know the generation of 1880 and to honor it in the person of Drosinis. Despite his weaknesses and his insufficiencies, the last representative of the great Phanariot generation, "the patriarch of the poetry of Phanariots in Greece," Rangavis managed once again to occupy a primary position in the new literary circles.

From this point of view, the brothers Soutsos revealed themselves as much more typical and more conventional representatives of Phanariot romanticism, not only in their work but also in their personal lives. With the brothers Soutsos, romanticism was not a theory; it was a way of life. Past and present criticism has detected foreign influences and traces of imitation in their work. It is evident that both were swept along by romantic intoxication, to which they abandoned themselves without reservation. In them, imitation, considerable as it might be, became a second nature, became a creator of life. Though Rangavis continued to place romanticism on a literary plane, for Alexander Soutsos, in 1839, the movement formed a way of life: "I have the misfortune to doubt the romantic love of the diplomats of Greece." And elsewhere, "Under the light of the moon, in the most romantic attitude. . . ." Romanticism was no longer a literary subject; it was a life style. Imitation was insufficient to interpret it: imitation expressed a choice.

Alexander Soutsos

Alexander Soutsos was born in Constantinople in 1803. He studied in Chios under Vambas, and later in Paris; he knew Koraes, to whom he had been recommended. In Paris, both he and his brothers found the romantic movement at its height. One name, above all, aroused the enthusiasm of the French public: Béranger continued and also restored the old tradition of the folksong by giving it a sharp political, sociological, and, let us say, even philosophical acuteness. Soutsos circulated in this romantic environment, was stimulated by it, and set out to become the Béranger of Greece. His early works in Greek were satires inspired directly by the ideas, the verse, and the tone of the French poet. Sometimes, he imitated; this was especially evident in the collection entitled *Panorama of Greece* (1833). The tone sought to be familiar. It is clear that the poet wrote with the hope that his satire would be sung, that it would become a song, that it would reach the people:

His Excellency embraces me every day.
When I pillage his cash box, he looks away, shows no interest.
The essential point is that, every evening, I whisper in his ear

What one person or another is thinking and doing.
Tra la la,
All is well.

What he sought was a simplicity, a charm that would recall the spontaneous element of the street songs. His satire was nourished by parody and imitation. Here is how he rendered the decree of Kapodistrias.

> *State of Morocco, Governor Count Nantes, Son of the Late Toni Maria*
> Considering that you all have rendered former services, it does not follow that we are blind, and seeing that it is profitable for the good of the people that only one should inherit the sacrifices of many, and that those who have a certain fame should go to the devil, ignoring, moreover, the advice of the Senate, we declare as culprits of the highest treason, the insolent Koundouriotis and his disloyal Zaïmis.

His political satire has perception. Sometimes the psychological analysis of people he ridicules is successful. When Augustin Kapodistrias left Greece, Soutsos recalled one by one his old honors, but occasionally he interrupted his discourse with the same refrain:

> Don't throw lemons, lads! One-two, one-two!
> There is a Count in the boat.

His satiric verse had no respect even for death:

> Two shots of the pistol resounded before the door of the
> Church.
> Tra la la, boom, boom,
> And instantly, you fall on your face, Kapodistrias!
> Tra la la, boom, boom.

Sometimes, though rarely, his style was elevated. The satiric character receded before an elegiac tone. Such is the case in a monologue of one of the brothers Mavromichalis:

> New imitator of Harmodios and Aristogeiton,
> I will cover my avenging sword with myrtle.
> I will fall before the tyrant, I will butcher him, and,
> courageously,
> I will be butchered like they were.

In the same collection, *The Panorama of Greece,* is also included "The Letter to the King of Greece, Othon," many of whose verses have survived to our day in the memory of the Greeks, as "To the beautiful Bosporos . . ." or "Kalvos and Solomos."

Such a witty satire, a realistic one based on facts, could only be effective. And, indeed, the polemics of Soutsos contributed to a great extent in the activity which characterized the history of Greece to 1863. Other causes also contributed in maintaining this brilliance. "The press was still in its infancy. Politics, to a great extent, were carried on through poetry. The sonorous verses of Alexander Soutsos exercised an influence on public opinion, unfortunately not a good one, but considerably greater than any that can be exercised today by the articles in the newspapers and even the verses of Souris." Vikelas's comparison is erroneous; in a later chapter we will examine the reasons that Souris's satire had no influence. But one reason is seen in the social satire of Soutsos, a satire which almost always had nothing to do with reality. He described morals, he satirized conditions unrelated to the first Greek society of Nauplion. There was no personal tone, nor a voluntary censorship; the only end Soutsos pursued was to arouse laughter by descriptions that evoked nothing of the real life of the period. The satire descended to shadow-boxing. The imitation of Béranger is evident here: criticism does not emerge from experience but from books. Béranger wrote *Mon Habit*; Soutsos wrote" To My Old Coat."

M'a-t-on jamais vu dans une antichambre
T'exposer au mépris d'un grand?
(Béranger)
No one has seen you frequenting the chambers of the Great,
And to this day you have never dishonored your old age.
(Soutsos)

This lack of a sense of reality brought Soutsos, who always followed in Béranger's footsteps, to reflections inappropriate to Greek sentiments during that period:

"Je veux bien que le diable m'emporte,"

says the God of Béranger, looking on the world.

"If only I were a God,"

writes Soutsos in his turn.

This same absence of contact with reality is found again in various theatrical works Soutsos wrote, such as *The Prodigal* (1830), *The President of the Council* (1843), and *The Rebel Poet* (1843). They were cold versified elaborations, without action; even reminders of Moliere failed to make them appear as art. Besides the plays, we should mention for its bad quality, his only work in prose, *The Exile* (1835), "full of tearful pomp and interjections . . . composed of reminiscences of various foreign readings," as Angelos Vlachos characterized it. His other prose writings were some dialogues and short texts of a political nature.

In the meantime, he continued his abundant production of verse, in which politics remained the principal subject. His verse, which remained undeveloped, is often prosaic; imitations (Barthélemy and Byron) are abundant. Thus, we have a series of journalistic articles in verse, written with an incredible facility. Every kind of patriotic and political subject inspired him during those years. Sometimes, he attained a certain height, but this was pure rhetoric:

> Saint and Almighty Spirit of Liberty! From the first day of creation, God has breathed a living breeze into all that He had created.

The aspiration for freedom and the revolutionary ardor of Soutsos often brought him in conflict with the authorities. He was persecuted, imprisoned, forced on many occasions to flee Greece. Death found him in Smyrna in 1863. The day before he died, he wrote to his brother Panayotis: "I have been, as you say, the projectile in the catapult which the Almighty has cast on the heads of two tyrants. But their heads were broken, while I, today, the projectile in His catapult, am driven as a stone in the dust and I have not even sung the praise of the victory of the Greeks." The National Assembly, on hearing of his death, decreed the publication of his *Complete Works* at state expense but this decree was never fulfilled. In 1874, John Papadiamantopoulos (later known as Jean Moréas) undertook to reedit the works of Soutsos. In his preface to *The Rebel Poet,* he wrote: "A pure language, picturesque and exact, healthy and poetic ideas, elegant and flowing verses, of which our young poetry offers few comparable examples are the qualities that ornament the drama and all the works of Alexander Soutsos, justly considered the father of neo-Hellenic poetry and reformer of the language." Moréas, at eighteen, gave the common attitude of the period; Soutsos, with all his faults and virtues, was the foremost scholar in Athens of this time because he characterized it. He affixed his seal on the technique of verse, of thought, and of politics. He created the special school of Athenian satire. His life, equally impregnated as his writing by romanticism, exercised its influence on the younger Athenians and he became their model in every way, in action and in poetry.

Panayotis Soutsos

Panayotis Soutsos, three years younger, followed a parallel line in his personal life and in his career. He was born in 1806 and died in 1868. Much more intellectual than his brother, it was only under the influence of Alexander that he became involved in politics. His world was poetry, lyricism, elegies. Because of this, his life was much smoother and much more systematically devoted to letters. His principal juvenilia were: in 1831 a first volume of *Poetry*; in 1834 the novel *Leandros,* and in the following year a new collection of poetry, *The Guitar*. The main body of his poetic production of 1831 is contained in *The Voyager*. Soutsos informs us that he was eighteen years old when he wrote this work. He says, moreover, that it was "conceived under the overcast horizon of Nordic Europe; it resembled the phantoms emerging from the darkness of the tomb."

His poetic work had dramatic form, but was not intended for the stage. Two lovers, separated by fate, meet on Mount Athos. The hero performs his duty toward his country before that toward his betrothed. After the war, he is informed of her death. Overwhelmed by grief, he travels widely to forget, and, one day, he arrives at Mount Athos. The girl, Ralou, who was not dead, continues to live with the memory of her beloved. The desire for vengeance for what he had done to her battles within her heart against her inexhaustible love. They meet and recognize each other. Ralou seems to the voyager a phantom come to reproach him for having abandoned her. He goes insane and commits suicide; Ralou dies. Soutsos weaves his verses on such improbable stories. They are not lacking in certain force and even grandeur. His search for sublime images was often crowned with success. Otherwise, there are the lengthy, rhetorical effects of a juvenile eloquence, which chill the feeble emotions and relative interest that this drama should have aroused.

The linguistic history of *The Voyager* reveals an interesting side to Soutsos's literary objectives. The edition of 1831 was followed by others in 1842, 1851, and 1864. Soutsos revised his work each time, not only to accord with the evolution of his linguistic convictions, but also to render it more accessible to the public. To these revisions can be added one more which was not completed, and of which we find traces in the *New School* (1853), Soutsos's famous linguistic manifesto, which we will consider later in this *History*. Thus we see Soutsos's incessant effort and his assiduous care to perfect his poetic form; always restless, always dissatisfied in his conceit, he sought to approach even closer the crests of the Parnassian idea. But such was not his fate. After his juvenilia, we find him lost on ambitious endeavors, in tragedies or in novels, for which he had no talent.

Some verses of *The Voyager*, particularly in their original, most simple form, could be included in a modern Greek anthology. The romantic themes, the fondness for solitude, the passion for escape, the sadness of love, are often encountered:

> The distinguished spirits seek solitude and would make commerce with ordinary men, as the great plane tree, which only sinks its roots where they are not touched by the trunks of other plane trees.

The alternate rhyme scheme, with its elegiac tone, prepares the way both for the heights of Athenian romanticism and its decline.

> What have I gained in leaving traces of my passage throughout the immense space of Eternity! What has the ship gained, which sails on the waves, leaving behind it the traces of the stern?

His romanticism, however, remained religious, as Soutsos himself remained a religious man to the end of his life: "Divinity, love, and liberty; this is the triangle in which Panayotis Soutsos created his own poetry," he later wrote about himself. Indeed, the religious element prevails even in *The Voyager*:

> O God, I sing Your glory night and day.
> You have covered the earth with flowers, the heaven with stars.
> The people on earth agree, in their discord, to adore You.
> Thousands of different languages praise You at the same time.

This same collection of poetry of 1831 contains a series of love poems and a third part, entitled *Elegies*, where he continually attacks Kapodistrias.

But Soutsos' lyricism was manifested more characteristically in
The Guitar. There we find numerous satiric poems, imitations of his
brother's satires, but with the lighter spirit or liveliness that characterizes Christopoulos. Besides these, his poetic temperament was
expressed in elegiac verses, where the romantic technique of French
poetry was associated with his dreamy mood:

> He did not die when, in Methone, he set fire to a ship with
> great clamor. He did not take the ashes from the inferno in a
> shroud. Nor did he have for a funeral bed the carcass of a
> double mast.
>
> (taken from *Our Farewell to Miaoulis Who Is Dead*)

The form of strophes in most of his poetry was clearly romantic:

> Roll your waters, river of Sparta. In your foam the dead yel-
> low leaves of cold autumn follow your dormant waters silently.
> As they, I will follow you in silence, a voyager in mourning.
>
> (taken from *The Ruins of Sparta*)

The Village Graveyard by Thomas Gray, one of the poems which
nourished Western preromanticism, was paraphrased in *The Guitar*.
But more than any other name, that of Lamartine should be mentioned here. The French poet very early moved the emotions of
Greek scholars: Constantine Ekonomos imitated Lamartine in one
of his discourses; Spiros Trikoupis thought about Lamartine in his
poem *The Lake of Missolonghi*. But it is with *The Guitar* that the
poetry of Lamartine truly penetrated into the essence of Greek literature. Panayotis Soutsos imitated Lamartine in *The Lake*. Soutsos
has:

> O sea! The moon, for the fourth time, has dropped on you its
> reflection of gold. But she does not see your glaucous mirror.
> Look, I am alone, seated on the solitary rock, where once I saw
> you sitting with me.

Here the poet of *The Lake* begins his long and glorious career.
The difference between the personality of the two brothers Soutsos
can be defined by the influence of Béranger on Alexander and Lamartine on Panayotis.

Almost contemporary with *The Guitar*, as we have seen, was the
first novel of Panayotis Soutsos, *Leandros* (1834). This work derives
directly from Western romanticism, more specifically from Foscolo's
Letters to Jacob Ortiz. Its form is epistolary; the romantic element

abounds here. The hero is presented as a man of "severe character, independent spirit, and fiery passions. For society, he feels the usual resentment which is habitually inspired by its requirements, its prejudices, and its ceremonies." His letters "are somewhat stoic, insolent, and sarcastic with respect to all societies." All the treasured commonplaces of romanticism, the moons, the storms, the torrents, the melancholy, and the nostalgia, as well as the exaltations, the visions, the phantoms, the tremors, are found here. "Come, Rousseau! Come Shakespeare! Come Goethe and Schiller!" All rush forward, not only these but many others, and offer to assist the publishing of the first romantic novel in Greek. Fifty years of romantic novel production were nourished by treasures borrowed from Soutsos. Despite these plagiarisms, however, the agreement between the poet's inflamed spirit and romantic exaltation is such that it gives us a homogeneous work, though a bad one.

Immediately following his early youth, Panayotis Soutsos lost his way, as often happened with the romantic poets. He tended to rise toward great intellectual conceptions and fall into a versified prosaism. In 1839 he wrote: "My Muse, O scholars of the Greeks! She no longer follows the transports of youth, but having an awareness of her sacred task, she goes forward prudently and gravely." Neither his *Messiah,* to which the above is a preface, nor the tragedies which followed, succeeded in recreating the atmosphere of *The Voyager* or *Leandros.* Finally, in 1864, after numerous metrical and prose works, he wrote one more novel: *Charitini, or the Beauty of Christian Religion, Antidote Against the Deviation of Ernest Rénan, Who Repudiated the Divinity of Jesus Christ.* Inspiration is lacking; he substitutes grandiloquence. His language is extremely archaic, which discourages even the best of intentions.

The Phanariots had given all that they had to offer. Certain works still survive, thanks to their suppleness, as in the case of Rangavis; but the new capital of Hellenism. Athens, will assimilate their heritage and will renew it. Indeed, beginning with the formation of the new Greek state, one observes a phenomenon whose consequences are felt even today. Whereas enslaved Hellenism and the Diaspora possessed numerous and important intellectual centers, matters changed after the insurrection; due to many causes, which we will not examine here, the colonies beyond Greece proper began to decline economically and intellectually. The Greek provinces, poor and with limited cultural resources, were unable to acquire intellectual autonomy; intellectual life was concentrated in the Greek capital. One good scholar of the time, George Serouios, who established himself in Hermoupolis after the revolution and whose activities were teaching and literature, complained in 1845 about the centralizing power of Athens. Only Athens could claim publishing facilities: "the Athenians have a passion for every kind of publication." The Athenian scholars were inconsiderate of their provincial colleagues; whoever nourished some kind of ambition, whoever sought to succeeed in literature, must transport his activity to Athens. In Constantinople, a few prerevolutionary scholars survived, but they no longer kept up; besides these, there were some younger writers, but their eyes also turned toward Athens.

Last of the Phanariots

Most of the scholars living in Constantinople had much in common with scholars of liberated Greece, as we can see in such poets as Christos Parmenides, prose writers such as Nicholas Argyriades, who will be discussed elsewhere, and playwrights such as Michael Hourmouzis (1801–1882), who belonged both to Athens and to Phanar. Parmenides, moreover, left Constantinople while still young. Hourmouzis spent a great part of his life in Athens, particularly during the revolutionary and early postrevolutionary years. In 1861, there appeared in Athens an anonymous translation of Aristophanes's *Plutus*. This work was attributed to Joseph Ginakas, but it appears to be that of Hourmouzis. The language of the translation is of exceptional cultivation, with very few signs of the decline of the *katharevousa*.

With Hourmouzis, I mention the comedy of Nicholas Avazidis, *The Imaginary Philosopher* (1840), published in Constantinople. Here also belongs the anonymous D. G. K., who published the comedy *Monsieur Kozis* in Constantinople in 1848.

Tantalidis

The true representative of Phanar in Constantinople during this period is Elias Tantalidis (1818–1876). He published various studies and collections of poetry: *Games* (1839) and *Intimate Poems* (1860).

Tantalidis preferred the *katharevousa,* but he also wrote poems in the spoken language. His technique was strictly Phanariotic. His early poems exhibited the strong influence of Christopoulos. A distinguishing element in his work was the ability to lower his tone and to restore the forgotten charm and jocosity of the Phanariots. Though he became blind at an early age, his poems retained this humor to the end of his life. Wherever we see this jocular humor associated with the language of Constantinople, the success of Tantalidis merits attention.

Thus, Tantalidis, whose entrance into the arena was hailed by A. R. Rangavis, can be considered the last Phanariot poet. He was a professor at the school of Chalki, where George Vizyinos was one of his students. He exhorted Vizyinos to apply himself to letters, and unquestionably influenced him in his poetry. However, culture was concentrated in Athens.

Only the Heptanesians were an exception to this rule. Their administrative autonomy was the greatest external cause of their intellectual autonomy. They also had a university, the Ionian Academy, with remarkable professors, where we find an intellectual life on a higher plane developing. And last, as a heritage from the Venetian occupation, the Ionian Islands had continuously cultivated literature, in fact with a local color that varied from island to island.

Chapter 19

The Heritage of Solomos

School of the Ionian Islands

The originality of the Ionian Islands, which benefited from the aggregate of modern Greek culture, was reinforced by Solomos's activity and brilliance. When his friends and successors were not following the tradition of the folksong, they were conforming to the rules of Italian versification, which gave a softness to verse. Generally, each of the Ionian Island writers accepted and cultivated one of the forms Solomos had employed. Ionian Island poetry was essentially nationalistic. Its usual themes also included love and nature. But this school was distinguished by the idealism with which the subjects were treated, and by a spirituality and a nobility oriented toward abstraction. We should recall that criticism and satire had their place in Solomos. The Ionian Island school had no great accomplishments to offer in imaginative prose. Not only was the production rare in this area, but the greatest part of it did not present specifically Ionian characteristics. In the Ionian school, it was poetry, and poetry derived from Solomos. It was not accidental that while Solomos lived, two collections of folksongs appeared, both emanating directly from this group. The first collection, published in 1850, was presented by Polylas at the age of twenty-five.

Matesis

When Solomos still lived in Zakynthos, we know that he was surrounded by a group of scholars, among whom Anthony Matesis (1794–1875) was most prominent. Matesis was influenced by Solomos, whom he admired from the beginning. He also wrote Italian verses; he wrote light poems, satires, anacreontics, idylls, but occasionally his tone was elevated to honor the beloved dead, to honor those who had fought for liberty. Parallel with this, around 1824, he was occupied with the problem of language and defended the popular language with fervor, in the same sense that Solomos defended it in his *Dialogue*. Matesis' style offered nothing new for someone who knew the verses of Solomos. However, from another point of view, it was more closely associated to the forms of the past, to anacreontics and to other forms. Because of this, later it was easy for him to turn toward archaism and to discard the precious influence of Solomos. His versification was quite neglected, but it contained a tenderness and dignity which one often encountered in the literature of the Ionian Islands.

> You are extinguished, dainty one,
> As the small flame is extinguished,
> And you have exhaled
> Your last breath.

His vocabularly was poor and uncultivated; the rhyme scheme accepted all kinds of compromises and expediencies.

As he was influenced directly and somewhat externally by Solomos, Matesis welcomed the romantic movement. He translated Ossian, *The Sepulchers* by Foscolo, and Gray's *Elegy*. The greatest work of his life, in my estimation, was *Basil*, which relied on the romantic influences he had accepted. He composed this theatrical work around 1830; it was marked by a complete opposition to the neoclassical style as represented in neo-Hellenic letters by the tragedies of Christopoulos, Neroulos, or Zambelios. Written in prose, it borrowed its subject from recent local history. The work is marked by an ardent liberalism and by a strong interest in the island folk life. Matesis later defined the work as "a historical novel presented under dramatic form."

We are in Zakynthos in 1712 at an aristocratic manor. The father represents conservative concepts; he cannot envisage another kind of marriage for his daughter than a union with an aristocrat. His son has progressive ideas, while the daughter is in love with a plebeian and has entered into relations with him. Following various vicissitudes, the father is forced to accept the marriage. Dialogue is rapid and lively, plot is skillfully woven. Psychology has no design here, hence the characters and situations are natural. The manners are well calculated and have been rendered as a slice of life. This presentation caused the work to be considered a study of manners. But the author's intention and his results surpass by far the objectives of a premature naturalism in letters: we have here an authentic social drama, the first to appear in Greece. It was not published until 1855, but it had already been presented on the stage around 1832.

Typaldos

The great brilliance of Solomos dated from the Corfiot period of his life. Julius Typaldos (1814–1883) was the most typical heir of Solomos in poetry. In this heritage, Typaldos appropriated the suavity and the idealism. His only collection published during his lifetime was *Various Poems* (1856), dedicated to Solomos. The following year, he rendered a memorial full of profound admiration to his master. Later, he continued to write, but this part of his work remained unpublished to our times. His inspiration was basically patriotic; however, the religious element was equally manifested in its most ideal form. Typaldos was dependent on Solomos, but he was also influenced directly by the folksong, which he greatly admired.

> See, in front, this huge and terrible mountain,
> Whose crest is so white and whose base so black?
> This is Kissavos, famous throughout the world,
> Who sends down to the sea his swollen rivers,
> And rains shots of the klephtes like lightning on the Turks.

These verses are found in a long poem on Rigas. The flexibility is associated with the fifteen-syllable verse, with the mysticism expressed at the end of each of the three sections of the poem in various meters. Rigas is transfigured in this poem and presented, in the words of Palamas, "in a kind of sacred pre-Raphaelite portrait." In reality, something obscure and misty, with muted colors, distinguished the poetry of Typaldos; it was bathed in a lunar light. Among his other poems, the most well known is entitled "The Imaginary Creature." The theme of the ideal woman, borrowed by the poet from foreign literature, is treated in soft, melodious verses to which an easy rhyme gives added softness:

> You who at first appeared
> As a dream in my eyes,
> You who aroused stormy passions
> In my innocent heart,
> Where are you, my love,

> Where are you, sweet hope?
> Are you living on earth,
> Or on celestial stars?

The synizesis is cultivated, avoiding the harsh consonants; the melodiousness marks a culmination of the poet's efforts. Many of his poems were set to music and survived as songs among later generations.

> Awake, my sweet beloved,
> The night is profound,
> All nature is sleeping,
> Everything is silent.
> Only the pale moon,
> Like me is awake,
> It sails in the nocturnal
> Calm of the sky.

The environment that suited Typaldos was a scholarly one; though in his art he borrowed indiscriminately from folksongs, we know that he succeeded in assimilating Western models in his poetry. His scholarship helped him influence younger poets in useful direction. From this point of view, he should be given first place among those who contributed to the decline of Athenian romanticism.

Manousis

Where the poets of the Ionian Islands departed from Solomos, we see a diminishing quality in their production. Anthony Manousis (1828–1903) published a long poem, *The Death of the Blind Girl,* in 1848. In the dedication, he spoke with extreme admiration about the poet Solomos. The subject of the poem is essentially romantic. Written entirely in Dantean tercets, it is impregnated with the idealism of Solomos and deeply influenced by his language, but one also perceives the author's individual charm:

> Crowned with celestial roses,
> As a young bride, smiling innocently,
> Aurora rises from the crusty sea.
> The kiss she plants on blue breasts
> Makes them sparkle like gold.
> And she awakens, radiant.

In 1850 he published a collection of folksongs, which Polylas praised highly. The strong influence of Solomos appears again in the Introduction. From this point on, Manousis oscillated between the Italian technique of Solomos and imitation of the folksong. His collections, *Sighs* (1857) and *Lyric Poems* (1876), are representative of both these influences, but the lyricism in the short poems, sonnets, and others is feeble. A slight tendency toward refinement of language made this weakness more evident. But certain satiric poems in the collection revealed a pleasant survival in Manousis of the authentic satiric spirit of Solomos and his predecessors.

Romas

In the lyric climate Solomos created in the Ionian Islands, the appearance of the same name of George Kandianos Romas (1796–1867) is most surprising. When he published his *Flowers* in 1853, dedicated to Solomos, Kerkyra praised him, as did Solomos himself. Zalokostas dedicated a poem to him, and the periodical *Euterpe* wrote in the same year: "Mr. Romas is the Young of our sister the Heptanese." Today thiis collection gives the impression that it was the honest and considerate citizen, rather than the poet, who addressed these praises. Furthermore, Romas wrote *Flowers* after his daughter's death which associates it with Young. The poet used artlessly the commonplaces of romantic sorrow in verses only slightly influenced by the melody of Solomos and written in a mixed language. Here and there, raw feeling provokes a certain emotion, but it is not an artistic one:

> I love you for the virtues
> That ornament you,
> I love you for the charm,
> That you diffuse around you.

His later collection, *The Cottage* (1865), where Romas's other love. that of country, was projected, merits only a simple reference. The poet detached himself completely from the Ionian Island tradition and aligned himself coldly, in hundreds of strophes, to a purist language. Solomos himself condemned the defection of his old friend toward archaism.

Melissinos

Parallel to Romas, but without his talents, was the work of Spiros Melissinos (1823–1888). He was a prolific writer, among other things, of tragedies, and he departed quite far from the example of Solomos, despite a theoretical fidelity which he retained. If his memory has survived, he owes it all to a few juvenilia.

> Your face turns to me; I still remember
> How, without thinking,
> I ran here and there, gathering flowers
> For your thick tresses.

These verses belong to his work *The Sepulchers* (1860), where he also preserved some personal memories of Solomos.

Single Survivals

The influence of Solomos, however, was so great that it was not rare to encounter Ionian Islands poets remembered only for a single poem that emerged directly or indirectly out of Solomos's world. This was the case with Spiros Zambelios, a detractor of Solomos, who borrowed directly from *Lambros:*

> Ποία μέσα στῆς νυκτὸς τὴ σκοτεινάδα
> εἰς τὴν ἀστροφεγγιὰ στέκει ἀποκάτου;
> Γλυκιὰ εἶναι τοῦ προσώπου της ἡ ἀχνάδα,
> φορεῖ στεφάνι γάμου ἢ τοῦ θανάτου;
> Στολίζουν τὴν ἀχνή της εὐμορφάδα
> τὰ ὁλόμαυρα μαλλιὰ ριμμένα κάτου,
> καὶ ὅλα λυτά, ὁλόλευκα ἐνδυμένη
> σὰν καθαρὴ παρθένα ἀποθαμένη.

Who, then, holds you in the obscurity of night, under the rays of the moon? It is sweet, the pallor of her face. Is it a marriage wreath or a death wreath on her black hair, falling to her shoulders, all bare? She is dressed in white, such a pure maiden, dead.

Later, along with other genres, he continued to write poetry. Inspiration for this was deeply influenced by Athenian romanticism. He was always indebted for form to Solomos, particularly Solomos of the Zakynthian period. Rarely does one encounter a more personal tone:

> I hear you in the murmur of the pines,
> In the murmur of the roses.
> I hear you in the brook that flows
> And makes the flowers blossom.

Spiros Xydias survived with a single poem, written sometime before 1840; we find it today in anthologies, even though it is attributed to someone else:

> The day has sweetly dawned; the morning star announces the appearance of the sun. Perhaps it is in vain that we are together, we two. The vaporous moon has departed, she who, one night showed me your face, and a tear, at the moment you said, "I love you."

Gerasimos Mavroyannis (1823–1906), known especially for his later works on the history of art and the history of the Ionian Islands, gave us a collection of poetry, published in 1858 in which was included, among various poems in a purist language, an imitation of a folksong in "The Sailor of the Ionian Sea":

> On the high sea, among the waves, between Skinari and Cephalonia, a beautiful ship journeyed; the wind caressed her white sails, the waves sweetly caressed her stern.

The typically romantic characteristic of poetry, which is associated with youth and vanishes with it, is found both in the Ionian Island and the Athenian Schools.

Elizabetios Martinengos (1832–1885), son of Elizabeth Martinengos, retained in his earlier poems something of the lightness of Solomos's early verses. George Martinelis (1836–1896) also began his poetic career with a certain charm and sentimentality, which later changed to affectation. In any case, he exhibited neither sensibility, nor elegance, nor melodiousness.

> Listen, young girl, when, with bitter melancholy, with harmony of verse, my unhappy heart says, "I love you."

We have nobility without richness, inspiration without spirit, and words without force.

In general, the Ionian Island school showed little innovation with the passing years. It was a closed world, which became increasingly impoverished and tended to die out. Nobility became debility, idealism was transformed to sentimentality, vocabulary was impoverished and unfolded with monotony, expressions and images became a langorous sentimentality: roses, flowers, maidens, harmonies, and the rest.

Panas

Panayotis Panas proved a stronger personality; his work survived. Born in a village of Cephalonia in 1832, he went into a variety of areas such as journalism and folk publications, until he committed suicide in 1896. As a liberal, he was occupied with politics and worked militantly for the Enosis (union) of the Ionian Islands. He was persecuted and exiled for his political activities. He became interested in letters early; his first literary manifestations revealed his admiration for the Soutsos brothers. In 1862, however, he published a translation of Ossian in fifteen-syllable blank verse in the demotic. The quality of his verses merit attention.

> Lovely girl of the sky, the silence radiates softly on your face.
> You come forth fascinated, and the stars in the East follow your
> Footsteps. You appear, and the clouds rejoice and gaily cover
> Their somber breasts with a brilliant light.

In 1833, he published a collection of poetry, *Works of Idleness,* where he collected a portion of his earlier production. He made new concessions to the purist language, but simultaneously he continued to cultivate the popular language. His satire combined the manner of Alexander Soutsos with the tradition of the Ionian Islands. But an important element, which should be underscored, was the literary satire found in this collection. His satiric poems, to which there is a reference in the chapters relating to the school of Athens and to Valaorites, exhibit the high culture and style that characterized the intellectuals of the Ionian Islands during this period.

Polylas

Criticism was also a part of the inheritance of Solomos and the most important representative of modern Greek criticism, Jacob Polylas (1826–1896), predominated as a worthy heir. A number of the critical works that appeared at this time in the Ionian Islands are due to the influence of Polylas; his systematic political activity made him a leader of a group of scholars, united not only by common aesthetic concepts, but also by political prejudices. Polylas's principal critical work was the *Prologomena* to the edition of Solomos in 1859. We should observe that Polylas was largely responsible for the edition itself and that it constituted a monument to criticism: the choice of variants, the organization of the text, and the scholarly, succinct commentaries made this publication a model in its time. Even today, the continuing research on Solomos increasingly recognizes the value of the work Polylas accomplished.

Polylas was deeply influenced by his friendship with Solomos, particularly during the Corfiot period, the poet's most meditative period. German idealism was at the base of Polylas's criticism, but his critical temperament went beyond any prefabricated system and permitted him to erect his critical edifice, independent of any preconceived theory. The two stages, the objective and the subjective, of criticism, knowledge, comprehension, and judgment were the basis of his effort. He began by conscientiously collecting and arranging all the historical, biographical, and personal elements necessary to our knowledge of the poet. Then he analyzed the elements of poetry, comparing them with all the elements previously indicated, and he concluded with evaluations which show an extremely delicate poetic sensibility. His observations on Shakespeare are equally relevant. They were made on the occasion of the translations mentioned below. Lastly, we should not forget his critical penetration as it was expressed in his controversy with Spiros Zambelios in 1859–1960. The latter, in his monograph *On the Origin of the Demotic Term 'I Sing,'* criticized Polylas's edition and, among many other sharp observations, he maintained that Solomos, during his Zakynthian period, had not used the popular language. Polylas responded to this attack in the following year with a publication he called *Whence the Phobia of Mysticism of Mr. Zambelios.* Here he again analyzed certain aspects of Solomos's work with sagacity and critical talent, pursuing the reflections observed in the *Prolegomena* and complementing these.

The language of Polylas in the *Prolegomena* was still the language that Solomos cultivated. Later, Polylas combined the influence of Athens with the teachings of Solomos for a more elevated language to harmonize with the elevated ideas. In the pamphlet published in 1892, *Our Literary Language,* we ascertain that he had departed considerably from the tradition of Solomos. He had lost nothing of his critical acuity, but we perceive a confusion between the legitimate refinement of language and its archaization. Polylas was primarily a critic, in the sense that he was more concerned with making critical examination of matter than contributing to creative imagination. He not only took into consideration other writers' critical thought, but he acted on it. His imagination made comparisons, but did not create. Thus, as his criticism was action, certain of his works do not require creative imagination. I refer specifically to his translations of Shakespeare and of Homer.

In 1855, he presented *The Tempest* by Shakespeare in popular prose enhanced with poetic elements. In 1889 he presented *Hamlet.* The popular language he used was rich and found a convenient vehicle in a wisely worked iambic thirteen-syllable verse. In the meantime, he had begun to publish his translations of Homer (the *Odyssey* in 1875, the *Iliad* in 1890). We have become accustomed, under the influence of Pallis and of certain other older Homeric theorists, to seek the morphological elements of the folksong in translations of Homer. Polylas followed an entirely different path in his translations; he used the fifteen-syllable verse, but one entirely free of the folksong tradition. On the contrary, he revealed a conscientious tendency toward archaic grandeur. His translation at no moment captivates us, but it very often inspires an admiration and a feeling of respect very close to those which a reading of the original inspires. Only the element of charm is diminished; and from this point of view, it can be said that the translation is inferior.

Hence, the lack of imagination is replaced by the imagination of the classics, and Polylas is clearly revealed as a great artisan of expression and verse. From the versification heritage of Solomos, he did not appropriate, like other poets of the Ionian Islands, the early melodic elements, but rather the full maturity of the last period. It is a robust verse, whose melody is only internal, a solid verse, without a crack. The thirteen-syllable verse, with its variety of accents and scholarly caesuras, constitutes a significant contribution to neo-Hellenic metrics.

The same charms encountered in the translations are also found in the few original works of Polylas. They posssess natural nobility of thought and language but simultaneously some antilyrical coldness. Moreover, even in these few original poems, the researchers have discovered borrowed elements. We have also a very few short stories from Polylas, but they add nothing to his fame. Polylas was primarily, and has remained, an important critic in Greek literature. His exclusive attachment to the memory of his master Solomos, his political battles, and a certain sterility of soul, which accentuated the age, deprived him of only one critical quality, breadth of spirit. Thus, he could not appreciate either the qualities of Valaorites or the virtues of Kalvos. He was unjust to both writers. He did, however, as we will see, praise the early efforts of Palamas and Eftaliotis's attempts at versification. The effective reunion of the demotic with the scholarly element was something which could not have left a disciple of Solomos unmoved.

Kalosgouros

The line Polylas traced as critic and as translator was followed faithfully by George Kalosgouros (1849–1902). He translated the Italian poems of Solomos, the Greek classics, and some Italian literature (*I Sepolcri* by Foscolo). In his translations, Kalosgouros is less an artisan of verse than Polylas; however, he is softer and more melodic. His criticism has a greater sensitivity but less acuity than that of his predecessor. As for the rest, however, we find him following his master faithfully; his critical essay on *Hamlet* exhibits an idealism carried to extremes. He also recognized in Palamas the successor to Solomos.

The Ionian Island school did not cease to exist with the writers we have mentioned thus far: it continued with its own original sensibility until more recent times. But methodic examination of the first postrevolutionary generations forces us to examine a certain number of chronologically parallel manifestations. Moreover, we know that the isolation of the seven Ionian Islands was relative. In the following two chapters we will examine the school of Athens and the intermediaries who linked the Ionian Island school with that of Athens. In the end, the last representatives of the Ionian Island school aided the Athenian scholars of the next generation in assimilating a large part of the heritage of Solomos.

Chapter 20

Romantic Excess

School of Athens

The school of Athens, as was natural, was profoundly influenced by the Phanariots living in Athens. The poets comprising this school came from different religious traditions or disciplines. They found in Athens a strong organized body and they tended to adopt it. Orphanides imitated Alexander Soutsos in his early works and professed a profound admiration for him. Karasoutsas admired Rangavis. Contacts with the popular language or with the Ionian Islands tradition were rare, especially in the beginning. Thus, we have a literature without roots or one not deeply rooted, that easily becomes a prey to all kinds of influences. The only authentic element in this poetry was patriotism, as even the contemporaries observed. Patriotic or political activity, which monopolized the attention of modern Greek society, was the most important experience of the writers at this time. Mixing the various groups that came to constitute the Greek state created dissensions, with leadership going to those who had the gift of expression. Moreover, the attitude of the writer toward life followed the example of Western romanticism, which radiated directly or indirectly from the Phanariots to Athens. Byronism was constantly felt in Greek literature throughout the fifty years of romanticism, 1850–1880. Afterwards, it was Béranger, with his strict political spirit who occupied first place, then followed Lamartine; dozens of writers translated *The Lake*. J. Isidore Skylitsis (1819–1890) translated the *Death of Socrates* in 1841. When Lamartine passed through Smyrna, he considered it opportune to visit his translator, Skylitsis, and Skylitsis put his emotions into verse:

> When I heard these words, 'Lamartine has come to you. He speaks your name, he is there outside and asks for you,' my spirit became numb, I believe, from reverence. This visit was the greatest moment of my life.

But all these foreign influences, to which Victor Hugo would be added shortly, should not make us ignore certain fundamental truths, independent of general theoretical observations associated with foreign currents in Greek literature. Hence, I will begin by remarking, first of all, that the generation which attempted to define Greek romanticism was the generation embittered by the successive defeats following the War of Independence and ennerved by the succession of hopes and deceptions that characterized the Greek experience at the time. The writers, who could not adapt to a society which increasingly had less need of them, fought, were crushed, and endured bitterness. The mournful spirit governing Greek romanticism had its effect on the life of most of its representatives: some committed suicide, others withered and died young. In those who survived, one often saw the loss of a poetic inspiration that had been romantically associated with youth. Illness, loss, and death pursued them; this cannot be called literature. Even though the romantic movement came from without, it survived in Greece because it resonated to some fundamental part of the Greek character: the pessimistic mood, the melancholy, the sadness of love. Finally, romanticism evolved a fairly stable form over its fifty-year development. Even if the forms were defective, when they were attached so strongly to life, they followed a certain path: after the first attempts, they attained a height and fullness that should neither be ignored nor judged unfairly.

Orphanidis

The name of Theodore Orphanidis (Smyrna, 1817—Athens, 1886), poet and university professor, appeared at the beginning of Athenian romanticism. His romanticism and his involvement in university contests made him concerned with neo-Hellenic criticism. Following closely in the footsteps of Alexander Soutsos, he published a collection of poetry called *Menippos* in 1836:

> And I explain at once without any hesitation:
> In range I wish to imitate Alexander Soutsos.

However, he remained far inferior to his model and produced vulgar personal attacks and insinuations that had no relation to satire. He resembled Soutsos in the facility but not in the quality of his verses. In 1840 he published a short-lived periodical of satire, *The Archer*. Here he was also insulting and lacked inspiration, but his gift of versification was evident. In the meantime, Kolettis, who feared the vulgar brand of satire of Orphanidis, preferred to know him at a distance and sent him on a scholarship to Paris. Orphanidis returned as a botanist, but he did not stop working with poetry. He wrote easily and abundantly, either epico-lyric poems such as *Without a Country* (1854), *Enslaved Chios* (1858), *Saint Minas* (1860), and others, or satires, such as *Tiri-Liri* (1858). The quality of his verses is entirely negligible. Neither image, nor imagination, nor rich expression exists. He was not an innovator in anything. But he now occupied a chair as professor and often was spokesman for the university contests, and he exercised considerable influence on the younger men. We can say that the easy spirit which later proved so detrimental to Greek letters had its origin in Orphanidis.

If, however, we associate romanticism organically with elegiac poetry, as it is convenient to do, Orphanidis is somewhat unusual. Typical Athenian romanticism was produced by other poets, such as D. Valavanis (Karytaina 1824–Athens 1854), J. Karasoutsas (Smyrna 1822–Athens 1873), D. Paparrigopoulos (Athens 1843), Spiros Vasiliades (Patras 1845–Paris 1874), and Achilles Paraschos (Nauplion 1838–Athens 1895). Some of the innumerable poets who appeared during this period are mentioned elsewhere, but here we should include Alexander Katakouzinos (1824–1892), from whom we have many colorless verses and some unsuccessful poems for children. But the most representative romantic writers were those who, without producing any significant works, associated poetry with their youth. We recall Xenophon Raftopoulos (1828–1852) who, "when he was only ten years old revealed himself as a lover of the Muses." Even Myron Nikolaïdis (1835–1898) abandoned his genuine talent in all its maturity while he was still a youth. Not to lengthen this list, we close with Nicholas Saltelis (1810–1849), an admirer and imitator of the Soutsos brothers, who wrote *Kydoniate* (1842); John Raptarchis (1838–1871), who committed suicide in early youth after writing a variety of literary works; and Andrew Rigopoulos from Patras (1821–1889), a dramatist, versifier, passionate politician, forerunner of Peranthis Yannopoulos, who committed suicide in the waters of the Aegean.

Valavanis

Among the poets who met a premature death, the most important is Demosthenes Valavanis. He left only a few poems, some of which were written in the purist language, and several pages of prose. His verses, which appeared before the height of romanticism with its exaggerations of passion, were remarkable compositions. One finds an inspiration full of nobility and restraint, a precise language, and a clarity of images. Though the elegiac tone tends to rhetoric, it never becomes grandiloquent, commonplace, or indecorous. When he uses the popular language, he adds a linguistic sense to his other qualities, a sense unique for his time in Athens, and a creative ability that reveals a born poet and simultaneously the successor of the popular creative tradition. The connection with the folk creative spirit also appears in the spirit that sometimes fills his fifteen-syllable line. He is a scholarly writer, certainly, but restrained by tradition. His work might be considered a continuation of A. R. Rangavis in content and versification.

> The roses were laughing, the flowers exhaled their perfume,
> Your eyes were jubilant, full of light and charm.

The Grave of the Klephtes by the same poet is very well known.

Karasoutsas

As Valavanis did, Karasoutsas also began his poetic career very early in 1839 with *Lyre,* his first collection of poetry. It was certainly natural that he also should sacrifice to the idols of his time. In his second collection of poetry, *The Nursing Muse* (1840), we find a long description of night presented with calm and majesty, then the moon appears, and suddenly, in the end, the demons arrive:

> They open the tombs with their profane hands,
> And throw the skulls and bones to one another.

But his romantic inspiration tends to clothe itself in somber form and classical organization. This element is accentuated by the language he uses, which, going beyond the purist, tends toward archaism. Karasoutsas also followed the current linguistic evolution, sometimes correcting his earlier poems in this direction. As a consequence, we can incorporate him without any reservation in the romantic movement of Athens. Nevertheless, if we exempt the influences that Alexander Soutsos exercised on him in his youth, he is revealed as a personal poet; very personal and somewhat isolated. When he took his own life in 1873, his death went almost unobserved by the public.

His inspiration was elevated: country, love, liberty. The new element he brought was a true sensitivity to the natural world. It was an idyllic sensibility, not a romantic one; he did not project personal conditions of the soul but was charmed by colors, lights, and odors. And even the patriotic element, when he recalled his beloved Ionia, was associated with the beauty of the landscape.

> There the sweet breezes blow: on the water the foliage of the plane trees shimmers. There the sweet-scented myrtle blossoms. All is pleasant and calm, safe are the tyrants.

Nature often served as inspiration. His verses were delicate and mellow. He replaced the distracting romantic lamentations with the clarity of his form:

> You have come, Ares, you have come at last.
> The plains are green again,
> And the look of springtime sparkles,
> Sparkles joyfully over all the earth.

Titles such as *Hymn to the Rising Sun of Attica* or *Sunset in Attica* were common. One poem in the demotic, *Autumn,* had a similar theme. This elegy displays the particular style of Karasoutsas:

> Among the branches of the willow tree, the birds were hiding. When they heard a noise, they flew away, frightened, with a light stroke of the wing.

Finally, I should mention one of the poet's typically romantic themes, which in Karasoutsas shows some very personal accents:

> Ἡ φυλὴ δὲν εἶναι μία τῶν πτηνῶν τῶν ἡδυφώνων,
> οὐδὲ ποιητῶν ὑπάρχει εἰς τὴν γῆν ἓν γένος μόνον·
>
> .   .   .   .
>
> Καὶ ὁ στεναγμὸς πολλάκις τῆς ἐσχάτης ἀγωνίας
> εἰς τὰ χείλη των ἐν εἴδει θνῄσκει θείας μελῳδίας·
>
> The species of melodious birds is not one
> Nor is the race of poets on earth only one.
>
> .   .   .   .   .   .
>
> And often the sigh of the last agony
> Dies on their lips in a kind of divine melody.

Karasoutsas left us one poem containing his aesthetic credo. He compares with André Chénier, certain of whose verses he echoes exactly:

Καὶ κόσμει, ὅσον ἐφικτόν, τὰς νεουργοὺς ἰδέας
διὰ πτυχῶν φειδιακῶν κατασκευῆς ἀρχαίας·

Ornament, as far as possible, with Phidias' drapes of an ancient
texture.

Paraschos

Before the culmination of the romantic movement, we should also
mention George Paraschos (1822–1886), not so much for his lyrical
production, which is not particularly original, but for certain war
songs *(Thourios)*, written in the demotic:

> Carrying the heavy helmet at night. . . .

During the entire period we are examining, the number of versifiers
is considerable; but since they are devoid of any personal character,
it suffices to examine only the more important to characterize the
movement as a whole.

Paparrigopoulos

We are rapidly approaching the height of Athenian romanticism.
Typical representatives were Demetrios Paparrigopoulos and Spiros
Vasiliades. Paparrigopoulos, son of Constantine, appeared early in
letters, but his early works were not poetry. In 1861, while still a
boy, he published anonymously a short pamphlet called *Thoughts of
a Brigand, or the Condemnation of Society*. The inspiration, the subject matter, and the manner of treatment are typically romantic. Already we encounter the grandiloquence that remained a flaw of
Paparrigopoulos but also an obstinate reflective and philosophical
disposition, which he never abandoned. His liberal, even revolutionary and anarchic temperament was manifested in "Brigand,
criminal! The wealthy tremble before them, the poor honor them.
Who has contempt for them? The law? Certainly not, because it
refuses to punish them." In 1864 he was awarded a prize for his
treatise *On the Duties of Man, As a Christian and As a Citizen*. Two

years later, he published his doctoral dissertation on a philosophical subject. He also published other short philosophical works, and imitating the example of his father, he wrote a short history of the War of Independence in 1869. In the meantime, he published the poem "Sighs" in 1866 and continued his lyrical production until his untimely death. But to the end he wrote on philosophical subjects.

His total lyrical output was small compared with the rest of his production, but it was through his lyrics that he survived, because his poems contained valuable personal qualities although these were combined with contemporary poetic defects. His was a moving thought, pessimistic, funereal, largely oratorical in tone, with an easy, but majestic, language:

> It was in vain that I sought everywhere for happiness. I found only sighs, sorrow, and bitterness. The hearts I touched did not have only one beat; beneath the beauty only vices are concealed.

His verses, lacking the easy flow that one finds in Alexander Soutsos, poured out more slowly, but with a far more regular quality. The hiatus, which the poet often explored artlessly, intensified the rhetorical tone and the sonority of his verses. The composition was insufficiently worked: a series of ideas without much interrelation. Imagery was rare: we have here a poetry that speaks to reason rather than to emotions. Only the philosophy is raised to a system: life is a valley of tears which ends in nonexistence. It is burdened with memories and the prospects are sinister:

> The future, a game of chance, an irony of life,
> Words signify nothing nor does passage of time,
> And remedy offered by bitterness is absorbed
> To bring tomorrow filled with the same suffering.

In conformance with the Greek temperament, even though somewhat artificially, given in the poet's theoretical and purely intellectual mode, pessimism leads Paparrigopoulos to an enjoyment of life. Direct pleasure is the only justification:

> When the crimson lips call for a kiss and when the swollen breasts of a beloved invite an embrace, it is no longer a dream, and even Ecclesiastes cannot say: "Vanity."

Though his language was poor, with a limited vocabulary, though his tone was rarely removed from the elegy, though his rather simple thought satisfied the reader, all this did not neutralize his genuine suffering, which appears even more authentic because of the simple means he employs to express it. Paparrigopoulos also left a certain number of theatrical works, most of them in prose. He called a large portion of these *Characters.* Their moralistic tendency was obvious and they were written in a cold official language, which diminished all life and chilled all emotion in the reader.

Vasiliadis

Spiros Vasiliadis was more artistic. His interests were more directly human, and his contribution to the literary movement of his time was much greater. We should seek neither depth nor philosophy in him; superficial and sensitive, he transmitted his emotions directly. Influenced by the spirit of the period, he sought, at times, to philosophize:

> A deceptive scene, a mirage, that is the world, nature.
> However, the spell is broken when one touches the world.

But we feel during these moments that his philosophy was a pure sacrifice to convention, in complete opposition to his relaxed lyricism. His first collection of poetry, *Images and Waves,* was published in 1866 and received the Voutsinaias prize. Here we find the favorite themes of romanticism, the graves, trees, deaths; but they all lack weight and appear as mere convention. In 1872 he published *Winged Words.* Vasiliadis attempted to liberate himself from the commonplaces of romanticism and turned to classical subjects which he treated with elegance, though somewhat coldly.

> I see the slave who holds you, standing erect, turning you this way and that, for the pleasure of his mistress. She combs her hair and pretends, in the mirror, to be a thousand beauties.
>
> (taken from *To an Ancient Mirror in Corinth*)

Vasiliadis participated with all his being in the life of the times. He was interested in his country's social and intellectual problems. In his prose writings and critical essays, we eventually find him attacking romanticism: "the superficial influence and the little philosophy of romanticism." Using a discussion of the *Study on the Lives of Modern Greeks* by Nicholas Politis as a point of departure, he praised the importance of the folksong. He attacked the theory of Constantine Paparrigopoulos on the three divisions of Greek history; that is, the ancient, the Byzantine, and the modern. "We scarcely recognize the impure Byzantine character in the genuine morals of the modern people . . . as the ancient character also rarely appears in the Byzantine decadence." Elsewhere he spoke about the admirable folksong. It was only through the folksongs, he said, "that we are able to initiate the beauty and truth of our people; it is only by making use of the folksong that we will be able to create a national poetry." Thus, he succeeded in reconciling romanticism with an admiration for antiquity. In a series of prose theatrical works, he was able to exploit classical and modern inspirations simultaneously. With *Galatea* particularly, he brought a subject borrowed from the folksong to the stage. But whatever he said, whatever he did, his personal milieu was clearly romantic. The great poet for him was Lamartine.

> It is you, Lamartine,
> Your verses are the myrtles of Paradise.
> The world has grown old, the world has grown old, Lamartine,
> And even love anticipates the tomb.
> The world has grown old, the world is weary
> Your voice is the swan song and the sweet epics. . . .

He also translated *The Lake,* as had Karasoutsos, Valaorites, and others. Generally, his scholarly technique bound him to the great poets of the West, but their example protected him from the dangers of exaggeration and verbosity.

Paraschos

Achilles Paraschos did not escape from any of the dangers of romanticism. Having far outlived the end of the romantic period in Greek literature, his accents were as disconcerting as a dissonant song. Without exception he was the greatest romantic poet in Greek literature; without reserve, without doubt. He gave himself entirely to romantic themes, to romantic forms of expression, and to the most empty romantic grendiloquence:

> I would like to open the tomb of my father,
> To dig it up with my hands, unearth the coffin,
> To see what has happened to my old father, lying there so long
> In the night and in the earth of the tomb.

The exclusive attachment to an ideal, to a style, helped him to impose himself on the society of his time and to be acknowledged the principal representative of poetry. And indeed, a society which was deceived by words and for which the high deeds of its ancestors, far from being a goad toward action, were only a comfortable pillow, could very well be mirrored in the poetry of Paraschos. All the elevated subjects were emotionalized in his abundant production; they inflated and deflated in a universe of words. In our hands only a few ashes remain, the residue of a truly human suffering, of a genuine emotion, which, however, could not be elevated to art.

The life of Paraschos was similar to his work; it was uneven and disturbed. Grandiloquent, enthusiastic, without foundations, he squandered the admiration of his contemporaries, and from one moment to another he passed from gratification to doubt. Handsome, with an imposing presence and voice, he was the symbol of poetry for the society of his time. The publication of his poems in 1881 was considered a national event. His memory remained alive long after he was gone, and the mediocre quality of his verses was harmful to the aesthetic conception of the generations that followed.

His production was bilingual. In any case, he honored the popular language: "The language of the people is a veritable mine;/it contains diamonds and much gold."

However, even when he imitated the folksong, particularly the heroic song of the klephtes, all the defects that characterized the pure romantic poetry of his time reappear in abundance: poverty of vocabulary, impropriety of terms, awkwardness in construction. As for his ideas, there is no doubt. Uncultivated, a spontaneous poet, he struggled with a few stock phrases to fill his verse. Absence of the intellectual element led him to search for rhetoric which culminated in a repetitious and intolerable verbiage. Before emotion could be expressed, before it could assume the final form of his poetry, he produced a verse that gushed forth or a revealing distich which showed that under different conditions Paraschos could have become a poet.

Often his first verse is direcly lyrical: "I still come to your solitary church," or "O, there is the cave of the nymphs, there is the footpath!" or even, "Voyager river, beloved river."

But immediately afterward, he falls into verbosity. Inspiration is dampened; the aversion to the river continues with a second verse that contains an inflexible interrogative sweep:

> Where do you dash yourself, unhappy one,
> Singing funereal lamentations?

This is followed by a banal comparison of human life with the course of the river:

> Ah, you are as we; he who goes before,
> He who always precedes, never knows where he goes.

This repetition of the same notions in almost identical terms, which perhaps Paraschos associated with the fifteen-syllable folksong, is his most characteristic trait and that which has been commented upon by his detractors. But a more serious fault is his quasi-fortuitous use of words:

> I want my friend ill now,
> Pale I want her and white as death's shroud.

Images oppose one another, from one hemistich to another, from one verse to another. and clash boldly under the tolerant gaze of the noble poet.

Achilles Paraschos was the poetic equivalent of the Grand Idea at its decline. It was for this reason that he became so popular. He took on his shoulders and carried to the end the burden of romantic excess created by the Phanariots of Athens, an excess accentuated by the Athenian romantics. Paraschos was the characteristic representative of romanticism, especially after the deaths of D. Paparrigopoulos and Vasiliadis. In 1878 he transported the bones of Alexander Soutsos to Athens and this act immediately confirmed his succession.

But the new poetic stirrings, precisely those destined to control both romanticism and rhetoric, could not endure the poet's faults without some protestations. In 1874 D. G. Kambouroglou presented to the Voutsinaias contest a collection of poetry composed of satires and parodies. The parody of verses by Paraschos is pertinent because it reveals the reaction of younger poets:

> I would wish her a tubercular, my friend, emaciated, ashen,
> Dust, a breath, a dying woman, a phantom, immortal;
> I would wish to have her only as my sister,
> But not as my wife, not as my wife.

Paraschos, on his part, remained insensible to the new activities; he condemned the movement of the 1880 generation, characterizing its main representatives as youngsters: "Whoever sees them, bursts into laughter."

The criticism that reacted against this attitude, or even endured it, is examined in another chapter. This element prepared for the new school of Athens. Here it suffices to observe that though Athenian romanticism was in perfect accord with the society of Athens, the Ionian Islands, true to their tradition, gave another evaluation to the problem. Panayotis Panas, who expressed the general opinion of the heirs of Solomos, published, in 1872 before the critical attacks of Roidis, a caustic satire against the inanities of Athenian romanticism:

> This night is bright with a radiant sun. All around pours the obscure glimmer of lightning flashes. The thunder rumbles in silence. Lights pierce the vault of the earth and the sun of heaven sadly rejoices. Though standing in wakefulness, I was sleeping on my bed, when suddenly before me I beheld a young old man. And with eloquent silence he spoke to me: "What troubled serenity! What radiant obscurity! What a time for joyous sadness!"
>
> (taken from *Neo-Hellenic Poetry: Romantic School*)

There is another reason to turn to the Ionian Islands. The somewhat restless isolation no longer culminates in exhaustion and wasting away. Between the Ionian Islands school and Athenian romanticism intermediaries exist now, and they will transmit the heritage of Solomos to Athens and make it bear fruit. The contribution of these intermediaries is important for the evolution of modern Greek letters. The work of the Ionian Islands was impeded, but in the end they gave a perceptible contribution to the structure on which the generation of 1880 erected its work.

Part Seven

Preparation for 1880

Factors in the Decline
of Athenian Romanticism

The unrestrained romanticism of the Athenian school encountered limits and also new influences that gradually increased. These influences came principally from the Ionian Islands. Limits were posed by prose and criticism, which, by their very nature, further submit to reason. As society evolved in this manner, Greek culture attained a maturity that delivered it from romantic excess.

Chapter 21

The Intermediaries

Ionian Elements

in Athens

Various links including intellectual exchanges appeared early between the Ionian Islands and the Greek state. The Ionian Islands, which had been rich in spirit, were injured by this, but Athens profited. The ties took various forms. I mention specifically some excellent periodicals published at this time in Athens: *Euterpe* (1847–1855), *Pandora* (1850–1872), *The National Library* (1865–1873). But the principal intermediaries were regional or literary or even personal.

Patras

A geographic connection between the Ionian Islands and Athens was constituted by Patras, which always had commercial and other contacts with the Ionian Islands and more particularly with Zakynthos. Oriented to perform this function, Patras received influences which, once developed, were transmitted to Athens. In 1836 Adamantios Papadiamantopoulos (1811–1896) from Patras, father of Jean Moréas, was inspired in his juvenilia by an unpublished first draft of Solomos's *The Free Besieged* which he was privileged to read.

In other verses, he attempted to associate a free use of the demotic with the early forms of romanticism. To Elias Kalamogdartis (1817–1849), also from Patras, was attributed the well-known song:

> O! do not sleep, awake,
> My charming friend!

whose melody obviously originated from the Ionian Islands. Anthony Kalamogdartis (1810–1856) also appeared to have accepted influences from the Ionian Islands. Panayotis Synodinos (1836–1914), who continued an unbridled romantic production to his old age and who was always mentioned as a model of bad taste, was inspired by the Ionian Islands while he lived in Patras. In the introduction to his collection *Greek Springtime* (Patras, 1857), he compared the purist poetry with the demotic and he praised the poets of the Ionian Islands. As an illustration of two great poets, he cited Hugo and Solomos. And in his own verses, he praised Solomos, "Who looks on the country/ Of the great Solomos!" Imbued with romanticism, he deteriorated with each succeeding collection as he departed from the Ionian influence and came under that of the Athenian purist language.

Tayapieras

In addition to the geographical association, we should not ignore the connection woven by men. Braïlas-Armenis, originally from the Ionian Islands, was an ambassador in the service of the state. George Tertsetis was a magistrate and later a functionary in the Chamber of Deputies. Demetrios Tayapieras (1777–1842), though he did not make a name for himself in literature, exercised a personal influence when he went to Greece from the Ionian Islands, first as a friend of Vilaras and later of Solomos. At Nauplion, the capital of Greece, he was a literary advisor of the younger poets. George Prantounas (1800–1861), who abandoned letters early, consulted Tayapieras when he wrote his tragedy *Athens Liberated* (1830). His influence was not deep, because he soon returned to the Ionian Islands, but the memory Tayapieras left with scholars in Nauplion exhibits his importance. The advice he gave to A. R. Rangavis was characteristic: literary works should present "a closed plan, so that they can have the unity essential to all artistic production." Alexander Soutsos dedicated *The Rake* to him, and in the preface, he expressed gratitude for all "the sincere and useful advice, fruit of an erudition full of modesty." It does not appear, however, that Rangavis exploited all these precious counsels; N. Dragoumis mentioned unfavorable comments Tayapieras made on *The Rake*. Athenian romanticism neglected his teachings, as it also ignored the advice of George Tertsetis, even though this scholarly friend of Solomos never ceased striving, in a series of lectures made in Athens and published later, to graft the intellectual buds of the Ionian Islands on the Athenian tree.

Tertsetis

Tertsetis requires a more analytical study. He was born in Zakynthos in 1800 and died in Athens in 1874. He studied in Italy. A relative of Matesis, a friend of Solomos, he brought with him when he came to live in liberated Greece the environment in which he had lived in Zakynthos beside Solomos. He was without financial resources. In 1830, we find him in Patras as a tutor to the Botsaris family. He asked Solomos for funds to go to Nauplion, where he found work. He was appointed a professor of history at the military academy. He left characteristic evidence of a classicism which predominated even in the academy. In 1832 he was reading *Crito* in modern translation to his class. Night fell; he prepared to leave. The students begged him to continue and the lecture was completed by candlelight. At this same time, the students of the academy presented classical tragedies. In 1833 Tertsetis became a magistrate. His refusal to condemn Kolokotronis, despite government pressure, forced him into exile. He returned after the political change in 1843 and the following year he was appointed librarian at the Chamber of Deputies. From that time on, except for a few trips undertaken for political reasons, he remained in Athens. He wrote a few verses, and almost every year published the speeches he presented each 25th of March, the commemoration day of the War of Independence.

His personality was exceptional; it was greatly superior to his work, though that did not lack merit. In 1833 he wrote "The Kiss," a poem dedicated to King Othon. His inspiration was intimately connected with the folksong and the popular language. This poem caused Solomos to advise him on the use of the demotic and the style of the folksong. Tertsetis "elevates himself to great heights," but in prose. In another chapter we will discuss the *Memoirs* of Kolokotronis, and Tertsetis's contribution to the study of the modern Greek spirit generally. In his speeches and prose publications, Tertsetis revealed an advanced culture, conscientiously based on elements of modern Greek civilization and associated with a high concept of the beautiful and the good. But his indecisive language harmed these texts, even though one discerns in the framework of his phrases an extremely personal style.

In his poetry, Tertsetis did not exploit the teaching of Solomos. Tertsetis published a collection of poetry in 1847 entitled *Simple*

Language and in 1856 two poems, *The Wedding of Alexander the Great* and *Corinne and Pindar*. In both the latter, the effort to remain close to the folksong diminished the spirit and rendered the expression monotonous. This monotony was accentuated by the narrative character of these poems and today they are read with difficulty. In his other poems, Tertsetis followed the example of Solomos during his youth, without approximating the high spirituality that characterizes his subsequent development. In *Simple Language*, Tertsetis published some foreign poems along with his own. We now know that the comedy, *Triumph of the Poetry Contest*, which was presented to the Ralleios contest in 1858, was his work. This comedy, only recently published, is insipid, quite opposed to the temperament of Tertsetis. At any rate, its intention was to ridicule the contests and to defend the right to current speech. The noble personality of Tertsetis, the prestige he enjoyed in Athenian society, and his teachings, which always remained in line with the Ionian Island school, made him one of the principal links between the islands and Athens.

Braïlas-Aremenis

The contribution of Petros Braïlas-Armenis (1812–1884) in this same direction should not be ignored. A philosopher and aesthetician, without great force but with a receptive nature and sensitivity, he left us various philosophical studies, where he proved to be a partisan of French eclecticism. He also left a great number of essays in the cultural tradition of the Ionian Islands, but written in the purest language, which were intended to inform the Greek public on Western culture. I should also mention his criticism of the poems of Typaldos, published in *Pandora* in 1858. These literary assignments increased contacts between the Ionian Islands and liberated Greece. The personal brilliance of Braïlas-Armenis also contributed in this, as in the case of his relations with Viziinos.

It is necessary here to mention Constantine Asopios. He not only brought the memory of Solomos to Athens, he also brought the heritage of Koraes. Furthermore, his academic and literary activities in Athens and his participation in the university contests place him more directly among the precursors of the generation of 1880.

His contribution is examined in the chapter on this subject. Naturally, during this entire period other writers originally from the Ionian Islands operated in the vicinity of Athens. Their work, however, was modest, their tradition limited, and finally, they were absorbed by the imposing character of the capital. Emmanuel Staïs and Anthony Phatseas belong to his category, so they cannot be considered as intermediaries between the Ionian Islands and Athens, but they did help prepare for the turning point of 1880. We should also note that the statesmen of the Ionian Islands often used the demotic in their propaganda pamphlets. Though it did not become general practice, this custom was transferred to Athens. I should also mention the pamphlet of John Spiliotakis, *Awaken Greek, and Down with Bribery!* (1881), which was written in a completely demotic language and in a rather spirited style.

Zalokostas

Despite the brevity of his career, George Zalokostas (1805–1858) contributed significantly toward familiarizing liberated Greece with the Ionian Islands. The lyrical quality of his verses helped reconcile Athenian society to the popular language, at least insofar as poetry was concerned. Zalokostas began to write verses in his youth, during the War of Independence; but later especially his literary activity became extensive (*The Khan of Gravia* was written in 1847) and his most abundant production came after 1850. Originally from Epirus, he studied in Italy, which aided him in forming a precise idea of the aesthetic attempt of the Ionian Island school. But the Athenian environment in which he lived prevented him from clarifying his true position, hence he appeared aesthetically and linguistically divided.

When he wrote in the demotic, he used the fifteen-syllable verse and attempted to follow the line of the folksong or to introduce into Greek assemblages of lighter Italian strophes. His poems in the purist language were influenced by the narrative form of the period but inclined toward a cold academism rather than the hollow grandiloquence of the romantics. At his worst moments, he was also Byronic after the fashion of the Soutsos brothers and was identified with them and their immediate successors. It is difficult to grade lyricism, but since the prevailing custom is to establish a formal division between major and minor poets, it is convenient to situate Zalokostas among the former. He had the feeling of tenderness, he loved the atmosphere of intimacy; emotions and passions of daily life inspired him more than did the dramatic grandeur of historical moments. This side of his nature is easily discernible, if we remember the manner in which he sang about the heroism of Missolonghi. He had participated in the siege, he had fought beside the men, as Solomos had not. And yet, though the spirit of 1821 palpitates in *The Free Besieged,* Zalokostas, in his poem on Missolonghi (1851), was unable to elevate himself beyond a common panegyric:

> The mouths of the bronze dragons, which spout flashes of light, speak in a mysterious language. All utter only a menacing cry: "Surrender," they say, "the garrison and cannons, surrender the keys."

This material was totally contrary to the intimate themes that suited his talents. Whether he paraphrased *The Kissing,* or was inspired by family misfortunes when he wrote *The Partridge,* or when he sang the eternal theme of a separation of lovers in *Her Departure,* we sense the breath of genuine poetry. But even in these poems the feeble imagination of the poet borrowed the theme. What was excellent in him and of value was form:

> When I awakened, they told me the young girl I love was gone,
> And I went down to the shore
> I implored the sea
> The bitter waves.

Sober means are used to express simple sentiments. A certain lack of vocabulary, easily interpreted, should not be condemned by the modern reader, because it agrees with the poet's simple concepts and emotions.

His literary personality, however, reached its heights in his aesthetics and his critical notes. Evaluations influenced by the Ionian Island spirit appeared in periodicals such as *Euterpe* and *Mnemosyne.* When in 1853, on the occasion of a poetry contest, an interesting controversy erupted, Zalokostas found the opportunity to criticize the poetry of Panayotis Soutsos. The remarks of Zalokostas were generally clear and used the proper words; here he approximated classicism. His critical evaluations of linguistic problems were less clear, because they were confused by the archaic language which prevailed at that time. He was unable to free himself from his period, but one senses the struggle which took place in his soul. It is only his admiration for Solomos, about whom he wrote that "he is the only poet about whom this unfortunate nation will be proud one day," that puts him much above the average Athenian aesthetics of his day. Poet and critic, Zalokostas gained more by his efforts at versification than by his successors; nonetheless, his contribution as an intermediary between Athens and the Ionian Islands and some of his verses secure for him an honorable place in Greek letters, not only for all he sought to achieve, but also for what he managed to achieve.

Valaorites

Aristotle Valaorites was the most eminent intermediary between the Ionian Islands school and that of Athens. He was born in Leukas in 1824; he studied in Italy, Switzerland, and France. Later, he participated actively in the political life and national struggles of Greece; meanwhile, he was also occupied with letters, where he devoted himself exclusively to poetry. He died in Leukas in 1879. In his youth, he had written verses in the purist language, which he left unpublished. His first collection of poetry was *Pieces in Verse* (1847). It was followed by *Memorials to Death* (1857), *Kyra Phrosini* (1859), *Diakos, Astrapoyannos* (1867), and various other scattered poems. Valaorites was from the Ionian Islands, but his family was originally from the mainland. In his veins flowed the blood and in his mind persisted the memory of ancestors who had been glorified in battles against the conqueror. The Ionian Island school and the example of Solomos taught him that only one language was suitable for poetry; this was the demotic, the language of folk creation. He used this language exclusively. An ardent patriot, he dedicated the major portion of his work to patriotic themes. The theme was common to both schools; but his language conformed to the Ionian Island teaching. In technique, Valaorites was attracted to the Athenian forms. In his most important poems, he was revealed as an absolute and unreserved romantic. We find in him the weaknesses of Athenian romanticism, the grandiloquence, the rhetoric, the shallowness. But his choice of the right linguistic means attenuated these weaknesses to a certain degree; verbal poverty, a sore spot with

Athenian romanticism, Valaorites avoided by using the rich popular vocabulary. Moreover, the poet's orientation toward patriotic themes often diverted him from the lugubrious tone of the contemporary Athenians; a desire for health and strength, a heroic tone, reigned in the major part of his work.

Preceding generations did not hesitate to compare Valaorites with Solomos. Even Spiros Trikoupis, at the death of Solomos, wrote the following verses for Valaorites:

> The nightingale is not dead,
> The nightingale lives forever.
> It has changed plummage,
> But it hasn't changed voice.

Let us accept the comparison temporarily. Immediately, we see two antithetical poetic worlds; Solomos developed, Valaorites only progressed. His poetry, from its first flights to his last efforts, never varied in essence; it improved but only in relation to form. For this reason, it is unjust to evaluate him simply on the basis of his earlier poetry, since the later poetry was differentiated by simple progress in the technique of the verses. In Valaorities we have no stages and successive periods of poetic creation but rather an uninterrupted, conscientious effort to perfect his immobile poetic universe. He worked on the fifteen-syllable verse; he worked on it without respite from the time of his youth. When he died, he left partially completed the poem *Photinos,* which offers us a vigorous and tight verse with heroic spirit and pace.

However, here we must note a difference between Valaorites and Solomos. Valaorites had an absolute facility in versification; his verse, which poured out with amazing spontaneity and ingenuity, did not satisfy him. He constantly struggled for perfection. His aesthetic, from this point of view, contained a certain external quality, the distinction between form and substance, but it also exhibited a high awareness and a great desire for what was good.

The second essential distinguishing point is that Valaorites always lived in the climate of romanticism with perfect contentment. Not for one moment did he seek to avoid it, to render his art autonomous. Finally, I should add that the greatest difference between Solomos and Valaorites was the absence of spirituality that characterized the poet of *Diakos.* Valaorites worked with only a few ideas, a few emotions, that had become a faith, and, above all, an impetuous and irresistible love of country.

Theoretically, Valaorites disavowed romanticism, but he understood by this term only the pessimistic tendencies of the Athenian school. In reality, he was a romantic. His subjects, taken from recent history, substantiate this, as do the sentiments he attributed to his heroes and especially his admiration for Victor Hugo. In one of his letters, he declared that he received from Hugo the mania for antitheses and the desire to allow "his imagination to gallop, at full speed, wherever whenever it desired." At another time, he affirmed: "I admit that each moment of inspiration is a moment of folly." One sees the image of the romantic poet appearing. However, let us consider it more closely, because his attitude illuminated even romanticism. Let us consider the word "desire." Valaorites's technique of creation was based on a voluntary element; it rested on a self-possessed, cool resolution. The meandering came later. With absolute judgment and great reflection, he sometimes betrayed the outline of the poem as he was preparing to work on it, but it was an outline that possessed a logical train of thought, a desire for unity, and a psychological concern. The awareness of these elements and their formulation created a special place for Valaorites and indicate that poetry produced in Athens was directed toward a methodic and cold exploitation of poetic talents.

Valaorites was particularly attentive to problems of metrics. He was concerned with the morphology of the fifteen-syllable verse, and he used a special popular eleven-syllable verse with the accent on the fourth syllable and a cesura after the sixth. This latter verse, when it is associated with regular verses of eleven syllables, sometimes creates a successful opposition and confers to the whole a dramatic breathlessness, but it becomes monotonous if used constantly. Solomos employed this form, but he divided it into two verses.

The great compositions of Valaorites were *Kyra Phrosini, Athanasios Diakos,* and *Photinos.* The latter was inspired by an episode in the medieval history of Leukas. Aside from the vivid imagination that characterized all his work, *Kyra Phrosini* and *Diakos* show the same weaknesses: a romantic exaggeration in the psychology of the heroes, in the expression, and in the dramatization of the myth. Byronism dominated these works. The cult of horror is found here, as it is in a great portion of Valaorites's works. Dreams, visions, ghosts, all the romantic undercurrents also characterize his art. However, out of these weaknesses the verse as we have it or the scholarly elaboration often surges: "Straight to the sky, the nightingale also flew."

The physical world also moved the poet, who sometimes succeeded in rendering his emotions with a certain simplicity.

> The dawn surges forth, furtive, behind Mount Pindos,
> And sprinkles each rose in its path with dew.
> The lake sleeps, calm, and on the bank
> One hears the froth playing softly, sweetly,
> As the tranquil breathing of a sleeping child.

Sometimes, his close union with nature led him to create poems of a purely allegorical character. His weaknesses, except for his verbosity, and his virtues are more apparent in his shorter poems:

> Two gypsies bound him to the anvil
> And aimed to strike him with the hammer.
> The bones flew in splinters, the marrow spilled;
> The muscles, pieces of flesh, littered the earth.
> And he looked at the sky and sang sweetly.

In *Astrapoyannos* and in "Escape," the rhythm agrees happily with the theme:

> The horse, the horse, Omer Vrionis!
> The Souliotes are coming to crush us.
> The horse, the horse! Hear the whistling
> Of their scorching bullets, menacing us.

And Astrapoyannos says:

> He runs this way, he runs that way,
> The poor footman on the mountain,
> Like a black wave, whipped by the wind,
> And cannot find a shore.

An idyllic element is introduced as a contrast to dramatic descriptions:

> My green oak tree, my pines, my fresh streams;
> Lambeti, they must not see me,
> They must not witness my deformity. . . .
> Come, let us go, not to embitter them.

When he succeeds in mastering his verse, his patriotic passion offers him a world of tightly woven images, which create a type of romantic superfluous epigram:

There is no migratory bird that for a day,
Traverses the clouds and passes, swift as the wind.
There is no ivy that insensibly encompasses the rock.
No flash of lightning is extinguished without thunderbolt.
There is no dead sea, no tremor without an earthquake;
I feel for you my country a laceration in my bowels.

Political oppositions and aesthetic divergencies provoked a rupture between the school of Solomos and Valaorites. Despite all he wrote, Valaorites was unable to understand Solomos. In time, the Ionian Island school attacked Valaorites. Panayotis Panas published two satires in 1868 that revealed the great division between the Ionian Island tradition and the technique of Valaorites. One accusation Panas made concerned the manner with which Valaorites appropriated the folksong technique. Such a remark, formulated so early, shows to what profound knowledge of the folksong the followers of Solomos had advanced already; they would not allow themselves to be deceived by a superficial resemblance:

It was a young noble who had disguised himself.

The other satire was entitled *Recipe for Poetry*. With satiric virtuosity, Panas accumulated there all the weaknesses of Valaorites:

Take two clouds, a liter of air,
Two grains of dew and a flute;
Three tons of Pindar, four of snow;
A liter of breath, and a nightingale,
Four sprigs of laurel, of myrtle;
Cassocks; rags; gypsies; dawns.

.   .   .   .   .

Two drams of savage, durable worms;
Rumbling of thunder, wind from the North, roses and
    seaweeds.

.   .   .   .   .

Countless oaths, some flesh, and a large dose of flowers from
    the cemetery,

.   .   .   .   .

Toss all these in a large pot,

Then add some ice-cold water,

.   .   .   .   .

Bring all to a boil only three times.

But the opposition proved more grave when in 1872 the University of Athens formally invited Valaorites to recite a poem at the unveiling of a statue of Gregory V. This invitation demonstrates the poet's great fame in this period; it also constitutes an overwhelming victory for the demotic language, which should be attributed to the prestige of Valaorites. But matters were more complicated; Valaorites inspired the Athenian public that heard and read him; two scholars, however, attacked him violently. One of these, Demetrios Vernardakis, proceeded anonymously to a harsh, close analysis of the poem, where it is evident that he wished to ignore all the poet's virtues. His criticism was essentially antiromantic, but Vernardakis's excessive attention to detail weakened his intentions. Independent of personal reasons and those of opposing temperaments, which could have led Vernardakis to this virulent attack, his criticism interests us because it reveals a certain satiety with romanticism in 1872 and the awareness of a need for new techniques, freed from the excesses of romanticism. The second criticism Polylas either wrote or inspired. This was also published anonymously. Valaorites was criticized for the improprieties of his vocabulary, for the lack of clarity of his images, and for much else. This criticism was not free from acrimony, from personal attacks, or from political passion. Nonetheless, I make the above observations to reveal that Greek literary history was specifically interested in the desire for the concrete.

Naturally, such criticism failed to diminish general public enthusiasm for the work of Valaorites, and I believe that because of this enthusiasm we can further discern a praiseworthy turn of the new generation toward an art which is closer to the human soul. To recognize the weaknesses of Valaorites's poetry presupposed an advanced aesthetic culture, which did not exist at that time among the Athenians. Valaorites's virtues, on the contrary, were evident. This observation could not constitute a more general evaluation of his art, an evaluation which simultaneously would justify it and explain his success. Other critics, who had less reason than Vernardakis or Polylas to evaluate Valaorites severely, showed greater understanding and greater justice. Roidis, in the year the poet died, published an

excellent study of his work. Laskaratos, with the reservations that
the Ionian Islands had contributed to his aesthetic formation, held
the poet in equal esteem.

Laskaratos

Andrew Laskaratos, originally from Cephalonia (1811–1901), can
be considered the most genuine intermediary between the Ionian
Islands and Athens. He was a fanatical Ionian, as was his idiom,
which he used to a great extent in his literary production; that is, he
brought to the capital an unadulterated Ionian Island atmosphere.
To the great extent that he influenced the Athenian intellectuals, his
contribution in this transfer of tradition is evident. He derived from
Solomos, whom he knew as a youth in Kerkyra and under whose
tutelage he bagan his literary career. However, it is likely that, aside
from his linguistic convictions, where he remained dedicated to demoticism, the moralistic and puritanical disposition of his mentor
Kalvos agreed better with his temperament. His entire work was
closer to the portrayal of manners than to the pure and more limited
literary creation. He wrote numerous works in prose and a few
verses, most of which were collected in 1872 in one volume called
Various Poems. They were dedicated to Tertsetis. Then followed
". . . Go then, go, my verses. It may be that you are not poems, but
that you will be something better, I hope, than poems. Today, you
will be an incentive to the sleeping Greek spirit, and tomorrow or
the day after, an evidence of our period. . . ."

> Free verses speak freely.
> Censure disgraceful vices everywhere,
> In the common people as in the clergy.
> Mock them wherever you see them.

His verses, neglected from the point of view of form, are mostly
satiric. They were social satires; he railed at the morals and concepts
of his contemporaries and disparaged those ideas he considered
contrary to the spirit of progress. His principal target was the for-
malism of the church. Even though he professed to be a Christian
and was considered a model Christian, in reality his religiosity was
limited to the belief in the existence of a supreme power. As for the

rest, he was concerned exclusively with moral problems. Because of this, his teaching offended; he presumed that his contemporaries had an infinitely higher intellectual level than they did. He imagined a morality liberated from all forms of worship, and in seeking to purify his ideal of all he considered false and superfluous, he did not hesitate to disparage even the nature of the divinity:

> He will laugh, the good God, when he comes to judge us. He will hold bis belly. What gestures of contempt he will make! O Time, O wonders! Happy is he who will live to see these things!

His language became even bolder when he judged the clergy:

> If this vestment that you wear
> Suffices not to make you live honorably,
> Why do you not cast it aside to become
> Peddlars or even coachmen?
> They also steal, yes they steal and pillage.
> But they at least do not profane the sacred.

At times, his mordant spirit led him to write verses which did not belong to true satire; they did not parody or ridicule natural weaknesses, nor were they simply for amusement. His genuinely lyrical poems, *Serious Pieces,* as he called them, are few. One of his sonnets was distinguished by its tenderness; he dedicated it to his wife and called it "In London in 1851":

> For I sense you so strongly mine,
> So closely bound with my own soul,
> That I no longer know in my thoughts,
> How to call you, my wife or my soul.

Apart from this, some of his juvenilia proceeded directly from contact with Solomos.

But his real tone was better in his prose; this was his craft. He wrote *The Mysteries of Cephalonia* (1856), characters under the title *Ecco Homo* (1886), and other shorter works, published individually or in his own newspaper, *The Lamp*. He also left several works that were published posthumously: *Morals, Customs and Beliefs of Cephalonia, Thoughts, The Art of Public Speaking and Writing,* and an autobiography written in Italian. In these works, the moralist prevailed, a moralist full of demands for the moral comportment of man and full of compassion for the weaknesses inherent in the human condition. His *Characters* were easy to distinguish from the usual types in such works; they had a clearly didactic purpose. The two books with Cephalonia in the title criticized provincial defects of the author's compatriots for a didactic purpose. Laskaratos had a lively spirit, his eyes discerned weak points fairly clearly, but above all, his thought was incessantly preoccupied with moral perfection. Even in his purely literary essays, his principal concern was moral order; he declared: "The author and the orator will have truth as a guide, as a measure of justice, and as an object of honest utility." It is characteristic that he placed *Thoughts* above all his other works. Here the satiric vein was lacking and the study of morals and manners predominated: "He is a liberal who seeks spontaneously to give freedoms. He who seeks to obtain freedoms, may or may not be a liberal." Religious fanaticism and superstition, which were often confused in this thought with attachment to forms, were criticized sharply in all his works. It was natural that he should arouse the church. Laskaratos was excommunicated for his campaigns against the clergy.

However, neither his excommunication nor his polemics following the excommunication isolated him from the intellectuals of his time. On the contrary, they aroused a wider public interest in both his work and person. He often went to Athens, either to escape local vexations or for other reasons. Though the language he used was strictly idiomatic, diametrically opposed to the tendencies of his Athenian intellectual contemporaries, the Athenians received him with expressions of respect and interest. *Parnassos,* still at its beginning stages, welcomed his works eagerly. In 1875 Palamas decided to adopt the language of Laskaratos, "because from this point on, in my prose and in my poetry, it will be the most beautiful and the most harmonious." The new generation saw Laskaratos as the herald of the approaching times. With him, something of the heritage of Solomos had been brought to Athens. Part of this heritage had also been brought by Gerasimos Markoras, who was also personally acquainted with the poet of the *Hymn.* Born in 1826, Markoras dedicated himself very early to letters. Athens took notice of some of his publications between the years 1870 and 1880: *Simple and Purist Language* (1872), satiric verses (1872), *The Vow* (1875), and an epic inspired by the battles of Crete. But his main literary activity came rather late, around 1890, when Athens, under the influence of the generation of 1880, had already rallied to the teachings of the Ionian Islands. By that time, Markoras could not be considered an intermediary; his writings were an integral part of Athenian literary production. The remainder of his work is examined later in this *History*.

Konemenos and Vergotis

The names of Nicholas Konemenos (1832–1907) and Panayotis Vergotis (1842–1916) should not be omitted from the list of intermediaries. The former, originally from Epirus but with an Ionian Island culture, prepared the way, as has been observed elsewhere, for the linguistic renewal of Psycharis. The remainder of his production, poetry and social essays, divided between Kerkyra, Patras, and Athens, present him, with his strong personality, as a kind of intermediary between the Ionian Islands and the capital. However, the works of his maturity especially contain a provincial eccentricity. When in 1879 he published a small collection of poetry, his moral quality showed he was close to Laskaratos, but we sense, simultaneously, that he belonged to a world already passed.

> They married off my poor beloved
> In a very distant country;
> She had reason to tell me
> That parting was a heavy burden.
> And I looked at the sea,
> And woe is me,
> Since I had no other love,
> Better that I should have drowned.

Vergotis published in 1865 a translation of Dante, where he brilliantly defended, in the preface to the first five cantos of the *Purgatorio*, the virtues of the popular language. A student of Menaya, who was also a Hegelian, Vergotis left us philosophical works, as well as polemics in favor of the demotic language. These did not pass unobserved in Athens.

Chapter 22

Return to the Soil

Prose as an Antidote

to Romantic Excess

The mode of Athenian romanticism was verse, it created a style, a school. Prose, which in mass appeared later than poetry, presented a greater freedom and originality. *Leandros* by Panayotis Soutsos naturally had imitators. One year after the appearance of *Leandros* in 1835, D. Pantazis, still young at the time, published a volume of prose translations taken from *Night Thoughts* by Young. At the same time, a great many foreign translations began to appear, among which French romantic novels predominated. These translations concerning unhappy love affairs, illnesses, suicides, knights, and ghosts, that is to say, the dual heritage of *Werther* and *Jacobo Ortiz* on the one hand and of Sir Walter Scott on the other, found many admirers but also a number of detractors. Indeed, though lyricism tolerated a division between expression and reality or common sense, the natural articulation of prose had much greater difficulty in masking such discrepancies.

Finally, creative prose and the various scientific publications both used prose discourse. This led prose writers to interpolate elements borrowed from science into their narratives, that is to say, elements associated with experience, with observation, and with knowledge. A number of short stories and novels of the period constituted simple extensions of the chronicles devoted to the War of Independence and reflected the historical or folkloristic interests of the moment. We can say that the post revolutionary novel had its source in contemporary interests and constituted, as did theatrical works, an expression of national neo-Hellenic awareness. Thus creative prose contained the germ of circumstances that would succeed romanticism.

Early Prose Writers

The Athenian Demetrios Pantazis (1813–1884) created a genre of his own: short narratives inspired principally by antiquity, attempting to use an archaic language, and associated with a search for elegance that approximated humor. His short narratives were cold, but one distinguishes certain elements of the ironic spirit that characterized the work of Roidis. We can say the same about the production of Constantine Pope (1816–1878), with the exception that Pope was more directly attracted by contemporary subjects and was influenced by romanticism. It was to Pope, who published under the pseudonym Gorgias, that the annals, that particular literary genre which took on certain original forms in Greece, was attributed.

The Orphan Girl of Chios, or the Triumph of Virtue (1839) was the work of Jacob Patsipios (died c. 1869) and represented one of the most magnificent attempts at novel writing that occurred early in this new period of Greek letters. The words "orphan" and "virtue" in the book's title reflect the modern Greek romantic environment. The subject was taken from recent history and was woven with a variety of adventures and an excessive imagination. The book was a precursor of the novel and it has been read widely down to our times.

Contemporary interests led Gregory Paleologos to write his novel, *The Artist* (1842). The author was better known for his activity in the area of Greek agriculture and for his writings on this subject. Also not to be ignored is a volume by John Anagnostis Deliyannis (1815–1876) that appeared in 1845. The author, a friend and collaborator of A. R. Rangavis, was inspired by contemporary subjects to which he gave a strong romantic coloring. Finally, we should mention *Thersandros*, a work by E. Frangoudis (1847), a romantic novel in epistolary form, whose theme was borrowed from the War of Independence. These three writers wrote in prose as an avocation or as juvenilia.

Xenos

The most imposing figure among the intellectuals, a prolific writer, was Stephen Xenos (1821–1894). *The Heroine of the Greek Revolution,* the best known of his novels (1852), was an example of this genre. Xenos's ambition was to write a romantic story of the War of Independence. After a conscientious historical preparation, he succeeded in his enterprise. Despite a somewhat hasty purist language and certain improbabilities and digressions that burdened the work at times, this novel had epic spirit and the composition was unified. Xenos wrote other novels as well, but these were done even more hastily, conforming even less to the rules of his art; they never had the persistent success of the *Heroine*. In any case, we should mention his oldest work, *The Devil in Turkey* (Greek edition, 1862), which is rich in incidents but obviously written with the intention of revealing the decadence of the Ottoman Empire. In some of his works we find interesting autobiographical elements.

Kalligas

In 1855 Paul Kalligas, a well-known attorney, statesman, and economist, who also wrote remarkable historical studies, published his novel *Thanos Vlekas* in the periodical *Pandora*. The work was taken from contemporary life, which is precisely what he described, but in a story raised to a much higher level than later portrayals of manners. Kalligas made no concessions to the demotic, not even in his dialogues. But certain of his artistically cast popular locutions gave his language a vigor that complemented the charm of his carefully worked style. Sometimes his expression seems cold to us. Perhaps this coldness was natural to the author, but in part it should be attributed to his period. At this time, prose writers had to choose between grandiloquence and dryness. The culture of Kalligas and his scientific turn of spirit deterred him from grandiloquence, and this resulted in the somewhat dry tone. The ironic spirit, which was not rare among the cultured intellectuals of the period and constituted an antidote to romantic sentimentality, completed the literary physiognomy of Kalligas in *Thanos Vlekas*. The manners of King Othon's period were described with care and with perfect knowledge of the craftsmanship of the novel. The psychology of the heroes was accurate and absolutely convincing in its simplicity. The author's social interests, the problems which concerned him, that is to say, the problems of contemporary society, were perfectly integrated in the story. Even if this work had no great variety of perspective, one could still say that it was the first social novel in Greek literature.

Melas

Alongside the work of Kalligas, it would be proper to place *Old Man Stathis* by Leon Melas (1812–1879), first published in 1858. *Old Man Stathis* was a recasting of a French work; it was not a novel. Written to edify the young, the book made its point in a variety of unrelated short stories borrowed from various sources, particularly from antiquity. The book, published at an appropriate time, was read widely. Even today, if its language did not present such difficulties, it would make good reading material for children, although its static form and the absence of plot greatly diminish its interest for young readers. Leon Melas, who was known for his social activities and pedagogical interests, also wrote other more specifically educational works and a verse drama called *Athanasios Diakos* (1859), about one of the most admired heroes of the War of Independence.

Ramphos

Constantine Ramphos (died c. 1871), whose principal works are of this same period, left a quantity of novels inspired by contemporary national battles: *Katsantonis* (1860), *The Last Days of Ali Pasha* (1862), and other works. In advanced age, after distinguishing himself in national activities, he became interested in the novel. Ramphos exhibited a talent for storytelling full of a youthful liveliness; he interwove adventures in tight episodes and animated his narratives with a true epic spirit. It was these qualities that made him widely read among the common people, who continued to read him until our time. He made some concessions to the popular language in his dialogues, but that did not suffice to invigorate his language, which lacks reflection and literary character.

Before passing on to the change which *Pope Joan* marks in Greek letters, we should mention *Perikles, A National Novel*, a work which was first published in Constantinople (1863) by Nicholas Argyriadis. This novel was very freely translated from English as a reaction to the bad romantic novels in translation that had infested Greek literature of the period. Other authors, contemporary with Argyriadis, also ridiculed in prefaces to their works the mania for translations of romantic novels, for example, Nicholas Votyras in his various works (*The Self-Styled Ghost*, 1860, and others).

Pope Joan by Roidis

Roidis's intentions were analogous to those of Argyriadis, but more complex, when he undertook to write *Pope Joan* (1866). He subtitled the work *A Medieval Study*. In the introduction, he referred to a great number of texts with critical commentaries, thus revealing not only his erudition, but also his desire to give a scientific appearance to his work. The numerous annotations accompanying the text had the same purpose. But Roidis was writing a novel and he knew the requirements of this genre. In the preface, he cited novel writers who were concerned with past periods; specifically, he mentioned Sir Walter Scott. He also remembered with pleasure Byron, from whom he borrowed much, both in style and in composition. Hence his subject was romantic, as were the subjects of his masters. From all this there emerged a chivalric romance with terrifying episodes and fanciful adventures. One can say that the author sought to ridicule the genre by weaving a simple plot, referring occasionally to contemporary events. Roidis reacted indirectly against the romantic excesses of his period and thus created a negative work. At the same time, however, he used the freedom offered by the novel to introduce into Greek literature a new spirit, positive, rational, and full of acuity. In the hazy atmosphere of Athenian romanticism, there suddenly appeared an aspiration for clarity, for simplicity of expression, for precision in descriptions. Roidis's initiative constituted an implicit protest against Athenian romantic grandiloquence. His style showed a repugnance for twilights; he sought a continual effervescence, he was ambitious to offer, above all, a treat to the senses, that is to say, a direct aesthetic pleasure. He often uses the word *pleasure* to express the feeling a well-written text gave him. For Roidis, the ideal relationship between text and reader was one of a sensual nature. When he wrote, he endeavored to hold the reader's interest with his phrase, to provoke an incessant renewal of the reader's attention.

The surprise created by unexpected comparisons constitutes the key to his literary technique. Simultaneously, he worked his phrase until he rendered it smooth, intelligible, and musical. Primary with him was the search for clarity. Nothing must escape us and nothing must be misinterpreted. The focus on aesthetics operated in a parallel manner: the position of accents in the phrase, the punctuation, and the conclusion preoccupy him greatly. We should mention the predominance of will power in his writings; he is not easily distracted. When he becomes hasty, his phrase gets long and cumbersome, following the meanderings of a detailed and exhausting thought. Roidis thus introduced a sense of style, a professional literary awareness, into modern Greek letters. Similarly, even when he composed his most important works, it was the desire for good taste, the submission of particular cases to more general aesthetic rules, that prevailed. We often encounter, either in the chapters of *Pope Joan,* or in the individual paragraphs, or even in the short stories Roidis wrote later, the constant repetition of the identical pattern. The passages open with a generally admissible idea, then follows, positively or antithetically, the application of the particular case that interests the author with the general thought expressed at the beginning. All this showed a man who believed in art more than spontaneity, in reason more than sentiment. This is Roidis; this is his novel. We do not demand imagination from him; he lacked this literary attribute to such an extent that his later works came to be identified with memory. We should not seek emotion in him; a dry, critical glance immediately neutralizes every moment of the spirit.

The values expressed in *Pope Joan* correspond to the theoretical considerations of the author. The liberation of thought, the relish for criticism, which often touched religious matters, and the crudity of his amatory scenes created a great scandal in Greek society of 1866. This book was a total refutation of the entire romantic aesthetic, the refutation of the entire psychic world and the close bonds with religious faith.

Naturally, *Pope Joan* was condemned by the church. A few months earlier, Renan's *The Life of Jesus* had created a unique reaction in Greece, as had the *Charitini* by Panayotis Soutsos. Religious factors aroused a strong disapproval. Within fifteen years, three authors of importance were condemned for their views on religion: Kaïris in 1852, Laskaratos for his *Mysteries of Cephalonia* in 1856, and now Roidis. This trend of the times should be interpreted as a composite of church anxiety at expressions that formerly

would have left it undisturbed, of national importance attributed to
the Grand Idea of a unified nation, and, correspondingly, of the
union of romanticism with religious sentiment. The medieval Christian world was now clearly interposed between the new Hellenism
and the classic vision of the ancient world.

Roidis replied to his critics with a couple of publications: *A Few
Words in Reply to No. 5688 Encyclical of the Holy Synod* and
Letters of a Man from Agrinion. The sharp attacks offered him an
occasion to exercise his acuity of spirit. Story, intrigue, imagination,
and their role in creation are entirely lacking here. For this reason,
when later Roidis compared *Pope Joan* to these short publications,
he did not hesitate to consider them "much inferior in importance
to *Pope Joan*."

Roidis

Emmanuel Roidis was born of a wealthy family in Syra in 1836.
From the age of six to thirteen, he lived in Genoa. Later, he returned to Syra where he pursued a regular course in education. At
the boarding school he attended, he lay awake nights secretly reading the novels of Alexander Dumas. It was at this time his literary
dispositions first became evident. While still a young boy, he again
travelled to foreign places; he lived in Germany, in Rumania, and in
Egypt. That is to say, until his twenty-first year, when he returned
to settle finally in Athens, he lived in a cosmopolitan atmosphere.
An assiduous reader, interested in the arts, he divided his time
among libraries, seminars, museums, and concerts. But cosmopolitan
life also interested him. He was a happy youth who cultivated the
sentiment of beauty, but who allowed his imagination to remain in-
active. Two successive misfortunes accentuated Roidis's personal
isolation: deafness prevented him from participation in social life
and a series of bad investments ruined him financially. The superiority complex he had developed in his happy youth now helped develop a rationalistic and sarcastic spirit. Roidis's nostalgia for the
past gradually diminished during the years he lived in Athens, enjoying the environment of a large city. But he was to remain a displaced Greek.

Reading, now his only pleasure in life, helped him sustain a simi-

338 Preparation for 1880

lar attitude. When he read Greek texts, he compared more than he evaluated. Nourished by the best French works of the time, he examined the Greek literary efforts unkindly. His analytical mind, which had never been initiated into a synthetic vision of life, found in the Greek texts abundant material for detailed criticism. Whatever pleased him was foreign. His incapacity to grasp beauty is characteristic; his criticism consists of censuring and refuting. This is not a position, but an opposition. When he attempted a creative evaluation, an exaltation of good, we find him moving with awkwardness. Criticism was his mode; and his critical acuity was an instrument of destruction and not an encouragement toward fulfillment. Bitterness emerged from all his works, whether he wrote a novel, a political essay, or criticism. Toward the end of his life, economic reasons, combined with nostalgia for his childhood years, led him to specialize in a genre that today we call the short story. These stories were autobiographical.

In an intellectual milieu, the artistic desire that characterized Roidis could not help but make the young intellectuals esteem him, much as they feared him and were displeased with his critical temper. Moreover, as we will see in the following chapter, his criticism was directed principally against the older writers and consequently could not have the approbation of the younger writers of the generation of 1880. In 1893 Constantine Manos expressed in an interview the opinion that was generally shared by the younger writers: "I think that of the older writers, he is the one who exercised the greatest influence on the literary generation of today."

Roidis first appeared in letters in 1860 with a translation of *The Journey* by Chateaubriand. His preface shows an early interest in matters of style and writing, which was rare at this time in Greece. In some of his passages where Western influence was evident, Roidis analyzed the charm of Chateaubriand's style successfully. He also showed, rather ostentatiously, the extent of his Biblical knowledge, and we ascertain that he kept up with most French publications. He enjoyed making references and flaunting his scientific knowledge. Finally, we see the pattern of his critical personality; he took pleasure in attacking the university contests, the translations of bad novels, and the purist language. In critical works he did not hesitate to use foreign texts, but in a manner prohibited by literary ethics.

His style, which is of interest in relation to this period's emerging verbal elegance, as in Pantazis, and the spiritual and jocose tone inherited from French journalism of the romantic period, as in Alphonse Karr, had already been somewhat formulated. It poured out unrestrained, however, in *Pope Joan*. The pyrotechnics of his expression are so excessive that, after the original surprise and first pleasure have passed, they provoke satiety: "Charlemagne, after he had overrun Europe, cutting laurels and heads with his long sword. . . ." "In Aix-la-Chapelle, a city famous for its sacred relics and for its needles. . . ." "England at that time had a monopoly on theologians, as today it has on the steam-machines." "Weaving eulogies for the Saints and baskets for the fishermen. . . ." Despite the indubitable quality that characterized Roidis, this surfeit permits us to understand the author's deeper personality. He did not attain control of his works as a whole. His entire thought—and this appears better in his criticism—consists of detailed observation out of which flows the essence of matters.

In *Pope Joan* he did not fulfill his promise to restore the atmosphere of the period, nor did he succeed in perfecting the character of Joan or infusing her with life. We have here as well a series of incidents and reflections that are characterized by observation and a great acuity of spirit; the expression is impeccable, but the work is loosely constructed. Since he did not succeed with the simplest genre, biography, Roidis had little chance with other genres, particularly criticism. What is good about *Pope Joan* is a magnificent narrative, a brilliant style obtained by very simply means, and finally, an energetic protestation against the errors of Athenian romanticism.

Military Life in Greece

After *Pope Joan*, but within this period which included the generation of 1880, we encounter few works in prose that merit attention. Extremely significant was the two-volume work published anonymously by Braïlas-Armenis in 1870–1871 under the title *Military Life in Greece*. I am inclined to attribute this work to the Greek scholar, C. Demopoulos, who lived in Rumania; however, the other known works by this author do not compare with the quality of *Military Life*. The narrative was written in the first person and was presented as a fragment of autobiography, but with many characteristics of creative prose; the tendency toward plot construction is visible, and the abundant dialogue frequently serves to present characters and events. The author was not insensible to the influence of Roidis. His style lacks the brilliance that charms us in *Pope Joan,* but it is distinguished by a much greater firmness. Moreover, the work is redeemed by a human accent, heavy in content and somewhat imposing, which add to the delightful expression. In these pages we find an author able to observe with accuracy, to distinguish important details, and to render these elegantly and exactly; a man who takes matters seriously and reflects on them.

His language tends toward the purist; however, despite this, the author likes to use an extremely simple vocabulary of popular words and a syntax strongly influenced by these words. This gives his style an unusual vivacity that is accentuated by his originality of images and clarity of thought, two distinctive characteristics of the book. The descriptions are rapid and suggestive; the dialogue, without departing entirely from the purist language, is natural and rhythmic. Manners and characters receive a lively accurate portrayal. The author is severely critical of administrative and military customs during the later part of King Othon's reign. But his writing talent permits him to clothe his criticism in a plot that gives us real aesthetic enjoyment.

Zambelios

In 1871 the *Cretan Weddings* by Spiros Zambelios (1815–1881) was published. This was a historical novel which takes place in the years of the Venetian occupation. Zambelios, who often exhibited an excessive imagination in his historical works, here offends by holding himself to historical reality. His novel never breaks its historical bonds to become a creative composition. The book's heavy and awkward purist language increases the reader's impression of historical research without literary pretentions. Nor is this impression dispelled by either rhetorical effects or the didacticism that was cultivated in the long pages or even by the portrayal of manners, which, by its exaggeration, forms a dry and loose contact with human reality.

But in leaving Zambelios, who will appear in many other chapters of this *History,* we would have difficulty assessing such original and

varied work as Zambelios did. Without doubt, he had great intellectual gifts, critical acuity, imagination, and originality. The extent
and variety of his writings show his ability in numerous branches of
culture, but his prolific output prevented his attaining distinction in
any one of these manifestations. His strong personality was unable
to triumph in the activity of his times and his image appears today
three-quarters effaced. But historical perspective places him at a
critical moment in modern Greek literature.

Vassiliki and Other Works

Another historical novel, *Vassiliki,* published in 1878 under the
name of Nicholas E. Makris, has aroused considerable criticism. It
is attributed to Constantine Versis (1845–1881). The plot was set in
the time of the Turkish occupation. The author proposed to render
attractive the history of this period by veiling it in a myth. The didactic commentaries in the book are not sufficiently linked to history, and the narrative itself is slow and lacks life. The book was
praised more for the information it contained than for its literary
quality. A few years later a prolific writer, J. Pervanoglos (1831–
1911), who was also concerned with the theater (*Thebes,* a tragedy,
1864), published a historical narrative called *Michael Paleologos*
(1833). Pervanoglos also attempts to render history attractive. At
this same period Papadiamantis began his literary career by also
writing historical novels. We should observe that during these last
years, as we see in Papadiamantis and others, Byzantium was beginning to provide an increasing proportion of inspiration for historical
novels. But the period of this genre was approaching its end. The
arbitrary limit is represented by Demetrios Vikelas (1835–1908)
with his work *Loukis Laras.* This book can be considered as beginning a new period in modern Greek prose.

Vikelas

In *Loukis Laras* Demetrios Vikelas narrates a true story of the War
of Independence. His narrative has simplicity and charm, and an
obvious desire to avoid the exaggerations of the purist language. At

the same time, criticism around the problems of the art and research into linguistic problems had significantly progressed and was preparing new developments. Around 1880 we ascertain that Athenian society established a certain equilibrium with the appearance of a large bourgeousie, important businessmen, and the establishment of a relatively stable political life. There had come to be statesmen and they, too, helped create an autonomous intellectual life that was expressed in specialized periodicals. The role of the literary man in politics was significantly reduced; other causes also contributed to his retreat from the political scene: the new bourgeousie distrusted the participation of literary men in political life, since they had generally been subversive and revolutionary in the early period. Society no longer aspired to agitation but to harmony. The home as a basic social cell began to have its own intellectual needs, its own particular charm, and awaited a literature that would express this charm. The poet, stepping down from the high political stage, entered the home, lowered his tone, and attempted to become intimate. Romantic excess no longer had a place here. Literature had to be renewed.

These needs coincided with the internal history of letters. Even more than the criticism of romanticism, it was the movement's own exaggeration that led to its refutation, to its abolition. At its height, the agitation created an impasse. The new writers moved, naturally, toward another extreme. They sought what had not been provided by previous generations, the sweetness, the peace, the tenderness, and the simplicity of everyday feelings. Moreover, Western culture had preceded in this direction, and thus again foreign influences assisted local necessities. In the following chapter, we will examine the different literary manifestations which contributed in the passage of Greek literature from Athenian romanticism to the new school of Athens.

Chapter 23

The Preparation

Contribution of

Criticism

In addition to its two fundamental forms, creative prose and poetry, the literature of the romantic period (1830–1880) presented other efforts and developments of an intellectual order. Criticism, naturally, was at the center of these, a criticism that developed only after the other literary genres, though we have already observed its early manifestations. The maturity of criticism, as a separate genre, was prepared to a great extent by the university contests (1850–1877) and owed its achievement to the critical activity of Roidis. However, the periodicals and various associations founded throughout this period also contributed to the development of criticism and to discussion of ideas. Parallel with this, in the last two decades of Greek romanticism, we have the crystallization of tendencies that we encountered earlier toward the study of history and folklore. Finally, a literary language was developing; after its attempts at absolute refinement, language was now ready for the campaign Psycharis launched. This is to say, different forces, tendencies, and forms of expression converged in a social and political framework to create an intellectual world which permitted, indeed imposed, the formation of the generation of 1880.

Poetry Contests

In 1850 a wealthy Greek immigrant, Ambrosios Rallis, decided to institute a poetry contest. We know how poetry was praised and revered during this period; we also know how close the connection was between poetic production and the exaltation of the War of Independence. "The poets," wrote Karasoutsos, "like the Vestal Virgins of Rome, guard the sacred flame of love of country vigilantly, console Greece, maintain hope, cheer the saddened heroes by singing of their exploits and live and die as they did, leaving a heritage to their descendants, some their sword, others their lyre." Rallis thought the university had as its destined function the elevation of Greek poetic creation, and more specifically that it serve as a counteraction to the demotic influence on Greek poetic expression. Hence, an annual contest was instituted in which a committee composed of university professors awarded a prize. The decision was greeted with enthusiasm. In 1851, while still in his youth, Sophocles Karydis wrote of Rallis in both prose and verse. "When Your hand wove the wreath for poets, another hand, that of Glory, was preparing a second wreath, more glorious, for your head." The long-range objective of Rallis's efforts was expressed in verse:

> Our liberated youth
> Will soon act with courage
> Will become involved in new battles
> And chase the Turk far away. . . .

If the poetry contest did not ameliorate poetic expression in the sense sought by the man who instituted it, as we will ascertain below, it is indisputable that the contests were in accord with the poetic climate of the period and for many years constituted one of the greatest points of contact between national awareness and poetry. This correspondence was particularly conspicuous during the reign of King Othon and the early years of King George I. Later, conditions changed. However, at the beginning, the poetry contests had the character of a national ritual. The day set for the reading of reports and awarding of the prize created a general gathering. One source reported: "On that day, all Athens was on the move; all classes of society expressed the same interest. The cafés and the bazaars were deserted; the squares were crowded with people who shouted, gesticulated, and discussed with the excitement natural to these people. After the report concerning the different productions submitted to the contest was read, the judge announced the winner, congratulated him in the name of the nation, recited his verses in a loud voice, and crowned him with laurel. The crowned poet was greeted by the acclamations of the crowd, which accompanied him almost triumphantly to his house."

One condition set by the founder of the contest was that the purist language should be cultivated. A. R. Rangavis, who chaired one of the first contests, gave his own interpretation: if the demotic was supported, there was danger this instrument might predominate and instead of fashioning a pan-Hellenic language, there would be only the "development of special dialects." But the demotic persistantly appeared at the contests. The committee praised a number of works written in this language, but awarded the prize to others. However, one must not consider that language was the sole critical criterion; the result the professors desired was the much more general one of making a certain aesthetic predominate by combatting romantic irregularities: romantic poetry "is foreign, and not Greek." The antiromantic attitude of the judges, as "foreign" as romantic poetry if not more so, nonetheless had a certain salutary effect: the judges required poetry to plunge its roots into reality.

With a certain naïveté perhaps influenced by his studies and his profession, Orphanides, himself a judge later, supported the idea that in order to compose beautiful poetry, a "buoyant and practical study of nature" was essential. In the same sense, Mistriotes taught that "great poets are not born, as Athena, out of the head of Zeus; they are representatives of the people with whom they live." A natural environment, a social environment were essential; a step further and we arrive at a natural language. And, indeed, among the chairmen and judges of the university contests, there were some lucid minds who could conceive what was just, who either pointed out the weaknesses of the purist language or the importance of the demotic for poetry. Other causes helped clarify this. The recognition that the folksong had contributed to the historical unity of the Greek nation led within measure to a recognition of the language in which the folksong had survived. The bad treatment a multitude of uninstructed versifiers had inflicted on the purist language exasperated the judges who were nourished on classicism. Furthermore, the excesses of those who sought rare words from the ancient language, a distinctive sign of romantic poetry, provoked disgust and disenchantment. The chairman of the 1865 committee complained that "the archaic manner of vocabulary has become an epidemic with us." Thus, even academic criticism was led to seek a conciliation. In the last contest, the demotic, whether in the dialogue of a comedy or in the lyrical pieces, was awarded the prize.

However, in both its aggregate and its detail, the contribution of the contests in the development of modern Greek poetry was negligible; university criticism was more a product of the new realities than a director of the movement. "If there ever was a product of the mind worth considering," Polylas wrote later, "it appeared in our time. Who ventures to affirm seriously that this happy event made something of those official poetry contests, or that the opinions of the literary judges succeeded in extricating the critical spirit in Greece?" Nevertheless, we cannot pass over the contribution, especially a negative one, these contests made in the development of neo-Hellenic criticism and of the new Greek literature generally. It is a significant fact that the influence of Koraes and Solomos were associated with the more important representatives with liberal aesthetic tendencies. From the beginning, in 1852, we see a radical disagreement with the founder of the contests, which was formulated officially by the rector, Spiros Pilikas, a friend of Solomos and trustee of his *Dialogue*. After having praised the efforts of Koraes, he protested, as rector, against the tendency toward archaism in poetic expression: "The wind from the cemeteries dessicates the delicacy of sentiment." Pilikas (1805–1861) left memoirs relating to his ministerial activities during 1853; these were published long after his death. Shortly after his term as rector (1853), the critical movement which culminated in the *Critique of Soutsos* indirectly penetrated the area of the poetry contests.

Asopios

Constantine Asopios from Epirus (1785–1872) also was fortunate to benefit from the teachings of both Koraes and Solomos. As a young man, while he studied and taught at the Greek colonies abroad, he was under the influence of Koraes and he assimilated this influence conscientiously and intelligently. Later, he went to Kerkyra and there became acquainted with the work of Solomos and admired it. He left us some remarks on the poet. When he went to Athens, where he finally occupied a chair as professor at the university, he brought with him and imposed on a circle of friends this double and doubly important critical tradition. Discontented with the poetry contests before becoming a judge in his turn, D. Vernardakis attacked Asopios, who for some years was the most eminent representative of Greek criticism, but mostly he complained about the exaggerated severity of Asopios's associates. Hence, we have here implicit acknowledgement of a school of criticism with Asopios as leader.

As one of the last representatives of the prerevolutionary generation having numerous humanistic concerns, Asopios did not express his entire personality in his works, important as they were. His direct influence appears to have been considerable. Specifically, he was in contact with the young Roidis, who left us a characteristic picture of him: "We find him each evening . . . the sorry old man . . . alone and abandoned, bending over a miserable table. . . ." Asopios corrected Roidis's first literary essays; he counseled and taught him: "Many evenings we spent together, and I heard numerous evaluations on modern Greek poetry from the mouth of the man who had spent all his life studying the poets." Asopios's critical theories are particularly evident in his introduction to Pindar (1843) and in the *History of the Greek Poets and Prose Writers* (1850) where he examined ancient Greek literature by means of a dictionary of proper names. His critical evaluations exhibit a continuous contact with the new Greek letters and a strictly aesthetic development.

In the *Critique of Soutsos,* whose main, if not only, editor he was, he systematically examined the poetry of Panayotis Soutsos. This examination was not limited to aesthetic analysis but often included purely linguistic observations. This work, through its requirements for poetry and its praise of the demotic poetic tradition, made an essential contribution to the formation of modern Greek criticism. Christopoulos, Vilaras, and Solomos were praised there; *Erotokritos* was utilized. The book created quite a commotion; the discussions it raised resulted in a greater familiarity with the teachings of Asopios. We should not forget that Zalokostas's fine critical efforts appeared in this same year, as did the important criticism of Emmanuel Staïs (1817–1895) on Solomos's *Lambros.* This criticism, written in the demotic, was published in Athens, but it is evident that his thought originated from the Ionian Islands. German realism associated with aesthetic culture predominated here. Staïs characterized Solomos as the "Homer of contemporary poetry." The analysis of *Lambros* was principally aesthetic; it followed the poem verse by verse, focusing on the art of the poet. Staïs attempted criticism again later, but with less success; he had also become disenchanted with Solomos.

We should mention further that, though the contests did not produce positive results, they stimulated rivalry and aroused and maintained public interest in the existence of a certain kind of high-level poetry. A great number of Greek intellectuals appeared for the first time through the university poetry contests. Kleon Rangavis (1842–1917), son of Alexander, was unable to offer any noteworthy contribution to the development of Greek literature because of the superpurist language in his later dramatic and poetic attempts. Nor did Timoleon Ambelas (1850–1926) offer anything outstanding with his abundant and varied literary production. But both contribute to the intellectual ferment that characterized their period, and both penetrated the world of letters by way of the poetry contests. I should also mention the prolific writer Anthony J. Antoniadis (1836–1905), who was awarded a prize almost every year from 1865 on, either for his long epic poems, usually inspired by the War of Independence, or for his theatrical pieces. If Antoniadis had devoted himself to modern Greek history, perhaps his conscientiousness and application would have made him a good historian; today, his works have fallen into justified oblivion and are interesting only for what historical information they contain.

Men who wrote in other genres also participated in these contests and they were undoubtedly encouraged by the popularity of the contests. Alexander Vyzantios (1841–1898), who later became one of the great figures in journalism, received a prize in 1862 for his long poem *Socrates and Aristophanes*. His cold purist language would suffice to relegate this work to oblivion, if his classical tendencies and his classical sobriety did not require mention of him. D. Vikelas, who later displayed such a great diversity in his intellectual and social activities, also began with poetry. In 1851, while still at the lyceum, he published a translation of Racine accompanied by some original verses; in 1855 he presented some verses to the contest instituted by Ralleios. Spiros Lambros, who later helped orient modern Greek thought toward recent periods of Greek history, participated in a poetry contest and was awarded a prize. I also mention D. G. Kampouroglou in connection with the contests, for they were the point of departure from which the future historian began his multiple activities.

Finally, among the young men who started on their careers with the university contests, we should mention Aristomenis Proveleggios, whose epic poem *Theseus* was highly praised in 1870; Vizyinos, who received a prize in 1874 for another epic poem *Kedros;* and Palamas, who presented his first collection of poetry, *Words of Love*, in 1876.

The importance of the poetry contest was further confirmed by the eager participation of men of first rank. Among these was Orphanides, professor at the university, who entered and reentered his poems until they were awarded a prize; he believed that an injustice had been perpetrated against him, and he attacked the jury and provoked long controversies. Alexander Rangavis entered his poem *The Swift Falcon* in a contest in 1871 and obtained high praise for it.

Koumanoudis

Stephen Koumanoudis, a most enlightened man who many times later served as a judge of the contests, entered his poem *Stratis Kalopichiros* in the first year. He was born in Adrianople in 1818, studied in Germany and France, and published his first study in 1845, in Belgrade, under the title *Toward What Does the Art of the Modern Greeks Tend?* Later, he went to Athens, where in 1851 he was appointed professor of Latin literature. His fruitful and varied activity, which included literary, archeological, and historical work, began at that time and continued until his death in 1889. Modern Greek folklore and linguistics concerned him greatly. And though these subjects were subordinate to his scientific activity, his esteemed personality and his immense knowledge permitted him to influence matters touching modern Greece. I make special mention of an un-published neo-Hellenic bibliography and a large *Collection of New Terms Created by Intellectuals from the Fall of Constantinople to Our Own Days.*

He was never indifferent to verse, which he wrote especially in his youth. I cite a series of sonnets to Venice written in 1845. The nostalgic attitude evident in these poems classifies them as romantic poetry; but their clarity and simplicity of language make them fore-runners of the new poetry.

> Closed windows of the palace, is it true, tell me, that a charm-ing crowd of women's faces have appeared already, or is it only a story?

A little later, he was inspired by the revolutionary movements of 1848:

> And already I see distinctly, O people, your colossal height standing behind the Alps and taking great strides; I see your bright face surrounded by a crown of rays.

I tend to believe that it was precisely his virtues, his love of pure ex-pression in both senses of the term, that took him entirely outside the lyrical aspirations of his time, and because of this, he quickly preferred to express himself in other literary forms. *Stratis Kalopichiros* was a long poem, in iambic trimeter, monotonous and lacking charm for the reader today. Koumanoudis, however, was extremely partial to the poem, and in its successive editions he revised it carefully without being able to free it from its initial coldness.

Hence, his real contribution to the new Greek literature came mainly in criticism. He belonged, first of all, to those forming the group around Constantine Asopios. He believed in the demotic and saw in it the form most appropriate to poetry. With his cultivated love of beauty, he was able to distinguish the most successful works of Greek literature, and he was among the first to render tribute to the efforts of the Ionian Island school. He helped judge contests; he wrote for periodicals and even edited them. And always his penchant for beautiful forms in Greek literature was obvious. With the passage of time, his intentions became clear and he rose in the esteem of the much younger intellectuals.

Vernardakis

In 1854 and 1855 Demetrios Vernardakis, while still a student, participated unsuccessfully in poetry contests. In 1856 his *Conjectures* was awarded a prize. It was a badly written epico-lyric poem inspired by Byzantine history. It abounds with contemporary defects: the verbal quest, the lack of clarity. Vernardakis first appeared in letters in 1854 with *Graemyomachia,* "a comic-heroic poem." His notes show an ironic turn of spirit and a certain fatuity. In the following year, he appeared fiery and combative in *The Delights of the Self-Styled Scholar.* This was a polemical pamphlet which continued the battle of the *Critique of Soutsos.* Vernardakis, who was born in Mytilene in 1833 of a family originally from Crete, studied literature at the University of Athens. The award for *Conjectures* aroused the interest of a national benefactor also named D. Vernardakis, who sent him to Germany on a scholarship. In 1857 he entered the contest with a drama called *Maria Doxapatri,* whose plot was set during the Venetian occupation. This work was not awarded a prize and Vernardakis launched an attack against the committee and its chairman, Koumanoudis. In his introduction to the drama's published edition (Munich, 1858), the author also attacked Asopios, who had defended the committee. This long introduction, where he discusses the theories of contemporary drama, provoked great interest. After Homer, he exalted Shakespeare as "the poet of all the people and of all centuries." Vernardakis had studied the possibilities and needs for a national Greek drama, that is to say, a romantic drama. As for *Maria Doxapatri,* the influence of Shakespeare is apparent, but he did not attain the heights of his model, not even to the extent of infusing his characters with life; he only succeeded in producing a cold purist language.

In 1860 a new drama called *The Beehives,* which again received no prize, provoked new attacks by Vernardakis. The author continued to write significant literary studies and theatrical works: *Merope* (1866), *Euphrosyne* (1876), *Faust* (1893), *Antiope* (1896, unpublished), *Nicephoros Phocas* (1905). Beginning 1861 he occupied a chair at the University of Athens, he published a variety of historical and other works, and he continued various attacks with a juvenile belligerence. He resigned from the university in 1869, was reappointed in 1882, resigned for the last time in 1883, and retired to Mytilene where he lived until his death in 1907. He played a major role in the battles over the language question. His role in this is examined later and there he is given a mere general evaluation. As for his theatrical works, it cannot be said that he surpassed the level of his period. However, it must be acknowledged that he helped improve the Greek repertoire and generally aroused the interest of that public connected with the theater.

Indeed, beginning 1854 one observes that the number of theatrical works presented in contests increased year by year. Antoniades entered theatrical works and won prizes; C. Versis, to whom *Vassiliki* is attributed, was awarded a prize in 1870 and another in 1875; Vlachos received a prize for his drama *The Captain of the National Guard* (1868); and P. D. Zanos (1848–1908), who entered his work in the 1868 and 1870 contests, wrote theatrical works to the end of his life. In comedy, the demotic language continued to reappear from time to time. The search for a living language able to serve the real needs of the new Hellenism appeared early and was reinforced by the interest which questions about folklore aroused. Emmanuel Staïs ascertained with joy in 1853 that even in Athens one saw "a certain number of poems written in the folk language . . . appearing, which proves to me that the truth has begun to find followers even there." In 1858 Tertsetis entered his comedy *Triumph of the Poetry*

Contest. The demands of the theater certainly helped promote the demotic language. Even though classicism demanded a more elevated language for tragedy, "the language of comedy is the popular language." In 1861 a translation of *Plutus* by Aristophanes was published anonymously; it was a free paraphrase in the Greek vernacular. The work is attributed to the educator Joseph Ginakas (1871) and M. Chourmouzis. At any rate, the former appears to have had a sound judgment on matters of modern Greek literature; in 1869, that is to say, very early in the history of modern Greek style, we find him working on *Erotokritos.*

In 1871 a comedy, *Bertoldos,* was entered at the Voutsinaios contest. The committee praised it, but did not award it a prize; it was written in the demotic, and in the long introduction the author expressed the national need for this idiom: "What profit for the nation if the idea of free development of the language expressed by Vilaras had prevailed! The nation would be wise and enriched, consequently, strong." The work was published in the same year. Because of its imperfections, exaggerated characters and awkward versification, we understand the reservations of the committee perfectly. The defects of contemporary society, the imitation and bad assimilation of Western tradition, were attacked with great linguistic freedom. The author of this comedy was Anthony Phatseas (1821–1872). He had undertaken early, in a series of studies and memoirs, the battle in favor of the demotic (1850, 1856). Later, he wrote gnomic verses. His comedy was inferior to his true quality. Phatseas was a man with liberal and progressive convictions and was distinguished by his courage and originality in the relative stagnation of his period.

The Voice of My Heart
by D. G. Kampouroglou

But the times had come almost full circle. Old forms no longer gave satisfaction, and even the contest judges felt the need of conforming to the new demands. In 1873 G. Mistriotes, as chairman of the committee of judges, awarded the prize to a lyric collection entitled *The Voice of My Heart,* a work by Demetrios G. Kampouroglou (1852–1942). All the pieces were written in the demotic, but this was not their principal originality; the atmosphere of this collection was antiromantic from beginning to end. A tone of informality reigned here, one that tended toward the most self-conscious prose The first poem was called "Love and Candy."

> I only love two things on earth, my friend: love and candy. It is for these that I live. It is for these that I die of envy. All the rest is nothing to me!

We have a smile, a good humor, a good appetite, a joyous heart. Presenting this work at the contest and awarding it a prize revealed a marked aversion for the funereal atmosphere of romantic poetry. The generation of poets who died young was exhausted; literature now began to enlist men who believed in life, who had a sound, vigorous constitution and were biologically strong. Let us remember that the generation of 1880 was remarkable for its longevity and its endurance. The choice of the jury created a furor, the newspapers participated, and this year was thought to announce the new times. We know that Palamas, who had "come to Athens with a group of young provincials," sought to make the acquaintance of the rebel poet Kampouroglou; undoubtedly, he must also have approved the necessity for renewal. In 1874 Kampouroglou entered a satiric poem in the contest. Although the committee did not award it a prize, nonetheless, they were greatly concerned with it, paying special attention to the parodies of contemporary romantic poets in it.

It is evident that when Karasoutsos, Paparrigopoulos, and Vasiliades disappeared, a new era opened for Greek letters. But the decline of romanticism could not come about indirectly or irresponsibly, without anyone assuming leadership. It was necessary that someone undertake to criticize and condemn the older poetry in a methodical manner. Emmanuel Roidis was found ready and well disposed to assume this task.

Roidis and Vlachos

The university contests, which were no longer able to respond to the demands of intellectual society, were replaced by other much younger and more liberated institutions. In 1865 the literary society *Parnassos* was established. Its founders were young men; they were anxious to work and they aspired to a renewal of the Athenian literary atmosphere. Even the excommunicated Laskaratos found *Parnassos* hospitable. Along with this organization, we also have other societies composed of young men: *Byron, Evangelismos, Society of Friends.* They all instituted contests and published new periodicals. The most lively was the *Parnassos,* which began publishing a periodical in 1877 under the same name. In the same year, which was also the last year of the Voutsinaias contest, *Parnassos* announced its own drama contest. Chairman of the committee of judges was Emmanuel Roidis, who was also burdened with excommunication for *Pope Joan.* But in the meantime, Roidis had come to influence the younger writers by his satiric acuity in the journal *Asmodaios.* His report was not content to condemn all the works entered in the contest; instead of entering into details and criticizing each one, Roidis preferred to develop a theory explaining why Greece of his period was incapable of producing poetic works. This is the famous theory of "the ambiviant milieu," based on the teaching of Taine. Roidis considered that "Greece cannot hope for poetry at the present time, since she has denied her ancestral customs, and since she has yet to participate in the intellectual life of other peoples."

To this provocation, Angelos Vlachos (1838–1920) gave an immediate response at a conference, in which he supported on the one hand the view that poetic creation depended on the divine gift of inspiration and on the other that a propitious climate for poetry did not exist in Greece at this time. Vlachos was the man best able to reply to Roidis. Young, in fact younger than Roidis, he had sacrificed to the romantic Muses with his juvenilia. In addition to his original romantic production, we should mention his translations of Lamartine in 1864. But his lucid mind had early permitted him to distinguish the inadequacies of Athenian romanticism and the necessity to use the popular language. In 1865 the university contest committee accused Vlachos of resembling Heine, which showed that his intentions were good. Moreover, he had already published in 1864 translations of the German poet. During a conference on Tertsetis (1875), he again paid tribute to the popular language. A studious man and scholar, a prolific writer, he lacked the intellectual ability of Roidis, but he radiated a serious sense of responsibility. Moreover, the theoretic disagreement with Roidis was quantitative, not qualitative. Vlachos raised no objection to the theory of environment, which we know had been supported already in Athens by G. Mistriotes, but exaggerated the importance of ability. In general, he tended toward idealism. This tendency, which he exposed systematically in 1879 in his attack on the naturalistic school of Zola, was already apparent in his attitude toward Roidis.

The debate, which provoked two replies from Roidis, passed from generalities to specific subjects, particularly men and works in the new Greek literature. Roidis used the occasion to attack his contemporaries, to praise writers of the preceding generation like Christopoulos, Vilaras, and Solomos, and also to exalt the poetic value of the demotic. Among the living, he praised Valaorites and Paraschos. (At the death of Valaorites in 1879, he published a good critical essay on his work. It is one of the rare contributions in which he successfully formulated a positive evaluation.) Roidis's arguments in the discussion were not original. For the most part they came from Asopios. Nor was his method very successful; it was based on references. What was original and successful was, as always, his style and acuity of spirit, with which, furthermore, it appeared that Roidis was victorious in the dispute that troubled the minds of his time profoundly.

Papadiamantopoulos

Other intellectuals also participated in the discussion. I mention among the older writers, A. R. Rangavis, who naturally attempted to remain conciliatory, and, among the younger, John Papadiamantopoulos. Though still very young (born in 1856), Papadiamantopoulos was to make a career in 1878 when he became involved in the debate and showed a noteworthy literary activity. For at least five years his name had appeared in periodicals and almanacs, where he published prose and verse, both original and translations. In 1873 he published an anthology of lyrics anonymously. This anthology displaced the new poetic tendencies, and for this was of greater interest than most works of this genre. The editor wrote in the purist language and expressed his admiration for the poets of the generation of the Soutsos brothers and Zalokostas. However, the new elements that he introduced employed the demotic: Julius Typaldos and the poems in the demotic by D. Valavanis and G. Mavroyannis. In subsequent years, Papadiamantopoulos was occupied with reprinting the works of Alexander Soutsos, which he prefaced with high praise. Parallel with this, however, both in the poems he wrote and in the works he selected for translation, he exhibited a need to go beyond romantic grandiloquence; he translated Heine and was influenced by Baudelaire.

In the debate on modern Greek poetry, he exhibited a youthful acuity and showed himself well informed on intellectual matters. He attacked Roidis violently, but one can say that he attacked a well-armed adversary with the same weapons: the same kind of mind, the same technique. And he was not distinguished so much on theoretical matters, where he contented himself with correcting Roidis as he was in his evaluation of modern Greek poets. We can say that he followed Roidis in theory, but that his style differed. He admired Solomos, Tersetis, Valaorites, Laskarates, and the representatives of the romantic school of Athens.

The irresolution he displayed in his preferences is also found in his collection of poetry called *Turtle Doves and Vipers*, which appeared in the same year, 1878. It is a bilingual work, where the demotic and purist run side by side. In addition to verses charged with romanticism, we also find the beginnings of the new poetry. The expression is more dense, the sentiment more reserved and more moderate; we have a desire for pliability. Heine also speaks here:

> Wherever I stop, wherever I turn
> In the world or in the desert,
> Everywhere and always your face
> I have before me.

From 1878 to 1881 Palamas published a series of poems under the title *Verses* in which he attacked Heine. Later, Palamas recalled his emotion on first encountering Papadiamantopoulos and the impression on reading his early poems: "The collection of Papadiamantopoulos, *Turtle Doves and Vipers*, seized my soul vigorously." But the collection also contained some verses in French: Papadiamantopoulos was ready to become Jean Moréas, and soon he was lost to Greek letters. At any rate, this collection, his first and last in Greek, announced the generation of 1880.

Part Eight
New School of Athens
The Generation of 1880

The work of the generation of 1880 combined elements of language and thought that had circulated in earlier years. This phenomenon undoubtedly corresponded to the evolution of society and expresssed a new Greek spirit. It was the beginning of a new Enlightenment. The initiator of this new movement was Psycharis, the great creator was Palamas; both were linked to tradition as well as to the renewal. It was around Palamas that the new tendencies of the Greek spirit coalesced.

Chapter 24

The Generation of 1880

and Psycharis

Verse, Inspiration, Language

"We have already observed that *Turtle Doves and Vipers* bade a farewell to something that was already passing, that the *Verses* of Kambas welcomed, for the first time, a new dawn, and that the *Idylls* (1884) of George Drosinis confirmed this new dawn." Thus did Palamas mark the passage of modern Greek literature to the generation of 1880. In many of his later prose works, he recalled the first awakening of his spirit and his thought, when, as a student, he travelled between Missolonghi and Athens. At the time, the memory of Nikos Kambas (1857–1931) continued to live for everyone. Two years older than Palamas, Kambas also studied law. He was versed in foreign languages but preferred the sustaining nurture of the great foreign models to the insipid fruit which declining Athenian romanticism offered him. This fondness and these interests he transferred to Palamas. But, as we observed above, the reasons which demanded a renewal in Greek literature had an objective character and were not simply an expression of a fondness for greater refinement.

The aspiration for a general renewal was manifested in the new periodicals. *Hestia* began to circulate in 1876; it proposed to become a family magazine containing both literary and encyclopedic material. In 1878 Kleanthis Triantaphyllos (1850–1889) and Vlasis Gabriilides (1848–1930) were exiled from Constantinople, where they had practiced journalism and published the *Rabagas,* a satiric periodical. Kleanthis Triantaphyllos, who was known under the pseudonym Rabagas, wrote satiric verses. Gabriilides was attracted by novelty and interested in every kind of youthful expression. Moreover, both were strongly liberal. The former took his own life when he was persecuted for his political articles; the latter, with *Acropolis,* the newspaper he published, later became famous for his long journalistic activity, which revitalized the Greek press.

Because Gabriilides will be of no further consequence to us in this *History,* a few words about his literary work and his criticism are in order here. Both he and Triantaphyllos were dominated by a journalistic awareness, and both had the *Acropolis* as an outlet. The style of Gabriilides is intentionally disconcerting; this he accomplished as much by his contrasts as by the introduction of demotic elements in the purist language. His style surprises, but it has no charm. It lacks harmony, symmetry, and clarity. But Gabriilides was very dynamic and despite the imperfections of his style, he exercised an influence on his contemporaries (Mitsakis, Yannopoulos). As for criticism, Gabriilides was always interested in all new intellectual movements and disposed to support them. He contributed greatly because of the prestige he had acquired in public opinion and among intellectuals in the renewal of Greek intellectual life; from Palamas to Papatsonis, a number of writers were indebted to him for their early recognition in neo-Hellenic society.

In 1880 he published, without Triantaphyllos, a new satiric publication, *Do Not Lose Your Head*. Both *Rabagas* and this periodical wanted light satiric verses and intended to support the younger writers. In both periodicals, the verses of Palamas, Kambas, and Drosinis were published anonymously or under a pseudonym. These verses differ greatly from those that the older lyricism had offered to the public. Rapid and light, they sought to charm rather than to attain sublimity. The satiric verses also were lacking in grandiloquence and overstatement. Men who remained attached to sanctioned matters read those verses with displeasure. Others who sensed the new needs welcomed them with satisfaction.

Kambas

In 1880 an enlightened man, Lambros Koromilas, decided to establish a publishing house and begin a systematic publication of the new poetic literary production, having as an example similar French houses. He published the *Verses* of Nikos Kambas, one hundred pages of poems, some in the purist language, others in the demotic. But the change in tone was more characteristic than the progress of language. These verses were written to be read, not from the politician's high platform, but in the warm atmosphere of a room. Violent passions were not expressed; rather the emotions were those concerned with the small daily pains and joys. Their expression was not pretentious; one can say that they were murmured with a soft smile intervening to disguise the emotion:

> Yes, she said, stubbornly, all is finished between us,
> And she begged me to return all her gifts.
> Here are your letters, a lock of your hair. Don't go,
> Take also the white almond blossoms and your kisses.

Very soon Kambas abandoned letters and turned to the practice of law. But his timely work and his brilliant personality reserved for him a place at the beginning of the new period of Greek literature.

Drosinis

Kambas also introduced Koromilas and George Drosinis (1859– 1951), who had published his first verses in *Rambagas* under the pseudonym "Spider." The collection was called *Spider's Web*. In place of an introduction, the book opened with a quote from Coppée. This choice constituted a profession of faith; the new currents in French literature under Parnassicism were echoing through Greece. Drosinis also sought to be gracious and simple. His preferences permitted him no violence of form or content:

> They say that only in April
> The roses and lilies flourish.
> At this moment, we are in January;
> But on your cheeks and lips,
> I see the lilies and roses blooming.
> But what a pity! They do not bloom for me!

These are short poems with an essentially amorous theme. We encounter these same characteristics in the second collection, *Stalactites* (1881). The only difference is that the tone sometimes becomes more formal, the spirit stronger and more sustained, and the subjects that inspired the poet more varied. We already distinguish a love of plot and a tendency to give value to the folklore element. These characteristics, combined with the poet's interest in recent historical events involving enslaved Greece, were reinforced in *Idylls,* published in 1884. The purist language, which appeared here and there in the earlier collections, now disappeared entirely.

In 1886 the first collection of poetry, *Songs of My Country,* by Kostes Palamas appeared. The title characterized the collection both in its broader sense of country and in the more narrow sense of that word. The poet exploited the richness of the folksong, of neo-Hellenic traditions, and of Greek history. Even though it was of a serious nature, he interwove light songs on the order of those by Kambas and Drosinis. His language in this collection was exclusively demotic. On the title page of the book, we read: "In Athens, bookstore of the *Hestia.*" The generation of 1880 had conquered the new periodical; after 1881, Drosinis and Palamas wrote for it regularly. The principal figure in the group at its formation was Nicholas Politis.

Politis

The contribution of Nicholas Politis in the development of modern Greek culture is one of the most significant. Politis was born in Kalamata of the Peloponnesus in 1852. Early he devoted himself to folklore research and in 1871 was awarded the prize at a university contest for his first book on folklore, *A Study on the Life of the Modern Greeks.* This book attracted the attention of Spiros Vasiliadis, who praised it highly and was influenced by it. Later, Politis instituted the science of folklore; he was to the end of his life (1921) an indefatigable pioneer. Meanwhile, with youthful enthusiasm, he studied the Greek folklore treasures and sought to share all the joys these offered him with his circle of friends. Drosinis wrote: "He led us to treasures, as yet unexplored, of traditions, legends, superstitions, and customs of the Greek people, and he urged us to study these national jewels and to make use of them." The new literary writers of Greece were influenced by their inspired elder. The *Idylls,* the *Songs of My Country,* and all the later literary exploitation of neo-Hellenic folklore material derived principally from Politis. "Folklore took in hand and guarded our poetry under its roof," Palamas wrote about this period.

But it was not folklore alone. Later Greek history also inspired the young writers. Here we must mention the contribution of Spiros Lambros (1851–1919). Following an early concern with literature, Lambros, who was very much involved in literary circles, studied Greek medieval history and literature. The books of Sathas on the history and culture of enslaved Greece, as well as the works of Paparrigopoulos, offered material for interests in this area. The history of the Turkish domination and Greek medieval literature, interest in which was stimulated by the recent discovery of *Digenis Akritas*, inspired the new writers, who chose to work on situations approximating real life and other subjects otherwise less exploited by past intellectuals. To these attractions was added another: the language of these texts, the language of the folksong, was the demotic. And the notion of reestablishing Greek values necessarily involved the question of language. The Ionian Island tradition had passed to Athens. Palamas discovered Solomos in *Songs of My Country*:

> You have entered so deeply into my heart
> That I tremble now at losing you.

The Question of Language

Two monographs appeared in 1873 and in 1875, which gave form to the new linguistic theory; they came from the pen of Nicholas Konemenos. The line of thought originated from an earlier period. It will be the thought that Psycharis will also follow: scientific arguments that reinforced a national desire. Psycharis was to say: "The intellectuals believe that the living language of the people is the living language of vulgarity and of impropriety. But with this fact, they condemn the entire nation, because the entire nation speaks this language."

The linguistic excesses and the mania for an archaism not always based on profound knowledge had provoked various reactions. Constantine Kontos, a scholarly Hellenist, in a long series of *Observations on Language* published as a volume in 1882, carried purism to the extreme. Pointing out the errors of all writers, even the greatest, who had undertaken to refine the language, he wrote: "In truth, it would be better to express oneself in the vulgar language than to cultivate the beautiful language and make horrible solecisms." Nonetheless, his activity showed him to be a partisan of the greatest linguistic extremes. This is how his contemporaries saw him. Paraschos attacked the two extremes represented, on the one hand by Kontos and on the other by Laskaratos:

> You with your oddities are the Kontos of the people,
> And Kontos is the Laskaratos of our Academy.

The *Critique of Pseudo-Atticism* by D. Vernardakis (1884) was a refutation of *Observations on Language* by Kontos. The book by Vernardakis, polemical, full of violence, but also of science, aroused the enthusiasm of partisans for a living language; it confirmed the position of Kontos as leader of the purist language exponents and made Vernardakis the champion of demoticism. One does not always choose his brothers-in-arms; they are chosen by the demands of Polemics. Vernardakis had no clearly defined linguistic theory. His quarrelsome temperament brought him to write admirable pages in favor of demoticism in *Critique of Pseudo-Atticism*. But he was never consistent in this matter, neither in practice nor in theory. In fact, if one pays careful attention, one can see that even this book contains the seeds of future attacks against the demotic. He wrote:

> We know of no poet who has composed a poem purely and authentically demotic, unless it is the late Zalokostas, who has composed two or three.

The *Critique* should be considered an admirably written personal libel, rather than a justification of the demotic language.

In the same year, when Vernardakis's work was circulating in book form, G. Hadjidakis (1848–1941) published a response under the title *Study on Modern Greek, or Examination of the Critique on Pseudo-Atticism*. The observations of Hadjidakis were also marked by a personal tone, and they did not originate from a well-defined linguistic theory. One senses that at the moment Hadjidakis, a young man with a solid linguistic orientation and a positive sense of language, could have become the champion of demoticism. To the end of his career, even when he was leader of the purist language partisans, he exhibited contradictions, hesitations, and indecisions. It was a desire for a method that determined his attitude each time, though simultaneously we are able to follow an internal drama: his knowledge brought him to the demotic, his method to the purist.

Pyscharis

Though Hadjidakis was considered an eminent linguist, he failed in the history of the linguistic campaigns to occupy a place commensurate with his knowledge and talents. This place was soon taken by

John Psycharis. A leader dedicated to the problems of life as well as science, possessing a highly developed sense of beauty, motivated by literary ambitions, and very talented in criticism and composition, Psycharis had the will to impose himself and he had the virtues and defects essential for assuming leadership in the linguistic movement. The leader's place was empty; he assumed it.

Psycharis was born in 1854 in Odessa of a good Chiote family, whose permanent home was in Constantinople. He passed his earliest years in Constantinople; but he was still a child when he left for France. There, and in Germany, he studied philology, after which he was admitted to higher learning in France. He first came to Greece in 1886. In the same year, he published a book in Paris, written in French, on linguistics, where even then he expressed his theory of the demotic in broad lines. But after his first contact with Greek reality, he produced another work in 1888, which began a new campaign around the language question. This book was called *My Journey*. The work had a mixed character. Under a literary guise and in a strictly demotic language, Psycharis propounded his linguistic credo. He did not consider that he was writing the work as a linguist: "If I had been only a philologist, I would never have dared to intervene in the language problem," he wrote a few years later. The campaign he conducted was national: "Language and country are one. To fight for one's country or for its national language is a single battle." Running through the entire book was a lively spirit, a desire to overturn established patterns; victory for the demotic would signify the liberation of Hellenism from its intellectual shackles. One might say that in large measure the criticism Psycharis made was more social than linguistic.

But actually Psycharis was less revolutionary here than he wanted to appear. In the year *My Journey* was published, theoretical support of demoticism had been made by many others. Indeed, in practice, we can say that the demotic had prevailed by this time as the language of poetry. Psycharis's contribution was above all personal. On the one hand, he used the demotic in a prose text that was not purely literary; on the other hand, he contributed the tone and the passion in defense of the demotic language. "I thirst for glory and brawls," he wrote in *My Journey*. With these words, he assumed his position in the battle. The young writers accepted his preaching with enthusiasm; the first of these was Palamas. What had been diffused, rejected, and special now took form, was organized, and became that toward which common efforts would tend. The partisans of the living language now had a common goal; they were aware they could win. Furthermore, they had the scientific reinforcement that Psycharis had already systematized; the demotic must prevail because of ineluctable natural laws. We find these writers dealing with a positivism that delighted the new Greek generation, that sought by every means to base itself on reality, and that believed in the power of science. Even the linguistic theory of Psycharis was presented as an antidote to the unreality of the romantics.

The *Journey* naturally provoked furor among the intellectual circles of Athens. A reaction was organized, just as the forces of demoticism were organized. In a long study, Roidis praised Psycharis both for his theories and for his work. Years earlier, Roidis had also announced a study on the language problem. This study did not appear until 1893; it was entitled *The Idols*. The book was written in the purist language, which, though always severe, was much warmer than Roidis's preceding works. The importance of *Idols* for demoticism was exceptional; the prestige of Roidis, the language he used, the grace and acuity with which he proposed his arguments, helped make this work read even by the most guarded, the most conservative men. Naturally, it provoked violent responses and criticism. It contained weaknesses which the detractors did not fail to point out. Borrowed knowledge, suspect references, and scientific insufficiencies were the weak points. But the position that Roidis had assumed was well chosen. He had not appeared as a supporter of the demotic. Rather he presented himself as a mediator, an impartial judge; but he gave final satisfaction to demoticism. The *Idols* sealed the authority of Roidis and simultaneously confirmed the theoretical victory of demoticism: "The appearance of *Idols* dated the separation between intransigent purism and the scholars deserving the name," wrote Xenopoulos in 1904, the year that Roidis died.

Kokkos and Koromilas

It was not easy for literary men who were already engaged in a scholarly career to adapt completely to the new linguistic reality. Some writers remained indecisive; death interrupted the work of certain others before they had an opportunity to evolve. One of the latter was Demetrios Kokkos (1856–1891). Kokkos embarked on his literary career with *Do Not Lose Your Head.* Later, he collaborated with Souris. His collections of poetry, *Laughters* (1880), *Memories and Aspirations* (1886), *Poems* (1889), and *Pearls* (1891) showed he was undecided but nonetheless attracted to the new popular language. He was moving toward ridicule in his poetry. However, what interests us in his case is that he belonged essentially to the generation of 1880. Also his first collection of poetry was published by the editor Koromilas, in the same collection with the poems of Kambas and Drosinis.

> Each time I see the moon in the sky, it reminds me of a charming evening when I was seated by her side. It was to her that the moon offered rays of gold, and she, she offered the moon . . . her beauty. Now, O moon, where has she gone, why do you display yourself? Hide in the abyss, and I will hide in my solitude. Or do you wish to offer me your stupidity and to receive from me . . . my ugliness?

When later on we examine the strange evolutions of Greek fondness for beauty, we should remember that the same needs gave birth to the responsible desire of Palamas or Drosinis and to the irresponsible spirit of the contemporary humorists.

The comedies of Kokkos, *The Lyre of Old Man Nicholas* and *Father Linardos,* were important for Greek letters. These works belong to a new genre for Greece, the musical comedy, whose beginning is placed characteristically at precisely these years. They were musical comedies combined with a study of manners. Of course, this genre, with the songs which accompany it, constituted an advance for the demotic. One of the better known musical comedies was *The Fate of Maroula* (1889). It was written in collaboration with Demetrios Koromilas (1850–1898), a prolific writer of dramatic works, who was unable, however, to perfect his work. He began publishing his plays early (*Mission of a Friend,* 1872). The influence of Vlachos brought him to the comedy of manners, which he used in the form of musical comedy (*The Fate of Maroula, The Lover of the Shepherdess,* 1892) to produce works that survive in the history of the Greek theater. He also sought to penetrate the authentic folk tradition, that of the provinces; he travelled from village to village attempting to arrive at an authentic expression of this tradition; the teachings of Politis had borne results.

As the last representative of musical comedy, in chronological order, we should mention Spiros Peresiades (1864–1918). Peresiades was more popular, and some of his works, such as *Golpho, Esme, The Young Turkish Girl,* succeeded in their purpose and survived long after their original success. However, we should not ignore Panagos Melisiotes (1845–1904), the author of *Haido.* The folk origin of this work brought him effortlessly to comedy interspersed with song, and because the folksong was still largely a provincial phenomenon, his verse and a certain dramatic originality were appreciated. This is one more case, though a somewhat artificial one, of the return of a scholarly genre to its folk sources.

Parallel with the musical comedy, we see the appearance of the dramatic idyll. One can also consider musical comedy, modeled on *The Secretary General* by Elias Kapetanakis (1859–1922), as an attempt at renewal. With such works, the theater helped extricate romantic idealism and create propitious conditions in the Greek milieu for the appearance of naturalism, whose expression in prose was the short story, which also took form during this same period.

Vizyinos

However, before passing on to creative prose, we should stop to mention some writers who came to maturity or had begun their activity during the generation of 1880, and who were influenced by the teachings of Psycharis. Vizyinos, Proveleggios, and Stratigis were not successful in completely assimilating the new teaching. Pallis and Eftaliotes, on the other hand, adopted the new teaching with fanaticism and followed it to its ultimate conclusion. George Vizyinos was born in a village of Thrace in 1849. Part of his education took place at the school of Chalcis beside Elias Tantalides. He published his first collection of poetry at that time in Constantinople, a collection which exhibited a remarkable sense of the demotic (*First Poems,* 1873). In 1874, he published *Kedros* in Athens. The following year, he went to Germany to study philosophy. He lived on the continent until 1884, though he made brief visits to his native country. His last stopping place was London, where he met Braïlas-Armenis, through whom he became acquainted with the Ionian Island tradition. But he had already turned toward demoticism, and he wrote in 1882, in verses left unpublished: "The new poet/Was persuaded in the West."

In London, he published his collection of poetry called *Breezes of Attica* (1883). His poetic work has been collected, but it is lacking in value. It contains an authentic sensibility but is without spirit; it turns away from romantic exaggerations and has a penetrating sense of language. When he writes in the purist language, he fortunately recalls Tantalides rather than Athenian romanticism. He is situated between Tantalides and the first movements of the generation of 1880. His demotic language is enjoyable and his provincial origin is evident. Some of his themes also exhibit an interest in neo-Hellenic tradition.

> His head is protected by the shield, and his girdle of gold, woven and ornamented with precious stone, circles his waist; on his left side, like a flash without lightning, hangs the sparkling scabbard—without a sword.

Whenever his melancholy is manifested, it associates him with Athenian romanticism and is always restrained and sober in expression:

> Yesterday, I saw in a dream
> An unfathomable river,
> —May God keep the dream
> From coming true!—
> On the banks of the river,
> I saw a young man I know,
> Pale as the moon,
> Silent as the night.

Vizyinos was fond of metrical narratives. He turned a myth, a popular tradition, an historical incident, into verse. Perhaps the old storytellers still spoke through his mouth. Perhaps the folklore interests influenced him even in the area of ballads. Perhaps we have a vestige of the epico-lyrical genre, in which he excelled as a child; perhaps he was even influenced by Western writers who wrote ballads. Among his last works was a study on *Ballads,* published in 1893. It was composed of translations of foreign poems and some examples of original poetry. His poems will be discussed in the following chapter. Vizyinos also had no time to complete his work. In 1892 he went insane; and after four years in a mental institution, he died in 1896. During his illness, he continued to write verses:

> Since I started mourning,
> My blond and blue,
> My heavenly light.
> The rhythm of the world
> Has changed for me.

Proveleggios

Aristomenis Proveleggios (1850–1936) also began his literary career early with the appearance of *Theseus* in 1870. He also studied philosophy in Germany. Besides his early epico-lyrics, he also wrote many theatrical works in his youth, most in verse form. His poetry was characterized by an intense idealism, associated with melody, and a nobility of sentiments and thoughts that borders on weakness. Proveleggios was unsuccessful in conquering the language problem. To the end of his life, he oscillated between the demotic and the purist. The demotic he used always had an archaic tone to it which chilled the reader, but which actually agreed with a style and vocabulary tending to abound in abstract terms.

> I climbed this evening to the hill.
> In its perfumes and the divine serenity,
> The sun was setting
> Into an ocean of purple light.
> All around, Creation was silent;
> Woods and valleys and the dome of the sky.
> But like an agitated sea, the uproar
> Mounted hollow to the city.
> That is life.

Removed from worldly preoccupations, he did not nurture his inspiration with violent passions, but with intellectual emotions. His poetry, which does not surpass dream and memory, expressed a quasi-effaced nostalgia of a past grandeur:

> And a desire possessed me, a desire stifled me. Each sound was a sob of joy, a joy which is passed. It was the divine sigh of a beloved world, of a world that has disappeared.

His lyrical work, for the most part, has been collected in the anthologies *Poems* (1896), *Poems* (1916), and *Before the Infinite* (1926).

George Stratigis (1860–1938) published in 1880 a collection of poetry, *Laurel-Roses,* where he vainly attempted to escape from the influence of Paraschos, both when he wrote in the purist and when he attempted the demotic. His later collections, *Songs of Home* (1902) and *What Say the Waves* (1919) always seem pallid, weak in inspiration and in form. Among his other literary expressions, I cite a short story written in the Tsakonian dialect. This attempt at creating an idiomatic literature should be included in the body of folklore, but also in the naturalistic movement of the time.

Polemis

John Polemis (1862–1925) was able to pursue the evolution of language in modern Greek literature closely. After his first collection of poetry (1883), he published many others, among which was the collection *The Old Violin* (1909). He also wrote a poetic drama (*The King Without Sun,* 1910). His material, inspiration, and language contained something soft and amorphous. His facility at versification is indisputable, especially since he was never strict in metrical matters; but his verse is weak and verbose and does not adhere to the rules of strict demotic. Platitudes do not alarm him; he cultivates everyday emotions and only a remnant of romantic grandiloquence tends to inflate the expression. He moves in a world poverty stricken of ideas and words. Let us recall Paraschos. His weaknesses were of aid to him in pleasing a large public and in circulating among the lower levels of the intellectual milieu. Nothing in him, not his images, his thought, his language, or even his inspiration surpassed the intelligence of the average reader. However, all these mediocrities sometimes brought him to a few poems of tender simplicity. The elegiac tone and the melancholy mood often found in his verses were the cause of his rare successes:

> I do not petition for a little joy for myself, unhappy creature. I no longer beg, happy beings, that you recount my sorrows. Erect I stand, without a word, awaiting death. It is useless to exhaust myself and live without a purpose.

In his better moments, he reminds us of the weakest moment of Drosinis.

Krystallis

Kostas Krystallis (1868–1894) wrote a small quantity of poems and prose that have the character of a study of manners. He collected most of his work and published it as folklore material. He first appeared in Greek literature with an epic poem in three songs called *Shadows of Death* (1887). His awkward verse showed the strong influence of Valaoritis. Two poems appeared in *Shadows,* one in the purist language with the title, "Memories," which contained an epigram to George Paraschos. In 1890 he produced a long narrative poem, *The Monk of Kleisoura at Missolonghi.* The influence of Valaorites and his technique predominate here as well. In 1891 we have *Pastorals.* They were awarded an honorable mention in the same poetry contest where *The Eyes of My Soul* by Palamas and *The Ruins* by Polemis were also awarded a prize. The committee of judges was composed of Proveleggios as chairman, Roidis, and Politis.

It was a sign of the times that folklore alone predominated. The entire collection was imitations of the folksong. The new poets attempted to write folksongs; their failure was painful. The refinement, the sobriety, the flexible restraints of the folksong, the scholarly and impeccable placement of the proper word in the verse, the epigrammatic expression of sentiment and psychology are replaced by a total poverty that attempted to conceal itself in an abundance of unbridled fifteen-syllable verse. Even worse is the fact that Krystallis sometimes introduced entire folksong verses into his poetry. Such verses are brilliant in isolation and render very opaque the obscurity which surrounds them. It is the same with the subjects he borrowed from the folksong; their unexpected intrusion is more disconcerting than charming. A similar judgment can be made about his last collection, *The Singer of the Village and the Fold* (1893), which was also praised at a poetry contest where Angelos Vlachos presided. In the following year, Krystallis, a child of the mountains who never became acclimated to the city, died of tuberculosis.

His contemporaries were still dazzled by the discovery of the folksong. Its interpretation was only beginning; its aesthetic foundation had yet to be studied. All were disposed to praise everything that recalled the folksong, that tended toward it, even though they were as yet incapable of exercising critical control. Krystallis said, "With respect to my last poems, I am greatly enchanted, because now I have taken my place as well in the contemporary Parnassus of Greece. My friends certainly never expected such poems. They were all amazed when they read them." Further the question of language was of high interest; in the eyes of the new demoticists, the use of the demotic itself constituted a poetic title. Then came the untimely death of Krystallis to help create the proper atmosphere of critical irresponsibility. The poet was praised excessively.

Naturally, even during his lifetime there were some reservations among the more cultivated, those who sought a more spiritual content in his poetry. "The exclusive attachment to popular models harms the poet. . . . / Poetry written in this vein will always have the same relationship to the folksong that artificial flowers have to natural ones." This was the opinion of Proveleggios. Vlachos praised him warmly, though he awarded him no prize. The innovators were unreserved. Gabriilides, in an editorial in his newspaper, wrote a long tribute to Krystallis: "His small book is not only one of the most charming that we have seen, but it is also a mountain, a valley, a fold, a forest, a crag, a plain, a bucolic poem, a love, a harvest, a strawberry, a summit, and a riverbank." Michael Mitsakis had written in one of his critical studies that many poems by Krystallis "can perhaps pass to the mouths of the people. In his verses beats a little of the spirit and life of true Greece." Today, however, when the folksong has become a study in itself and we possess a more profound knowledge of the recent history of Greece, the work of Krystallis is seen in its true proportions. The treatise by Apostolakis on this subject definitely has closed the debate about Krystallis.

Pallis

The influence of Psycharis and Politis was the basic incentive for the work of Alexander Pallis. He was born in Piraeus in 1851 of an Epiriote family, which produced other men of letters as well. He began by studying letters, but he abandoned them early (1859) to turn to a more lucrative career, without, however, abandoning his interest or activity in literature. After 1859 he lived the greatest part of his life away from Greece; he died in England in 1935. His early literary interests took the form of an edition of *Antigone*. To the end of his life he was concerned with classical letters; he translated and wrote commentaries on the ancients. But the soul of this man responded to the real necessities of life; a collection of poetry for children (1889) revealed his interests in a living education for neo-Hellenic youth. Political matters equally concerned him and the destiny of modern Greece generally was at the center of his restlessness. It was with this same concern that he considered the matter of language. He saw in language a solution to the general cultural poverty which the new Greece suffered. The accent on life prevailed in all his works; they emanated from life and turned toward life. The masculine lyricism which sprang from every page of his works had its source in the inexhaustible surge of life.

His songs for children constituted a sudden advance in comparison to earlier attempts in this genre, such as those by A. Katakouzinos. The difference was not so much in language; certainly, we do have a genuine inspiration, but chiefly, we have a different attitude toward the child. In this respect, Pallis appears as a precursor to the new pedagogy, which was based on an awareness of the child's particular needs, on a respect for the child's psyche, and on knowledge of his needs. When Pallis wrote his poems for children, or when he translated them, he created a freshness, a gaity, and a joy of life. These poems also revealed a great dexterity in versification: a play on words created to become songs.

The same freshness and desire for life was also apparent in his few poems for adults. Dynamic in his joys and his passions, he often displayed a tendency toward didacticism: the man of letters became an educator of the people. Here again we find an elevated didacticism. He presumed knowledge of the spirit; a powerful and courageous lyricism was his method of expression:

> The council of notables gathered at the pier decide that they should encounter the Turks on firm ground. Then, removing my fez, I advanced and said: "All this, gentlemen, will serve no purpose. It is only the beat which counts. . . ." When one of our big brass heard me, he became inflamed and poured forth rancor: "Who is this man who gives such advice? What is his name?" That's how Psara was lost. And I, with fire in my hand, left and went toward Chios, and from there I cried with bitter voice—I could no longer restrain myself—"There! That's what I'm called!"

> (taken from *To Kanaris*)

His tendency toward realism led him to the epigram, which was often satiric. His desire for good always prevailed and he censured

all weaknesses. Above all, Greek reality was censured for its evils
and exalted for its virtues.

> You have undertaken to reform the state, and for this you have
> begun with your own promotion. It is true that, when a Greek
> takes a comb in hand, he begins by combing his own goatee and
> mustache.
>
> (taken from To Zerbas)

It was in this same spirit that he approached his translation of
Homer. He was consumed by worship of the folksong. Influenced by
the Homeric theories of his time, he sought to give life to the
ancient epic, to refashion it into a folksong. The epic assumes a
Doric form, which corresponded to the translator's ideals.

Pallis's effort, whose objective was the modernization of the epic,
produced many beautiful verses, but they were removed from the
tradition of the original and lost the epic's specific flavor. He utilized
his abilities as translator to put many texts into modern Greek. I
mention *The Merchant of Venice* specifically, a fragment of Kant,
and the New Testament, which created a great furor.

To the problem of language he brought the same passion and attention. He had fixed ideas: even where we don't expect it, the linguistic problem appears. He translated *The Cyclops* by Euripides:
"The Cyclops, a giant with one eye and a trowel-like beauty." He
struggled with every intellectual and material means to promote the
demotic language. His *Brousos* (1923) merits special mention. Written as a travel book with numerous digressions, Pallis here gives us a
violent and perhaps sometimes unjust criticism of neo-Hellenic social, intellectual, and political life. The spirit of the writer is poetic,
and his lyricism is natural, quite apart from his literary preoccupations and the forms they took. Though his restlessness and his
criticism have always been meaningful, the passage of time has redeemed the poet. The most essential contribution of Pallis to Greek
letters was his poetry.

Eftaliotes

Argyris Eftaliotes should be mentioned along with Pallis. Their lives
ran a parallel course; Eftaliotes was born in Mytilene in 1849. At the
age of eighteen, he was already in England pursuing a commencial

career. He lived the greater part of his life on the continent and died in France in 1923. He began his literary career with verses in the purist language. It was through Pallis that he became familiar with the teachings of Psycharis. He became enthusiastic immediately and he dedicated himself faithfully to the demotic. In 1889 he was praised for a collection of poetry in a contest which had Nicholas Politis as chairman of the judges. It was no small honor. *The Hymn to Athena* by Palamas was awarded first prize in the same contest. In 1891 he presented a new collection to a contest. Vlachos was committee chairman at this contest. It was Eftaliotes's greatest moment. The collection contained a series of sonnets without strict form but written in the exquisite thirteen-syllable verse. The poems were not awarded a prize, but they were published the same year in *Hestia* and received wide acclaim. Polylas, who could not remain insensible to such quality of expression and treatment of verse, was inspired to write his pamphlet *Our Literary Language*. Palamas was already inspired to publish a series of critical articles on the same subject, which were among the best articles of his early period.

At this point, one could have expected great accomplishments from Eftaliotes. However, a personal harrowing, or perhaps other causes of which we are not aware kept him from maintaining the height he had achieved. He continued his now infrequent production with various poems, short stories, plays, translations, and historical studies, all of which he wrote in the strictly demotic language of Psycharis. We will be discussing his short stories in the following chapter. Among his other works, we should mention here the collection of poems, *History of Romiosyne,* and his translation of the *Odyssey.* As for his theatrical work, first published in 1894, it is perhaps worth mentioning that his subject was taken from the folksong.

The remainder of his poems also show excellent technique and exhibit, now and then, a desire to revive the folksong: one more form of preoccupation with folklore material added to his interest in the popular language.

> Take a dagger and hack me, and cast away the pieces, love.
> Cast them into the sea.
> From the moment you left me, I have hated the world,
> I have lost my head,
> And I hope for nothing good.

Realism tended to penetrate his poetry, an antilyrical element whose perfection of form and richness of expression did not succeed in achieving the sublime. Furthermore, when he tried elevating himself to the summits of lyricism, there was a discrepancy in the very essence of the effort. His translation of the *Odyssey* was influenced by preoccupations similar to those of Pallis; his was less bound to the theory of folklore, less Doric, but also much less lyrical.

Prose expression was better suited to him, whether he wrote short stories or criticized the new Greek society. *The History of Romiosyne* represents one of the early attempts at writing a scientific work in the demotic. When the work was written (1901), we cannot say that it constituted a contribution to the science of history. Furthermore, it remained in a fragmentary condition. *The Notebooks of Old Man Demos* should be mentioned among the prose works of Eftaliotes. His intention here was to criticize modern Greek affairs. In his dedications to Psycharis, with which *The History of Romiosyne* opens, Eftaliotes left no doubt as to the origin of this subject. He also showed that art did not constitute a way of life for him. "Ever since our country has been released from the torment that kept it down for more than three years, I have lost my fondness for verses or for history. In fact, I thought it a sin that our nation should still be suffering from such a dreadful catastrophe and we should wish to lull it to sleep with songs, instead of reflecting on what we should or should not be doing to avoid submitting again to a similar humiliation. I thought it a sin to play with the imagination, instead of working with the mind." Neither art, then, nor history; action, critical works were needed.

This critical attitude of Eftaliotes, which we encountered in Psycharis and later in Pallis, forces us to reexamine these authors and to attempt a more general observation. All three lived on the continent and were professionally and socially independent of the Hellenic milieu. This independence permitted them to judge the realities of Greece and to compare them without being influenced by any psychological factors that fatally inhibit thought. But we can also reverse our approach to the phenomena and observe that these psychological factors constituted the essential coefficients in the formation of society. Hence, the Greek milieu, as it appeared to these three men and was criticized by them, was an excessively rationalistic theoretical elaboration: they saw modern Greek reality as an empty form, without taking into account the psychological conditions which governed neo-Hellenic life. Our remarks concerning their attitudes on the questions of language could be analogous. Their absolute orthodoxy regarding language also results from a unilateral conception of the language problem. In an absolute intellectual context, outside social reality, the question of language perhaps could have been resolved according to the theoretical bases posed by Psycharis, even though his linguistic positivism was not scientifically approved. But when we integrate the question of language in Hellenic life, we observe two extralinguistic limits: on the one hand, the language problem was an expression of a universal innovating spirit, on the other hand, it was subjected to all kinds of psychological limitations, precisely because of its universal character. Hence, the reaction in favor of demoticism is owing not only to theoretical causes, but also to a different attitude toward life, an attitude which to a great extent was legitimate and dictated by historic Greek reality, but it could not be understood by men who lived outside Greece. They imagined that they were seeking to impose a living language, but, in reality, they carried with them only a theoretical elaboration. On the whole, it was natural that the intellectuals established in Greece should be closer to reality; they could give a much broader dimension to the reformation of the language and were free to deviate from strict linguistic orthodoxy.

Chapter 25

"Prose, We
Want Prose!"

Prose

We already know that creative prose was less dependent on Athenian romanticism. It was destined by its very nature to serve the classicist tendencies of neo-Hellenism in a more positive or rather a more prosaic manner. Contact with neo-Hellenic life and particularly that of the provinces arose from these tendencies. The interest aroused by folklore prepared the way for a study of manners favoring Western currents centering around realism and naturalism. In 1880 J. Kampouroglou (1851–1903) published his translation of Emile Zola's *Nana*. The translator, whose original works have little merit, rendered a great service to Greek letters with his translations. *Rabages* by V. Sardou (translated 1878) was adopted by Greek letters. *Nana*, both because of the linguistic freedom it advocated and because of its naturalism, profoundly influenced the new writers of Greek literature.

Hence, the passage from the historical novel with Greek plots to the novel of manners was natural. However, the new mood was formulated in the milieu of the generation of 1880; here we have one more withdrawal from the epico-heroic character of the romantic school of Athens.

Vikelas

We have already observed that *Loukis Laras* can perhaps be considered a transitional element closing one period and inaugurating another. The work was first published in *Hestia* in 1897. Drosinis pointed out in his memoirs the success this book enjoyed with readers of the periodical and emphasized how much this success encouraged intellectuals to write short stories, since they were assured publication in *Hestia*.

This is not the first time that we encounter the short story in modern Greek literature. But until now, it always appears as an exception to the rule of the novel. Normally it was a reduced model of the novel: plot, numerous episodes, a tendency to exalt heroism, and an historical inspiration. Now, the short story became a separate genre. It conformed to the general characteristics of the period, it lowered its tone, and it turned from the external world to internal life. The family home in all its aspects contributed to the genesis and development of the new genre. Even the tragic episode was presented here in the most everyday atmosphere. But it was especially the ordinary existence of men that writers sought to paint. One more door opened to the study of manners. Certainly, both in life and in most early modern Greek short stories, purism was an obstacle which discouraged even the modern reader. The path followed by Greek prose writers was approximately the same as that of the poets. The older writers remained true to purism, while the others passed to the demotic; in later editions, even the purists modified the initial form of their works.

Vikelas published a number of short stories during this period. He was interested in Greek provincial life. However, with him, it was never simply a study of manners: plot was always at the base of his narration; a simple plot was sought to put the central figure of the work in relief. The heroes of Vikelas were good and brave men. The author had an edifying intention, but it was never projected in an offensive manner. His words were cold, his narration lacked enthusiasm, and his descriptions were colorless. Nonetheless, once we have accepted the purist language in which they were written, his short stories charm us with a nobility of soul, a sense of equilibrium, and a desire for the best which characterizes them. "Father Narkissos" and "Philip Marthas" are among his best short stories, those which arouse the greatest sympathies and in which the author's weaknesses are least evident.

Vizyinos

It was Vikelas who urged Vizyinos to write short stories. The poet from Thrace brought with him a world of childhood memories, which easily led to the study of manners. His temperament helped him distinguish what was original from what was banal and emphasize the most unusual qualities in men's characters. Most of the themes of his short stories were related to Thrace; in addition to being a study of manners, they also were a penetrating psychological study. The author often smiles in his melancholy nostalgia, and his soft smile passes into his work as a lyrical breath. Even without particular preparation, the reader becomes involved in this atmosphere. We do not seek technique in the short stories of Vizyinos, with the exception of "Consequences of an Old Song," where he sought to achieve a composition. The others are lightly sketched portraits with simple contours, colorless, and lacking chiaroscuro; but they charm us precisely because of their simplicity. But here, as well. the purist language is a barrier.

Drosinis

Drosinis and Palamas also wrote a few short stories in their youth. The latter will be discussed in the following chapter. Drosinis published his first short stories in the purist language. Later, he adopted the demotic in his prose. His original short stories, which are travel impressions, are found at the crossroads between his lyrical meditation and his folklore interests. His important collections were: *Idylls: Rustic Letters* (1882), *Three Days on Tinos* (1883), *Short Stories and Memories* (1886), *Amaryllis* (1886), *Short Stories of the Fields and the City* (1904). Later, in 1932, he published a novel called *Ersis*. This work, in which Drosinis attempted to assimilate recent trends in prose, was so intimately associated with the poet's temperament that it can be included in the general examination of his earlier Greek prose writings.

The narrative work of Drosinis always tended toward simplicity and sought to express the author's personal impressions and sentiments. The work had a lyrical tendency, but it was the author's own lyricism; that is to say, it was modest, reserved, and marked by an intense spirituality. His heroes, either provincials or urbanites, were always simple men, animated by good sentiments. One should not think that because of this Drosinis was satisfied with a study of manners. His essential objective was always much more the portrait of individual psyches and his preoccupations largely surpassed description. A delicate and idyllic poetic spirit prevailed in Drosinis' prose works.

Eftaliotes

As we have already noted in the preceding chapter, Argyris Eftaliotes exhibited a prosaic element in some of his poems, moved with
ease in the short story, but never approached a true composition.
The *Island Stories* are narratives written with emotion and love for
the simple men he described. But his characters resembled one another greatly and were somewhat schematic in a way which recalls
youthful sketches. His works seem to lack maturity and completeness; they are like fragments of a composition left unfinished. Psycharis had praised the prose of Eftaliotes warmly and his evaluation to a great extent was justified. But the absence of a strong spirit,
which prevented Eftaliotes from giving value beyond his technical
abilities in poetry, was equally an obstacle in his prose: the portrayal
of manners was the dominant characteristic of his short stories.

Psycharis

Compared to the boredom, monotony, and lack of personality that
characterized the older Greek short stories, those of Psycharis, as all
his other works, stand apart. A vigorous temperament, complex and
animated by a strong spirit, he attempted great accomplishments. He
introduced all his virtues in his prose works, both short stories and
long novels. They were always inspired by the desire to express
something, to inform readers about something. Besides, as we know
already, he believed in his literary talents and he worked his expression with precision. We must not forget that, though poetry can
sometimes achieve important accomplishments through a temporary
inspiration, the demands of creative prose are different. These concern technique, an elaboration based on study and a knowledge of
this genre. It also presupposes great culture and constant study. Inspiration does not suffice; work is essential. Psycharis lived in a great
intellectual center. He followed French literature, to which, moreover, he contributed regularly. He thus secured two important advantages: perfect knowledge of genre and a renewal of subjects and
central interests.

To what extent he had knowledge of the genre and to what extent questions of technique concerned him, Psycharis revealed in his critical works. Though he wrote few critical essays ("I am not a critical writer," he insisted, and "criticism is not my medium"), whenever he did concern himself with criticism he exhibited an exceptional ability in this area. Criticism was not his profession; in his hands it was a weapon with which to attack his adversaries; this weapon he handled with dexterity. When he treated of Renan or Solomos, when he attacked Souris or Palamas, when he praised mediocre writers, his observations concerning style and the art of writing always carried an exceptional weight. He utilized his knowledge even in his original prose works; their composition was artistic, possessing an architecture, a sophisticated plot, a judicious distribution of values. His prose work was considerable. He wrote many remarkable short stories, but he was specially attentive to the novel, which he believed represented the best form of literary prose. More precisely, he believed that technique and perfection of expression alone were insufficient for writing a good novel; society should prepare "years and years" for this genre. He also believed, referring to himself (but his opinion was valid for the entire generation of 1880), that Hellenism possessed the degree of maturity to demand prose: "Prose, we want prose!" In the same article (1927), Psycharis wrote: "I am also a period in history; I represent the period of prose." In an earlier text (1903) he had written that "the critical hour for a nation is that in which it can begin to write in prose." In his enthusiasm for his own contribution and for linguistic rules which he believed would transform Greek letters, there was one matter that he was unable to evaluate. Though he had proclaimed that he was not a critic, we are in a better position to ascertain his incapacity to criticize himself. He also wrote theatrical works, but they were mediocre. Their form and their allegorical intention defeated his hope of creating life. Prefacing his work, he said: "However, I count on the centuries to be mine." And in another place: "One day, they will produce them [the plays] in Greece, they will produce them often. Not only am I certain of it, but I know even now that they will earn much money."

Let us add that Psycharis also lacked the prophetic gift, and let us return to his efforts at writing: *The Dream of Yanniris* (1898), *Life and Love in Solitude* (1904), *The Two Brothers* (1911), *Agnes* (1913), and still others. The absence of critical sense prevented Psycharis from understanding that creative prose was not the natural instrument for expression of his thought. His novels, though they displayed all the desirable technical facility, were lacking in only one thing: literary talent. If the novel is technique, it is not that alone. It requires something more, which was lacking in Psycharis. The life which struggled in his writings was not the life of heroes. Psycharis did not succeed in creating living human types; it was his own personality that he projected in the characters of his novels, and the emotion that he aroused was the result of his personal temperament.

For this reason, perhaps the most characteristic of his novels was *The Dream of Yanniris*. In effect, it is a fiction through which he expressed his own personality and destiny, as he conceived these two and wished them to be. The young Greek who became an expatriate attempted everything, succeeded in everything, and finally became involved in amorous passion. In short, it was an image, certainly idealized, of the author himself. Palamas praised this work as "the novel of the Greek soul." The characterization was not exaggerated; here Psycharis effectively found in himself the insatiable thirst of the Greeks; their wide-ranging curiosities, which became a form of discipline and virtue; their individualism, associated with love of their land; and the passion that so often led them beyond the limits of personal interest.

That this and all the other works of Psycharis were read less than they should have been can be attributed both to the author and to his public. The technical qualities Psycharis displayed were not those that the Greek people were accustomed to seeking in a novel. Then there was Psycharis's language. On the one hand, his extremism, his scientific severity in linguistic matters, made his language somewhat artificial and unnatural. On the other hand, Psycharis was never able to grasp the difference between the demotic and familiar speech, or, let us say, between the demotic and the everyday spoken language. His morphology attempted to be that of the demotic; but he did not attempt to elevate his language in this morphology to a cultivated demotic; that is to say, to make something equivalent to what Koraes sought to do, to what Solomos sought, to what Palamas created in his maturity. In Psycharis we have an imitation of the spoken language, marked by naïveté and an affected simplicity. The constant tone of extreme familiarity in his work exhausts the reader very quickly after the first surprise has passed. Yet the defects in his work should not cause us to lose sight of the virtues.

Psycharis offered to the novel precisely that which the novel lacked: a general rule, a modern Greek prose, a technical refinement, a sense of totality. This was his basic contribution. We should add culture and one other interesting manifestation, because it was a more general characteristic of the period: the irony and the humor that one often encounters during these years as a national antidote to the grandiloquence and the exaggeration of romanticism. In summary, we can say that Psycharis is found, along with Gregory Xenopoulos, at the origin of the modern Greek novel. His fame and his essential contribution to the new linguistic campaigns assured him an important position in the new Greek letters.

He died late, in 1929. His grave is in Chios, where, conforming to his last wishes, his remains were transported. On the white marble plaque is an inscription he had composed: ". . . Sing me a funeral lamentation, one of the lamentations I heard you sing when I was a youth and came to the villages renowned for their mastic liqueur, to learn your language, the Greek Romaic language. Who knows, perhaps they will awaken me suddenly from the grave, so much did I love them, so deeply were they imbedded in my Romaic heart. . . ."

The End of Roidis

But though the teaching of Psycharis could have borne fruit easily in poetry where matters were more receptive, in prose it encountered greater difficulties. For a long time after the initial appearances of the new demoticism, the purist continued to be cultivated in prose with greater or lesser consequence. Along with the craftsman Psycharis, if we examine the purist language survival, we should mention another craftsman, Roidis. We already know that Roidis had no imagination. After *Pope Joan,* he published a series of narratives set in medieval times; they appear to be the residue of his study for *Pope Joan.* Then came his political preoccupations, the main portion of his critical work, and later, after the short story had been established in the new Greek literature, Roidis began to publish those works that we call short stories. He had lost his fortune. Several times he was appointed, and then dismissed, as warden of the National Library. Let me remark that his passage through the National Library gave him the occasion to write two of the most libellous pamphlets. The deficit in his personal budget had to be filled by whatever resources he could draw from his pen. Not a prolific writer by nature, this indefatigable sculptor of expression began to produce with greater abundance.

We are now in the period around 1890. Roidis, fatigued, poor, embittered, turned with nostalgia to his childhood years. His readings were reduced by his indigence; it was memories that he sought as a new source of inspiration. He entered into the narrative period of his life. The passage of years tempered the initial harshness of the author of *Pope Joan;* nostalgia for the past, in particular that of his childhood, softened the tone of all his new writings, not only those works properly called short stories. His memory came to the aid of his atrophied imagination. On the other hand, his analytical mind did not succeed in giving these stories the minimum composition that the genre demanded. Intermixing memories with brilliant descriptions and meticulous narrations, he succeeded in creating an elegant totality, where the plot is thin or sometimes altogether non-existent and where the author usually speaks in the first person. This was no technique for a writer. It was reality as it suited him. Even when he wrote on inconsequential matters, he did so in a subjective manner. The great difference during this period of his work was just this subjective element. It was this subjectivity which first revealed Roidis's tenderness and finally established a sentimental relationship between reader and author.

The decade between 1890 and 1900 was significant in the life of Roidis because of these works. He hesitated to open his heart about men; his sympathy was manifested toward animals: hence, the stories of horses, dogs, and other animals. His childhood life in Syra inspired many individual pages; it was about Syra that he wrote his only well-constructed short story, "Psychology of a Husband from Syra" (1894). We do find in these pages a desire to analyze psychologically and create a type, but this desire was facilitated because the type of indifferent hedonist he presented reminds us of Roidis himself. Moreover, once again we ascertain for another time that what the author portrayed was more than a type to charm us; he described provincial life, revealed it with fine observation, an ironic spirit, and an artistic expression. His other narratives had themes taken from foreign lands, those he had known, especially Egypt and Italy. His style was always impeccable; in fact there is less strained originality and brilliance so that we appreciate it more than in his preceding works, particularly in *Pope Joan.* His language was always the purist, but without the exaggeration which his earlier works had exhibited. We have only one narrative in the demotic, written like a folktale, called "The Apple Tree." Perhaps in writing this story, Roidis was replying to those who had accused him of not knowing the proper use of the language he was supporting in theory.

In conclusion, I think that we should praise Roidis once again for not becoming involved in the study of manners of the time. A critic more easily censured than praised, he gave us in his old age, along with his creative prose, another sample of his dual capabilities by successfully criticizing in 1899 the overstatements of the neo-Hellenic provincial study of manners and praising, less successfully, an obscure short-story writer, C. Metaxas Vosporites, who was attempting to avoid these subjects: "Our public has begun, we do not say to be disgusted, but to weary of sheepfolds, caves, flutes, comrades, beautiful youths, beautiful young girls, funereal lamentations, gold and silver jewels, and strokes of horns from goats." It was always the expatriate Greek who was talking.

His attitude, moreover, toward Greek letters became increasingly reserved and sorrowful as he grew older and lost his liveliness. In 1900, when he was closing the period of his narrative work, he wrote an article supporting the fact that literature was composed of reminiscences, and that the Greek people, having lost contact with the ancient tradition and not having found "sentimental adventures" in recent history to nourish its memory, was in no state to forge a literature. The young writers admired and feared him, but they also frequently complained about him, accusing him of criticizing them without even having read their works. Then, following the disaster of 1897, we find ourselves in a period that desires a general renewal. The majority of literary men sensed the necessity to serve; they were presssed, and they did not linger over questions of style, on which Roidis had spent his best hours. What appealed in his work were also its most striking characteristics, because they were exterior: the tendency toward good use of words, the display of wit. The great master craftsman found disciples among the most superficial journalist. The most antiliterary element of the period, Souris, Anninos, and Tsokopoulos, were ambitious to appropriate something of the elegance of Roidis. Generally, the critical method and profound awareness of responsibility which characterized Roidis, was inherited by one writer, Kostes Palamas, who was to bring these to fulfillment.

Episkopopouluos

Roidis died in 1904. Thus, he survived many younger contemporaries who had also submitted to his influence. We mention here two prose writers, whose lives extend much beyond this period, but whose work stops well before their disappearance from the literary scene: Michael Mitsakis and Nicholas Episkopopoulos. The latter was born in 1874; he began by publishing various short stories and other works in Greece; then he went to France and devoted himself to French letters. Episkopopoulos early exhibited the desire to escape from the portrayal of manners. In this respect and also considering the influences he received from Anatole France and the attention he paid to refining his language, he could be placed among the continuators of Roidis. But his juvenilia, full of sentimentality, set him apart and bring him close to the efforts of neo-Hellenic symbolism.

Mitsakis

The personality of Michael Mitsakis was much stronger. He was born in 1868 and devoted himself to letters and to journalism as a young boy. In 1894 he began to exhibit symptoms of imbalance and two years later he was finally and irrevocably lost to Greek letters. He died in 1916. Mitsakis was, first of all, a style, a style that was not only created to charm but, if possible, to enthrall and, in all cases, to surpise. Moreover, this desire to be distinguished from the ordinary, to express with words an original personality, is visible not only in the narratives he left us but even in his violent critical work. His language expressed a particular time and special turn of spirit in Greek letters. Let us recall Gabriilides: he did not adhere to the linguistic movement of demoticism, but grafted elements of the demotic onto purism, carefully constructed in order to give it color and life.

Color and life were the literary ideals of Mitsakis. He can be considered the most conscientious and most responsible representative of Greek naturalism; what was of special concern to him was description, the animation of objects through expression. Description of objects, scenes of the streets, and visual and auditory reproduction of daily reality composed the materials of his narratives. Story was often totally absent. He used to say to D. Tangopoulos: "Let us go to my library," by which he meant go on the long walks where, with minute attention and indefatigable observation he would note the forms and types destined to pass into his novels. His only well-constructed story is called "An Athenian Gold Seeker" (1890), but even here the predominant intention was to reproduce accurately a short phase in the history of Athenian society, when the vision of the treasures at Laurium had turned the heads of the Greek people. This literary attempt interests us because it indicates, very characteristically, the extreme limits of Greek naturalism, but it must be pointed out that Mitsakis was unsuccessful in his intention to create a style. His phrase, which follows the meanderings of thought and loses itself in material details, is often extended and sometimes becomes hopelessly confused. Subordinated and parenthetical expressions are wedged into his prose, which is ornamented with brilliant adjectives, in such a way that often the first reading is insufficient to render a meaning, even the simplest one. To this disorder, his lack of homogeneous language adds a burden.

Among the short-story writers who were unable to assimilate the new orientation of language, even though they had lived in the greatest period of demoticism, we should mention Emmanuel Lykoudis, John Dambergis, Alexander Moraïtides, and the more important Alexander Papadiamantis. Lykoudis (1849–1925) published short stories, memoirs, and essays, written with nobility and attention, but which were cold and lacking spirit. Of the prolific writer J. Dambergis (1862–1938), a volume of short stories with the title *My Cretans* is the only meritorious work to have survived. These narratives are distinguished by a psychological analysis of simple people, written with elegance and precision.

Papadiamantis

Alexander Papadiamantis was born in Skiathos in 1851. His family was austere and religious; his father was a priest. He went to Athens and began his studies in philology, but he failed to complete his work toward a degree. He was attracted to writing. He studied foreign languages, he wrote verses, he translated and wrote original prose. In addition to his few poems, his early works were historical novels of epic style: *The Expatriate* (1879), *The Merchants of Nations* (1882), *The Gypsy Girl* (1884). We have a series of adventures, a dramatic plot, but poor characterization. His early works did not surpass the average of the genre, which was at that time in its decline. Papadiamantis turned to the short story. In 1885 "Christos Miliones," inspired by a folksong, marked this new orientation and the beginning of a production where folkloristic interests took the form of portrayals of manners. From that time until his death (1911), almost his exclusive production was in short stories, which number approximately two hundred. His entire life was confined between Athens and his birthplace, the island of Skiathos, where he returned every so often to remain for several months. He went there for the last time in 1908 and remained until his death. The inspiration and life of Papadiamantis was marked closely by the religious element. He had the religious tradition in his blood. As a child, he sketched the saints in his notebooks which he also ornamented with subjects from liturgical life. Before he started his university studies, he spent a few months in Mount Athos and throughout his entire life he enjoyed chanting in church. His short stories abound in reminiscences of religious ceremonies and pious people. His religiosity, however, never went beyond simple piety—simple and sometimes gently simplistic—and the attachment to an ecclesiastical ritual and the narrowest conception of tradition. He was conservative; in him the religious spirit of Byzantium at its decline predominated. He had a hatred for the Franks and a horror for every kind of innovation. We found this same attitude in a great number of intellectuals after the War of Independence. We should also attribute a Byzantine origin to the fondness Papadiamantis had for parodies of religious texts, which he took pleasure in reciting or which he improvised himself. He lived outside the problems and distresses of the Greeks of his generation. Surnamed "the Saint of modern Greek letters," Papadiamantis had only the sainthood of an anchorite and remained strange to compassion for man.

His novels were juvenilia, ambitious compositions which were not supported by sufficient preparation. In any case, they exhibited an effort toward composition which Papadiamantis quickly abandoned. Later, what we still call short stories were only short narratives depicting certain moments of life or presenting some psychological episode and a study of manners. At times they were composed only of descriptions. Papadiamantis was fond of minute details in his descriptions and often interrupted the unity of his narrative by introducing an extravagant proportion of descriptions. His heroes came from the island environment and usually expressed the ordinary pacifist mood of these inhabitants. Papadiamantis was sympathetic to these simple people, not only conforming to the mode of his times, but also because these men were in accord with his own states of soul. However, the folklore element abounds in his work, and, if an intention at psychological analysis was not apparent, and if a diffuse lyricism did not run throughout his work, we could say that it set the tone.

The folkloristic element emerged from a true familiarity of the author with his subject. He lived the life he depicted; he had observed the manners carefully and with love; his descriptions, when he succeeded in elevating them as an objective narrator, constituted faithful portrayals of life and the mentality of the inhabitants of his own island. More often, however, the narrator interposed with commentaries and gave to the work an edifying tone that detracted from the benevolence and native wit Papadiamantis had for his heroes. His psychological analysis was usually understated because often his characters were voluntarily comic. They had imprecise contours, they were neutral, because that is how their creator wanted them. Moreover, the types present little variety: there are three or four men, the same number of women, and only the names change. Sometimes, stronger personalities appeared, as the one in *The Murderess*. In this novelette, Papadiamantis presented a woman whose sadism, her perverse mysticism, led to a series of infanticides. As for lyricism, the particular atmosphere that Papadiamantis created in his short stories consisted of nostalgia, reverie, reminiscence, and religiosity. His technique was simple, always the same; in its repetitiveness, it became monotonous. The author projected himself indirectly in the narration in order to express his own emotional world. All this, however, was offered in a harmonious reproduction of the atmosphere of Greek folk life and especially that of the Greek islands.

When one reads a short story by Papadiamantis, he is charmed by the material and by its presentation. When he reads two stories, the impression is attenuated. When he reads many, the impression disappears, not only because of the monotonous technique, but also because the same themes and motifs are encountered: there is neither development, nor even restoration. A closed world, pleasant on first contact but oppressive in the long run, exists in all his stories. Furthermore, the entire prose work of Papadiamantis, if one excepts his early novels, is marked by a total negligence, which is contrary to all notion of art. Style, expression, and language are governed by chance; he had no success in this sense. The narrator's intervention becomes burdensome and awkward, an insipid play on words, references to events that are about to follow, inversions, parantheses, points of suspension, exclamations—all the defects of careless writing are constantly found in his work. The verbal expression presents the same defects; it is cursorily written and lacking in limpidity; the distribution of parts is defective. Sometimes, the first reading does not suffice to give each verb its complements. At other times, we have the absence of the principal after a hypothetical proposition. Adverbs often are placed at random; adjectives are poor and conventional or so rare and elegant that they evoke no response in the reader.

This evaluation of Papadiamantis, to a great extent, can be considered an expression of today's opinion. Among the first to examine his work critically were Gregory Xenopoulos, who published a brilliant critical work the year before Papadiamantis died, and Kostas Hadzopoulos, whose study appeared in 1914. But, while he was alive, a legend was created around him, whose origin should somehow be explained. He was known for his purist language, bad technique, and folklore; that is, those qualities essential to reconciling the undistinguished society in which he lived and all that was essential to be reconciled with the intellectuals who warred against the demotic and simultaneously praised the study of neo-Hellenic manners. Papadiamantis was read with pleasure by men who were not accustomed to good quality writing or one for which any preparation was required. It was natural that the generation which considered Souris a great poet should consider Papadiamantis a great prose writer; the significance of art existed only in the other camp, with those who labored to create, who struggled to climb slowly in an environment of public indifference and disapprobation by the intellectuals, who considered themselves as depositories of tradition. Poverty was characterized as sobriety, the recondite was called art, punning was considered wit.

However, even later, other generations and other intellectuals who confronted the Greek literary situation with awareness and responsibility praised Papadiamantis extensively. The "nationalist" line, which began with Perikles Yannopoulos, could not but cherish the sensitive painter of the Greek island atmosphere, the glorifier of Greek tradition, the scorner of new trends imported from the continent. Photos Politis was also fond of Papadiamantis for the same reason. He found the simple narrator's purity of spirit a respite from the astute efforts, the rationalizations, and the experiences of more recent writers: "He carried in his work a Greek conviction and sentiment. An authentic Greek and a powerful writer, he produced pages of admirable purity and moral force, while he himself was devoured by nostalgia for a remote fairy-like island, bathed in blue light, where the plains spoke and where the grottos chanted funereal lamentations, where the flowers, the trees, and the birds scattered gaiety and where men were true children of God."

Admiration for Papadiamantis became profoundly rooted in Greek letters. It was thirty years after his death before many voices, more or less courageously and more or less clearly, tended to re-establish a more accurate hierarchy in the new Greek prose.

Moraïtides

Alexander Moraïtides (1850–1929), a relative and friend of Papadiamantis, followed a similar career. Imitator of Papadiamantis on many points, he had greater variety in his works. He began with theatrical works, *Vardas Kallergis* (1875), *The Massacre of the Island of Psara* (1876), and with a prose work inspired by history called *Demetrios Poliorketis,* "private biographical notes" (1876). He wrote many short stories and left us a great number of travel impressions and other memories, as well as works with religious content. He was cold, lacking in inspiration, but he paid close attention to form. The fame of Papadiamantis certainly harmed Moraïtides, and even Papadiamantis himself, since he enjoyed his position as foremost writer. But in any case, the work of Moraïtides, even though it appears modest and coherent, constitutes a survival. The fate of modern Greek letters was in other hands and animated by another spirit. It was during this same period that Palamas created the new literature.

Chapter 26

Palamas

The New Synthesis

Not only in literary history, but also from a more general historical viewpoint, the work of Kostes Palamas shows characteristics comparable with the work of Solomos. Both writers expressed great moments of the Hellenic race and new forms of Hellenism; both expressed these moments in a personal manner. Finally, both affixed their seal on the destiny of Greek literature. Historical differences, which even intruded in their personal contributions, made the diversity between them. In his composition, Solomos expressed the height of Hellenism at the moment when the nation attained its freedom. The composition of Palamas expressed a turn of the new Greek history, the moment after the synthesis, when the bourgeois structure prevailed in society. The personal element appears from this point on: what was faith in Solomos recedes in Palamas and becomes knowledge; what was inspiration in the former becomes thought in the latter. However, as we look closer into the personal history of the two poets, we observe a distinction that was remarked on by Palamas. He wrote that the poet of the *Hymn* was "one of those who prepared his poetics first and then his poetry." In the case of Palamas, the need for poetry did not proceed from a concept of the world, but from a purely psychological necessity.

The family of Palamas, a solid, ancient one, was able to produce a long line of intellectuals, all equally devoted to the national cause. His great-grandfather was Panayotis Palamas, whom we have encountered already among the associates of Voulgaris. Panayotis was involved in the Russo-Turkish Wars of Empress Catherine. His son John, grandfather of the poet Kostes, was also a professor in Constantinople, Athens, Missolonghi, and elsewhere. The intellectual and spiritual gifts, even the physical characteristics, appear to have been inherited most persistently in the long line of the Palamas family. We have works of Kostes's ancestors, and descriptions of them and their activities. All the evidences and testimonies exhibit remarkable resemblances that are perpetuated in the Palamas family to the time of Kostes. In all the national struggles, from the expedition of Orlof to the Cretan Revolution in 1886, we find repeatedly the honored and famous members of the Palamas family.

The poet was born in Patras in 1859 of a father who was a magistrate. He spent his early years there. At the age of seven, Kostes lost both his parents and spent the remainder of his childhood and adolescence in Missolonghi with his uncle Demetrios, a professor and writer. His new home was composed of intellectuals, inspired by love of culture, poetry, and country. His uncle wrote, his cousin wrote, other relatives in Missolonghi also wrote. But the loss of his parents created difficulties in the soul of the orphan. He was deprived of mother love; the attention surrounding him could never replace this. What aided him was his memory and imagination. Escape from reality became one of the first experiences of the young Kostes Palamas. We find him immersing himself deeper and deeper in the complexes created by this need for escape, removing himself farther from the normal life of a child of this age, avoiding his peers, living in solitude. And very soon this attitude incurred the malevolence of the other children and increased his isolation, which ultimately made him hostile toward the whole of society. Later, he was to say about this period: "Negation nurtured me, hatred impregnated me."

Escape and imagination constituted the first deliverance of the child. Books, familiar in his home at Missolonghi, shaped the world of his imagination, and the future poet came early to his first literary essays; at the age of nine, he had already written his first verses.

A fundamental dichotomy provoked by the heritage of the Palamas family and by the childhood life of Kostes, was accentuated by the atmosphere at Missolonghi during these years, "saturated by memories and the glorious narratives of the War of Independence." In the poverty of contemporary life, Missolonghi lived the still recent battles of the insurrection as though in a magnificent dream. We must keep in mind the shape of postrevolutionary Greece as it was discussed in the preceding chapter. Action had been transubstantiated into dream, into nostalgia. The past and the present now were blended into an animated dream. Even for members of the household, passion for country combined memory with action. We are at the height of romanticism, but also at the height of the Grand Idea denoting a greater Greece. "The home is animated by patriotism, but it does not scorn cosmopolitanism." Kostes's uncle was the head of the household. One writer wrote of him that he was "the master, as everyone called him, the Hellenist, the theologian, the philosopher, the mystic, the Hesychatist, the craftsman of expression and master of the Word, stamped with a mysterious grace, the strange and confined man, the declared interpreter of the prophecies of Agathangelos, which at that time were the authoritative sources, the pride of the agathangelists."

Dream and reality, thesis and antithesis collided in the spirit and life of the child. A rhythm of contrasts predominated in all his work. The synthesis encountered in his home was realized for him through art. The final liberation was provided by artistic creation. In Palamas, dialectic movement characterized this creation which was elevated to a symbol of universal order, thus participating in a divine creation. Palamas conferred a mystic content and value on the work which helped establish him in life. Inspiration was qualified as "equal to God." He will say:

Everything, even the impious, is sanctified by rhythm.

We already know from the preceding chapters about the society and intellectual climate of the period in which Palamas matured when he went to Athens in 1875 to enroll at the university. However, we should remark here that life and letters increased the original division we noted in Palamas. In what concerned his life, Palamas was affected by a new society being shaped with great dynamism, but remaining tragically attached to the past. "This world which emerges brings revocations wtih it, dreadful dead residues of a glorious history, contradictory psychology, and lack of internal unity," write M. Avgeris. We must remember, as well, the thirst for knowledge which characterized the rising new classes. The generation of Palamas was a scholarly one: science, Science, was the order of the day, shattering internal harmony that before this had been secured by faith. Palamas wrote:

You, O Science
And you, O Knowledge!
Religion of man
And glory of the valiant. . . .

In letters, the question of language also provoked an internal conflict. The young and indefatigable reader, who became intoxicated with the verses of the Soutsos brothers, of Karasoutsos, of Paraschos, knew the demotic language now, the battles that languages raised, and the opposition between the love of older things and the aesthetic necessities, which the purist language could not satisfy.

It was in such a psychological and social environment that Kostes Palamas took his first steps. His long life constituted the uninterrupted effort of a "thinker poet," as he labeled himself, who intended to conquer and unify the world. And though he failed in theory, he succeeded in practice by means of art. The stages of his journey as poet toward perfecting art, toward perfecting technique, should be established, according to the biological curve of human life, as follows: the beginnings (until around 1900), to the height (until around 1920), and to his long and ripe old age.

Juvenilia

After his early childhood efforts, from which a few poems in the purist were published in a newspaper in Missolonghi in 1874, Palamas appeared at the age of sixteen in 1875 in the Athenian publication, *Attic Calendar,* which was published by Irinaios Asopios. A young student at that time, he travelled between Missolonghi and Athens, collecting impressions from contact with life in the capital. He was attracted by what was new, revolutionary, and heretic. Already in 1875, he praised Laskaratos and J. Papadiamantopoulos; Valaorites influenced him. Even in his first Athenian publications, we find a purely Valaoritic echo: "You who, as a timid young maiden, sprouted from our mountains. . . ."

Later, when Palamas was writing about his childhood, he remarked that he had lived "as though hypnotized by verses," or even, "the worst poet was able to hold me in ecstasy." In 1874 he wrote in his diary: "My hand was bound by the pick of my lyre, which is ever dear to me. She is the only comfort and only confidante of my joys; she is my wealth, she is my only treasure; she is my sister; she is my jewel. It is to her that I always have recourse. It is with her that I will live, and my final glance will be on her." It is in the purist language that he wrote his first collection of poetry, *Words of Love;* he presented it to the last university contest of Voutsinaias in 1876. The judge was Orphanides, who dismissed the collection with only a few words. The poems were characterized as "cold exercises in versification by a learned scholar." in 1878 Palamas published a long poem in Missolonghi. In the following year, he began collaborating on *Rabages* and on *Do Not Lose Your Head.* He was associated with Kamlas and Drosinis. The generation of 1880 was in full formation.

Songs of My Country

However, his first collection of poetry was not published until 1886. This collection was entitled *Songs of My Country*. The objective importance of this collection is mentioned elsewhere. Here we must observe, first of all, certain weaknesses that were the result less of the poet's youthfulness than of the bad instruction he received from the school of Athens. Though the collection was written entirely in the demotic language, the technique of the verses and the handling of language had a visible purist origin, such as the verbosity and the intellectual linguistic forms. The hiatus, which later Palamas judged so harshly, appeared in this collection more frequently than synezisis. In any case, the poet's desire to turn to folk tradition either directly or through the efforts of Valaorites is evident. It was from Valaorites that the older fifteen-syllable verses of Palamas originated, verses with sonorous cesuras, enjambments, and insertion of the seven-syllable or second hemistich in the flow of the fifteen-syllable verse:

> Νεράιδ᾽ ἄλλοι τὴν ἔλεγαν, καὶ ἄλλοι Παναγία
> κι ὅλοι θεοῦ εὐλογία.

It appears that the opposition of ideas also originated from Valaorites. We must not forget that these ideas were in full accord with the psychology of Palamas and generally belonged to romanticism.

This brings our attention to the poet's metrical efforts: a quest for a great variety of verses, strophes, and personal experimentations. Here we also distinguish the desire to reconcile folk tradition with cultivated poetry. Palamas made use of refrains from the folksong and the meters of the dirge, as he also made use of the demotic twelve-syllable verses used by Mavroyannis earlier. Hence, the refrain:

> Καὶ θρέφ᾽ το μὲ τὰ χάδια καὶ μὲ τὰ φιλιά,
> τὸ καημένο
> τὸ παραπονεμένο !

Or the meters of the dirge:

> ῎Αχ ! τοῦ πολέμου ἡ φωτιὰ
> καίει καὶ τρώει τὴ λεβεντιά !

Κ' ἐμᾶς, κ' ἐμᾶς τὶς ἄμοιρες
μαύρη μοναξιὰ θὰ φάγει
καὶ θὰ κάψουνε οἱ πάγοι.

Or the twelve-syllable verses:

Καὶ μέσ' στὴ λαύρα πῶχει τὸ τραγούδι του
γελοῦν οἱ ἐμορφάδες τῆς 'Ανατολῆς...

This tradition calls for closer attention. Palamas not only had the folksong in mind; he attempted to exploit the folk vocabulary and grammar, to exalt the common speech: ἀρχόντοι καὶ φτωχολογιά, κυρὰ μεγάλη, or βάστα καημένη Πόλη. This effort was not always successful, because the poet was still undecided about the language he would adopt ultimately. But he also went farther back into the past. We have already noted his interest in Byzantium; words, such as ἀποκρισάρης, βούλλα, and many others, as well as Byzantine subjects, are encountered in *Songs of my Country*. It is evident that he tended toward a synthesis. Subjects from contemporary folklore especially, but also from the national history and traditions, cut across more subjective inspirations. Significant, as well, was his contact with the Ionian Island school. He discovered Solomos and wrote, quite dazzled:

You have penetrated my heart so profoundly
That now I fear I might lose you. . . .

The fact that he used the iambic eleven-syllable verse in this homage to Solomos was not accidental in a period when the verse form was still used in Athens.

On the whole, in studying this first poetry collection by Kostes Palamas, we see, despite its many weaknesses, that he was carving his future path, his faith in the great power of art:

I love you and I have fame to petition from you,
O Verses. . . .

His apparent desire to create a unity, such as would enclose all the elements of Greek tradition, the classical, Byzantine, modern, and the instruction of the Ionian Islands and the school of Athens, is evident. Foreign influences were less perceptible, as was the grandiloquence that characterized his later work. On the contrary, we still find him closer to the early tendencies of his generation in certain short poems where the familiar tone clearly approaches antilyrical forms. He is closer to Kokkos than to Kambas:

> What then is woman?
> —Don't ask: a bird, a doll,
> A flower, a log, gold, Charon, angel, plague,
> Or a rag for a cart, or a queen on a throne.
> But she is no human being.

But certain tender and delicate accents often compensate for this weakness.

Two years later, he wrote a long poem called *Hymn to Athena*. Here, the tone was constantly elevated. The fifteen-syllable blank verses revealed a remarkable technical perfection with its solid structure, as with its easy flow:

$$\Sigma \epsilon \iota \sigma \mu \grave{o} \varsigma \ \xi \epsilon \sigma \pi \acute{a} \epsilon \iota, \ \tau \grave{a} \ \pi \acute{\epsilon} \lambda a \gamma a \ \chi \omega \rho \acute{\iota} \zeta o \nu \tau a \iota \ \kappa a \grave{\iota} \ \phi \epsilon \acute{\nu} \gamma o \nu \nu \cdot$$

Furthermore, Palamas occasionally attempted in this poem to surpass the classical form of the fifteen-syllable verses. We have the feeling that he was close to acquiring mastery of a national Greek verse form. An equal assurance is encountered in the language of the poem. The element of grandeur predominates in the poem's inspiration, its verses, its language, and its proportions. His inclination, his admiration for great poems henceforth matured.

The poem was awarded a prize in the Philadelphian poetry contest of 1889 with Nicholas Politis as chairman of the committee. Politis formulated a characteristic evaluation: "Only a truly living language can communicate the breath of life to people of past and related periods and unite these two worlds, the classical and the modern, with invisible chains; the two worlds that a vast span of time has kept apart." In the same year, Vikelas addressed to Palamas a poem, inspired by a reading of *Hymn to Athena*:

> For us, it is as though an ancient poet had composed this hymn, and not Kostes Palamas.

Eyes of My Soul

In 1892 a new collection of poetry entitled *Eyes of My Soul* appeared. The title was taken, significantly, from a verse by Solomos, which had a variety of meters, rhythms, and inspirations. The verse is full and rich; the hiatus has disappeared. In his language one senses the influence of Psycharis, whose instruction Palamas was among the first to praise. In the preface, the poet speaks about a *national language,* "as the demotic should be called more accurately." He employed the demotic here with great authority. The themes of his inspiration were those that we already know, but with an added element, a more spiritual one. The figure of woman rises more familiarly associated with passion. We are approaching the feminine type that marks the maturity of Palamas: a figure that is, simultaneously, ideal and sensual:

> You stand apart from the crowd, one among so many women,
> You pass by and raise a tempest in men's hearts.
> And in my soul, a deep serene sea,
> Your passage, like a breeeze, gives birth to dreams.

Parallel with the waning influence of the Parnassian School, which prevailed in *Songs of My Country,* one senses the breakthrough of the new symbolism. To this we can attribute the appearance of free verses—more precisely, the verse "with multiple turns," as Palamas called it—in the poet's new collection.

In 1892 Stephen Stephanou (1868–1944) also published a purely symbolist collection of poetry in Athens under the title *Sonnets.* J. Gryparis, in the following year, published a series of excellent articles on symbolism in the periodical, *Philological Echo,* which was appearing in Constantinople.

Eyes of My Soul had been awarded a prize in the Philadelphian poetry contest with A. Proveleggios as chairman. Criticism was now seriously concerned with the work of Palamas. Gabriilides, Demetrios Kaklamanos (1868–1949), who began with literature but later devoted himself to diplomatic service, and many other writers praised the poet and recognized that he was first among his generation. The attitude of the Ionian Island school with regard to Palamas had special significance. Severe in its criticism, as we know already, and little inclined to compromise, it quickly distinguished the value of Palamas and officially declared its esteem for his work. From this point of view, the criticism of G. Kalosgouros on *Eyes of My Soul,* published in *Hestia* (1893), was of particular significance. The critic wrote about Palamas: "These last few years of national independence have permitted the Greek spirit to constitute itself by drawing considerably from the treasures of Western wisdom." The principal reasons Kalogouros had to honor Palamas were his Hellenicity, while he simultaneously turned toward the West, and his recognition of the heritage of Solomos. Much later, a letter from Polylas to Drosinis was made public: "I am grateful especially to Palamas for having been the first to render to Solomos, my true spiritual father, the place he deserves."

We can say that Palamas had already secured a place for himself. The decade between 1890 and 1900 established his reputation. In 1895 it was he who was charged with writing the hymn for the Olympics: an official recognition. In 1900 an Athenian newspaper conducted a survey among the intellectuals to designate the poet laureate of the living Greek poets. Xenopoulos, Malakasis, Papantoniou, Porphyras, Karkavitsas, and many others voted for Palamas. C. Hadzopoulos, who also voted for Palamas, stressed how important was "the indisputable influence that he had exercised on the younger generation." Naturally, critics were encountered at the same time. Among these were G. Pope in 1898, P. Dimitrakopoulos, who parodied a poem by Palamas in the same year, and N. Laskaris, who, a year later, was witty at the poet's expense. Of greater interest were the criticisms from some of his more reserved colleagues. In 1895 there was a violent attack by Mitsakis, who already was showing signs of losing his memory. The accusation of obscurity, which concerned Palamas from the time he prefaced *Eyes of My Soul* and haunted him to the end of his life, was exposed in a critical article by Polemis in 1897. Polemis wrote that the verses of Palamas were "obscure without justification, either because of the unmethodical combination of different ideas, or because of the insufficiency of phrases."

Polemis was referring to the collection called *Iambs and Anapaests,* which circulated shortly before the calamitous war of 1897. Today the work appears as a model of clarity and sobriety, at the same time showing great richness. The broad intellectual area within which Palamas moved henceforth is found in its entirety in the unaffected classical verses of his small collection:

> I love you as a heroic
> Song of Epirus!
> You have never been intoxicated
> By the wine of dreams.

National tradition, Western wisdom, and more narrowly, science govern the world. This collection includes one of the best-known poems of Palamas, "Charon Gallops on a Horse. . . ," as well as one that begins with the verse: "Inflexible Science strikes with a hatchet swift as lightning. . . ."

But the collection interests us for other reasons. First of all, we have the poet's declaration (1925) that, with Kalvos as his guide, his metrical quest has led him to the assemblages of strophes in *Iambs and Anapaests*. Thus, his composition was enlarged. Then, for the first time in Palamas, we have an entire collection where inspiration flows through similar poems. Finally, we have a collection whose title does not indicate content, but rather the verse forms which compose it. These two observations, which will be repeated often in studying Palamas, are of exceptional interest; they prove that the poet's inspiration was essentially metrical. It was in metrical versification that the poet found his spiritual balance, the reconciliation of opposites which harrowed him. With the passage of time, meter acquired an even greater importance in his consciousness; to a point, in fact, that one day he wrote:

> Everything, even impiety, is sanctified by rhythm,

or even,

> And Galileo, with his stars, and the earth of Euclid,
> All are meter. . . .

He even wrote that "verse is the symbol of universal order," or that verse "in its microscopic, rhythmic step, is the symbol of rhythm that governs the Universe." Similarly, the poet was strengthened and rose to a height, becoming the greatest among men, from whom he had formerly fled in terror. After this collection, we can say that Palamas no longer developed or changed. He had conquered his universe; he now moved within it and brought it to perfection with art and meditation.

His personal life was also balanced during this same period, which closed approximately at the end of the century. In 1887 he married a young girl from Missolonghi, Maria Valvis, whom he had known and loved for years. Best man at their wedding was V. Gabriilides. Among the poems inspired by his wife, perhaps the most representative for its simplicity and tenderness, and because it was written in later years, was "The Hearth" (1930).

> To die on the same day, to be interred on the same day.
> I hope that Death has reserved the same hearth for both of us.

Maria Palamas preceded in death by only a few days the husband to whom she had devoted her long life.

In 1897 Palamas was appointed secretary at the University of Athens. He occupied that position—with one brief interruption in

1912—until he received his pension in 1928. His was a simple, straightforward destiny. His books were his work; his thoughts and passions were his adventures. However, in 1897 the national disaster of Greece and in 1898 the death of his youngest son, Alkis, cast him into profound grief for the remainder of his life. After these two ordeals, the tone of his work became definitely serious. The result of the war of 1897 on his intellectual world and his work will be analyzed later. As for his son's death, there is a long poem, more precisely a collection of poems in the same form, entitled *The Grave* (1898):

> In the calm and in the silence,
> Accompanied by our kisses,
> You left our embraces
> To return to the unknown.

Perhaps better than any commentary, the creative genius of Palamas was characterized by the phrase he wrote in 1929 regarding his child's death: "How crushing for the father! And also, what a wealth of inspiration for the poet!" Again, in 1906, the death of his son inspired a poem, "First Words of Paradise," which the poet published in 1909.

In 1900 a long poem appeared separately with the title *The Greetings of the Sun-born Maiden*. It was a partial draft from *Our Periodical,* which Gerasimos Vokos (1869–1927) was editing in Piraeus. In this poem, with its national symbolism gradually elevated to a cosmology, we have perhaps the poet's first reaction to the debacle of 1897:

> The roses are about to blossom,
> Some here, some over there,
> In their ancient beauty.

Palamas increasingly came to see his artistic ideal, that is, the long poems which were centered around his country.

Immovable Life

With the collection *Immovable Life* (1904), we can say that the first creative period closed for Palamas and that the second period began: an end and a beginning simultaneously. It was an end because it contained a collection of material belonging to various earlier periods;

an end also because after this we encounter the two great works of the poet's maturity. It was a beginning because we find in *Immovable Life* the entire universe of Palamas, impeccably orchestrated, an inimitable record of meters and rhythms. From simple tenderness to the highest philosophical thought, from passion to ascetic serenity, all that constitutes the originality of Palamas is found in this collection. And above all, there is the poet's awareness of superiority.

> Such as I am, with such a heart, a bird trembling in a sick breast, I am much closer to light and to truth than the mighty and strong of the world. It is for this that I understand myself at depth, despite my weakness and my physical misery; that I whisper contempt for all the strong and mighty of the world. And this suits me. . . .

Criticism, Short Story, Drama

We should stop for a moment to cast a backward glance and to look at certain other works Palamas wrote: criticism, prose, drama. I also mention that he intermittently, throughout his long life, translated verses and prose.

An objective evaluation would classify the critic and essayist Palamas on an equal plane with the poet. Considering the rest of neo-Hellenic production, the critical work of Palamas remains unique, since no one surpassed or even equalled it. At the beginning, he was presented as a continuator of Roidis's technique: frequent references to Western thought, a tendency to consider literature from a scientific viewpoint. Very quickly, however, we perceive a difference; there is a literary quality, a profound knowledge of technique, and a breadth of documentation. All these are encountered early in his vast critical work. An indefatigable reader, receptive to all Western movements, knowing fully the older Greek literature, Palamas was for the historian of letters and for criticism the model of modern Greek literary thought. Eclectic, without weakening his personal contribution, he tracked down and investigated beauty, which he proclaimed wherever he distinguished it. He proved equally penetrating when he analyzed his own work. His critical ability was confined only by his poetic personality. Though the contribution of Valaorites did not escape him, though he had remarked early on Kalvos (1889) and

Solomos (1886), though he had praised Psycharis as he deserved praise, Palamas was incapable of appreciating the poetry of Cavafy or of enjoying verse forms that digressed entirely from traditional forms. We must observe, as well, that many times, especially when he was involved in the battles for demoticism, he praised the new writers to excess. In any case, his critiques and other essays, both those he collected in volumes and the great portion he left scattered here and there, constitute an exceptional contribution to modern Greek culture. The edition of Solomos, which Palamas prefaced and published in 1901, marks a new stage in the research around Solomos.

The short story also attracted him very early (1884), but he did not use this form regularly. When later, in 1920, he collected his old short stories in a single volume, he reworked their language. Those written in the purist, he recasts in the demotic. Most of his short stories have a strong autobiographical character. The most important one, "Death of a Youth," was published separately in the periodical *Hestia* in 1891. Folklore is found at the base of this narrative, but originality is equally manifested. The beautiful adolescent who dies so that he will not have to live as a cripple becomes, in Palamas's short story, a living symbol of Hellenism, the symbol of the modern Greek who cannot tolerate lame solutions and compromises, and in whom an ideal of pliable beauty inherited from antiquity survives.

Of equal symbolic importance is the heroine of his drama *Trisevgheni (Thrice-Noble Maiden,* 1903). She is a symbol of the Greek spirit, of the folk language, and in a more universal sense, of beauty. The framework is also folkloristic in order to present the symbolic intention in relief. But as Palamas did not write a study of manners, so he did not turn to allegory. The characters in *Trisevgheni* are living beings; they are taken from provincial life, though the language is sometimes more lyrical than realism would require. On the other hand, movement and plot are adequate enough that we can speak here about a work destined for the stage and not simply a prose work in dramatic form.

The Height

We have seen that around 1900 the younger writers considered Kostes Palamas their master. At this time his first period had terminated. Central to the goals he pursued, aside from his literary efforts, were two preoccupations: language and the nation. Perhaps it would even be more appropriate to speak about a single assertion on which the two preoccupations were based: a *national language*. Conditions were conducive to this endeavor. First of all, there was the defeat of 1897, tragic consequence to the abusive exploitation of the Grand Idea. Though this disaster was painful for Hellenism, the passage of years revealed it to be salutary. The younger writers, particularly those who had not settled on specific forms, awakened under this rebuke; they saw the truth, and the truth was that action should replace hollow words, that expression should be given to the service of action. It was from such a common point of departure that national spirit is revealed on Macedonian soil, that which restored the campaign in favor of a national language. *The Flute of the King* was a product of this climate. Furthermore, from a more general viewpoint, the generation of Palamas, after twenty years of action, gave a new meaning to Hellenism, which also in the interval was formed. The younger members no longer sought but demanded that Greek society express their will: the frontiers of Greece which were sufficient for the older ruling social groups were too restricted for the young; they could no longer be satisfied with a pretentious rhetoric. The same processes caused the generation of 1880 to raise, not without pains, not without battles, not without hesitations, the complex vision of the new Greece: "I believe in one Greece, great and indivisible, thrice-glorious and eternal, country of the spirit of enlightenment, of wisdom, and of science, of all that is perfect; creator of art, of beauty, of civilization, and of all progress." So wrote in 1905 Manuel T. Cheretis, an uncle of Perikles Yannopoulos.

Common Struggles

Parallel with the battle which took place internally for reorganization of the nation and externally for the Turkish-occupied regions, new Hellenism sought obstinately the right to speak its language. A series of diverse manifestations during these years revealed the aspirations of the younger writers and the reactionary forces to which they were opposed. In 1901 the partial publication of the New Testament, translated by Pallis, provoked from the conservatives very strong polemics, which came to have violent manifestations of a more general character. Two years later, a production of the *Oresteia,* translated by G. Sotiriades in a language which today would be classified as mixed, provoked a new conservative attack. The production was preceded by a request for recitation of a poem by Palamas, "Salute to Tragedy." This invitation is evidence of the authority that the poet enjoyed at this time, but it also helped make him a target for a new attack. During tumultuous demonstrations, the students cried: "Down with Palamas, down!" His position at the university was endangered. In the same year (1903), the new periodical *Noumas* began to circulate. Its purpose was fairly general at the beginning; later it became a specialized outlet for the partisans of demoticism, with all the broader views that characterized their renewal efforts. The periodical was edited by D. P. Taggopoulos (1867–1926). He also wrote a good deal, but he is remembered above all because of his activities with the *Noumas.* Around this periodical the older and newer writers were united in the common objective of a national language.

This was the heroic period of the demotic, which coincided with the heroic period of Hellenism. In 1902 a volume entitled *The Linguistic Problem and Our Educational Renascence* appeared, consisting of various articles by Photis Photiades, articles that had been published a few years earlier in a newspaper in Constantinople. Photiades (1849–1936) was a physician who had evaluated the disastrous effects of the purist language on enslaved Greece; he became an ardent defender of the demotic. The work he left us is not very abundant, but it is of quality. I mention an interesting effort, a scientific work written in the demotic called "The Innate Glow" (1935). "With Photiades," wrote M. Triantaphyllides, "commenced the fermentation that he sought to give to neo-Hellenism with a language and true culture." When we see how the educational side of the language question developed ("The Association for a National Language," 1905, "The Education Association," 1910, "The Friendly Companions," 1910, "Teaching Reform," 1917), we can estimate the true value of this precursor's thought. At any rate, he sought to have the Greek people continue their national traditions in order to be in a better position to assimilate Western civilization.

In 1907 the first volume of the *Grammar* by Menos Philintas appeared. A partisan of an extreme orthodoxy on linguistic matters, Philintas left us, in addition to his theoretical contributions in the demotic, a certain number of literary works in verse and in prose, which we should not omit. They were distinguished by a very fine sensitivity and attention to form. I also mention here Elissaios Yannidis (pseudonym for the mathematician S. Stamatiades, 1865–1942). One of his works, *Language and Life* (1908), which was reprinted a number of times, contributed significantly to the popularization of the theory of the demotic. Written simply, in an intelligible and convincing manner, it constitutes even today the best apology for the linguistic movement. Yannidis published other works later, whose content was either linguistic, philosophical, or scientific. I mention the following: *The Great Problem* (1925), *Critical Essay on Materialism*, and *Elements of Geometry* (1938).

Vlastos

Among the other champions of demoticism, using the same method as *Noumas*, were Alexander Pallis and Eftaliotes. We should also mention Petros Vlastos (1879–1941), who began his writing career under the pseudonym Hermonas. Vlastos maintained the same linguistic orthodoxy that characterized Pallis and Eftaliotes. Furthermore, he also had lived outside Greece and his total production was characterized by an abstract view of the Greek problems. His first work, *Of Life*, was published in 1904. It consisted of original texts and translations. Among his abundant later literary production specific mention should be made of his translation of *Physics* in the demotic (1912), *Critical Voyages* (1912), *Argo* (1921), a reedited collection of his poems, including some that had never been published before, and *Synonyms and Related Words* (1931), where he attempted to classify the rich demotic vocabulary. His efforts in this area of language, as well as his literary production and his theoretical tendencies, were marked by the absence of direct contact with Greek reality. It was Greece seen from a distance, with an idealism that attempted to conceal itself behind harsh forms and all kinds of extremes. This same harshness reappeared in his poetry, which was distinguished by an exceptional application. It was inspiration and poetry of the study, which, nonetheless, sought to be natural and enthusiastic. This contrast, characteristic of his diverse work, diminished significantly from its value and created only isolated successes without interrelationship. The closing verses of a short poem called "Greece" read:

> O Goddesses, you are not dead!
> It is light, the earth covering your tombs;
> Bowing to the sun in the forests,
> I have heard your immortal corpses,
> Stirring in their tombs!

Yannopoulos

This nostalgic vision brings us to another aspect of the renewal effort during his period, an effort in a purely national expression. In these same years, Perikles Yannopoulos (c. 1869–1910) was attempting to improve the total picture of Greece by relying on his love of country, but also on every kind of knowledge and experience. He studied history, art, Greek landscape, and assembled a vision of perfection:

> Everywhere light, everywhere day, everywhere charm, everywhere ease. Everywhere order, symmetry. Everywhere purity of lines, the versatility of Odysseus, the melodiousness of the *palikare*. Everywhere gentleness, grace, smiles. Everywhere the sport of Greek wisdom, the desire for laughter, the Socratic irony. Everywhere philanthropy, sympathy, love. Everywhere a passion for song, for embracing. Everywhere a desire for the material, the material, the material. Everywhere a Dionysiac pleasure, a desire for intoxication through light, a thirst for beauty, a cherishing of felicity. Everywhere a breath of air full of war songs, a vitality, a gallantry and an ardor everywhere, and, simultaneously, a breath of air of melancholy beauty, a sadness of beauty, a lamentation of a dying Adonis. And everywhere the air of a bright war song, and at the same time the air of the flute softening the body with a voluptuousness. And everywhere a breath of air, everywhere the lamentations of Aphrodite, and simultaneously, a very strong acid satire (1903).

This was Greece. The Greek ideal consisted of drawing near to Greece, of making her a way of life. "And when GREECE is silent, HUMANISM disappears. And when the GREEK imitates the BARBARIANS, he commits suicide and there is no longer a GREEK on earth. There is no longer a NATURE. And there is no longer a SPIRIT. And there is no longer BEAUTY" (1904). Yannopoulos died young, a suicide. He was unable to write the great composition he had dreamed of writing. But with his personal brilliance, he occupies a central place in the history of modern Greek culture. "His appearance," wrote Sikelianos later, "among the Athenian bourgeousie, was as the picture of her mountains, which rises before us from any road we look." The thought and imagination of Yannopoulos played a basic role in the early stages of Ion Dragoumis and Angelos Sikelianos. We will discuss Sikelianos later at the greatest moment of his career. As for Dragoumis, he wrote in his journal on hearing of the suicide of Yannopoulos: "It appears to me, now that he is gone, that I must assume all the burdens he carried on his shoulders. And for this reason, I have much work to do, very much work. I must not lose a single minute of my life."

Dragoumis

Ion Dragoumis (1878–1920), who sometimes wrote under the pseudonym Idas, also carried out a political activity parallel with his literary activity; theory was complemented by action. In 1907 his first book, entitled *Blood of Martyrs and Heroes,* contained verses taken from Palamas as its motto. The work was inspired by the Macedonian battles and culminated with the death of Paul Melas in 1904. The hero, Alexis, was an intellectual devoted to patriotic activities. In 1909 Dragoumis published *Samothrace* and in 1911 *All the Living.* Both works follow the line of his first book. The later works, in fact, have a markedly political orientation.

What characterized the literary side of Dragoumis was that, for the first time in modern Greek literature, an author turned to his inner world. He studied his reactions, he attempted to discover the deeper motivation behind his actions, he analyzed his psychic states. This man who believed in force and taught it, searched his inner self indefatigably. In his work and thought, echoes of Nietzsche and Barres often recur. Here again we find foreign influences attracting the attention of Greek writers. During these years, German philosophy and French writers exercised an indubitable influence on European literature. Hence, it was natural that a young thinker who was following Western currents closely should be influenced precisely by these same authors. But the influence coincided with the direction toward which historical causes led neo-Hellenism. Dragoumis found what he sought in Barres and Nietzsche.

The literary works of Dragoumis that were published posthumously were only improvisations and were marked by a provisional character. What remains to us of Dragoumis are the three books mentioned above, and especially the image he left us of neo-Hellenism, that which issued from the collapse of 1897 and which was expressed by the politics of Venizelos.

The Dodecalogue of the Gypsy

The catastrophe of 1897 and the national burst of energy that followed were the partial origin of *The Dodecalogue of the Gypsy* and the entire origin of *The Flute of the King,* the two extended poetic works by Palamas. *The Dodecalogue of the Gypsy* was published for the first time in 1907. The preface was dated 1906, but the dedication was given as 1899, when composition of the work was first begun. Effectively, we know that from the end of the nineteenth century Palamas was preparing a trilogy in which, through three symbolic heroes, he would unfold his scientific scepticism, his love of art, and the exaltation of individualism. Throughout the years, the trilogy developed into a dodecalogue, the three heroes were reduced to one, who combined the characteristics of all three. Hence, contrast passed from the surface to inspiration itself, while the work of art acquired the necessary unity. At any rate, the work draws from all the poet's emotional sources; analysis reveals the poet's revolutionary spirit first, then his faith in science, followed by his national aspirations, and finally, beyond every kind of opposition, the creative serenity that art offers.

All the poet's knowledge and interests, all his preoccupations assume a lyrical meaning, where narration alternates with description, grandiloquent meditation with fiery passion, slow majesty with dramatic swiftness. The imagination is given freedom of expression, the images are set in relief. Colors, forms, the external world, dramatic episodes, scenes of passion, dialogue, pieces of eloquence hold the reader's attention alert. Positive science, folklore, traditions, ancient history, Byzantine and modern history, childhood recollections readings, all these are stirred in a gigantic melting pot and poured out in twelve lays of varying meters. But, in addition to this material, we should observe that the work contains echoes of recent Greek texts in the purist language, the texts of Karasoutsos, Demetrios Vernardakis, and others.

The metrical and linguistic wealth of the *Dodecalogue* marks the greatest heights Palamas attained and, simultaneously, a sublimity that has not been surpassed in Greek literature. Meters and rhythms follow the movement of inspiration, sometimes impetuous as a torrent, and at other times as calm as dormant waters. In his language, Palamas exploited the entire national heritage and more particularly the Byzantine vocabulary. Moreover, parallel with the *Dodecalogue,* the poet was working on *The Flute of the King,* whose purely Byzantine subject had plunged him into Byzantine readings. Furthermore, we should not fail to observe the poet's admirable creative talent and his aptitude for enriching the language.

The *Dodecalogue* constitutes a genuinely lyrical composition, despite its numerous extralyrical elements. In the final analysis, the central hero of the poem, the gypsy, is himself a poet. Because of this, the composition is complete and expresses the multiple personality of Palamas. In *The Flute,* on the contrary, which was published in 1910, the epic element prevails, while the national preoccupations predominate as inspiration.

The Flute of the King

The sources which sustained *The Flute* were also multiple. The principal source was undoubtedly the patriotic exaltation, the aspiration for a rehabilitation after the disaster of 1897, and the Macedonian battles against the Bulgarians. For this reason, the poet related the high exploits of Basil Voulgaroktonos. However, besides this fundamental inspiration, we encounter the poet's personal bitterness and disillusionment, which sometimes gave an ironic coloring to his verses. Then there were the campaigns favoring the demotic; folklore interests were represented as well in portions of this composition.

My observations about the *Dodecalogue* can apply equally to *The Flute;* it shows richness, force, imagination. Nonetheless, his verses, which number more than four thousand and are nearly all in fifteen-syllable blank verse, and which are worked with absolute mastery and brilliance, exhaust the reader. Furthermore, in *The Flute,* inspiration functions inversely to its function in the *Dodecalogue.* The entire poem developed a very slight initial inspiration. The magnified extension of this initial idea weakened the work. The seed was lost in the outburst of expression. *The Flute* can only be read in fragments.

Along with the great works that Palamas composed at the dawn of this century, and as though he sought respite, he wrote numerous short poems that were soon collected into two volumes, *The Sorrows of the Lake* and *City and Solitude* (1912). In both collections, but particularly in the first, a tender and soft inspiration prevailed; nostalgia recalled childhood years which were always opposed to accents of passion. But a collection like *The Sorrows* suffices to prove how unjust were the attacks that Palamas was not an erudite poet:

> My early years, unforgetable years,
> I spent them beside the sea,
> Beside the sea so deep and calm,
> Beside the sea so wide, so grand.

The collection interests us further because "Satiric Exercises" (1907–1909) was published for the first time in the same volume. Here, as well, the wind of regenerated Hellenism blows. The satire Palamas wrote was scorching and it purified. It was in complete opposition to all that the period called satire: the humoristic writings. He called these poems exercises, and yet each one was an absolute success. It was the most courageous political satire in modern Greek literature.

The City and Solitude lacked the unity of inspiration found in *The Sorrows.* As Palamas grew older, he produced a long series of poetry collections containing poems assembled from various periods. In the period of his height, which saw a continuous ascendancy, we can place the collections *Altars* (1925), *Unfortunate Occurrences* (1919), and *Pieces of Fourteen Verses* (1919). A mature expression, organically enriched by assimilated traditional elements; a constantly elevated inspiration, rich in imagination and tenderness; and a verse entirely subject to its creator's will; these characterize the collections. At the same time, the poet had a profound awareness of the responsibility conferred upon him by the eminent position he occupied in Greek letters. The events of contemporary history, the wars, the interests of men, moved and inspired him.

In *Unfortunate Occurrences,* we find the long, typical Palamas
poem called "Dialogue." It is a dialogue between the Muse and the
poet. The Muse begins:

> Unworthy, among my faithful,
> And to all that take life and breath
> From my spirit.
> Unworthy he who cannot
> In the midst of defeat and chaos
> Erect a fortress of his opinion,
> Who waits,
> Who says: 'I'll see' and cannot,
> Whose soul sways slowly,
> As the cypress tree.

And again the Muse ends, thus giving meaning to the poem:

> O butterflies of children and of hearts,
> Unsuspecting in the mass of grasshoppers!
> The fame of works and the joys of songs
> Result from the happiness of nations.

A date at the end of the poem, New Year 1917, is indicative. The
poet, having full awareness of his duty, published this poem in February, 1917, in the troubled political atmosphere of his time.

Fourteen Verses, with its characteristic title, is an inspired collection consisting of 102 sonnets. "It was sonnets that the poet desired
to fabricate," wrote Palamas in 1931 when he commented on this
collection. "From that moment, the world appeared to the poet, emo-
tionally and intellectually, as a mold fourteen-feet high that demanded replenishing." In this collection, we find a unified and integrated universe for the last time in the poet's maturity.

During the same period, Palamas also continued his critical and
journalistic work in books, periodicals, newspapers, and lectures.
Henceforth, he would offer to new Hellenism a linguistic instrument
which, without departing from the demotic, would be capable of expressing the most subtle nuances of thought. "The treasure of our
thought in a national garment" had also been sought by Solomos.
What merits special attention are the penetrating and luminous
pages of autobiography and self-analysis in the two volumes entitled
My Years and My Papers.

The later collections of poetry include: *The Pentasyllables, The
Pathetic Whispers, The Wolves, Two Flowers from Foreign Places*
(1925), *Timid and Frustrated Verses* (1928), *The Cycle of Qua-*

trains (1929), *Passages and Salutations* (1931), and *The Nights of Phemios* (1935), which was the last collection of poetry published by Kostes Palamas.

The Wolves, a collection of many strophes of various rhythms, was inspired by the disaster of Asia Minor. The poet projected his calm sentiments of superiority in the world and in history:

> A jealous destiny, a bad moment of terror,
> And the flowers and fruit all crushed by the storm.
> If all passes away, then this too will pass.
> Peace to you and serenity.

Some new verses are included with older ones in all these collections. In the new verses, we observe no drop in tone, no impoverishment of creative imagination or versification ability. I refer particularly to the poem "Aristotle Valaorites" (1924) in the collection *Timid and Frustrated Verses.*

> The enchanting dance of your hundred years carries me on
>   high
> Where the din of battle has been transformed to musical
>   murmur,
> To heavenly worlds of poets and of heroes, where
> The suffering and the tumultuous battle of men cannot
>   reach.

Last Collections

Two collections, *The Cycle of Quatrains* and *The Nights of Phemios,* were distinguished by their particular form. Indeed, we have here a unity of inspiration in a cyclical form; both collections were composed exclusively of quatrains. The poet was now more than seventy years old; that is to say, this was his spiritual testament. His cosmic experiences were summarized with epigrammatic conciseness that touched abstraction. All the themes known to us recur here in a compressed, distilled expression. The mind is ageless, but the spirit, formerly so strong, has disappeared. Hence, the ideas and images become increasingly more difficult to grasp, and, simultaneously, they acquire greater relief; there is a lyricism without flowers, only fruit.

The old oppositions have been surmounted; they have been defeated by the meaning of art, and the poet finds himself possessing an ideal synthesis of the world and the spirit.

> Often, in the One, a division like a falsehood appears,
> And his life becomes another drama and his thought a
>   stranger.
> Though images are so unlike, they are still by the same
>   hand.
> Though different in the eyes of everyone, art perceives
>   them as one.

The poet is elevated above men; he has become a divining prophet, thanks to his gift of poetry. In *Nights of Phemios,* he recalls a verse from *Songs of My Country,* written in 1882:

> I live with meter and with rhythm, I breathe with rhyme.
> Verses, you are my companions both in Love and in the tomb.
> The first note of song that always changes, never rests.
> "I love you, and I have to petition you for fame. . . .

His poetic life had come full circle.

The End

Kostes Palamas lived long enough to know the horror of invasion in 1941. Honored, covered with glory, he bent slowly toward the grave. Public reaction to his death in February 1943 showed the profound response his work had aroused in the souls of the Greek people. The eulogies to him had the character of a majestic national ceremony; when the crowds assembled at his graveside, they sang the national anthem by Solomos.

Antiintellectual Society

Though we have seen the most vital elements of neo-Hellenism passing through the long life and work of Palamas; though we have seen the poet expressing his uneasiness over the new Greek conditions, on the one hand, and on the other hand giving form to neo-Hellenic achievements; though we have seen further how the younger generations revered him, how they were guided by him in their divergent paths of art and thought, we should not believe that his expressions were acceptable to the entire society in which he lived. This recognition came later and had only a short duration; it coincided with the moment when the older literary representatives began to decline and the new writers had not as yet surpassed the investigations of Palamas. The society within which Palamas had labored, struggled, and created had other intellectual ideas. It was not the society that emerged in 1897, but one which had been responsible for the disaster. It was not composed of men who cherished words and avoided all that could disturb their newly acquired equilibrium. We should recall the demands that brought forth the generation of 1880: the home, the peaceful existence, the smile that succeeded polemics, the murmur that succeeded eloquent oratory. The path carved by Roidis with his literary production, the soft passage over matters, the sceptical mood, all agreed with this society, but it failed to persevere in the quest for beauty. Effort was not suited to the idiosyncrasy of these men. Most of the older writers honored Paraschos; their sons appreciated Polemis. The presence of Papadiamantis calmed their consciences, insofar as their obligations toward tradition and the Greek people were concerned. Above all, they sought no new problems, no quests and anguish. Such had been the attitude of the generation of 1880. The new attitude was expressed in the best possible manner by the work of Souris. The exceptional success of his work gives evidence that it corresponded precisely with the aspirations of his time.

Souris

George Souris (1852–1919) dedicated himself to letters quite early. He first appeared in 1873 with verses; from 1879 we find him publishing satiric poetry along with Drosinis, Kambas, and Palamas. In 1882 he undertook the publication of a weekly periodical in verse called *The Greek*. Other writers collaborated in the beginning, among them Kokkos and Polemis. Later, Souris continued the publication alone until 1918. This abundance, to which we should add other poems and short verse comedies, amazes us. We must admit, first of all, that he had an exceptional versification facility that was integrated with nationalism. But in reading these verses, we discover that the natural talents of Souris were supported by a mixed language, which, in accord with the needs of versification alternated between forms and vocabulary in the purist language and in the demotic. This multiplied the possibilities offered to the poet. Insofar as content is concerned, we naturally find in the verses of Souris, and particularly in *The Greek,* a vast panorama of Greek political and social life. Souris often exhibited wit, sometimes difficult to perceive, at other times so artistically presented that it easily brings a smile. He possessed enthusiasm, he imitated and parodied with dexterity, and he had no fear of implications. His verse was always ready to run, to pour forth under the most varied pretexts:

> "To be or not to be?" asks Shakespeare.
> "All right, to be or not to be?" I ask in turn.
> I like nothing of either of these,
> Each is an insupportable evil. . . .

Here are some verses from his *Don Juan:*

> Riaro announces the arrival of the stranger
> To Madame X and she announces it to Madam Y.
> One transmits the message to the other.
> And an elegant dribble begins:
> "Is it true that this famous Don Juan has arrived?
> And my husband, the brute, has told me nothing."

But it is his satire that interests us. He is outstanding in this area; in the profusion of his verses, where everything, characters and situations are touched upon, the point of satire is entirely lacking. He called it satire, but it is never provoked by anger or suffering. He simply sets out to amuse the reader. There is no question of revealing concealed wounds, but of rendering them painless with a pleasantry and punning. The good and bad traverse the panorama in the same manner; the good is treated without respect, the bad without passion. Souris was aware of this. He wrote about himself: "He mocks everything, and he parodies everything." The public devoid of faith, was satisfied and accepted all his jesting with pleasure and indulgence. It was invited to laugh without endangering anything in which it was interested. And this society which boasted of creating and defending Greek tradition, this society which went up in arms indignantly when someone presumed to translate the New Testament or the *Oresteia,* when someone attempted to use the demotic language, applauded Souris unreservedly. *Fasoulis* and *Periklitos* (the two principal figures in the Greek version of Punch and Judy), who appeared in *The Greek,* were for many years the joy of the public which waited impatiently for their weekly appearance. And Souris, without awareness of his responsibility, sought subjects wherever he could find them. On many occasions, religious festivals furnished him with material. The fifteenth of August at Tinos was one of the more appropriate subjects for him:

> If the Mother Virgin wishes in Her goodness
> To cure such a large crowd of fools,
> She will not be restricted by so much folly,
> And perhaps even Her own mind will twist.

And for New Year's Day, the holiday of Saint Basil, he wrote:

> And once again the same old story. . . .
> Saint Basil has arrived from Caesarea. . . .
> Truly, I am bored by this imbecile.

And here are the resolutions he formulated for the New Year in an epigrammatic manner:

> In this nation, which honors asses without packsaddles,
> I wish blazes for the past year and blazes for the new.

We are in 1904, the year Paul Melas died, the year of the *Life Immovable* by Palamas appeared.

Psycharis devoted some pages to Souris: "All that was noble, sublime, or good and honest in the Greeks, Souris systematically avoided examining; even more, he had no eyes to see." Naturally, neither poetry nor satire could emerge under such conditions. The evaluation of Psycharis remained definitive: "Souris was not a poet." This criticism condemned the poet and the antiintellectual society which looked on Souris with pride. Palamas, a truly satiric poet, considered society and the poet as one:

> Fasoulis, away from us, and you Punch and Judy!
> Guard yourselves against such thoughtless people.
> Satirist, you pay tribute to enslavement.

A good many writers lived in this same climate, with more or less apparent dignity, with greater or fewer capabilities. They could all be considered humorists. Their precursor was Irinaios Asopios

(1825–1905), son of Constantine, who retained something of D. Pantazis. Then there were Babis Anninos (1852–1934), Constantine Skokos (1854–1925), George Tsokopoulos (1871–1923), and George Pope (1874–1946). Some rare writers survived in their cold purist language, but they were without literary value even though they had a high awareness of their mission. Among these were Timoleon Ambelas (1850–1926) and Spiros Papanelis (1852–1933). The latter, in fact, devoted all his attention to language. His direction leaves us indifferent today, but the application with which he deployed his energies in the midst of general negligence characterizing the end of Athenian purism is praiseworthy.

As for the others, they wrote as they pleased and whatever they pleased. These were prolific mediocre writers, who were especially often humorists. They wrote novels, comedies, theatrical revues, but also studies and treatises on philosophy and politics. It was an enormous production, much admired in its time, but one that disappeared within a few years. Talent was lacking in all these writers. Moreover, they often collaborated, hence one complemented the other. Anninos sometimes arrived at a tolerable badinage. Laskaris knew how to compose a theatrical plot. Pope was mordant. But what harmed these writers was their facile spirit, their lack of awareness that they had a mission as men of letters, and their uncritical spirit. Yet, until 1915, Pope's newspaper, *Athens,* published coarse parodies of the verses of Palamas.

Part Nine
**Under the Heavy
Shadow of Palamas**
Later Years

The last significant mature period in modern Greek culture was that of Palamas's generation. The best successors were able to convert the forceful spirit of 1880 into action. In the following chapters, we will analyze the changing times in a chronological order. First, there was the direct succession of Palamas, which retained the spirit of its predecessors and their characteristic traits. Sikelianos succeeded in this effort, but simultaneously, signs of a growing fatigue began to appear. In the last chapter, the decline is apparent; faith has been shaken. Even the writers who were able to establish faith, for example Cavafy, are interpreted as dissolute, conforming to the spirit of the period. This intellectual development, as always, has its correspondence in political history: the height is reached in 1912, the disintegration occurs in 1922. But the fall awakened dormant powers: a new literary history began, one which continues today.

Chapter 27

A Flame Rekindled

1890 to 1900

The society which could not assimilate the efforts of Palamas was not representative of the period's society. Similarly, the men of letters who debased the efforts of the generation of 1880 did not constitute their period's totality of writers. In truth, there was a misapprehension over what should be sought. Certain harmonious voices, certain dispositions better adapted to fundamental realities replied to the lack of contact with reality and the grandiloquence of the romantic period. The result from such a point of departure, and through informality, was an imperfect expression which was contemptuous of speech. Contact with life inundated literature with the sense of mediocrity and the commonplace. This was the misapprehension that the humorists of Palamas's generation expressed. On the other hand, a few writers working under these same conditions found the human tone through informality and the problems of living men through contact with life. Here we will relate the history of those writers who, in varying degrees, had understood the requirements of the generation of 1880.

Drosinis

First among these writers was Drosinis. Though his expression was never elevated to the sublime, though his imagination was never in the service of great compositions, still, after his early work, we find him firmly pursuing the perfection of his art. He had no imagination; his inspiration always emerged from direct experience. He had no flights, but he maintained a tone elevated by intellectual culture, delicacy of sensibility, and nobility of spirit. His sense of symbol, whose presence we constantly perceive, confers a lyrical brilliance on the most mundane matters. We find the old poetic theme once more:

> I see the immense plain, with its flowers,
> In a drop of pure honey;
> And I see in the blood-red wine,
> The green vineyard, full of grapes.

Drosinis offered nothing new to verse technique. On the contrary, imperfections of versification were common in his poems. His language was the same way. Though he attempted to maintain the creative qualities of the demotic, his contribution in this area was negligible. With the passage of time, his language and verse became somewhat more weighty and serious, which corresponded with a more responsible confrontation of life. The most important among his later collections of poetry were *The Luminous Darkness* (1915) and *The Closed Eyelids* (1918). His love of beauty, goodness, and truth were associated in these collections, as in all his mature writings, with a persistent interest in the great problems of life and history. Drosinis did not avoid actual events as a source of inspiration; these events were in line with direct experience. But he did give them a broader and more universal content. Drosinis did not create a different world out of the demands of the generation of 1880; he did integrate the substance of these demands in his poetic work. The following verses are a dedication to Palamas, written in 1927:

> Fellow traveller, yes, we set out together
> On the radiant morning of Art—but
> With the passage of time, a separate path
> Was carved for each of us.
> You sought Beauty in the sublime;
> And I sought it in the humble, in refuse.
> You worked with bronze and marble,
> And left the clay of earth for me.
> You climbed the Alpine summits;
> I stood on hills lit by the sun.
> Your muses were queens and ladies.
> Mine, the fisherwomen and shepherdesses.
> You extended your hand toward highest laurels,
> And I toward every blade of grass and herb.
> You wore of crown of laurel leaves.
> A little thyme from the mountains sufficed for me.

Conditions were much easier for those who came later. They found a more cultivated language and verse technique and the Greek world almost coordinated with the foreign accomplishments of the period. They found a propitious atmosphere within which to create. A group of remarkable poets soon appeared to create on the terrain of Kambas, Drosinis, and Palamas had prepared for them. Such men were Constantine Manos (1869–1913), Constantine Hadzopoulos (1869–1920), John Gryparis (1872–1942), Zachary Papantoniou (1877–1940), and Lambros Porphyras (pseudonym for Demetrios Sypsomos, 1879–1932). Some other writers should be mentioned as well. John Pergialites from Spetsos (pseudonym for John Yannoukos, 1866–1945), who was especially known for his fables. Three writers came from Smyrna: Michael Argyropoulos (1862–1949), Anghelos Simiriotes (1870–1944), and A. Photiades (1870–1943). From Roumeli came Mark Tsirimokos (1872–1939), a competent writer of verses who fought hard over the language question; from Livadia, Petros Zitouniates (1875–1909); and from Asia Minor, Paul Mamelis (1876–1935).

The New Type of Literary Man

From this moment on, we see a new type of literary man being molded, who practiced with the authority and seriousness that characterized the efforts of Palamas. Literature ceased to be an avocation; it became the center of the literary man's life. This was something new. If we take the most prolific writers of the preceding period, during the time that Roidis declared he was a writer despite himself; if we take Rangavis, Orphanides, and Antoniades, all of whom had a profession outside literature and who wrote only to express their literary interests, this explains why the poets of the romantic school were so numerous. Now we are no longer concerned with amateurs. The writer certainly had a secondary profession in order to earn a living, but his social position was determined by his literary qualities. Thus, the number of those who wrote diminished, while, on the contrary, the class of literary men increased. Most of the literary men named above were born within a decade of one another. They were ten to twenty years younger than Palamas and Drosinis. If the onerous prestige of Palamas had not existed for them, we could speak about a new literary generation. But, in reality, we have only a continuation. The line remained the same; and as none of these writers possessed the force of Palamas, they all appeared, willy-nilly, to be following in his footsteps. Their reservations and restraints could not endure and eventually even the most irregular writer submitted. Hadzopoulos engaged in a violent polemic against Palamas but ended by appreciating him. It was to Palamas's influence in combination with other exigencies that we can attribute the sudden interest of these first post-Palamas literary men for the little-known areas of Western literature.

Hadzopoulos

Hadzopoulos was primarily a receptive type. His personality was not striking, nor was his theoretical universe or his aesthetic direction. Both his theory and practice changed with the times. What remained stable and characterized him was his literary awareness, his unflagging quest for form, even though the ideal form altered. In 1898 he published two collections of poetry, *Songs of Solitude* and *Elegies and Idylls,* under the pseudonym Petros Vasilikos. An elegiac tone predominated. A musical quality and a certain attentive cultivation of verse he had were remarkable for that period.

> I do not seek something foreign, I demand nothing secret,
> > I wish for no favor.
> They have taken you from me, from my spirit,
> > They have taken something.

We sense that symbolism—temper and expression—passed through here.

At this time, Hadzopoulos was editing the periodical *Art* (1898–1899). It was an avant-garde publication, with which most literary men mentioned above collaborated, as did Palamas, Episkopoulos, Eftaliotes, Kambysis, and certain other writers encountered elsewhere in this *History*. The periodical was concerned greatly with Western literature, specifically English, French, German, Russian, and Scandinavian. This same line was also pursued by *Dionysos* (1901–1902), a periodical edited by D. Hadzopoulos, Constantine's brother, under the pseudonym Bohemian (1872–1936), and by J. Kambysis. Bohemian, who had received a Western cultural education, devoted his genuine talents to journalism; no work of note carries on his memory. Because Bohemian left no significant work, it is easier to discern the influence of John Kambysis in the periodicals' orientation toward the continent. As a young man, Kambysis studied in Germany. Because of his immaturity, early contact with unknown worlds was a source of astonishment to him. His letters, critical essays, drama, and other works often display a certain arrogance and an excessive influence from his readings. In any case, the orientation he gave his circle by systematically pointing toward new literary movements, quite unknown until now in Greec, was a milestone for Greek letters. We find other movements in the group contributing to *Art* and *Dionysos* and more specifically taking a critical attitude toward Palamas. The younger writers wanted to shake off his influence.

It was with such a receptivity toward foreign influences that Hadzopoulos went to Germany and came under total German influence. The ten years that he lived in Germany oriented him toward social problems; he ultimately became a socialist. Thus the short stories "Love in a Village" (1910) and "The Castle by the Edge of the Water" (1915) are, despite their study of manners and morals, works with a social content. In these works, we discern a realism expressed in a style employing a firm and tightly constructed rhythm and a rapid, natural dialogue. The change from his early works was great, but the attention he paid to form remained unaltered. In 1915 he published another short story called "Superman." Here he ridiculed all superficial contacts with German intellectual life. In the following year, we again ascertain the predominance of symbolism, this time in a volume of short stories. In 1917 the same symbolist atmosphere, but associated with northern influences, was found in his novel *Autumn*. Hadzopoulos succeeded here in suggesting the troubled and elusive states of the soul. Many writers attempted to imitate this work, but they were unable to maintain the same quality. We should stop a moment on his last collections of poetry, *Simple Manners* (1920) and *Evening Legends* (1920). His verse here attained a fullness, which occasionally showed a more forceful tone. But always in *Evening Legends* we find a haziness and suggestion of symbolism:

> He said, in talking of the two: They had come
> Late in the evening and had been seated—
> Earlier, they had stood on the rock
> And they had looked far out at sea.

> They had been seated near the water,
> On the edge of the green prairie,
> And they had looked at the water flowing past,
> And they had looked at the fork in the road.

This stanza is in the past perfect tense. The discourse is about to dissolve and with it the world of the poet. There is no clarity, no plasticity. But within this fluid mass, we discern, despite the lack of composition, the pure metal of lyricism.

Porphyras

Along with Hadzopoulos, and from the viewpoint of lyrical mood, we should mention Porphyras. His work was not abundant: one collection of poetry called *Shadows* (1920) and a second one, *Musical Voices* (1934), published posthumously. In both collections, poems of various dates were assembled. Porphyras also was included in the circles of *Art* and *Dionysos*. Reveries, nostalgia, and melancholy were the natural themes of his poetry, which was always noble, modest, given in half-words, and in nuances. When he attempted to raise his voice, the lyricism disappeared. He was unable to carry through on technique; his language was poor, often awkward, his versification weak. But these defects, though they cause lacunas without adding any charm, do harmonize with his image and complement it. Porphyras belonged to an advanced stage of symbolism, and the form he used tended to moderation and restraint:

> Do not cry, do not say that nothing remains for you here.
> What remains on the mountains is the passage of the
>   storm,
> What remains is the distant dawn, far out at sea, and the
>   day
> Down below on the plain, and the olive trees and the
>   murmur of the city.

Gryparis

The creative work of Gryparis was also slight; it belonged to the same period and milieu. He published only one collection of poetry, *Scarabs and Terracotas* (1919), an assemblage of earlier poems. In

the course of his brief creative period, Gryparis showed a double influence from France. He was influenced by symbolism, and the
Parnassian School. The sonnets of his collection have an austere
technical elaboration with the concomitant cultivation of language.
The poet enriched his vocabulary with elements from medieval and
folklore texts. Moreover, his effort was not confined to assimilating
linguistic elements. Contrary to the folksong imitations which predominated during the creative period of Gryparis (1890–1900) was
his attempt to assimilate various traditional elements in an artistic,
scholarly composition that conformed to the new Western tendencies. The contribution of Gryparis, from this standpoint, was considerable for Greek letters. His poem entitled "Satire" can be considered the synthesis of his theory:

> But Art trims off the common elements
> From the blossom of matter
> And harvests thrice
> To draw the essence.

According to his successive orientations, his poems expressed
either the pictorial intentions of the Parnassian School or the musical intention of symbolism. His technique was almost always impeccable; the rare hiatus that we encounter in his verses, when it was
not deliberate, was a remnant of his period. Palamas had yet to be
purged from verses. The noble elegiac strophe, where the two styles
encounter one another, was perhaps the manner which best agreed
with him and expressed him completely:

> This night—whose piercing sadness awakened me,
> As though the night had thought on our own sadness—
> This night, the seventh heaven opened
> And a deluge of water poured over all creation.

What the poet lacked was imagination. Because of this we see him
early abandoning original creation and turning toward the classical
masterpieces, which he translated into modern Greek. Thus, his
virtues of pure technique were manifested directly, unhindered by
foreign inspiration, and he gave us some of the most brilliant translations of classical texts, especially of tragedies. His verse, in these
works, possessed a certain harshness, but he retained the sense of the
sublime from the ancients.

Malakasis

Malakasis adhered to no one school, nor did he submit to any particular style. What we distinguish in his work is the influence of whatever school predominated at any given moment; these influences were not profound and were neutralized by their very variety. It is impossible not to mention Moréas, whose work Malakasis translated and whose influence obviously showed. But for Malakasis, poetry was an expression, above all, of melody. He wrote mainly in verses, and everything that he left in prose was incomparably inferior to his poetry. He was a born singer; he had the sense of rhythm and melody. In him, we have no elevated subjects, no great inspirations, no strong spirit; only an authentic lyricism. He gives us no feeling that he sought some kind of technique and we sense that his verse is naturally musical. He published several collections of poetry between 1899 *(Fragments)* and 1939 *(The Book of Love)*. The main subject was love, which inspired some of his best strophes. The other emotions and problems of life left him indifferent. When he did sometimes turn to these, we sense that he is no longer in his natural element. For him, love was primarily an overwhelming love, tender and sweet, followed by desire, but one that was gentle and serene; nostalgia came next, and finally the wise acceptance of the new conditions:

> And learn this, the piercing clarity of December,
> And the beautiful moonlit mists of January,
> One cannot find in capricious April,
> Nor in the beautiful monotonous summer days of May.

Melancholy agreed with the poet as suffering never did, but even this was attenuated with a smile. His inspiration often began with childhood memories of Missolonghi, and then the urban poet retrieved the joy and spirit of life close to nature. Such was "Batarias," one of his better known poems. It was to this same inspiration that a series of poems belonged, among which was the equally well-known poem, "The Swallows Say. . . ."

> Oh! How it beats, sometimes, this heart, and finds wings again,
>   Now, in old age!
> Like a young man to enjoy the moon, the day, the bright stars,
>   The twilights, and the soft dawn.

Papantoniou

In Zachary Papantoniou, who expressed himself in various genres, what predominated was technical skill and the quest for artistry. His poetic work is not abundant. We have a collection published in 1931 with the title *Divine Gifts,* which contains the poems that the poet himself desired to preserve for posterity. Inspiration is not always clear in his impeccable technique, which has no fear of difficulties and, in fact, seeks them deliberately. With Papantoniou we tend to speak about dexterity. Such an example is found in the last verses of the poem "Euthanasia":

> A blessed death has cast to earth
> The whistling blackbird at the moment
> When it plunged its amber beak
> In the honey of the fruit.

But the elaboration of the verse is so skillful that it returns us to simplicity. His cultivated language ignores all affectation and thus is presented with elegant simplicity. The subjects that inspire him contain nobility; they avoid humiliation but do not reach the sublime. A world of spiritual serenity is presented wherever convenient. Emotions also are balanced and sometimes they are extinguished entirely in a Parnassian tranquillity. However, more often we find a human tone and a comprehension of life, of natural creations, of nature. A philosophic resignation is elevated to melancholy:

> Wait. There are even more difficult hours.
> Do you think that destiny has forgotten her mission?
> Be calm! Suffering is no traitor.
> Your future holds many more storms.

Aside from poetry, Papantoniou also left novelettes, always elegantly and skillfully composed but without a strong spirit, and prose poems with the title of *Prose Rhythms,* which were the original models of this adulterated genre. He also was concerned with the theater; he wrote travel impressions and essays and distinguished himself in journalism. His participation in the educational reform of 1917 should not go unmentioned. He was principally responsible for writing the book of readings called *The High Mountains,* which was considered one of the great successes of this reform.

Markoras and the Last Writers of the Ionian School

Before passing to writers who utilized prose as their principal means of expression, we should mention the last manifestation of the Ionian Islands school, which produced its work principally between 1890 and 1900 but also continued into the next decade. First, we should mention Markoras, who came to attention in Athens with two collections of poetry, *Poetical Works,* published in Corfu in 1890, and *Short Journeys,* published in Athens in 1899. Markoras retained the intellectuality of the Ionian Islands, but also the weakness of tone, which we have observed elsewhere. His collections were composed in old age, but this did not prevent them from surviving; they are certainly marked by melancholy, but also by a serene contemplation of death. I mention an epigram called "To a Photograph of Jacob Polylas":

> They say, dear friend, that Death has not carried you off.
> Here, the light has been honored to reproduce your image with
>   fidelity.
> The other—the eternal light, irradiated by a great spirit,
> Leaves your brilliant image on all you've written.

The influence of Athens prevailed in his last collection. We have an epigram written to Maria Palamas:

> I asked: with his brilliant beam
> What is the source of beauty in Palamas?
> But when I saw you, such questions
> No longer came from my mouth.

He also dedicated verses to the death of Alkis Palamas. The ardent spirituality that characterized the work of Markoras was expressed beautifully in a sonnet to his sister entitled "Two":

> Two of us have remained! Who knows
> What the book of Destiny has reserved for the future!
> Which of the two will go first to the sunless country,
> Which of the two will remain alone?

> If we pitiful, childless old ones should live,
> As the austere, divine will commands,
> Let each of us hold the hand of the other,
> Until we feel it go cold and insensible.

Such a favor—let us ask for no other—
In the flame which has seared us deeply,
Is, my sister, a great consolation.

Oh, on the day when even this shall cease,
If the world is to shed one single tear,
Let it be for the survivor, not for the other.

Gerasimos Markoras died in Corfu in 1911. His fame in Athenian social circles was great. And it was Palamas who helped make the poet known and appreciated: "Markoras taught me my verse," the poet of *The Flute* wrote later about the poet of *The Oath*.

Among the other Ionian Islands writers who were active in Athens or who distinguished themselves during these years, we have the satiric poet Mikelas Avlichos (1844–1917), Dennis Eliakopoulos (1855–1895), Stephen Martzokis (1855–1913), and especially Lorenzos Mavilis (1860–1912). Along with these, we should mention some other satiric poets, as John Tsakasianos (1853–1908), who created a type, the Count Sparrow, and George Molfetas (1871–1916), who published the satiric periodical *Zizanion* in Cephalonia from 1892 until his death. We should also cite some older poets, such as Stelios Chrysomallis (1836–1918), who distinguished himself in satire as well as in translations, Nicholas Koyevinas (1856–1897), known especially for his translations, and the lyric poet Dionysios Margaris (1859–1895). Finally, among the younger writers who maintained elements of the Ionian Islands school we should mention Marinos Sigouros (1885–1961), Gerasimos Spatalas (b. 1887), and Spiros Nikokavouras (1883–1952).

Avlichos reminds us greatly of Laskaratos. However, the satiric element predominated in him and the intellectual world from which he drew his source of satire possessed a more notable social content. On the other hand, even his lyrical elements were greater. He characterized himself in verses to Palamas (1911) as:

But as for me, I am a small source, springing from a solitary rock,

That pours in solitude toward a solitary shore,
That flows as though crying for solitude.

And only night and day, evening and dawn,
Talk with the murmuring sea. . . .
And with a winged voyager, where he comes to drink.

Mavilis

In Lorenzos Mavilis, we have the final brilliance of lyrical creation from the Ionian Islands. Study of philosophy in Germany fortified his idealism, which, moreover, was one of the distinctive features of the Ionian Islands school. He was well read, and he left us translations from different languages, even from Sanskrit. We should observe here that, within the Ionian Islands cultural world which was constricting little by little, and whose center of interest was being increasingly transferred to the past, creativity tended to give way to memory. The spirit turned toward knowledge. To our times, the Ionian Islands have given us intellectuals with an exceptional culture.

Of his not very abundant original work, the sonnets of Mavilis early occupied a distinctive place in the public consciousness. For a world that had shared the heritage of Solomos, Mavilis retrieved the accent that had been lost and succeeded in rendering again the elevated inspiration in an adequate form. An indefatigable writer of verses and a perfectionist, he transmuted his wisdom and knowledge of technique into lyricism. His inspiration, whose source was always a personal experience, with ease attained the sublime in his inner world. In *The Olive Tree* we read:

> In the hollow of your trunk, a bee has come to live,
> Ancient olive tree, bowing
> Under scant foliage still covering you
> As a funereal dress.
> And each bird, intoxicated
> With love, chirping, flies around your branches
> In amorous pursuit,
> On your branches that no longer blossom,
> How much more sweetly they repay your death
> With their enchanting noise,
> These young beauties full of life,
> That press against you like memories.
> Oh, if others could thus die,
> Other souls, the sisters of your own.

A first contact with the sonnets suggests a connection with the Parnassian School. But the human tone, the personal desires of the poet remove us from the tranquillity of Parnassianism. I mention a sonnet inspired by the death of Alkis Palamas and another dedicated to Jacob Polylas. But his great passion was love of country. All his activity beyond the study of letters was devoted to his country; he fought with the insurgents in Crete in 1896 and in Epirus in 1897. Elected deputy of the revisionist House of Parliament in 1909, he defended the demotic language with passion. He was killed in the Balkan War in 1912, where he fought as a volunteer. One of his early poems, "Country" (1878), expressed the idealism of the Ionian Islands with a fervor which was rarely heard at this time:

> Greece, my Mother, why are you not
> Standing erect as before, tall, crowned
> With laurels; why do you not carry gifts,
> And why are you not decorated with eternal Victory!
> Alas, when will it come, when will the hour come
> When your sad face will shine once more?
> When will you light with hope
> Your deserted, valorous land?
> My Country, arise! Let your shining face
> Be bright again, lift it high in the air.
> The day of Freedom will emerge,
> And your divine face
> Will sparkle like the sun.
> You will be great, and woe to your enemies!

Prose

All the writers mentioned in this chapter displayed a characteristic trait that regulated the linguistic development of the period. The demotic language was on the way to dominance in Greece. The purist language, fabricated from diverse elements, without roots in life, contained something impersonal in its very essence, something which situated it beyond place. It was an antipoetic element and this sufficed to destroy the strong poetic temperaments. The demotic, especially in the early stages of its utilization when it was still closely associated with its natural roots and the world of folklore, needed the enrichment of an unadulterated vocabulary and the pure modes of expression that still survived away from the capital where people used an unformed linguistic mixture. All these writers who came from the Greek provinces brought with them the living offerings of the folk language. There had been no scholarly linguistic instrument for the demotic. Palamas shaped one, along with those of his circle who were partisans of demoticism. In later years, broadening of geographic boundaries and the creation of a cultivated demotic greatly reduced the importance of the provincial contribution. The result was the pure urban literature of the next generation. In the meantime, the prose writers of this period showed the same distinctive characteristics. These writers were Gregory Xenopoulos (1862–1951), the most significant prose writer of his time, the Epiriote Christos Christovasilis (1861–1937), John Kondylakis (1861–1920), Andrew Karkavitsas (1864–1922), Paul Nirvanas (1866–1937), Anthony Travlantonis, originally from Missolonghi (1867–1943), John Vlachoyannis (1868–1945), Constantine Theotokis (1872–1923), Spilios Pasayannis, originally from the Peloponnessus (1874–1910), and Constantine Parorites (1878–1931). I should also mention Constantine Christomanos (1867–1911) and Stephen Granitsas from Roumeli (1880–1915). As for Demosthenes Voutyras, because of the influence he exercised, he belongs to a later period, where he will be examined with more recent writers.

Christovasilis, Travlantonis, Pasayannis, and Granitsas were never able to go beyond the inspiration of folklore; the first two left us studies in manners: Christovasilis with a greater talent, Travlantonis with a better technique. *The Ravaging of a Life* (1936) of the latter presents, in the form of a romance, the author's social preoccupations, which were not based on doctrine but on a profound sense of humanity. Pasayannis left rather imaginative folklore material and verses influenced by symbolism. One work of Granitsas, *The Savage and Tame of the Mountain and the Forest,* described the animals of the Greek countryside with vividness and with numerous folklore elements. Writers like Kondylakis, Karkavitsas, and Vlachoyannis in his short stories also maintained their roots in folklore and in portrayals of manners, but their personalities allowed them to write works which made them more than anonymous documentaries.

Kondylakis, Karkavitsas, Vlachoyannis

Kondylakis, of Cretan origin, devoted a great part of his writing activity to journalism. Under the pseudonym Passer-by, he wrote chronicles where the desire to attain a style was counteracted by the purist language he used and by his spirit of cultivated irony. He left us a volume of short stories called *When I Was Master of a School* (1916), a remarkable novel called *Patouchas* (1916), and several other works. The same qualities that distinguished his chronicles also distinguished these works. Though *Patouchas* was presented as a study of manners, its psychology did not lack profundity and his heroes were designed with force.

Karkavitsas published many volumes of short stories, among which was *Words of the Prow* (1899); he was at his best when writing sea stories. As for his short stories generally, we should emphasize their unity of theme, their penetrating knowledge of simple men, and, above all, their admirable handling of language, which was exemplary for those years. Indeed, though Karkavitsas began by using the purist language, he welcomed the new linguistic instruction and rewrote in the demotic stories he had earlier written in the purist. *The Beggar, a* novelette with many elements of manners, was one of the most advanced neo-Hellenic naturalistic works. Nonetheless, all the prose writers mentioned here had no genuine intellectual culture. Their intellectual world was a closed one. At best, they attained elements of psychological truth or some commonplaces of a humanistic kind of writing. When Karkavitsas decided to elevate his tone and compose a short story that would expose contemporary problems, as they appeared to the group of young innovators of demoticism, he wrote "The Archeologist" (1903). It was a poor allegory which attempted to fictionize the new ideas of demoticism; the cause of neo-Hellenic misfortune according to him, was ancestor worship.

More important than these two writers, and more dynamic, was John Vlachoyannis, who published his early works under the pseudonym Epachtitis: *The Stories of John Epachtitis* (1893). His complex personality, his stylistic virtues, and his combative attitude attract our attention. Vlachoyannis had a passion for history. Though he appeared early with short stories, it was actually history that attracted him; what he attempted was a resurrection of the recent glorious years. During his entire later life, if we except a few verses and certain attempts at poetic prose, he oscillated between two poles: literary revival and historical research. Hence, he left significant work in both history (he was the first editor of Makryannis and of Kasomoulis) and short stories, most of which were inspired by the War of Independence and the Turkish domination. In these narratives, written in the brilliant and pure language of Roumeli, he was unable to dissociate himself from the historian. On the other hand, in his historical essays, he had a passion that greatly diminished from his objectivity and thus he was unable to compose. The burden of his knowledge and his excessive passion for detail always kept him from the synthesis he dreamed of attaining. In any case, with Vlachoyannis we arrive at the maturity of modern Greek historical awareness, which we saw outlined in preceding chapters. The activity of D. Kampouroglou was also mixed; he wrote history as well as literature. But the rise in both literary and historical standards between Kampouroglou and Vlachoyannis shows maturity of the generation we are considering here.

Theotokis

After the early social preoccupations the older writers exhibited, and we could even include *Thanos Vlekas,* social prose writing was realized with this generation. We have already noted it in Hadzopoulos and we find it more meaningfully in Constantine Theotokis. We must not forget that these are the years when Skleros was laying the theoretical foundations of socialism in Greece with *Our Social Problem* (1907). Certainly, Papadiamantis and Karkavitsas had earlier come under the influence of the great Russian novelists, who were highly respected in the West. This influence was even more evident in Theotokis. Originally from Corfu, Theotokis grew up in the climate of Polylas and Mavilis. After being influenced by many of his numerous readings, he finally turned to socialism. He lived in Germany for two years and on returning to Greece in 1909 he decided to devote himself to his country's politics. From that time he began to publish his most imporant works: *Honor and Money* (1912 in *Noumas*), *The Condemned* (1919), and *The Life and Death of Karavelas* (1920). Finally, in 1922, he published *Slaves in Their Chains,* a work of a purely social character, whose composition appears to have occupied him for many years. Most of the works by Theotokis have a social orientation, that is to say, they contain a message. But this does not diminish their considerable literary value. The works did not intend to prove something, as did the "Archeologist" by Karkavitsas, but were literary successes by a writer who had social convictions which he expressed in the story. In his last works, his talent was fully cultivated: dialogue, description, psychology, and language all contribute in creating strong, poignant works of prose.

We should also mention Constantine Paroritis, whose pseudonym was Leonidas Soureas. He too worked in social prose but without success. From him we have simple compositions on diverse subjects which attempt in vain to attain a literary form.

Xenopoulos

The great prose writer was Gregory Xenopoulos. His prolixity, the result of professional obligations, harmed him, because a great portion of his work obviously was written in haste. I should also add that his professional spirit and his obligation to please a large, literarily uncultivated public led him to make concessions incompatible with art. But even his prolixity was an expression of a strong personality; it was equally true that all his prose, without exception, showed indispensable architectural qualities and the requisite unity based on a strong plot; his stories were enriched by incidents which tended to maintain the reader's interest. I also note that in the study of manners, which concerned all the prose writers, good and bad, mentioned in this chapter, as well as most of those encountered in later modern Greek literature, Xenopoulos was able to produce not simply a study of manners; he could recreate contemporary Greek society, both provincial and Athenian. Xenopoulos combined a strong literary temperament with a perfected technique, which, as we know, is one condition of prose writing. His orientation and interest in technique were illustrated in his critical work. With an ease and authority that were rare in Greek criticism, Xenopoulos taught how to analyze prose, what demands it generated, and what conditions were essential for its success. We can say that he arrived at the ultimate limits of objective criticism. However, the reader approaching his criticism should be cautious; here, too, his professionalism had drawbacks. The theater also attracted Xenopoulos. He worked in this area with great success and displayed qualities that already had been revealed in his prose. Among the writers who set a precedent, who experimented, who gave us self-conscious works, and who constantly produced fine work, Xenopoulos was like a master builder who worked with confidence and reduced to a minimum the risks of failure.

Christomanos

In the development of the modern Greek theater, the contribution of Constantine Christomanos has remained important, not so much because of his own theatrical works as because he was the moving spirit in the establishment of the group called The New Theater. The founding charter of The New Theater (1901) contained the signature of Palamas as the first one on the list and that of Christomanos as the last. Among the works of Christomanos, we should mention *The Book of the Empress Elizabeth* (1907) and *The Wax Doll* (1911). In both works, a suggesive, poetic language, a faculty of understatement, and remarkable descriptive abilities served Christomanos in an analysis of the most delicate psychological situations. The rest of his work is entirely different from these two. The nostalgic reverie and latent eroticism of his other work is entirely contrary to the passion and realism of *The Wax Doll*.

Nirvanas

Among the attempts at drama in this same period, I should mention the plays of Paul Nirvanas (pseudonym for Petros Apostolides). He was influenced by Ibsen. Though this dramatist was without great personality, he did show application and careful attention to style, which characterizes precisely the whole of his abundant and varied work. He wrote verses, both in his early youth (1884) and in his maturity. He also wrote short stories, novels, essays, critical studies, and memoirs. Besides these, we have his chronicles, thousands of chronicles, which delighted the public of his time. Nirvanas possessed charm, elegance, culture, and civilization. The desire for meter and balance guided his thought. This attitude generated a danger: he had in common with the worst representatives of his period the tendency to be witty about everything, to treat the most serious subjects lightly. But what saved him from an unmerited failure was his artistic awareness and his sensitivity toward every new movement being manifested in Greece or that came from the West. As a consequence, he was distinguished from the facile, second-rate writers mentioned at the end of the preceding chapter and was able to occupy a place, not significant but meritorious, in the first post-Palamas generation.

Chapter 28

The Call to Arms Ends

1900 to 1912

The Melting Pot of Athens

Advancing chronologically, we come now to the period of Greek culture from about 1900 to the revolt at Goudi or the Balkan Wars. More than in the preceding decade, and we might add at once, more than in the following decade, we see the movement of the generation of 1880 being realized and maturing. Earlier, we considered the advance of this generation and Palamas's first period of creativity. Now the generation of 1880, as well as the intellectuals who followed, were at their height and at the summit of their literary production. The young writers who appeared after 1900 found a new world already somewhat established and they worked with material that had already been prepared. The melting pot of Athens had largely succeeeded in creating the essential mixture; just as ideological considerations had been formulated, so the language of the new writers had been formed. In the ideological area, we have essentially the two directions which characterized Palamas: first, an attempt at synthesizing the Greek idea into a lyrical unity, and second, a systematic study of foreign cultures and a conscious tendency to assimilate them. It was the time, as we already know, when Greek awareness attained its height with Yannopoulos and Dragoumis, when the foreign element erupted into Greek life with Hadzopoulos and Skleros. Provincial influence diminished, first of all because the cultivated demotic had now been constituted, but also because the provinces increasingly assumed more urban characteristics and thus assimilated with Athens. It suffices to observe certain provincial manifestations in order to be convinced that the Athenian character was found everywhere. All evidence shows that even the efforts apparently produced under local influences proceeded from the capital. The preceding chapter dealt with the end of the Ionian Islands school, or more precisely, its absorption by Athens. Exceptions always exist, but these exceptions alter nothing of the general orientation.

Constantinople and Other Regions

As exceptions, we can recall Photis Photiades or Yannidis from Constantinople. A large portion of Gryparis's early verses were published in a periodical that circulated in Constantinople, the *Philological Echo*. In 1902 another literary periodical called *Life* appeared; it was edited by Apostolos Melachrinos (1883–1952). Melanchrinos was deeply influenced by symbolism; he believed in the charm of musical expression. Among Greek writers he was influenced by the symbolist technique of Gryparis. Later, the poet went to Athens where he continued his production, always in the same direction. Along with his original work, he made some remarkable translations of the ancient tragedies. It was also in Constantinople that Antonis Yaloures (1876–1945) carried on his activity. He was a prose writer and critic who preferred to borrow his subjects from Byzantium and Phanar without, however, giving a particular character to his art. We should also mention among the intellectuals of Constantinople Homer Bekes (1886), who was active in Athens as well. He created a varied poetic work; his technique was brilliant and his inspiration vigorous, whether it sought to express passion or was transferred to satire in the world of ideas.

We will discuss Alexandria and its literary activity later when we consider Cavafy. Here, I should mention C. N. Konstantinides (b. 1889), who was essentially a follower of Palamas, but who also showed influences of Cavafy. Aristides Karavas (1880–1943) from Chios composed distinctive and understated verses. He also participated in the Athenian literary movement. The same can be said about other poets, such as John K. Zervos (1884–1959), originally from Kalymnos, and Anthony Kyriazis (1883–1950) from Roumeli, both of whom sought to retain contact with their roots, but who did not remain faithful to their origins except in choice of subject. Their works belong essentially to the capital. A closer relation with the provinces is found in the poems of G. Athanas (b. 1894, pseudonym for G. Athanasiades-Novas). Beyond the themes, one finds in his work excellent versification and linguistic elements taken from Roumeli tradition. But even his poetry and short stories should be included in the Athenian production, which was the only one alive during those years.

An Abundant Production

Production abounded during the years we are examining here and was manifested in a variety of ways. It was a continuation of the previous production, except there was an elaboration of technique and a greater facility in use of language. The importance of *Noumas* had not diminished, but many other literary publications appeared, which were more independent in certain aspects and increasingly removed from the linguistic orthodoxy of *Noumas*. On the whole, the literary production was easier, more abundant, and the writers were more numerous.

The most prolific writer was Elias Voutierides (1874–1942), who worked in all the literary genres. Today, he is best known for his volumes on the history of literature. Thrasyvoulos Zoiopoulos (1882–1947) and his wife Emily (1887–1941), who wrote under the pseudonyms Stephen and Emily Daphnis, C. Athanasiades (1878–1957), and Leander Palamas (1891–1958), son of the poet Kostes Palamas, are among the intellectuals who should be mentioned particularly for their lyrical production. Theoni Drakopoulou (b. 1883), under the pseudonym Myrtiotissa, wrote verses impregnated with an ardent sensuality. Thrasyvoulos Stavros (b. 1886), in addition to his brilliant translations of Greek and foreign classical authors, as a young man wrote symbolist poems of exceptional quality. I mention his useful *Metrics*. N. Poriotis (1870–1945), a scholarly translator, could not surpass the stage of technical application with either his translations or his original works. Rigas Golfis (1886–1957), pseudonym for D. Dimitriades, proved an accomplished artist in versification. Kartheos, N. Petimezas, and George Delis left a mature literary production. Kartheos (1878–1955), pseudonym for K. Lakos, worked at his verses and wrote remarkable translations; he also worked effectively on the problems posed by the demotic in its scholarly use. N. Petimezas (1873–1952), who also wrote under the pseudonym Lavras, cultivated poetry, the short story, and the chronicle. George Delis (1874–1954) wrote verses with an elevated inspiration and spirituality.

Among the literary periodicals of the time, we should distinguish the *Akritas* (1904–1906), both for its severe literary principles and for its various interests. On the linguistic problem, in fact, it exhibited a flexibility which essentially was evidence that the demotic had won the battle. The *Akritas* was simultaneously concerned with politics, history, and literature. The breadth of spirit that characterized the generation of 1880, in association with a patriotic fervor manifested at this time, found its application here. Director of the periodical was Sotiris Skipes (1879–1952). Skipes was a prolific writer, but the greatest part of his work was lyrical; he published a number of poetry collections and some theatrical works, essays, and criticism. In his poetry, which was mediocre in language and technique and without density, we find influences of French symbolism and those of later French literary circles. He further believed in the continuity of Hellenism throughout the ages and expressed this in his work. Fondness for the idea of Greece was a special sign of the times that concerns us here. We also encounter other names in the periodical. There was Anghelos Sikelianos, who first appeared in *Dionysos*. Others were A. Kambanis, Nicholas Hadzaras and Romos Philyras. The latter is examined at the end of this chapter. Kambanis (1883–1956) produced only a few poems in which neoclassicism caused concern for form and absence of imagination. His later work was principally critical. I mention his *History of Neo-Hellenic Literature*. Hadzaras (1884–1949) left us several poems in which an idyllic tendency was manifested. His restrained production, however, should be attributed to poverty of inspiration rather than desire for perfection.

Sikelianos

Out of this group, we quickly distinguish the dynamism and lyrical qualities of Angelos Sikelianos (1884–1951). While still in his youth, he consecrated himself to art, to lyricism. Originally from Leukas, he combined elements of the Ionian Islands tradition with a sense for the language of Roumeli. From the beginning, his poems exhibited an ease, a maturity and force, and an evident assimilation of the tradition of Solomos: "Rock which spouts forth water and murmurs sweetly." We regularly find one of the most original characteristics of his later work, that is, the union of a spiritual torment with sensual passion. "I pressed my thought against your lips as though to a vessel." Further, we should notice his use at this early stage of traditional verse forms, particularly the fifteen-syllable; his abundant expression submitted to the strict rules of form.

A few years later, in 1909, he published *The Visionary*, which had been written in 1907. It was the first great stage of his future work. In full possession of the means of expression, master of his creative originality, the poet here presented an accomplished lyrical construction. In later years, we will have an admirable development without departing from the world defined in *The Visionary*. Naturally, what prevailed was the young man bedazzled by the beauties offered him, the beauty of the world and the beauty of expresssion. These overflow in an intoxication and exaltation: "I extended a sonorous voice, / Murmuring as the plane tree." Even the verse overflowed. The hallowed forms no longer sufficed, so he liberated himself from these. There were moments when the poet appeared enchanted by the charm of words. Similarly, he was transported by the joys the senses offered. He was like a part of the natural world, and he was possessed by a passion for this union with nature. He expressed this with divine wisdom:

> The murmur of the sea floods
> My veins.
> Over me grinds,
> Like a wheel, the sun.

He also sang of man, of the human body as a component part of the natural world. He is aware that the natural world, and even expression, both of which give him joy, is a Hellenic world and expression. The richness of his vocabulary corresponded with his limitless needs.

In his later work, he subjugated his expression to the rule of his poetic will. His sensitivity to the physical world led the poet to the esssence of matters, to mystic communion with material things. His love for actual human beings led him to a universal love of man. We now pass to the mature stage of his creativity. We have *Prologue to Life,* four small volumes published from 1915 to 1917. Their titles are indicative: *Awareness of My Land, Awareness of My Race, Awareness of Woman, Awareness of Faith.* A fifth part, which was known only in fragments in 1943 but was completed in 1947, was entitled *Awareness of Personal Creation.* The entire journey of Sikelianos, from diffusion to intensity, from outer to inner world, was expressed in this succession of titles. The verse was free; the musical elements we encountered up to this time receded before more versatile elements. He presents the world of the senses not only subjectively but also objectively with admirable descriptive ability. This is particularly true in "The Village Wedding" found in *Awareness of Woman*. However, at the same time, we are profoundly immersed in a mystical world. Some of the fundamental figures in the later poetry of Sikelianos, the mystical Divine Mother and Dionysos-Christ, were already in a mature state here.

Furthermore, in the same abundantly productive years, we have numerous lyrics he published in various periodicals. Worship of country did not prevent Sikelianos from training his antennas toward Western culture and constantly borrowing from the new forces in order to perfect his own art and thought. *John Keats, The Mother of Dante,* and *Thalero* were first published in 1915. Sikelianos shows that he has conquered the impulse of his psychic world; he here touches classicism. An equilibrium reigned, a serenity resulting from restrained forces. It was something much stronger than the spirit of man; it was the will of the poet. The idyllic harmony that enchanted Sikelianos was not endangered by an underlying ardor of becoming mawkish. The intense pulsation was always held in check by the discipline of form. Even his most ordinary and weakest physical images assumed something of their creator's power:

> Enkindled, laughing, warm, over the vineyards
> The moon looked down.
> And even the sun warmed the bushes, as it set
> In double tranquillity.

The next period was inaugurated with the great poems *Mother of God* (1917) and *Easter of the Greeks* (1918). We could expect them, however, as a natural result of the mystic depths of *Prologue to Life* and the classical intention of his lyric poems. *Mother of God,* in its simple form of fifteen-syllable couplets, arrived, in the final verses, at a mystical deliverance from death.

> You who watch over my sleep are first to witness, sister,
> If in dream I did not hear the lyre of your voice!
>
> And at the last communion, I saw no trembling lips,
> As the four winds attacked your heart,
>
> And as I saw your dying face remaining
> Bathed in a thrice-deep smile, failing,
>
> And as you crossed your hands over your breast yourself,
> And as hour by hour death covered you like snow,
>
> Though you did not bid me sweetly to put aside the veil
> Of my bitterness, to portray you as ever-living!

The great dimensions of this poem, or of *Easter of the Greeks,* or even *Delphic Discourses* (1927), which allowed Sikelianos a prolixity quite natural to him, did not lead him astray. The tightly constructed verse and the sobriety of his rich phrases agreed precisely with his elevated inspiration. In *Easter of the Greeks,* the poet's personal experience, which was still sovereign even in *Mother of God,* receded before a more objective creative stimulus. The uniqueness of Hellenism for him now assumed mystic proportions and combined with the story of man. Figures of religion, history, and mythology became universal symbols. As he combined the religious traditions into one, and as he exalted the significance of man, so he balanced the epic and lyric elements, the musical and plastic elements:

> As though a wave from God rhythmically propels them forward,
> They do not walk, they sparkle on the white incline. . . .
> Their angelic footsteps measure the abyss
> And the dawn ever beats over their saintly forms.

Delphic Discourse followed precisely the same line. Expression did not exhaust the poet's creative needs. He believed that his titanic synthetic visions should mark the history of the world; that expression should precede action. It is thus that we can explain the earlier works of Sikelianos (1922) and his later, more delphic attempts (1926–1932). Similarly, the later preoccupation with problems of action should be interpreted by his universal love for man; so should his high concepts of the delphic endeavors where he sought the creation of a universal, spiritual kernel on the ancient, mystic soil of Delphi, on the omphalos of the earth. These aspirations were only realized in part; two theatrical productions, in 1927 and in 1930, combined with elements of modern Greek tradition were all he gave. But relating to this attempt, we possess some prose texts by Sikelianos, as well as the *Delphic Discourse:*

> Help me, Earth! What urged me deeply toward the first order?
> The action of the world is smoke and for me, thought is action.

The creative desire and the determination for action were bound to bring Sikelianos to tragedy. Indeed, during this period, we find him methodically working on tragedy while simultaneously pursuing and developing his lyrical work. *The Last Orphic Dithyramb or the Dithyramb of the Rose* was published in 1932 as a prelude to his theatrical work. In 1940 he wrote *Sibylla,* which, in a classical form, externalized the poet's new anxieties. The subject of the work was

Nero's visit to Delphi. Sibyl, a symbol of Greece, expressed the will for freedom and fidelity to tradition worship. It was written before the Italian attack on Greece in 1940 as a premonition of approaching events. *Sibylla* remained unpublished until 1944. In the meantime, Sikelianos published *Daedalos in Crete* (1943), *Christ in Rome* (1946), and *The Death of Digenis*, written in 1947. The theatrical production of Sikelianos was inferior in the narrow, technical sense of stage action. But the spirit animating these works suffices to enliven them for the theater. Large portions of the tragedies have an elevated lyrical character. As a whole they show impeccable quality in language and verse.

The same characteristics appear in his later lyrical production: a tight phrase full of grandeur and perfect balance, a tight, disciplined verse despite the external liberties he sometimes took. The new Western techniques, including surrealism, did not leave Sikelianos indifferent. Without acknowledging these influences, he assimilated them with Greek tradition, thereby multiplying his potential expression. Actually, he needed all means of expression at his disposal, because all his desires and anguishes, his passions and emotions had attained a high spiritual meaning without losing anything of their force and impetuosity. The creator's responsible maturity returned him to an unreserved lyricism where he expressed subjectively the most objective assumptions that the world was organically unified, free of contradictions. Substance and form exhibited through their homogeneity the desire for Hellenicity, but a Hellenicity that contained the entire human tradition and beyond that the essence of the universe. Thus in the poem "The Sacred Way" (1935), after having described the dance of a bear and her cub, a scene exhibited by gypsies on the streets, he concluded with these narratives:

> And my heart, while I walked, groaned:
> "Ah, will it never come, will the hour never come,
> When the soul of the bear and the soul of the Gypsy
> And my own soul that I call the Initiate,
> Will celebrate together?"
> And as I walked on
> And as night fell, I sensed from the same
> Wound that Fate had struck me, the darkness
> Entering my heart with force,
> As the wave forces its way through a crack
> In a ship as it slowly
> Sinks—And yet, as though it thirsted

My heart overflowed and then it sank
As though swallowed whole by the darkness,
A murmur spread over me,
A murmur,
    And it seemed to say:
      "It will come."

The poet believed in synthesis; he believed in beauty and in harmony of the world. Taking an apocryphal story of Christ, where he showed His disciples the white beauty of a dead animal's teeth, Sikelianos ended one of his poems, written during the German occupation, with these verses:

Grant me also, Lord, as I walk
Always outside the city of Zion,
And from one to the other end of earth
All is wasted, all is littered,
All are unburied corpses that choke
The divine sources of breath, inside the land
Or outside the land. Lord, grant me
In this dreadful odor through which I walk,
Your divine serenity for a moment only,
That I might stop calmly in the middle
Of the carrion and stop somewhere
And to my eyes a white sign
Like hail, like the lily,
Something suddenly reveal itself
Beyond the senses, beyond the decay
Of the world, like the teeth of that dog
That, O Lord, seeing them that twilight,
You had admired them, You made an enormous promise,
A reflection of the Eternal, but also
The cruel lightning of Justice and hope!

The Contribution of Sikelianos

The effort of the generation of 1880, its desire for a synthesis combining the various elements of Hellenic tradition with Western intellectual attainments, reached perfection in the work of Sikelianos. What that generation had desired, Sikelianos achieved. The initial search for the idea of Hellenism had scattered in many directions: the material of tradition first had to be found and assembled. The search for a systematic contact with the intellectual West had the same character; there was scattered material which required classification and an attempt at collection. After such an effort, a poet was necessary who could transmute this intensity of thought to lyricism. That poet was Sikelianos.

The Hellenic Problem

We should mention Sikelianos's other concerns. On the one hand, we have his Hellenic awareness, and on the other, his increasingly deeper examination of more general problems, either isolated or associated with the West. The examination of neo-Hellenic problems spread and was systematized throughout these years. Writers endowed with a critical sensibility and scholars with an artistic sense worked and produced writings that were concerned with the development of research devoted to modern Greece. In architecture, I mention Aristotle Zachos (1879–1939) and D. Pikiones (b. 1887); in the study of folk art, Angeliki Hadzimichalis (1895–1965); in the collection of folklore material, D. Loukopoulos (1874–1943), who wrote most of his studies in an admirably pure demotic. Spiros Theodoropoulos (1876–1961, pseudonym for Agis Theros), who wrote verses, was concerned as well with collecting and publishing folk-songs. Kostas Karavidas (b. 1890), along with his literary work, did research on the communal institution of modern Greek life. Other aspects of modern Greek history and life were examined and evaluated in the same spirit: C. Amantos (1874–1960), a specialist in Byzantine history, extended his research into neo-Hellenism. N. Beis (1887–1958) combined modern Greek literary studies with Byzantine studies. Stilpon Kyriakides (1887–1964) systematized folklore studies and made a comparison between ancient and modern aspects of Hellenic civilization. In a similar manner, the archeologist C. Romaios (1874–1966) offered his contribution to the examination of modern Greek customs.

Penelope Delta

The literary importance of these tendencies, however, was assured by the work of Penelope S. Delta (1871–1941). She first appeared in letters in 1909, during one of the most significant moments of neo-

Hellenism, with a short story significantly titled "For the Motherland." In the following year, she published "A Tale Without a Title," and in 1911 a long historical narrative called *In the Time of Voulgaroktonos*. I mention in addition her *Life of Christ* (1925) and her other long historical narrative, *The Secrets of the Swamp* (1937). Most of her works are intended for children. From earlier periods in our *History*, we know that application to pedagogical matters revealed a more general spirit of renewal. This was precisely what took place here. After early attempts in this direction which produced insipid works or ones written in a language that failed to communicate with a child's heart or imagination, we now have a writer of superior talent who devoted herself to a prose intended to charm and instruct the young. It is characteristic that we encounter allegory among Delta's early works. *The Tale Without a Title* expressed the faith in the potential of neo-Hellenism. Something similar had been offered in *The Archeologist* by Karkavitsas, but Delta's culture allowed her to work successfully in this delicate genre and to create forms of life. The other works of her early literary career refer to the battles of Byzantium against the Bulgars. Here she explored the Macedonian problem. Her later works were narratives for children, written with an autobiographical coloring. *The Secrets of the Swamp* was also inspired by the Macedonian battles. Penelope Delta left other works, narratives and essays, where she expressed more direct concern for the child.

The Education Association

It is with this same aim of examining and giving value to Hellenic matters that we should place recent developments of the linguistic problem already mentioned. The Education Association proposed to apply a new linguistic education in Greek Schools. This effort was supported by three specialists: Manolis Triantaphyllides (1883–1959), Alexander Delmouzos (1880–1956), and Demetrios Glinos (1882–1943). The last had participated in the movement of 1916 to reorganize the educational system. When this movement succeeded in 1917, the three theoreticians of the Association undertook to implement their program and were named to responsible positions with the Ministry of Public Instruction. Later, however, it appeared that this enterprise was so broad that efforts diverged. School reform faced great opposition from reactionary circles and was, for the most part impossible. But,what interests us here were the program's two drives; the one was to give value to Hellenic tradition and the other was concerned especially with freeing Hellenic education from foreign culture and the entire Western spirit. There thus came an eventual division in the group. Delmouzos and Triantaphyllides were interested primarily in research of modern Greek materials. Glinos was definitely oriented toward politics and sought the revolutionary application of the reform. And here the work of these three men leaves the framework of literary history. The principal preoccupation of Delmouzos always consisted of first establishing a school and later teaching. His writing served his pedagogical passion. Only toward the end of his life did he also publish works with a more general content, among others a study on Photis Photiades (1947). Triantaphyllides, after a series of works on the history of modern Greek language and other related subjects, published a *Historical Introduction to a Neo-Hellenic Grammar* in 1938. In 1941, as chairman of the commission instituted for this purpose by the Greek government, he published a *Modern Greek Grammar*. Glinos, who had a philosophical orientation, was soon attracted to action, but he did leave, along with less impressive works, a translation of Plato's *The Sophists,* which he began with a long introduction and published under the pseudonym Demetrios Alexandros (1940).

Kazantzakis

Indeed, the many preoccupations of the generation of 1880 were intensified at this time because of Greece's ever-increasing contact with the Western world. In the earlier period, Nietzsche's influence prevailed, notably in the work of J. Zervos (1875–1944) and in the juvenilia of Nikos Kazantzakis (1883–1957), who first published under the pseudonym Petros Psiloritis. The insatiable intellectual greed which characterized the generation found its most typical expression in Kazantzakis. With exceptional receptivity, ready to grasp each vibration of foreign intellectual life, he expressed himself in a variety of ways, such as translations, poems, philosophical works (*Spiritual Exercises,* 1927), tragedies, travel impressions, in the long philosophical poem *The Odyssey* (1938), and even in the novel, which occupied his maturity and made him internationally famous.

Thus, the world he created was composed of heterogeneous materials, from the most primitive mysticism to the most evolved expressions of realism. This universe took its unity not from a nonexistent organic homogeneity of materials, but from the personal intensity of its creator. This unity does not happen in the realm of accomplishments, but in the more cerebral domain of theoretical elaboration and aspiration. Similarly, the morphological manifestations of Kazantzakis, whether metrical works or prose, carry theoretical problems and solutions to problems rather than a need for artistic renewal of forms. And though he dedicated his energies to literary creation, on the whole, this productive and diverse writer, who participated so completely in the intellectual life of the period, belongs more to the general history of culture than to the narrow limits of modern Greek literature. At the convergence of movements and currents, Kazantzakis could be the point of departure for a variety of researches in the Greek intellectual world.

Varnalis

A greater unity and a more conscientious literary concern characterized Constantine Varnalis after he had passed a youthful period of irresolution. He began by writing verses similar to those of Sikelianos; his evocations of the ancient work exhibited an excessive sensuality. His scholarly verse technique did not diminish from his poetic force or spirit. The influenec of Palamas was evident in his juvenilia. Later, his preoccupations acquired more reality, and under Western influence, he turned toward Marxist theories. From that point on, his literary work was impregnated with Marxism, whether he wrote verses, narratives, or criticism. The technique of his verses remained solid and forceful. *The Light That Burns* (1922–1923), in verse and prose, as well as *The Besieged Slaves* (1927), in verse, belong to his second period. In both works, satire and sarcasm alternated with human suffering. In "Mother of Christ," we read:

> Ah! how as a mother I too had longed
> (It was only a dream, a mist that was dissipated)
> As though I had borne you as I had your brothers.
> Far from glories, and far from hatred. . . .

He also published his poems in literary periodicals. The presence of contemporary man is intensely felt in all this part of his production.

Among his critical works, we should mention a study called *Solomos Without Metaphysics* (1925). Varnalis here applied the theories of historical materialism with knowledge and aggressiveness. His point of departure was the interpretation John Apostolakis gave Solomos. In the narrative genre, we have *The Race of Eunuchs* (1923), *The True Apology of Socrates* (1931), and *The Diary of Penelope* (1947). His attention to form and spirit we find here mitigate, to a certain extent, the hasty and conventional theme and its exploitation. Finally, I should mention a volume of personal reminiscences that appeared with the title *Living Men* (1939).

Karvounis and Avgeris

It would be appropriate at this point to mention two writers who left no extensive body of works, but whose excellent writing and personal brilliance left its mark on Greek letters. Nicholas Karvounis (1880–1947) passed successively through a number of convictions and many intellectual disciplines, to which he applied himself with the same assurance and the same force. This attitude toward the fundamental problems of life helped all who came in contact with him to attain quality in their own work. The publications of Karvounis did not constitute a unified whole, and for this reason, they do not suffice to give us an understanding of his personal contribution. Mark Avgeris (b. 1884, pseudonym for George Papadopoulos) wrote verses, but it was especially in criticism that he distinguished himself. His more recent critical works, scattered in newspapers and literary periodicals, are based on the method of historical materialism and are models in this area.

Politis

Criticism was also the most basic expression of Photos Politis (1890–1934). An intellectual life so deliberately open to foreign influences could not fail to provoke the reaction of a critical spirit. Hence, Politis, writing the greater part of his work for the columns of the daily newspapers, incessantly criticized Greek values, whether they were ancient, deeply felt ones or those enjoying an ephemeral success. Encouraged also by the critical attitude of John Apostolakis, Politis condemned with intransigence and passion all in Greek culture that he considered unresponsive to the demands of an elevated idealism and an intense spiritual life. His criticism was productive and helped raise a new aesthetic of neo-Hellenic society. Exaggeration was not lacking from his work, and sometimes it bordered on injustice. But the injustice was done in good faith. Thus, in a conventional world, as an inevitable product of a newly organized intellectual world, he was able to constitute an effective barrier to personal compromises and irresponsible manifestations. Nurtured exclusively on esteemed writers, especially foreign ones but some Greek writers as well, Politis had created in their measure a standard by which to evaluate matters of his country. It was a conception based on hero-worship, which was useful, despite its exaggerations, for a society that never was distinguished by the severity of its critical criteria.

Politis's style was powerful and highminded. Accustomed to elevated spheres, he knew how to treat lofty subjects. However, let us mention at once that a problem exists in the above attitude. This problem affected all those who sought to follow Politis and Apostolakis but who did not have the essential ability to do so. Even Politis and Apostolakis faltered each time they dealt with less exalted subjects. First of all, culture is composed of some important concerns and a great number of minor ones. Both are necessary; each should be treated according to its own merits. To grant merit exclusively to important subjects when considering an entire culture can be unjust and either distort the important things or make them meaningless. This kind of criticism shows the difficulty of evaluating all the works that were not considered great; because criticism lacked the necessary standards, it was not always fair in the evaluation of certain works. The use of absolute criteria which lack historical awareness presupposes great personalities in criticism. When such personality is lacking and only method remains, the high ethical judgment becomes irresponsible rhetoric.

Besides criticism, Politis also worked on drama. He wrote original plays and translations whose stagecraft was quite well done.

Apostolakis

John Apostolakis (1886–1947) wrote critical works exclusively. He began with a biography of Thomas Carlyle that was destined to mark his entire later production; it was governed by German idealism. The principal target of his early critical works was Kostes Palamas. It was the moment when the mature creative work of Palamas invited critical evaluation. Apostolakis, as we have observed in Photos Politis, placed Palamas beyond history; instead of evaluating him, he compared him with the ideal figure of Solomos. In this fashion, neither Solomos, nor Palamas, nor even their critic gained anything. If one excepts some scattered aesthetic observations, the image Apostolakis presented of Solomos adds very little to our knowledge of the poet; it is a hazy image, existing outside time and space. Palamas was also distorted, because the critic praised his weaknesses and neglected to examine his more general contribution to modern Greek culture. Hence, the sensibility, the aesthetic experience, and the critical talents generally of Apostolakis remained unexploited in a great portion of his work. Similar observations can be made about his studies on Kalvos and Valaorites. The critic saw clearly, but his evaluations were false. We could say that the critic had left work of intensive effort and elevated thought, a high example of a man and the memory of a purely moral personality, if along with this work, we did not also have the contribution of Apostolakis in the study of the folksong. He was the first to consider the folksong from a purely literary point of view. He studied its aesthetics and went a step further, more precisely, he renewed our knowledge of the folksong. From such a profound knowledge of the folksong, he also wrote his criticism on Krystallis.

Other Genres

In these years when criticism was devoted to the early successes of Greek literature, the production of poetry continued. Strong personalities in this area were more rare than they had been in the years which followed the great spirit of 1880, but the new means appeared with greater clarity. I mention, in the theater, Pantelis Horn (1881–1941), who created successful works inspired by naturalism; Theodore Synadinos (1880–1959), who particularly cultivated what is known in France as comédie; Spiros Melas (1883–1966), who passed through various genres and wrote social and historical drama influenced by Ibsen. But his production was not confined to the theater. Along with the daily contribution to an Athenian newspaper, his prolific pen permitted Melas to give us a large body of prose work. His historical narratives, inspired by the War of Independence, had particular success for works of this genre; tales include *The Old Man of Moreas* (1931) and *Admiral Miaoulis* (1932). I also mention among the prose writers Dennis Kokkinos (1884–1967), who cultivated the novel of Athenian life and wrote carefully composed short stories and historical works. Irene the Athenian (1890–1955, pseudonym for Irene Dimitrakopoulos), achieved a lyrical inspiration in her texts and was influenced by symbolism.

Voutiras

During these years the name of Demosthenes Voutiras (1876–1958) began to be known among the intellectuals. His production included many short stories and novellas; these first appeared in the literary periodicals at the end of the last century and continued indefatigably. The world of Voutiras was that of the city bourgeois and laboring classes. Hence, we speak of a portrait of urban manners. Though Voutiras was fond of detail, long descriptions, lack of composition, and psychologcal portrayals of manners, his personal tone, which showed his aversion for the concrete and the attraction he felt for the troubled atmosphere of ambiguity and obscurity, differentiated his work from the typical portraits of manners, so we are obliged to set him apart. His technique resists any kind of aesthetic analysis; the random writing, the indifference to any effort at construction, the absence of verbal elaboration, and the absence of cultivated elements create amorphous masses of prose within which originality is difficult to detect. Of course, Voutiras's writings were popular at a particular moment in the country's cultural development, and since he has no objective virtues, or reveals them insufficiently, we should attribute his success to a correspondence between his peculiarities and his readers' demands. It is evident that the efforts of the generation of 1880 was past its peak. Furthermore, Russian literature, which had stamped Greek prose since the time of Papadiamantis, cultivated in the people a preference for imprecise and impartial psychological studies, which were echoed in the work of Voutiras. An awakening interest in social classes, which until that time had not been fully exploited in Greek literature, was an additional reason for his success. The intellectual group now being formed was no longer content with the objectives characteristic of those whose beginning we conventionally placed around 1880.

The Disintegration and New Formations

From this point of view, the critical works of intellectuals such as Photos Politis and Apostolakis and similar public critical manifestations, expressed in the success of Voutiras, have a close rapport despite their differences. It is characteristic that they are not isolated expressions; numerous men of letters who appeared toward the end of this period, that is, shortly before the Balkan Wars, showed that the disintegration of the old world had already commenced. Plato Rodokanakis, Nicholas Nikolaïdes, Manuel Mangakis, Photos Yophyllis, Romos Philyras, and Constantine Ouranis were symptomatic of the new formations. Strict observance of the rules of art and strict attachment to Greek life in that order receded now before a clear tendency toward dissolution; to keep the old attachments became a negation rather than a positive position. They became an expression of weakness rather than of an imperious creative spirit. Certain prose pages in Plato Rodokanakis (1883–1919) were full of a mystic beauty, which could only be based on adolescent inquietudes and the conviction that art was an end in itself. N. Nikolaïdes (1884–1956) sought in his short stories and narrative poems a haziness and a suggestion of a troubled spirit which he created uncertainly and by implication. His world was ethereal and lacked material foundation. Manuel Mangakis (1891–1918), an experienced translator of English literature, also expressed in his slight original work the desire to escape from life and to overthrow the absolute values in which the preceding generation had worked. Even more characteristic was Photos Yophyllis (1887, pseudonym for Spiros Mousouris). In his language, he utilized elements which until this time had been used exclusively in poetry:

> Then: Manitoba, 7 and 5 cents
> And Harvinter, 6 and 40.
> (F.O.B. Piraeus, delivered at the end of the month).—
> Woe is me! They always enchain me,
> Your eyes and your caprices, Medea!
> (taken from *The Anguish of the Wheat Merchant*)

Philyras

Romos Philyras (1889–1942, pseudonym for J. Ekonomopoulos) reflected in his verses the image of a world without precise limits, a world that belonged equally to dream and reality. The eroticism that prevailed in his work was weak and shallow. He believed in the unimportant and was incapable of recognizing that larger laws beyond the daily conventions governed life. Constantine Ouranis (1890–1953, pseudonym for C. Niarchos) also expressed his lack of faith in life, his desire for escape. Cosmopolitan poetry thus penetrated Greek letters; the journey became the metaphoric expression of escape.

A climate similar to that at the beginning of Athenian romanticism, a generation aware of its insufficiency in the face of the great problems of life, a generation that was attracted to all kinds of subversion or revolutionary thought, to language, Greece, knowledge in its more rational sense, and to all that had nourished its predecessors, no longer existed. Certainly, the older efforts had come full circle. The new Hellenic effort now bore fruit in the form of the politics of Venizelos and the two victorious wars of 1912 and 1913. The ambiance created in Greek intellectual circles by these wars was bound to precipitate this disintegration of literary mode; there was a feeling of success and security, unsuitable for inspiring courageous efforts or reinforcing renovative tendencies. The euphoria that followed these wars lacked the elements of anxiety, desire, and passion, which could have given impetus to expression. In the decade that followed, we will see the realization of all that was in preparation toward the end of this period. Impending dissolution was the reigning motif and even appeared in works which would not naturally have taken this tone. It was now that the work of Cavafy came to have value for men of letters, but it was badly interpreted and viewed from a single narrow focus. In the following chapter, we will examine the turning point that we have observed here and the work of Cavafy. As always, within this disintegration, we will observe the first signs of a renascence. Furthermore, let us keep in mind that during this entire period the great writers who had matured under very different circumstances continued to produce and hence to create the particular conditions necessary for an eventual renewal.

Chapter 29

New Flights and

New Aspirations

1912 to 1922

Normal Evolution

The group of intellectuals associated with the years 1912–1922 had a normal development out of the preceding years, as is witnessed by the verses of Spiros Panayotopoulos, the literary work of L. Koukoulas and Constantine Tsatsos, the theatrical work of D. Bogris and Linos Karzis, and the literary production of Alkis Thrylos, Petros Haris, and Phanis Michalopoulos.

Spiros Panayotopoulos (b. 1894) pursued his poetic career along restrained lines: noble inspiration, careful technique, clarity of language. His work was static. L. Koukoulas (1894–1967) published translations and original works whose soft tone place him both in conservative romanticism and in neoclassicism. Constantine Tsatsos (b. 1899) began to publish, under the pseudonym Ivos Delphos, theatrical works and poems strongly influenced by Palamas. His later development, insofar as it belongs to literary history shows him extending the traditon of 1880, based on a solid foundation of careful cultivated philosophic thought (*Palamas*, 1936). D. Bogris (1890–1964) wrote for the theater portrayals of Athenian manners which were done with competent technique. L. Karzis (b. 1894) began with poetry like that of Sikelianos and later devoted himself more particularly to the classical theater and to scenic problems posed by the theater. Alkis Thrylos (b. 1896, pseudonym for Helen Ouranis), after a variety of efforts, devoted herself to criticism, both of the theater and of literature. Her attitude was definitely conservative and tended to express the conceptions of the average reader who had a moderate sensibility and a relative culture. Petros Haris (b. 1903, pseudonym for John Marmariades) concentrated especially on prose and criticism. His narrative work had good composition, good technique, and a fine psychology. His criticism revealed his sensibility and wide information and tended visibly to reconcile foreign currents to Greek needs. Phanis Michalopoulos (1895–1960) began with literary interests very similar to those Sikelianos had for Greece. But the center of his preoccupations soon passed from literary creation to criticism and the history of culture. His contribution in these areas shows him to be a conscientious defender of modern Greek tradition. In works devoted to this subject, he was distinguished by abundant documentation which was not always the most selective and by a historical intuition which always led him to research the most important changes in modern Greek intellectual history. Even though his documentation and conclusions are of dubious value, his creative vitality distinguished him in the area of modern Greek research. In language, the frequent use that Michalopoulos made of unassimilated purist elements placed him precisely at the intersection between earlier efforts and the newer tendencies.

Research

The new research, however, was better expressed by a group of poets, among whom I mention the following: Napolean Lapathiotes (1893–1943), Constantine Karyotakis (1896–1928), Tellos Agras (1899–1944), Nicholas Hayer Boufides (1899–1950), and Demetrios Papanikolaou (1900–1943). Maria Polydouris (1905–1930) also travelled the same path. We have already observed that lack of faith characterized the attitude all these writers had toward life. The values for which Hellenism had only recently struggled were no longer alive in their souls. Karyotakis wrote about the Delphic festivals:

> At Delphi the spirit of two Greeces was appraised.
> Aeschylus recalled the echo of the Phidriades,
> *Lorgnons, Kodaks, operateurs,* to the suffering of Prometheus
> Added a special, a very picturesque tone.

What they retained of the original Greek was love of research and the effort to assimilate foreign movements. In a conservative form, Lapathiotes expressed his pessimistic attitude and hopelessness in the face of life and the beauty of things that die:

> The roses filled me with sadness
> When tonight they scattered their evening scent,
> As though announcing I do not know what distant deaths
> And suffering silently for something no longer present.

His colors are misty, his subjects are those of death and decay. We can say the same about Tellos Agras (pseudonym for Evangelos Ioannou). The words "gray" and "somber" recur in his poetry. As a more thorough and more reflective researcher, Agras succeeded in giving a more technical form to this: verses that fade into suggestion, rhythm that expresses the monotony of life:

> In the house, it rains in droplets,
> And life becomes sleepy and drab,
> It is limp and has no value.

Sensitive and cultured, Agras left critical works and thoughts on art, or rather on the technique of art. The critical effort that he devoted to the work of Cavafy, one of the first systematic studies on the poet (1921), expressed with both its subject and content the turning point of this generation. Reference to Agras will be made later along with the discussion on Cavafy.

We should perhaps place the pale poetry of Maria Polydouris beside the artistry of Agras. She did not have his technical application, nor his literary culture. The two are comparable for their nobility and minor key. Though we find some passionate accents in Maria Polydouris, actually these are only what the poetess dreamed of being; melancholia, reverie, and withdrawal are her habitual tone:

> She stood sadly before us,
> She sought something, who can say what?
> How did she come? Is she forgotten?
> What was it this stranger sought?

Karyotakis

Papanikolaou cultivated free verse in a spirit that expressed the last exhalations of symbolism mixed with more recent experimentations on verse forms. Boufides, on this same point of omissions and unsuccessful efforts, began to write verses in traditional forms, but went to the most perilous acrobatics. In language, all these poets exhibited a preference for purist expressions, those already formulated or given as immediate linguistic material.

From this point of view, as from many others, Constantine Karyo-

takis should be considered the principal writer of the group. He left
many poems scattered throughout the literary periodicals and three
collections of poetry: *Suffering of Man and Matters* (1919), *Ne-
penthe* (which was awarded a prize in a poetry contest in 1920), and
Elegies and Satires (1927). His life was without incident; he studied
law in Athens and became a public official in 1920, in which capacity he passed the greater part of his life in Athens. A few journeys
on the continent complete the picture. As for his literary career, we
should also mention his work on the publication of a periodical with
the suggestive title *The Leg* and his collaboration on a theatrical re-
vue. His poetry, on the whole, was conservative. Its versification was
without great application, it expressed a pessimistic mood and contained a bitter taste of disenchantment, which cannot be explained
from what we know of the man. It is the poet's period that was expressed in his verses:

> We have remained symbols of times that weigh us down,
> Insoluble puzzles that only speak to themselves,
> Graves that ever with an unknown time abide,
> Letters that never reached their destination.

In this toneless world, sarcasm was all that could provide some kind
of life. And certainly in the work of Karyotakis the poems inspired
by sarcasm are the most outstanding. Important events inspired the
poet's sarcasm, but so too did the subject of daily life. He was moved
to sarcasm by the city of Preveza, where he lived for a month in his
official capacity as a public servant and where he committed suicide
in July 1928.

> If at least among these men
> Only one dies of disgust. . . .
> Silent, sad, with manners correct,
> We would all be festive at the funeral.

This solution was the ultimate consequence of the absolute negation that overwhelmed this generation. Faith could have produced
another result; not faith in the traditional ideals combined with action, national life, and the life of men, but the other kind of faith,
the one that was a form of reaction to traditional pessimism, a religious faith. A number of literary figures did express themselves in
a religious manner during these years. The movement was felt as a
kind of lyricism, which derived, more or less, from Sikelianos.
Among these writers were Takis Barlas (b. 1894), George Douras

(b. 1895), and Takis Papatsonis (b. 1895). We can also add Joseph
Eliyah (1901–1931). His early writings were inspired by Judaism and
a mature humanism. Eliyah's expression was easily molded and
sonorous; it was elevated to the ideal while simultaneously being an
instrument for the warmest lyric tones. In verse that was conservative and lacked linguistic richness, Douras expressed his passionate
religious faith.

Papatsonis

In addition to lyrics, Takis Papatsonis's multiple talents gave us a
number of essays and translations from foreign literature. His juvenilia were basically inspired by his religious convictions. His was
a rich body of work with a variety of nuances; it was distinguished
by a personal liveliness and an original contribution to language and
verse:

> It was a passing flock of birds, I know,
> But neither for its fatigue, nor for its annihilation,
> Did we show love or respect, and now that they are gone
> Compassion is upon us and the burden of awareness,
> For our joyless action, for our shameful attack,
> And look at us, as we are left, unfit,
> Slow to understand the meaning of these apparitions,
> Abandoned, without a message from the north,
> With our usual *mea culpa*
> And the useless accusations toward ourselves.

Naturally, faith provided a certitude and with that a joy; contrary to
the toneless poetry also encountered in this generation, in Papatsonis
we find a euphoria and expressions of the joy of life.

> Since early morning, the influences are magicians.
> Kindness is deceived with its visible wings.
> So few things suffice for such an impression.
> Two kind coincidences that we do not expect.
> A charitable mood that is transformed to action.
> A change of wind. . . .

Moreover, one fundamental inspiration for Papatsonis was his constant contact with life. His heights tended to be elevated, but his
roots were planted solidly in the earth. The work always had per-

sonal experience as a source, no matter how far away from this it moved. On the other hand, the receptivity of the poet, the general culture, the liberty he took with metrics and language, which was the only real association he had with his generation, allowed him in time to assimilate the recent attainments of lyricism. This assimilation comes about in slow rhythm and organically. After his collection of poetry *Selection I* (1934), which contained poems written during a twenty-year span, he produced a second collection, *Ursa Minor* (1944). Religious faith brought the poet close to man. His tone was always elevated, but a lyrical mood reigned which expressed everyday emotions more directly. His technique showed a parallel phenomenon, that is to say, he developed a renewed form, without altering his individuality:

> You have the courage to adorn yourself
> With carnations, and I admire you,
> Not only because you are lovely
> And fresh and they become you
> But because you assume the wounds,
> You become the image of a legion new martyrs.

Prose

Prose, as we know, is always less free in its movements, more conservative, more traditional in manner. This is certainly true of the period we are examining. In prose we have a closer continuity than in poetry; the younger prose writers followed in the footsteps of their predecessors and advanced farther in directions already indicated. The element of renewal appeared less in form and more in subject matter, in the ideological or religious world of the writers. We should mention the realistic, social production of P. Pikros (1900–1956). B. Daskalakis (c. 1899–1944), alongside his numerous translations of Knut Hamsun, who influenced the thought and style of the young prose writers, also wrote a novel, *The Uprooted* (1930), which was distinguished by its accurate linguistic developments.

Stratis Myrivilis (1892–1969) worked on his style, which was rich in images, vivid and brilliant, and realized the literary ambitions of a Karkavitsas or a Petros Vlastos in a superior fashion. His language belonged to the richest tradition of demotic orthodoxy. His demoticism was intensified by the richness of his lyrical elements. We can now speak about an ideological development emerging from the atmosphere of disintegration in 1912–1922 and moving toward a greater Hellenic tradition. However, Myrivilis lacked a renewed inspiration and his technique, each time it went beyond the simplest forms, a narration in the first person or a short story, it lost its suppleness and the work lost its force. Hence, the clearest contribution Myrivilis made in modern Greek letters was limited to his style and linguistic elaboration. In this area he perfected older forms, without enriching prose with new elements.

More audacious in his search and consequently more uneven in his successes was Photis Kontoglou (1897–1965). In his early works he sought to color his orthdodox demotic with folk elements and thus wrote an artistic reproduction of popular narratives. His imagination, rich in itself and enriched further by his readings, helped him create narratives of unusual intensity and exceptional life, where art found its way again toward the Eastern folk legend. The travel element and the love of adventure and the exotic add a cosmopolitan tone to Kontoglou's earlier literary works. In his later work, he found subjects that corresponded to his linguistic tendencies and immersed him deeper in the Eastern Byzantine roots of the new Hellenism. This new orientation in turn produced a new language colored by an ecclesiastical language. The causes were diverse, but the result was the same: liberation from the essential tradition of demoticism.

Constantine Bastias (c. 1901), who saw increasingly greater possibilities in the folk language, persisted in holding on to it with a desire to render it worthy of serving even the highest intellectual demands. Besides theatrical production, he wrote in a vigorous demotic short stories and novels which, with a deliberately naive expression, revealed a comprehension of humanity and a profound religious faith. In his novel *Papoulakos,* where he revived the religious movements of Hellenism around 1850, he created a genre which pretended to address the religious spirit of the people directly: Papoulakos had visions and accomplished miracles at the time of King Othon. The novelist succeeded in communicating life to his creation and justifying a genre which, though perhaps it did not meet the requirements of the reading public, nonetheless expressed the uneasiness of a generation. Once again, literary creation became a means to express an attitude toward life.

Thrasos Kastanakis (1901–1967), a student of Psycharis, also remained faithful to the demotic orthodoxy. He was a prolific writer, who produced short stories, novels, other prose writings, and a few verses, which expressed divergent interests, both toward cosmopolitanism and toward a deeper acquaintance with the Greek spirit. Experience of life, knowledge of technique, and vivacity are the distinctive characteristics of this author. His psychological observations were excellent and full of nuances. Sometimes, despite his affectation and deliberate style, he attained remarkable results. But his elaborate plots, the artist's constant presence behind the works he offered make the production of Kastanakis somewhat cold and calculated. These characteristics often prevent the reader from enjoying all the good aspects of his works.

As was natural, this period gave rise to a new criticism which reflected above all the critic himself and his anxieties; it was willing to accept, to assimilate, and to express itself through the works it evaluated; it was less successful criticism when it had need to remain objective about the works themselves. Kleon Paraschos (1894–1964) can be considered the characteristic representative of this new criticism. In his restricted lyrical works, the lyrical manifestations of his generation were evident. His theoretical preparation was extensive and varied. Naturally he was close to the authors whose orientation was similar to his, the moralists. His sensitivity, not to immutable beauty, but to the battle for form, was intense. His critical pages, which he dedicated to modern Greek poets in whom the struggle for form was most evident, exhibited the extent of his critical abilities. In the essay, especially in the introspective essay, he did work that reveals both sincerity and critical sense. In such a manner he approached the most important figures of Greek literature. In these works of his maturity, he showed that he was capable of associating his lyrical virtues with the application required in a literary work. I. M. Panayotopoulos (b. 1901) also took a subjective critical approach to the new literature. In addition to his critical works and the variety of his other literary manifestations (*Elements of Modern Greek Literature, History of Art,* and other works), he also wrote purely literary works: verses, novels, travel impressions. The critical and lyrical spirit are combined in his work.

Cavafy

In general, the group examined in this chapter marked the disintegration of traditional values, while waiting for the strongest personalities to detach themselves from the group and create a new world. However, each generation, whether it tends toward creativity or toward criticism, needs to examine its past, or its forebears in the more recent past. During these critical years of the new Greek literature, the necessary seminal figure appeared. This was Constantine P. Cavafy. Despite the fact that Cavafy rarely published his verses, he had long been known in intellectual circles. It suffices to mention the critical commendations of Gregory Xenopoulos (1903). In 1903 Cavafy's hour had not yet come; his fame would not be heard before critical evaluation had undermined that of Palamas. Furthermore, in 1903 Cavafy had only produced a slight body of work; and though it showed signs of originality, it could only be approached with difficulty. The generation that matured after 1912 found the work of Cavafy quite developed; it found, or thought it recognized, in his works the elements the generation was cultivating simultaneously. This generation was influenced by his linguistic originality and his technique; they approached him philologically and developed their critical thought around his work.

Thus, while the older writers of the preceding generation disapproved violently of Cavafy, the younger writers of the period turned their attention to him with affection. Critiques came from various directions. There were Palamas and Psycharis, Petros Vlastos and Photos Politis. Points of irony and anger were made. But the literary periodicals of the younger writers, *The Altar* (1919) and *The Muse* (1922), assembled in their issues both the earlier productions of Cavafy and the more recent. Contemporary critiques dated to around 1921 the beginning of Cavafy's influence, avowed or disavowed, on the younger poets. Some of the new critics who wrote about him included Tellos Agras (1921), I. M. Panayotopoulos (1922), Alkis Thrylos (1924), N. Lapathiotes (1924), and many others. In 1924 the periodical *New Art* dedicated a panegyric issue to Cavafy. It was the poet's official acceptance in Athenian circles. Naturally, this recognition came after analogous moves by the Hellenic circles in Alexandria. There a vigorous literary movement developed, with Cavafy as central figure and whatever good periodicals there were to serve as outlets. Included in the group were C. N. Konstantinides (1880), Timos Malamos (1896), who expressed himself mainly in criticism, and Glafkos Alithersis (1897–1965). But we are interested in knowing how the new generation in Athens saw Cavafy and what it saw in him. Agras spoke, in discussing his work, "about his contemptuous scepticism with regard to every faith." Thrylos affirmed that Cavafy "believed in negation." The *scepticism,* the *irony* of Cavafy were the subjects that attracted criticism. As always occurs with great writing, the current generation was reflected in the work of Cavafy and recognized itself in it.

Biography

Before we turn our attention to his work, we should place Cavafy in history in order to get a more objective image of him. Constantine Cavafy, son of Petros Cavafy and Chariclea Photiades, was born in Alexandria in 1863. He signed his juvenilia by prefixing the family name with a Φ, the Greek initial of the name Photiades. I believe we can here discern a special tenderness for his mother. Moreover, the mother figures in the poems of Cavafy are all of remarkable quality. The poet was seven years old when he lost his father. Chariclea assumed the financial burdens of the family, along with the problem of the children's education. She went to live near them in England, where she had economic interests and permanently established relatives. In 1880 Cavafy returned to Alexandria. He went to Constantinople where he lived for about three years with other relatives. In 1885 he returned to Alexandria where he became permanently established; several short trips to France and Greece interrupted the monotony of his clerical work, which was prolonged until 1922. Then he retired from service and lived another ten years, dedicating himself exclusively to his poetic production. He died in the spring of 1933.

He had no systematic education, but he was an avid reader and possessed a great curiosity; thus very early and on his own he acquired vast knowledge, especially in literature and history. We should mention also the culture and experience he gained at the great cosmopolitan centers of London, Alexandria, and Constantinople where he lived during his crucial adolescent years. English literature, the Alexandria milieu, and Byzantium marked his work profoundly. But this life, which passed far from the Greek capital, also produced certain other characteristics of his writing temperament. The poet grew up and lived in foreign Greek communities, which always, as we know, evolved more slowly linguistically than did the center. The archaic element of the poet's language, independent of its theoretical foundations, of which we will speak below, can be explained in large measure by the society in which his work was created. Also, we must not lose sight of the chauvinism that characterized the Greek communities in foreign places. Cavafy was a fanatic nationalist, as those who knew him testify, and as his activity in Alexandria and his poetry demonstrate. It would have been astonishing if his life had not brought the poet to such an exaltation of Hellenism. In addition, one can perhaps attribute to his community's narrow social circle another trait that appeared much later in his art, his complex concealment.

The Point of Departure

The earliest evidence we possess of Cavafy's literary activities appear around 1883, during his sojourn in Constantinople when he began to write poetry. Scarcely ten years had elapsed since the death of Karasoutsos and D. Paparrigopoulos and only nine years since the death of Vasiliades. Achilles Paraschos was at the zenith of his glory. In all the travelling Cavafy did during those years through the foreign Greek communities, the Greeks of the diaspora received him with enthusiasm. The voices of the younger writers that had begun to disturb Athens had not reached here. Furthermore, we should not forget that the generation of 1880 had been bilingual in its early works as was also at this time the poetic production of Athenian romanticism. The early works of Cavafy were also bilingual and were strongly colored by romantic commonplaces, philosophic pessimism, and Epicureanism:

> Tired of the deceptive instability of the word,
> I have found calm in my glass.*

From that time, the theme of the poet occurred persistently throughout the work of Cavafy, as it later returned with persistence. We must observe here that the poet, even in his juvenilia, placed art on a very high plane.

Naturally, along with declining Athenian romanticism, Cavafy

---

* All translations of the poetry of Cavafy included in this chapter are from *The Complete Poems of Cavafy,* trans. Rae Dalven (New York: Harcourt, Brace, & World, Inc., 1961).

also had other sources of inspiration, which were more musical to use for poetic instruction. French Parnassianism, cold, noble, full of minutiae, was at its height; it was an excellent antidote for romantic excesses. Cavafy was to find there a number of attractive elements: the objectivity, the descriptive and pictorial tendency, the development of a historical spirit. To this descriptive tendency, he would very soon add another; symbolism, with its half-tones, its atmosphere of suggestion and abstraction, completed the elements which young Cavafy would use to prove his powers.

He worked constantly, he wrote much, he preserved little, and he published even less in the literary periodicals of the capital or of the expatriate Greek communities. One can say that only death interrupted his incessant metrical revision of the few poems which he appoved. When in 1904 he published his first collection of poetry, entitled *Poems,* he included only fourteen of the odd poems he had published to that time. Some of these he had altered profoundly; the poet was close now to finding his particular form to establishing his poetic art. Six years later the second edition of *Poems* was enriched with seven new poems, which brought the total to twenty-one. Cavafy did not produce another collection. He circulated his poems on loose sheets to friends with prudence and selectivity. From time to time, he would print a cover for a limited group of previously published poems with dates affixed and at times he would add the date in his own handwriting. A table of contents was also included. Thus the notebooks were composed of loose sheets from different periods, sometimes in chronological order. When a printing of one of these loose sheets was exhausted, Cavafy had it reprinted. It was characteristic that from one printing to another there sometimes appeared noteworthy revisions or alterations made in the manuscripts' marginal notes. His vigilant concern for perfection was incessant.

Classification

In order to explore texts so minutely elaborated, we must have recourse to detailed research. Certain suggestions from the poet himself aid us in our classification. These suggestions are, first of all, of a chronological order. Later tables of contents divide the poems into two groups; there are those "before 1911," which form a unity, and then the later poems whose date is noted with precision. We can say that the poet made a profound division in his work around 1910, and further, that he attributed a particular value to his later production. On the one hand, his earlier writing was mixed together and undated, while on the other, his more recent works were classified year by year. We must not forget that in 1910 the poet was forty-seven years old. Later he would say: "I am a poet of old age." Indeed, if we examine the two-hundred odd poems known to us chronologically, we observe that his most abundant production appeared around 1917 when Cavafy was about fifty-four years old. Poet of old age perhaps he was not, but he certainly was a poet of maturity.

Conforming to his own directions, if we seek to classify his work according to content, we ascertain the existence of three groups: there are the philosophical or "thought" poems, the historical poems, and the "hedonistic" or sensual poems. These three groups correspond to the three influences he felt in his youth. We can associate the philosophical poetry with romanticism, the historical with Parnassianism, and the sensual with symbolism. This division is convenient for research, but only for research. We can be certain that beyond these divisions and classifications, there must be an essential unity which alone is capable of furnishing the interpretation of his art and his aesthetic. Indeed, when we try to divide the poems of Cavafy into these three groups, we very often find that the groups overlap to a great extent. Sometimes, the historical character of a poem can be deduced from the title; at other times, its historical character appeared in a few verses at the beginning or the end and suppression of this section causes the poem to become purely sensual or philosophic. Finally, in a number of cases, the poet creates imaginary people, supposedly historical, whose presence in the poem has no other purpose than to transfer the theme beyond our times.

Melancholy of Jason, Son of Cleander
Poet of Commagene, A. D. 595

The growing old of my body and my face
is a wound from a hideous knife.
I no longer have any endurance.
I take refuge in you, Art of Poetry,
who know a little something about drugs,
and attempts to numb suffering, in Imagination and Word.

It is a wound from a hideous knife.
Fetch your drugs, Art of Poetry,
that make one unaware—for a while—of the wound.

Cavafy was fifty-eight years old when he wrote this poem, and Jason was an imaginary person. Imenus was also an imaginary person in "Imenus."

> ". . . Sensual delight sickly and corruptively acquired
> should be loved even more;
> rarely finding the body that feels as it would wish—
> sickly and corruptive, it furnishes
> an erotic intensity, unknown to health. . . ."

> Fragment from a letter
> of young Imenus (of a patrician family) notorious
> in Syracuse for his wantonness,
> in the wanton times of Michael the Third.

Similarly, study of the philosophical or sensual groups leads to the conclusion not only that the nature of poetry in Cavafy defied classification, but that the poems are not adequately represented by any of the three groups. Thus, just as in the historical poems we encounter reflections or hedonism, similarly in the philosophical poems we find a strongly marked history; in the sensual poems, the element of memory prevails. These sensual poems whose lyrical quality is very clear, allow us to make a basic observation: it was never the immediate that was expressed. Enjoyment was always generated by memory.

Titles such as *Days of 1903,* or *of 1910,* or *of 1896,* are frequent in the work of Cavafy and apply to poems written at a much later date. Cavafy was not inspired directly by events; he needed the passage of time, the exercise of memory, for emotion. The early designation, "poetry of maturity," became more clearly "poetry of nostalgia."

Parallel with this, another observation should be made: in the poetry of Cavafy, wherever the poet utilized history or the past, we see an objective narration breaking through. Very rarely did the poet speak in his own person in a poem. He often narrated the events affecting third persons. When the first person was used, Cavafy was careful to convince us, through means we know already, that he was not the speaker. A date or a reference sufficed to establish an alibi in other poems. In such cases, the poem had the air of a mime. As we continue our study, we will have the occasion to compare certain poems of Cavafy with the classical mimes. In any case, we already know that whether he escaped into the past or assumed the role of a third person, Cavafy was attracted by indirection.

This nostalgic displacement in space or time constituted a characteristic trait of Cavafy's inspiration. The rejection of actuality unites the various forms of his poems. Inspiration for Cavafy was offered not by what existed but by what was missing. In "Morning Sea" we read:

> Let me stand here. Let me also look at nature a while.
> The shore of the morning sea and the cloudless
> sky brilliant blue and yellow
> an illuminating lovely and large.

> Let me stand here. Let me delude myself that I see these things
> (I really did see them for a moment when I first stopped);
> and not that here too I see my fantasies,
> my memories, my visions of sensual delight.

In this last chapter of the *History,* we should return to its early pages. The folksong allowed us to state that nostalgia, an ardent desire for what was missing, was the essence of lyrical language.

Cavafy A Lyric Poet

The inspiration of Cavafy appeared to be constantly lyrical: he was neither a gnomic nor a historical poet, despite his penchant for history or for didacticism. Cavafy was a lyrical poet. It was here that his originality began. We have detected a constant displacement of emotions toward other points in time or space, other periods and other persons. This insight can guide us to more general observations. Cavafy presented a permanent phenomenon: a displacement from inspiration to expression, corresponding exactly to the displacement of emotion. In any case, I would observe that the sensibility of symbol, a distinctive characteristic in Cavafy's poetry, was obviously connected with the performance of displacement. At the same time, however, we are concerned with a constant fulfillment of concealment, entirely conscious in the poet himself. Among the many examples that we could cite, perhaps the most significant is that found in the poem "Temethos of Antioch, A. D. 400." Cavafy presents us with a nonexistent poet called Temethos, who writes verses to commend a very much older person, Emonides, a friend of an ancient king of Antioch:

> Verses of young Temethos   the lovelorn poet.
> With the title "Emonides"—the beloved companion
> of Antiochus Epiphanes;   a very good-looking

young man from Samosata.   But if these verses have
turned out ardent and moving   it is because Emonides
(from that ancient epoch   in one hundred thirty-seven
of the kingship of the Greeks!   perhaps a bit earlier)
was added to the poem   merely as a name;
yet a proper-enough name.   The poem expresses
a certain love of Temethos.   A beautiful love
and worthy of him.   We, the initiate,
his intimate friends;   we the initiate,
The naive Antiocheans   read only "Emonides."

Informed by such confessions, we should at once seek beyond
the subject chosen by Cavafy for the real lyrical source of his inspiration. Further, in commenting on his poems, Cavafy insisted on the
subjective character of his inspiration: "It is not a matter of destiny,
the destiny of humanity, but of the destiny of a few men." Another
time about another poem, he said, "The poet, of course, does not envisage generalities in the poem but a particular case." Hence, we
have a poetry of nostalgia, a transformation of the real object of the
poem, and a lyricism. These are the elements we have now to help
interpret the poet. But already we can draw two conclusions. The
first is that the didactic tone often contained in the poems does not
suffice to classify Cavafy as a didactic poet; behind his theories,
there is the lyrical emotion. The second is that the normal eroticism
which sometimes appears in his poetry can also constitute a displacement of inspiration. Cavafy has something to conceal, and this something is hidden behind false confessions, which often have a certain
haughty element:

And I have drunk strong wines, as those
Who give themselves to pleasure drink.

We are brought to reality: when the poet makes discreet allusions to
*the enjoyments which were partly real and partly from memory, they
haunt his mind,* or about the intoxication by which he is seized *in his
solitary home.* This solitary intoxication is perhaps the key to his art.

Vision

Reality does not constitute inspiration for Cavafy. This, to a point,
could explain that suggestion was a characteristic trait of his. We will
return to this subject later. One should understand further that in ab-

sence we have clear images, which is another fundamental characteristic of Cavafy's poetry. The interpretation again is furnished by the
poet himself, who frequently reminds us of the importance of visions
in his poetic creation:

> The task of collecting them, poet,
> Even if you are able to retain only a small number.
> The visions that your sensuality suggest to you.

or

> Thus in imagination I will see visions
> And they will come, the shadows of Love.

In another poem, "Caesarion," he analyzes the technique of his inspiration. The name of Cleopatra's son passes across the pages of the
book through which the poet thumbs, and this gives birth to inspiration:

> . . . .
> Ah, see, you came with your vague
> fascination. In history only a few
> lines are found about you,
> and so I molded you more freely in my mind.
> I molded you handsome and full of sentiment.
> My art gives your features
> a dreamy compassionate beauty.
> And so fully did I envision you,
> that late last night as my lamp
> was going out—I deliberately let it go out—
> I thought I saw you enter my room,
> you seemed to stand before me as you must have been
> in vanquished Alexandria,
> wan and weary, idealistic in your sorrow,
> still hoping that they would pity you,
> the wicked—who murmured "Too many Caesars."   (1918)

The poet, then, has visions, and his poetry has its source in these
visions. He possesses the technique of visions, principally of erotic
ones, which makes it difficult for us to distinguish the sensual from

the historical vision. In this way he arrived at his unique form of suggestion, which was not created by abstraction or by imprecision, but, on the contrary, by a multitude of very concrete details. That is, the poet did not suggest by giving the reader's imagination an opportunity to work, but by enchaining and subjecting it, through precise descriptions, to his own visions:

> . . . .
> Caesarion stood more to the front,
> dressed in rose-colored silk,
> on his breast a bouquet of hyacinths,
> his belt a double row of sapphires and amethysts,
> his shoes tied with white ribbons
> embroidered with rose-colored pearls. . . . (1912)

But Cavafy extended himself further in his use of vision and came to its limits with his active participation in the vision. In staging his creations, he was not content to see, but he himself participated in the imaginary action; he assumed the roles. It has been said rightly that some of his poems recall the classical mimes; they are like mimes, certainly, in which he participated. Hence, along with clarity and evocative power, Cavafy's poetry presents another fundamental element: drama. It is because drama is an integral part of his inspiration that it has been investigated in his poetry. And here we should make an observation: under such conditions, doctrine or the didactic element passes to a secondary position. Our questions about whether one or another opinion reflect the author's personal conviction are no more relevant if we wondered whether an actor shares the theories of the heroes he incarnates on the stage.

Hence, clarity, suggestion, and dramatic force are the characteristic traits of Cavafy's lyricism. These are the simple means his inspiration uses. But to complete the picture, we must add further a few words relative to how he expressed his inspiration. Two opposing forces governed his lyric need and his desire for concealment. Concealment appeared in his austere technique and sobriety of verse, language, and expression. A disciplined need vibrated through his entire work, which thus succeeded in transmitting emotion, even where it appeared prosaic at first sight. After that, a lyrical need broke out; at such moments the poet had allowed it break out. Then the opposition between surface serenity and prosaism at the beginning and lyrical excess at the conclusion conferred an exceptional force on the whole.

Verse and Language

We can say the same about technical means, such as versification, meter, rhyme, language, adjectives, adverbs, and comparisons. He did not use technical means to express emotion, but rather as a way to conceal it. His meter was iambic, which agrees so perfectly with Greek prose. It was worked so artistically that sometimes the untrained ear cannot distinguish Cavafy's verses from his prose. In this same way he exploited rhyme, which often is lacking entirely, while at other times its excessive richness creates a sensation of antilyrical coldness. The particular language Cavafy used, a mixture of the scholarly and demotic idiom, was naturally the result of various causes. The historical and biographical causes were mentioned above. Here it remains to say a few words about the aesthetic objectives of his language. It is not enough to say that it was a sober language, without adjectives or adverbs, images, or those common elements that can pass unobserved. Sometimes more must be said: his language was intended to conceal the emotional world, not reveal it. A neutral, conventional language, purged of all rhetoric and at the same time antilyrical became his ideal and the one to which, in time, he conformed in a decisive manner. But again, under this conventional dress, passion seethed and was reinforced by constraint. The compelling power of this language, which is so cold, allows us to understand how he governed the passions artistically.

The Archaic Character

Of course, all these elements were made to captivate a generation that was tired of sincere spontaneity in the expression of emotions, as well as weary of every kind of orthodoxy, linguistic and otherwise, and of every kind of faith. This, however, does not mean that Cavafy was a recognized representative of the generation Karyotakis and Lapathiotes spoke for, of the generation characterized by uncertainty, irony, and pessimism. Cavafy believed in ideals, he respected the Christian religion, he exalted humanism and Hellenism. Profoundly humanistic, he stood before man in an attitude that had nothing ironic in it. His human ideal was generous and elevated. He expressed himself in verses which should be constantly in the minds of writers whose business it is to create human souls. In "Thermopylae" we find him saying:

> Honor to those who in their lives
> are committed and guard their Thermopylae.
> Never stirring from duty;
> just and upright in all their deeds,
> but with pity and compassion too;
> generous whenever they are rich, and when
> they are poor, again a little generous,
> again helping as much as they are able;
> always speaking the truth,
> but without rancor for those who lie.
>
> And they merit greater honor
> when they foresee (and many do foresee)
> that Ephialtes will finally appear,
> and in the end the Medes will go through.

The heroes he honored were those who confronted life with courage and pride. And when we see him bowing to others, to those who destroyed their lives through negligence, it was always to confirm the words of Socrates, that "character is the destiny of man."

The Greece of Cavafy

Cavafy also had great faith in Greece. As did all the intellectuals of his time, Cavafy conceived of Greece as a historical unity, and he attempted to project this unity in his work. It is significant that his elevated examples were always taken from Greek history. Patriotic emotions inspired some of his best verses. Indirectly, he often expressed his personal patriotic emotions. His faith in the Greeks was expressed particularly well in an impeccable epigram entitled "Those Who Fought for the Achaean League":

> Valiant are you who fought and fell in glory;
> fearless of those who were everywhere victorious.
> If Daos and Critolaos were at fault, you are blameless.

When the Greeks want to boast,
"Our nation turns out such men as these," they will say
of you. So marvelous will be your praise—
Written in Alexandria by an Achaean;
in the seventh year of Ptolemy Lathyrus.

The poem interests us not only for its faultless style, for its grandeur and sobriety in the use of adjectives, and for its elevated and balanced expression. Certain other aspects should be mentioned. It was published in 1922, shortly before the Asia Minor catastrophe, when the spirit of the Greek world had fallen prey to the anguish preceding the inevitable castastrophe. At this moment, Cavafy once more turned to the past and selected another disaster, when Rome subjugated Greece, in order to exalt Hellenic virtue. The vanquished Greeks were the valiant, the irreproachable, and they merited magnificent praise. But this time also, we see concealment operating: the last two verses armed the poet with an alibi and simultaneously created a greater reality by attributing the writing of the poem to the period of Hellenic decline it describes. This technique characterizes precisely Cavafy's poetic creation.

Greece of 1922

The disaster was approaching. It was something immeasurably more violent and more tragic than the debacle of 1897. Greece was more mature, better able to meet the new attack, but the attack was also more intense. As for literature, though the generation that was currently writing was incapable as a whole of reacting to the national misfortune, some of its more noteworthy representatives, continuing the tradition of Palamas or pursuing independent paths, gave a more positive national content to their thought and writing. But from this point on, a new generation was coming into life, a life tried internally by the refugee problem and misery and externally by the shame the military collapse brought about. This generation grew up with a shadow over its soul. It confronted the questions touching literature with responsibility, sometimes with a seriousness devoid of grace, sometimes with harshness and pedantry, but always with a lively desire for good. One observes here again the persistent pattern of the spirit passing from disintegration to a desire for synthesis. This generation, which produced some characteristic works around 1930, continued its work during the next thirty years without, however, completing its message. It posed the Hellenic problem again, it attempted a new classification of Hellenic values, and it proved the maturity of Hellenic culture, particularly as it worked in prose. However, these phenomena do not constitute literary history. They belong to a broader study, which is not within the scope of this *History*. A supplement follows which attempts to formulate the broad lines of the generation of 1930 and of the younger writers who followed.

Supplement

In this supplement we are interested in writers who appeared around 1930 and whose expressions, consequently, have still not taken a definitive form in literary history. That is to say, we observe in these writers more distinctly the phenomenon which also characterized the last chapters in this History, *the search for more fluent materials. The examination of this transitional period stops around 1940, at the point where the work of younger writers would risk becoming simply an enumeration of unclassified material. Furthermore, World War II and its aftermath create the most recent natural landmark between the past and now. For this reason, writers who appeared after 1940 are excluded from this survey, but, as in the body of this* History, *all writers who appeared before this date are examined up to their most recent works. In any case, only those considered representative of main currents in contemporary modern Greek literature are mentioned. Very possibly the reader will encounter fewer writers in the following pages than he expected to encounter.*

The Asia Minor disaster in 1922 found modern Greek literature at the most thankless hour of a painful adolescence. External intellectual incentives able to support the inspiration of the younger writers no longer existed. The historical dreams of Hellenism appeared to have been realized. The patriotic and political ideals that nurtured the preceding generations failed to warm the soul of the young writers now that those ideals were no longer in demand. This spiritual decline produced other, corresponding ideals, especially the linguistic one, which was always associated with national awareness. In August 1922, as the Asia Minor front was collapsing, D. Ginos was confirming for the younger writers the existence of a "spiritual languor," a "spirituality of little faith," which was being expressed with *linguistic anarchy,* with an indolence of thought.

Naturally, even the representatives of the linguistic battle, the representatives of traditional faith, lost their ability to impose themselves in such a climate. The ideological tone that this suppression of values took is of no interest to us here. What does interest us is the spiritual atmosphere which permitted the suppression of these values. In 1922 Constantine Varnalis wrote:

> I am the Art of foolish men, of charlatans,
> The Art of adulterers and of eunuchs,
> Sold, dishonored,
>
> .   .   .
>
> I am *The Flute,* I, *of the King*
> And *The Easter of the Greeks!*

At the same time other writers proceeded to corresponding formulations of their faith or lack of faith. Once more, the political decline caused a corresponding vaccilation in traditional values.

The disaster came with all its moral, political, and economic consequences. The various reactions of the older writers were well-known to the Greek people. The young men between fifteen and eighteen years of age would reach maturity with anxieties, perplexities, lacking ideals or faith. "Our elders sank in the port of Smyrna, not only their forces but also their ideals and self-confidence," wrote George Theotokas in his first literary work in 1929. The usual attitudes of that age group, both revolutionary and imitative, accorded not only with their experience but also with the example of the earlier generation. Other young men came from the opposite shores of the Aegean. The nostalgic vision of a lost birthplace lived in their souls. And they grew up with regrets and perplexities.

If we now seek a precise understanding of the psychic and intellectual composition of the young men interested in letters, we will encounter two different heritages. On the one hand, there is the royal path of tradition, the path followed at that time by Palamas in his declining years, the path that Sikelianos was treading with soft footsteps. Tradition, as Solomos had shaped it, was all owing unreservedly to grafting of the foreign element on the national trunk. Tradition also believed in the obligation of the citizen, in the organic function of the writer in society. This attitude had some natural consequences certainly: it produced a gravity of discourse and at the same time a tone of objectivity, or more precisely, of universality, however subjective the source of inspiration might be; the writer was aware now of his literary responsibility.

On the other hand, it was a negation of the past, an infinite desire for reversal and an unlimited renewal. Old values were examined in a critical spirit or even discarded without examination. The traditional verse forms were deemed outmoded. All kinds of experimentation became legitimate. We should observe, however, that the radical spirit, though it denied all asociation with the past, did not lose contact with foreign currents. The relation we have regularly observed between tendencies and influences holds true; the young writers of the period found outside Greece, and particularly in France, the examples they sought of comparable extremes. Futurism, which had begun before the war, continued its evolution in the world of letters and art. Dadaism, which emerged during the war years out of cubism, was at its height. In 1924 we have the first manifesto of surrealism in Greece.

It is in this negative aspect, tragic and absurd, that life appeared to the younger generation after the Asia Minor disaster. George Seferis wrote later about these years, "In our country there began a period of ideological balancing of accounts and transformations which can be compared to the period of reform which followed the War of 1897." Distinctive signs of the coming generation were determined by its education: gravity, a sense of responsibility, a need for faith. The orientation would be toward establishment of a balanced world. Reflections, research, and self-analysis lead to prose writing, while free expression of the introspective life favored outbursts of the purest lyricism. Hence, we should expect a prose sustained by reflection and reasoning, by examination of conscience, and a poetry that was violently antirational. The potential of prose would expand in two directions. The one direction tended toward the

proper limits of prose expression whose ideal form was logical argu-
mentation. What resulted was the narrative, the essay, the article.
Introspection in this latter case took a strictly scientific form and
tended to the constitution of a new literary genre, to the constitution
of modern Greek literary science. The other orientation expressed
introspection with the aesthetic means that foreign literature offered
at that time; the interior monologue became one of the principal
means of this expression. Correspondingly, poetry demanded from
surrealism the satisfaction of deeper needs and arrived thus at the
absolute purification of automatic writing.

However, we should state that this assimilation of new elements
from Western movements occurred not only because they corresponded to the new psychic needs of Greek literature, but also because the element which had renewed Western literature from the
time of romanticism to more recent quests appeared to have an organic place in the history of modern Greek literature. Progressively,
from investigation to investigation, the West was able to isolate the
meaning of lyricism. The word, in its autonomy, either with psychological or phonetic resonances, had found its central meaning in
the framework of poetry. Poetry became distinct from prose; it assumed precedence and became the free field of experimentation, an
authentic expression of pure literature. Form obscured subject,
which, in many instances, became a secondary element. Sometimes
the rational element disappeared entirely in order to give way to the
mystical or magical radiation of expression or to the unbridled exercise of imagination in its most visionary manifestations.

In a country such as Greece, where all literature has been marked
by the elaboration of lyricism, it was to be expected that the seeds
of such inquiries were to be encountered. A brilliant and glaring
word, an elliptical turn of phrase, an autonomy of imagination, a
contempt for rationalism, these are indeed the characteristics that we
find, more or less accentuated, in the Greek folk poetry as well as in
the scholarly poetry. Greek romanticism's search for appropriate
words was not a fortuitous phenomenon. The contemporary poets of
Greece, even those who adopted the boldest techniques, could not
boast that they were continuing one or another current of modern
Greek lyric tradition. And certainly, they had not denied the past,
but, on the contrary, they gave meaning and value through criticism
to what in tradition corresponded to their needs: the folksong, Solomos, Kalvos, Cavafy thus assumed an individual and distinctive
place in Greek letters and a new light shone on them.

I would propose a third, negative cause that produced the revolutionary attitude of the younger writers. From whichever point of view we examine this matter, we can state that the early decades of our century were under the weighty influence of Palamas's rationalism, intellectualism, and science. In the first profound break with the past, the dialectic mind demanded that the spirit should move in the opposite direction and arrive at the extreme limits of direct expressions of the soul. The sudden change would also influence aesthetics, or, more precisely, it would find a response in aesthetics. At the beginning of the century poetry moved in the world of ideas; the newer poetry concentrated principally on the world of forms. In this way, the conscious reaction of the younger writers against the influence of Palamas would direct them ultimately to poetic freedom in all its aspects and consequently toward tradition. We should keep in mind the contrast between Palamas and Solomos.

The new generation, concerned with seeking its ancestors and consecrating its masters in accordance with a law that surmounted the most revolutionary aspirations for renewal, discovered Solomos, who had preceded Palamas, and reclaimed his position. Linos Politis, in describing the aspects of modern Greek lyricism, found no difficulty in passing from Greek folk tradition and the Cretan and Ionian Islands schools to Sikelianos, Seferis, Elytis, and to Greek surrealism. Such are the essential characteristics of the intellectual world of the generation which became known as the generation of the thirties. They were a bit premature, perhaps, because on the one hand the representatives of this generation simultaneously in their production widened the gap while they exalted their common elements; and on the other hand, because of the political events that followed the natural development of this generation was disturbed. In any case, in surveying the generation of the thirties, we can say that it had two main interests: cultivation of lyricism and cultivation of prose.

The most recent interest was perhaps the renewal of prose. We say most recent because, with the exception of certain matters pertaining to morphology, where the seal of Palamas remained deeply engraved, it is difficult to associate the later prose with the earlier. The new prose was entirely liberated from the lyrical elements of expression; plot was liberated from the elements contained in studies of manners. The attention of the writer was constantly directed toward the psychic world of his heroes. The epic concept of the novel, abandoned since the years of romanticism, or neglected in folk publications, again assumed a place which corresponded with the narration. Content of the new prose was an epic of the mind, an epic of the soul, adventures of man. The narrative was expanded and similarly the animation strengthened: the short story gradually gave way to the novel.

The most representative writer of this change is Angelos Terzakis. His early works, short stories, date to 1925. But already in 1932 he presented a two-volume novel whose theme and characters had not quite been liberated from elements found in the novels of manners and from the influence of the older writers. In the following year, *The Fall of the Ruthless Men* created a landmark in the epic concept of themes. This path brought him to a true epic composition, *The Princess Izambo* (1938, but first published in book form in 1945). In one of his succeeding works, *Without God* (1951), he returned to his earlier anxieties on the social development of our period. We should add to this later rich production, where the essay competed with the novel, one called *The Secret Life* (1957).

In Terzakis we find the most acute awareness of the modern Greek novel. A passion for narration dominates his work. All the abilities of the author, the images, descriptions, and dialogue, tend exclusively toward the same end, toward creation of atmosphere which justifies and imposes the unfolding of the plot. Revelation is prudent and characters are sketched with clarity and verisimilitude. His expression lacks brilliance, his phrase is not extended; but his works move in a responsible world, which is also tightly woven and succeeds in an aesthetic compassion. The dialogue contains realism, ease, and natural articulation. These talents also brought Terzakis to the theater for which he wrote an abundant production, but he also worked on the essay and on critical studies.

A strong epic spirit runs through *Earth and Water* (1936), the first novel of G. N. Ampot. This has since been followed by a rare production in which a remarkable attempt at the epic of the Greek diaspora is distinguished in the novel called *Demetrios Gabriel* (1960). However, he has yet to fulfill the expectations of his first work. In Loukis Akritas and in T. Petsalis, on the contrary, one notes a steady ascendancy from their early to their later creations. Loukis Akritas's *The Armed Men* (1947) is the most important neo-Hellenic work dealing with World War II. The characters are clearly described and its pace, despite the length of the book, continues undiminished to the end. T. Petsalis, after having attempted the urban novel, was attracted by later Greek history and wrote *Mavrolykoi* (1947–1948), a novel of a Greek family living during the Turkish domination. This work has become a national epic. Such a brave attempt was not unsuccessful and it secured for the author an eminent position in Greek letters. Petsalis's later three-volume novel *Hellenic Orthos* (1963) followed the same direction.

In this same manner, but with greater dexterity and more competent language and a greater challenge, Pantelis Prevelakis succeeded with his works, *The Chronicle of a City* (1938), *Forsaken Crete* (1945), *The Tree* (1948), *The First Freedom* (1949), and *The City* (1950), in giving us broad epic compositions. The last three constitute a trilogy, *The Cretan*, in which the struggles of Crete for freedom during the years of Venizelos, who appears in the work, are forcefully and artistically presented. Of his later production, we should mention two additional novels, *The Sun of Death* (1959) and *The Head of Medusa* (1963). Prevelakis was also occupied with other literary expressions and with the history of art. M. Karagatsis (died 1960) was also an epic writer, an exuberant temperament, gifted with narrative talent. He gave examples of a strong creative imagination in his numerous volumes of work (novelettes and novels). Lilika Nakou, Kosmas Politis, Elias Venezis, all exhibited great talent in their early works, but this talent was developed unevenly in all three. Lilika Nakou did not exploit here genuine talent. She was content with the facility with which she wrote and allowed her talents to deteriorate into smaller and more incomplete units. The aesthetic, rapid, and sometimes elliptical style of Politis, consisting of a continual series of outbursts, forces the reader into an emotional condition of relying directly on psychological derivations. The order of events are also basically psychological, thus diminishing and weakening the plot, which, in any case and despite the dramatic element, is not of primary interest in the totality of his works. His images are original; they are racy, fascinating, and are one main element of his charm. Nonetheless, one can say that all these proceed from a richness which is never refreshed. The satiety that they finally create is perhaps related to a similar satiety found in the author. Perhaps this observation explains, to a degree, the spirit of rebellion which dominates his later works and of which there was no foreshadowing in the earlier ones.

In Elias Venezis, as well, the repetition of technique from one book to another is clearly evident. His easy narration, varied with lyrical elements and the feeling of humanity characteristic of all his works (short stories and novels), charm the reader on his first contact, but satisfy him less with repeated readings. His themes are taken principally from life on the shores of Asia Minor before World War I, and from the Asia Minor disaster and its consequences. He is essentially an author whose soul was nurtured on the first impressions of the generation of the thirties. World War I inspired a theatrical work and a volume of short stories. Among his most important works are *Peace* (1939), *Aeolian Land* (1943), and *Ocean* (1956).

George Theotokas (died 1966) was the most Cartesian of the modern Greek prose writers in his early works. This characterization assumes fuller meaning only when we consider the burdensome heritage of lyricism which until recent years had been suffocating modern Greek prose. His style is clear, brilliant, straightforward; insufficient only, perhaps, in flexibility and delivery, the negative aspect of his Cartesianism. His images speak more to the mind than the emotions. Even though he has the basic ability to see, this virtue which permits him to extol details and to give life to his heroes, never impels him toward expressive means dependent on extraneous associations. He presents words, especially adjectives and adverbs, even when they are unusual, without any interruption in the smooth flow of thought. A consequence of these characteristics is the compact articulation of his works, where native wit and a play of imagination, though they attract him, are consciously and purposely subjugated to the entire architectural concept of his creation. His thought is likewise brilliant and well defined, delicate but without weakness, clear but without deep feeling. I would go so far as to say that he stands apart in his generation for aspiring to psychological analysis and for his general interests: all the contemporary problems concerned him in his creative literary output and in his essays.

The Free Spirit, his first intellectual work, published in 1929 under the pseudonym Orestes Digenis, continues to remain the manifesto of the generation of the thirties. A significant work also is *Argo* (1933; final form 1936). There he presents, aside from a developed picture of adolescent life, a portrayal of Hellenism in Constantinople during the Asia Minor collapse and in Athens during the disturbed years that followed. However, even his other genres have attracted attention: short stories, essays, plays, and poetry. I mention specifically a novelette called *The Demon* (1938), where, with acuity and artistry, the basic sides of the modern Greek character are analyzed. Also another long narrative, *Leonis* (1940), is a delicate, sensitive analysis of adolescent youth, a well-loved theme of the author. *The Game of Folly vs. Wisdom* (1947) is a Byzantine fantasy of unique quality. In the essays and travel impressions, Theotokas is always critical; he searches for the internal man and renders the conscience of the critical hours during his period. His effort in theory and practice aims to weave folk tradition into the treasure of the intellectual modern Greek production. Of his later works, where the restless observation of his period's problems is crystallized around religion, we have the following: *Journey to the Near East and to Mount Athos* (1961), a play called *The End of the Road* (1963), and a novel, *The Sick and the Travellers* (1964), where he incorporated an older novel, *The Sacred Way*, written in 1950 and inspired by the experiences of World War II.

Stelios Xefloudas, John Beratis, George Delios, Alkis Giannopoulos, and John Sfakianakis sought a more personal expression. Xefloudas began his writing career in 1930 with *The Notebooks of Pavlos Photinos*. He introduces the interior monologue into Greek literature. Xefloudas's expression is allusive, a hazy atmosphere of a wounded sensibility, a mood of revery. His subsequent works failed to use these characteristics in a visibly fresh way and only his war novel, *Men of Myth* (1946), was outstanding because, with the same technique, he presented the strong emotions war exploits create. Among other works, he published two more novels in the last years: *You, Mr. X and the Little Prince* (1960) and *Don Quixote* (1962). John Beratis (died 1968) travelled on a similar path, but he trod it out for himself. *Diaspora* (1930) is a book where the dream-vision is transferred to the reader. His prose and his few verses are given in a narration which is not internal monologue but thought externalized. His technique of narration was fulfilled early with exceptional completeness in *Travellers' Guide to 1943* (1964), a book about the resistance, in *The Wide River* (1946), a book about the war, and in the novel *Whirlwind* (1961). The author's awareness is a strange mirror reflecting the external world. The reader finds this picture: the world emerges from the consciousness. The expression always comes from the author, but indirectly, like an involuntary imprint of a thought put on paper. Phrase, description, narration envelop the reader, who loses his own personality and is entirely subjugated by the author's charm. All this is done with the simplest expression, sometimes with an excusable negligence and an indifference toward grammatical and syntactical rules. It is a new, very original, technique, which proved successful and effective.

It was natural that this period of research and experimentation should also incite critical reflection. Working along with the older writers, the younger writers came to establish their own rules, to put into practice and to justify the efforts of their generation. Here we observe two parallel manifestations: most of this period's men of letters cultivated the essay and criticism, but there also appeared the type of researcher, the erudite scholar, who did not practice literary creativity. Panayotis Kanellopoulos, Petros Spandonides (died 1964), Demetrios Kapetanakis (died 1944), George Sarantaris (died 1941), T. Xydis and George Themelis did some work with creative literature, but the main body of their work belongs to the essay and determines their special place in Greek letters. Particular mention should be made of Kanellopoulos's *History of the European Spirit.*

Among those who worked systematically with literary criticism, I mention first of all Anthony Karandonis, Vasos Varikas, John Hadjinis, Emile Hourmouzios, and George Katsimbalis; Katsimbalis's principal conrtibution is in bibliographies. Numerous are those who worked systematically with the science of modern Greek philology. Though their accomplishments are unquestionably uneven, their great number proves that the efforts at giving studies in depth to the knowledge of modern Hellenism has borne fruit. B. Tatakis, who is specifically interested in Byzantine philosophy, also extended his research to the history of modern Greek thought. I also mention, closer to our subject, Emmanuel Kriaras, especially for his work in the Cretan theater, G. Valetas, N. Tomadakis, G. Zoras, and Sophia Antoniades. Linos Politis was chiefly occupied with studies of Solomos.

We should mention here the characteristic orientation of modern Greek thought toward philosophic research made by E. Papanoutsos and John Theodorakopoulos. Finally, modern Greek problems within a larger framework, a phenomenon that took place from one generation to another, we have J. Kakrides and J. Sykoutris, whose interests were classical literature, and Chris Karouzos (died 1967), whose interest was in archeology.

It is thus that the modern Greek consciousness matured critically and creatively around the thirties. But the conquest of lyricism, as well, though essentially less subversive in its essence insofar as tradition was concerned, brought a profound renewal to Greek letters. Furthermore, here the transition was smoothly accomplished, either because we find an increased awareness of new forms of art in the poets themselves, or because we discover poets who remain somewhat on the lines of the older poets or those poets who confront their themes with an entirely new perspective. N. Kavvadias. with his collection *Mirabu* (1933), only accentuated a stance taken by Kostas Ouranis: the poetry of nostalgia and the distant harbor, and he adds a touch of Karyotakis's expression:

> And I who so desired to be buried one day
> In some deep ocean in the faraway Indies,
> I will have a death, common and very sad,
> And a burial like that of most men.

In his early work, *Poems* (1933), Alexander Baras combined Karyotakis's element of disintegration with certain elements from Cavafy. But his more vigorous personality was affirmed in new concepts:

> Without maneuvers, without meanderings,
> Without hesitation
> Or fruitless shrieking of sirens
> They turn their prows toward open waters
> THE CLEOPATRA, the SEMIRAMIS, and the THEODORA.
>
> (trans. by K. Friar)

The later collections, under the same title (*Poems*, 1938, 1953) are almost identical in character but somewhat denser and more responsible in expression; at the same time, his originality has matured and has escaped the danger of a purely formal technique. But the theme of weariness prevails with the direct or indirect heirs of Karyotakis.

It was with classical forms of verse that G. Vafopoulos (1931), John Ritsos (1934), Nikiforos Vrettakos (1929), and Zisis Economou (1934) began. However, all four felt the need for renewal of forms, thus each took his own path until he achieved strictly personal contributions in the new poetry. We also observe a tendency which perhaps began with Palamas: the glorification of a scientific culture. It appeared in Niketas Rantos (1933), who abandoned Greek letters early, after having given the first intimations of surrealism. We find the same situation in Zisis Economou. A writer and thinker of a varied production (poetry, essays, plays), concerned especially with philosophic problems, Ekonomou greatly subordinated his art to his themes, thereby performing an injustice to his inspiration which, however, never ceases to be strong and boldly visionary, and it emerges from the restlessness of our times. It is the same with Ritsos. After having circulated demonstrably in the milieu of a scientific culture, he later found an inspiration which was in accord with his own nature and gave soft tones and hazy images. Perhaps his later intense postwar political activities altered the purity of his inspiration. Something similar can be said about Nikiforos Vrettakos, in whom, however, the artistic eventually prevailed.

Vrettakos conceals, in a form that is entirely free at times, a sober and classical inspiration of admirable purity in concept and in inspiration, as we see in "Without You They Would Not Find":

> Without you the doves
> Would not find water
> Without you God
> Would not illuminate His fountains
> An apple tree sows flowers
> In the wind; you carry water
> In your apron from the sky
> The lights of sheaves of wheat and over you
> A moon of sparrows.

His religious spirit, toward which faith he inclines, as well as the clarity of the world within which he circulates, brings him close to Sikelianos, but without Sikelianos's imagination and power. The inspiration of T. G. Vafopoulos also contains philosophic, or more precisely, religious roots. In him also faith masters the destiny of man. This generation of poets seeks light and certitude.

Light and faith are the ends sought by surrealism, whose principal representatives are A. Embirikos (b. 1935) and N. Engonopoulos (b. 1938). Both men seek an unconditional liberation of the internal world and total contact with reality. Embirikos showed a rare visual imagination in his poems. In Engonopoulos, despite his incontestable poetic quality, technique is of greater concern.

Odysseus Elytis (b. 1935) also began with surrealism. And in the work of D. I. Antoniou (b. 1939), the presence of surrealism is strong. In Antoniou, a writer with small output, we find a tendency toward abstraction which often makes his true inspiration appear cold. In Elytis, on the contrary, we find a characteristic concentration of his generation's virtues. He began with amiable compositions, full of light and charm, but lacking force and tending toward monotony. As he advanced on his artistic path, he found more profoundly human and firmer tones, and at the same time, he achieved form in his poems. Though he succeeded in expressing the Greek spirit with its charm and grandeur, we should not forget that he simply succeeded better in rendering what already existed in the soul of his generation:

With luffing soul with brine on the lips
With sailor's dress and sandals red
He climbs to the clouds
He treads the sea-weeds of the sky.
The dawn whistles through its conch
Foaming a prow approaches
Angels! Forward the oars!
That Evangelistra may land here

The Albanian war inspired Elytis with a significant poem, the *Heroic and Elegiac Song for the Dead Second Lieutenant of the Albanian Campaign*. It is a lyrical cry of anguish before death, but also an expression of the unyielding faith Greece has in herself:

Now anguish bowed on bony hands
Grasps and crushes the flowers against her;
In the ravines where the waters have stopped
The songs lie starved for joy;
The hermit cliffs with hoary hair
Silently break the bread of solitude.

.   .   .   .   .

In the distance the crystal bells ring out
Tomorrow, tomorrow, tomorrow: the Easter of God!

George Seferis is the most distinguished poet of the period we are examining here. He appeared in Greek letters with the collection of poetry called *Strophe* (1931), followed by the long poem *The Cistern* (1932). In 1935 the second collection of poetry, *Mythistorima*, appeared. In that same year he also presented three volumes: *Poems, Notebook of Exercises,* and *Logbook I*. The first period closes. In 1944 we have *Logbook II,* and in 1947 a long poem called *The Thrush*. His personal experiences in Cyprus inspired a series of poems called *Cyprus . . . Where He Prophesied that I . . .* (1955). Parallel with these we have translations of T. S. Eliot (1936, 1963), various essays collected in a volume in 1944, an essay on *Erotokritos* (1946), travel impressions of the sculptured Christian churches of Cappadocia (1953), an essay on Delphi in 1963, the same year he was awarded the Nobel prize for literature.

Seferis also began with traditional verse forms. His milieu is French, somewhere beyond Mallarmé but in a world established by him: something between the whimsical and Valéry. But already he shows himself an absolute master of language; he knows most of the secrets of verse and displays an exceptionally developed feeling for symbols, evident in the quality of his images and the grasp of his inspiration, as we see in "Denial":

> On the blond sand
> We wrote her name;
> But calm breezes blew
> And blotted out the writing.
>
> With what heart, with what breath
> What desires and what passions
> We lived our lives; a mistake!
> And we altered our lives.

This same collection contains the impeccable fifteen-syllable verses of "Discourse of Love":

> On the field of separation may the lilies bloom again
> Days of perfection dawning, embraces of the sky
> Sparkling in the reflection of those eyes alone
> The purity of soul inscribed like the song of a flute.

Already in *The Cistern,* the tone is elevated in a severe verse form, and sensible alliterations combine the old with something new:

> Here in the earth a cistern has been implanted
> A cavern of secret water hoarded there.
> Its roof, noisy footsteps. The stars
> Don't mingle with its heart. Each day
> Extends, opens and closes, without touching it.

With *Mythistorima,* we see Seferis passing from traditional to free verse. This change coincides with the influence of T. S. Eliot. Simultaneously, we see that free verse can retain the perfect frugality of the classical.

> One more cistern in the cave.
> At other times it was easy for us to draw idols and ornaments
> To gratify friends who were always loyal to us.
>
> The ropes broke; only the furrows on the well's mouth
> Recall our past happiness:
> The fingers on the rim, as the poet said.
> The fingers feel the dew of the stone a little,
> Then the body's warmth conquers it
> And the cave gambles its soul and loses it
> Every moment, full of silence, without a drop of water.

The figure of the poet now appears in all its purity, and his intellectual and spiritual world have been perfected. Out of the folk tradition the poet has found his way back to antiquity and has organically bound the past expression with the new. Antiquity no longer constitutes an object of study but is a way of life. The historic conscience of Seferis and the tragic feeling of the destiny of Hellenism are thus shaped. Light exists, but the faith of the poet is not supernatural; it is faith in human weakness. Seferis, who came from the shores of Ionia, carried with him the special synthesis of Greek civilization in Asia Minor which combined the wisdom of the East with Greek rationalism, as we see in "The King of Asine":

> And the poet loiters gazing on the rocks and asks himself
> Does there still exist
> Among these broken lines, angles, points, caverns
> Does there still exist
> Here where one meets the course of rain and wind and decay
> Does there exist the movement of the face, the shape of
>   tenderness
> Of those who were taken so strangely from our life
> Those who remained shadows of waves and thoughts with the
>   vastness of the open sea
> Or perhaps not, nothing remains but the burden
> The nostalgia for the burden of a living existence.

In the tragic fate of Hellenism, in the tragic fate of his generation, Seferis grasps the universal anguish of our times. In his second creative period, the experience of the war and the later developments of Hellenism add still greater gravity to his lyricism. But the poet here surpasses himself. The verses of this period present, beyond the sense of symbols, the sense of solidarity of phenomena. Desire for an increasingly more difficult technique in its forms binds inspiration and disciplines it with a bold originality. The wealth of neo-Hellenic lyrical tradition is found in its entirety, but it is also entirely renewed in his expression. The clarity and originality of images remain on the classical order, disciplined to be free of any superfluity. Even in the freer and bolder verses, Seferis presents a balanced harmony, a moderate grandeur, and the human dimensions of classical beauty. In "Stratis Thalassinos Among the Agapanthi," we read:

> It is painful and difficult, the living do not suffice me;
> First because they do not speak, and then

Because I must ask about the dead
Before I can proceed on my way.
It cannot be otherwise, when sleep overtakes me
The companions cut the silver cords
And the flask of winds empties.

However, we must not forget that his prose follows on the same line as his poetry. His principal concerns are with art and the problems of Hellenism. In his essays, he touched on the crucial moments in the intellectual life of Hellenism, as we see in *Erotokritos,* Kalvos, and Makriyannis. The two subjects, art and Hellenism, are divided in his mind. We perceive this dichotomy in most of his prose texts; it is particularly evident in the essays having to do with Hellenicity in art, which became the matter of a debate in 1938 between Seferis and Constantine Tsatsos. Perhaps the position Seferis took was a responsible expression of his generation's expression. The debate itself revealed the direction of the new intellectual culture: Greece, as an independent concept, not static, is characterized by the constant renewal of a century-old tradition.

Selected Bibliography

The selected entries in this bibliography are intended to serve
as a guide to further reading. A more complete bibliography,
Modern Greek Culture, a Selected Bibliography, has been compiled
by C. T. Dimaras, C. Koumarinou, and L. Droulia and published
in Athens, 1970.

ABBOTT, G. F. *Songs of Modern Greece.* Cambridge: 1900.
ANTHONY, ANNE. *Greek Holiday.* Athens: 1957.
ANTONAKAKI, DEDRINOU KALLINIKI. *Greek Education.* New York:
  1955. (Bibliography).
ARGENTI, PH. *Bibliography of Chios.* Oxford: 1940.
ARGYROPOULOS, P. A. "Les Grecs au service de l'Empire Ottoman."
  Le cinqcentième anniversaire de la prise de Constantinople.
  Ed. L'Hellénisme Contemporian. Athènes: 1953.
ARNAKIS, G., Démétracopoulou, Evro. *Americans in the Greek
  Revolution: George Jarvis. His Journal and Related Documents.*
  Thessaloniki: 1965.
ARNAKIS, G. *Samuel G. Howe. An Historical Sketch of the Greek
  Revolution. Part I. Books 1–4. Revised edition with Introduction
  and notes.* Austin, Texas: 1966.
BAIRD, H. M. *Modern Greece: A Narrative of a Residence and Travels
  in that Country.* New York: 1856.
BENGESCO, G. *Essai d'une notice bibliographique sur la Question
  d'Orient.* Brussels: 1897.
BLACKWELL, B. H. *Byzantine Hand List. A Catalogue of Byzantine
  Authors and Books on Byzantine Literature, History, Religion,
  Art, Archaeology, etc.* Oxford: 1938.
BOORAS, H. *Hellenic Independence and America's Contribution to the
  Cause.* Rutland: 1934.
BOWER, L., BOLITHO, G. *Otho I, King of Greece.* A Biography.
  London: 1939.
BOWRA, C. M. *The Creative Experiment.* London: 1949. (Cavafy).

BUTLER, E. *The Tyranny of Greece over Germany*. Boston: 1958.

CASSON, STANLEY. *Greece and Britain*. London: n.d.

CAVARNOS, C. "Science and Modern Greek Thought." *The Carolina Quarterly* 4, 1952.

CLINE, M. A. *American Attitude toward the Greek War of Independence*. Atlanta: n.d.

COBHAM, CL. *An Attempt at a Bibliography of Cyprus*. New edition by G. Jeffrey (first edition in 1886). Nicosia: 1929.

COROMILAS, D. A. *Catalogue des livres publiés en Grèce depuis 1873 jusqu'a 1877*. Athens: 1878.

CRAWLEY, C. W. "John Capodistrias and the Greeks before 1821." *Cambridge Historical Journal* 13, 1957.

————. *The Question of Greek Independence, 1821–33*. Cambridge: 1930.

DAKIN, D. *British and American Philhellenes during the War of Greek Independence, 1821–1833*. Thessaloniki: 1955.

————. "The Origins of the Greek Revolution of 1821." *History 37*, 1952.

DALVEN, R. ED. *Modern Greek Poetry*. New York: 1949. (Bibliography).

DAWKINS, R. M., ed. *Forty-five Stories from the Dodecanese, From the Mss of Jacob Zarraftis*. Cambridge: 1950.

————. *Modern Greek Folktales*. Oxford: 1953.

————. *More Greek Folktales*. Oxford: 1955.

————. *Recital Concerning the Sweet Land of Cyprus entitled "Chronicle"*. Oxford: 1932, 2 vols.

DEMOS, R. "The Neo-Hellenic Enlightenment, 1750–1821." *Journal of the History of Ideas* 19, 1958.

DENHAM, H. M. *The Aegean. A Sea-Guide to its Coasts and Islands*. London: 1963.

DIEHL, CH. *Figures byzantines*. Paris: 1917–1918. 2 vols. (Theodore Prodrome, Digenis Akritas, Belthandros and Chrysantza, Lybistros and Rhodamne).

DONTAS, DOMNA. *Greece and the Great Powers, 1863–1875*. Thessaloniki: 1966.

————. *The Last Phase of the War of Independence in Western Greece*. Thessaloniki: 1966.

DRIAULT, ED. *La Grèce d'aujourd'hui et la Grèce éternelle*. Paris: 1934.

————. *La Renaissance de l'Hellénisme*. Paris: 1920.

EARLE, ED. "American Interest in the Greek Cause, 1821–1827." *American Historical Review* 33, 1927.

EMERSON, J. *The History of Modern Greece from its Conquest by the Romans B.C. 146 to the Present Time.* London: 1830, 2 vols

EMERSON, J., Pecchio G., Humphreys, W. H. *A Picture of Greece in 1825. London.* 1826. 2 vols. (The French translation of this work, made by J. Cohen, Paris 1826, *"Journal ..."* of W. H. Humphreys.—Italian translation by G. Pecchio Lugano, 1826.)

FINLAY, G. *A History of Greece from its Conquest by the Romans to the Present Time: B.C. 146 to A.D. 1869.* A new edition by Rev. H. F. Tozer. Oxford: 1877. 7 vols.

FORBES, N., TOYNBEE A., MITRANY D., HOGARTH D. G. *The Balkans: A History of Bulgaria, Serbia, Greece, Rumania and Turkey.* Oxford: 1915.

FORSTER, E. S. *A Short History of Modern Greece, 1821–1956.* Third edition revised and enlarged by Douglas Dakin. London: 1960.

FOTHERINGHAM, D. R. *War Songs of the Greeks and Other Poems.* Cambridge: 1907.

FRIAR, K., tr. "Greek Poems of the 20th century." *Poetry* 78, 1951. (Sikelianos, G. Seferis, N. Kazantzakis, Papatzonis, Embirikos, D. Antoniou, N. Vrettakos, N. Engonopoulos, O. Elytis).

GENNADIOS, J. *A Sketch of the History of Education in Greece.* Edinburgh: 1925.

GIANOS, MARY P. *Introduction to Modern Greek Literature. An Anthology of Fiction, Drama and Poetry.* Edited and transl. by. . . . Poetry translation by K. Friar. New York: 1969.

GORDON, T. *History of the Greek Revolution.* Edinburgh: 1832. 2 vols. (second edition. Edinburgh: 1844).

GREECE, "Hachette World Guides." 1955.

HARTLEY, J. *Researches in Greece and the Levant.* London: 1831.

HARZFELD, J. *La Grèce et son héritage.* Paris: 1945.

HENDERSON, G. P. "Greek Philosophy from 1600 to 1850." *The Philosophical Quarterly* 5, 1955.

HEURTLEY, W. A., DARBY H. C., CRAWLEY C. W. and WOODHOUSE C. M. *A Short History of Greece, from Early Times to 1964.* Cambridge: 1965.

HOUSEHOLDER, F. W., KAZAZIS K., KOUSTSOUDAS A. *Reference Grammar of Literary Dhimotiki.* Indiana University, 1964.

HUTH, B. *Map of Greece.* London: 1937.

JELAVICH, BARBARA, *Russia and Greece during the Regency of King Othon, 1832–1835. Russian Documents on the First Years of Greek Independence.* Thessaloniki: 1962.

———. *Russia and the Greek Revolution of 1843.* Munich: 1966.

JELAVICH, CHARLES and BARBARA, ed. *The Balkans in Transition: Essays on the Development of Balkan Life and Politics since the Eighteenth Century.* Berkeley: 1963.

JENKINS, R. *The Dilessi murders.* London: 1961.

KALTCHAS, N. *Introduction to the Constitutional History of Modern Greece.* New York: 1940.

KAYSER, B., Thompson, K. et al. *Economic and Social Atlas of Greece.* Athens: 1964.

KEELEY E., SHERRARD, P. *Six Poets of Modern Greece.* Chosen, translated, introduced, by. . . . London: 1960. (New York: 1961). (C. Cavafy, A. Sikelianos, G. Seferis, D. Antoniou, O. Elytis, N. Gatsos).

KINROSS, LORD. *Portrait of Greece, with photographs in color by Dimitri.* London: 1963.

KOUTSOUDAS, A. *Verb Morphology of Modern Greek. A Descriptive Analysis.* Indiana University: 1963.

KYPARISSIOTIS, NIOVE. *The Modern Greek Collection in the Library of the University of Cincinnati. A Catalogue.* Athens: 1960.

LADAS, S. P. *The Exchange of Minorities: Bulgaria, Greece, and Turkey.* New York: 1932.

LEAR, E. *Edward Lear's Journals.* Ed. by Herbert Van Thal. London: 1952.

LEGRAND, E. *Bibliographie Hellénique ou Description raisonnée des ouvrages publiés en grec par des Grecs aux 15ᵉ et 16ᵉ siècles.* Paris: 1885–1906. 4 vols.

———. *Bibliographie Hellénique ou Description raisonnée des ouvrages publiés par des Grecs au 17ᵉ siècle.* Paris: 1894–1904. 5 vols.

LEGRAND, E., PETIT, L., PERNOT, H. *Bibliographie Hellénique ou Description raisonnée des ouvrages publiés par des Grecs au 18ᵉ siècle.* (Up to 1970). Paris: 1918–1928. 2 vols.

LEGRAND, E., PERNOT, H. *Bibliographie Ionienne du 15ᵉ siècle à 1900.* Paris: 1910. 2 vols.

LEVANDIS, A. *The Greek Foreign Debt and the Great Powers, 1821–1898.* New York: 1944.

Lists of works in the New York Public Library relating to the Near Eastern Question and the Balkan States, including European Turkey and Modern Greece. New York: 1910. Part I–IV.

LOVINESCO, E. *Les voyageurs français en Grèce au 19ᵉ siècle, 1800–1900.* Paris: 1909.

MACMILLAN'S GUIDES: *Guide to Greece, the Archipelago,*
Constantinople, the Coasts of Asia Minor, Crete and Cyprus. . . .
London: 1908.

MALAKIS, E. *French Travellers in Greece, 1770–1820: An Early*
Phase of French Philhellenism. Philadelphia: 1925.

MATSAS, A. "Contemporary poetry and drama in Greece." *Bulletin*
of the John Rylands Library. Manchester: 1942.

MAVROGORDATO, J. *Digenes Akritas.* Oxford: 1956.

———. *Modern Greece. A Chronicle and a Survey, 1800–1931.*
London: 1931.

MELANITES, M. "Educational Problems in Modern Greece."
International Review of Education 3, 1957.

MENARDOS, S. *The Value of Byzantine and Modern Greek in Hellenic*
Studies. Oxford: 1909.

MILLER, W. *Greece.* London: 1928.

———. *Greek Life in Town and Country.* London: 1905.

———. *A History of the Greek People, 1821–1831.* London: 1922.

———. *The Latins in the Levant. A History of Frankish Greece,*
1204–1556. London: 1908. (Bibliography).

———. *The Ottoman Empire and its Successors, 1801–1927. With*
an appendix, 1927–1936, Being a revised enlarged edition
of the Ottoman Empire, 1801–1913. Cambridge: 1936.
(Bibliography).

MORPHOPOULOS, P. "Byron's Translation and Use of Modern Greek
Writings." *Modern Language Notes* 54, 1939.

———. *L'image de la Grèce chez les voyageurs Français, due 15ᵉ*
au début du 18ᵉ siècle. Baltimore: 1947.

MURRAY, J. *A Hand-book for Travellers in the Ionian Islands,*
Greece, Turkey, Asia Minor and Constantinople. London: 1845.
(Seventh edition. London: 1900).

MYRES, J. L. *Geographical History in Greek Lands.* New York:
1953.

PALLIS, A. A. *Greece's Anatolian Venture—and After.* London: 1937.

———. *Greek Miscellany. A Collection of Essays on Mediaeval and*
Modern Greece. Athens: 1964.

———. *The Phanariots: a Greek Aristocracy under Turkish Rule.*
(n.p., n.d.)

PANTAZOPOULOS, N. J. *Church and Law in the Balkan Peninsula*
during the Ottoman Rule. Thessaloniki: 1967.

PAPADOPOULOS, T. H. *Studies and Documents Relating to the History of the Greek Church and People under Turkish domination.* Brussels. (Bibliotheca graeca aevi posteriois, I).

PHILIPS, W. A. *The War of Greek Independence, 1821–1833.* London: 1897.

PSICHARI, J. *The Language Question in Greece.* Three Essays by J. N. Psichari and one by H. Pernot translated into English by Chiensis. Calcutta: 1902. I. *The Literary Battle in Greece.* II. *The Gospel Riots in Greece.* III. *A Glance on Vulgar or Modern Greek Literature.*

SERGEANT, L. *Greece in the Nineteenth Century. A Record of Hellenic Emancipation and Progress, 1821–1897.* London: 1897.

SHERRARD, P. *The Greek East and the Latin West.* Oxford: 1959.

SOPHOCLES, S. M. *A History of Greece.* Thessaloniki: 1961.

SPENCER, F. *War and Postwar Greece. An Analysis based on Greek Writings.* Washington 1952.

ST. CLAIR, WILLIAM. *Lord Elgin and the Marbles.* London: 1967.

STANHOPE, L. *Greece in 1823 and 1824; Being a Series of Letters and Documents on the Greek Revolution, written during a visit to that Country.* 1824.

———. *Greece in 1823 and 1824; being a Series of Letters and Documents on the Greek Revolution, written during a visit to that Country. New Edition containing numerous supplementary papers illustrative of the state in Greece in 1825.* London: 1825.

STAVRIANOS, L. S. *Balkan Federation: A History of the Movement Toward the Balkan Unity in Modern Times.* Northampton, Mass.: 1944.

———. *The Balkans since 1453.* New York: 1958. (Bibliography).

———. *Greece: American Dilemma and Opportunity.* Chicago: 1952.

SWANSON, D. C. *Modern Greek Studies in the West. A Critical Bibliography of Studies on Modern Greek Linguistics, Philology and Folklore in Languages other than Greek.* New York: 1960. (This bibliography as far as scholarly literature is concerned includes only works up to the seventeenth century).

SWEET-ESCOTT, B. *Greece: A Political and Economic Survey, 1939–1953.* London: 1954.

THOMSON, B. *The Allied Secret Service in Greece.* London: 1931. (French translation. Paris: 1933).

THUMB, A. "The Modern Greek and His Ancestry." *Bulletin of the John Rylands Library,* 1914.

TOPPING, P. "Greek Historical Writing on the Period 1453–1914." *The Journal of Modern History* 33, 1961.

———. "Modern Greek Studies and Materials in the United States." *Byzantion* 15, 1940–1941.

TOYNBEE, A. J. *Greek Policy since 1882.* Oxford: 1914.

———. *A Study of History.* London, 1934–1954. 10 vols.

———. *A Study of History. Abridgement.* London: D. C. Somervel, 1960.

———. *The Western Question in Greece and Turkey.* Oxford: 1922.

TOZER H. F. *Lectures on the geography of Greece.* London: 1873.

TRYPANIS, C. A., ed. *Medieval and Modern Greek Poetry; An Anthology.* Oxford: 1951.

U.S. LIBRARY OF CONGRESS. *Greece: A Selected List of References, compiled by Ann Duncan Brown and Hellen Dudenbostel Jones under the direction of Florence S. Hellman . . .* Washington: 1943. (Mimeographed).

VASDRAVELLIS, JOHN C. *The Greek Struggle for Independence: The Macedonians in the Revolution of 1821.* Thessaloniki: 1968.

VASILIEV, A. A. *History of the Byzantine Empire.* Madison: 1952. (French Edition, 1932).

VLASTO, P. *Greek Bilingualism and some Parallel Cases.* Athens: 1933.

VOUMVLINOPOULOS, G. E. *Bibliographie critique de la philosophie grecque, depuis la chute de Constantinople à nos jours, 1453–1953.* Athens: 1966.

WADDINGTON, G. *The Present Condition and Prospects of the Greek or Oriental Church.* London: 1829.

———. *A Visit to Greece in 1823 and 1824.* London: 1825.

WARE, TIMOTHY *Eustrtios Argenti. A Study of the Greek Church under Turkish Rule.* Oxford: 1964.

WEISS, R. "The Greek Culture of S. Italy in the Later Middle Ages." *The British Academy,* 1951.

WHITMAN, C. H. *The Vitality of the Greek Language and its Importance Today.* New York: 1954.

WILCOX, M. G. *Education in Modern Greece.* New York: 1933.

WILLIAMS, G. *The Orthodox Church of the East in the Eighteenth Century.* London: 1868.

WITT, R. *Greece the Beloved.* Thessaloniki: 1965.

WOODHOUSE, C. M. *The Greek War of Independence: Its Historical Settings.* London: 1952.

———. *The Philhellenes.* London: 1969.

XYDIS, S. *Greece and the Great Powers. A Prelude to the Truman Doctrine.* Thessaloniki: 1963.

YOVANOVITCH, V. M. *An English Bibliography on the Near Eastern Question, 1481–1906.* Belgrade: 1909.

Index